NELSON STANDARD GRA
BIOLOGY

Alastair Hay   Michael Roberts

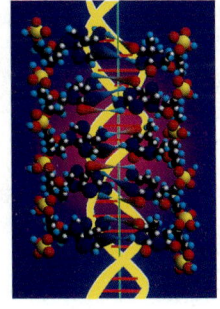

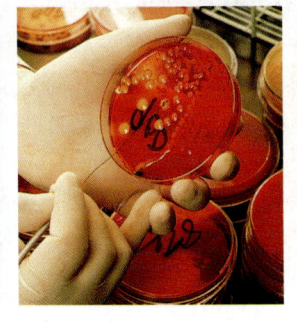

Nelson

Thomas Nelson and Sons Ltd
Nelson House Mayfield Road
Walton-on-Thames Surrey
KT12 5PL   UK

Thomas Nelson Australia
102 Dodds Street
South Melbourne
Victoria 3205 Australia

Nelson Canada
1120 Birchmount Road
Scarborough Ontario
MIK 5G4 Canada

© Alastair Hay and Michael Roberts 1997

First published by Thomas Nelson and Sons Ltd 1997

I(T)P   Thomas Nelson is an International Thomson Publishing Company
I(T)P   is used under licence

ISBN 0-17-438713-X
NPN 9 8 7 6 5 4 3 2 1

All rights reserved. No paragraph of this publication may be reproduced, copied or transmitted save with written permission or in accordance with the provisions of the Copyright, Design and Patents Act 1988, or under the terms of any licence permitting limited copying issued by the Copyright Licensing Agency, 90 Tottenham Court Road, London W1P 9HE.

Any person who does any unauthorised act in relation to this publication may be liable to criminal prosecution and civil claims for damages.

Printed in Croatia.

Acknowledgements

The publishers are grateful to the following for permission to reproduce photographs. While every effort has been made to trace copyright holders, if any acknowledgement has been inadvertently omitted, the publishers will be pleased to make the necessary arrangements at the first opportunity.

A–Z Botanical: 61 *middle*; ACE: 80; Aerofilms: 47 *bottom*; Allsport: 165; Heather Angel: 22 *middle, bottom*; 28, 32, 47 *middle*, 57 *top*, 58 *middle*, 61 *bottom*, 66, 68, 70 *middle*, 183; Ardea: 37, 64 *top*; ARP: 201; Bensons International Press Service: 184 *middle*; Biblioteca Ambrosiana: 82 *bottom*; Biophoto Associates: 84, 88, 162; Anthony Blake: 112 *bottom left*, 189 *bottom middle*; Brewers Society: 189 *top right*; Isobel Campbell: 184 *middle*; J Allan Cash: 8 *top right, bottom right*, 11 *middle left, middle right*, 12 *top*, 13, 22 *top right*, 30, 48 *left*, 58 *top right, middle*, 71 *middle*, 86, 136, 183; Chelsea & Westminster Hospital: 132; John Urling Clark: 61 *top*, 103, 170, 183, 184 *top*; Bruce Coleman: 12 *bottom*, 56 *top*, 58 *bottom left*, 169 *left, right*, 182 *top*, 183 *middle left, bottom left, middle*; Colorific: 200; Gene Cox: 114 *top*, 117 *left, right*, 194 *middle*; Cystic Fibrosis Research Trust: 177; Danish Dairy Board: 189; Ecoscene: 69, 189 *top, middle*; Environmental Images: 198 *top*; Farm Electric Centre: 70 *top*; Farmers Weekly: 187; Flour Advisory Bureau: 46 *top*; Garden Picture Library: 62 *bottom*, 175; GeoScience Features: 118 *right*; Glasshouse Crops Research Centre: 70 *bottom*; Sally & Richard Greenhill: 78 *top*, 168; Robert Harding Picture Library: 8 *bottom left*, 47 *top*, 125; BJW Heath: 24, 58 *bottom right*, 65 *top, bottom*, 78 *bottom*, 112, 121; Holt Studios: 51, 197 *bottom*; Hulton Getty Collection: 178 *left, right*; Image Bank: 164 *bottom*; Dr MW Jenison, Syracuse University NY/Society of American Bacteriologists: 193 *top*; Frank Lane Picture Agency: 182 *bottom*; Anthony Miles: 8 *middle*; Thomas Nelson & Sons: 62 *top*, 89, 113 *middle, bottom*, 114 *middle*, 122 *top, middle*, 142, 145, 152, *top left, middle*; Natural History Picture Agency: 45 *middle left, bottom* (×2), 50, 51, 56 *bottom*, 193 *bottom*; Oxford Scientific Films: 7, 8 *top left*, 11 *bottom left*, 14 *top, bottom*, 22 *top, middle*, 27 *top, middle, bottom*, 33, 35, 41, 45 *middle right*, 46 *bottom*, 53 *top*, 58 *top left*, 64 *bottom*, 71 *bottom*, 150, 161, 183, 188, 196 *top*; Photo Deutsches Museum: 122 *bottom right*; Planet Earth Pictures: 31, 59 (nos: 1, 2, 3, 4, 5), 110, 111 *top, middle, bottom*, 171, 196 *bottom*; Rex Features: 36, 92, 134; Chris Ridgers: 52, 79 *top, middle*, 15 *bottom*; MBV Roberts: 67, 79 *bottom*, 83, 127; Royal College of Surgeons: 91 *top*, 113 *top*, 130, 133 *top*; RNIB: 155; St Bartholomew's Hospital: 148; St Mary's Hospital Medical School: 203 *left, right*; Science Photo Library: 6 *top left, top right, bottom left, bottom right*, 9, 11 *right*, 42, 45 *top*, 53 *bottom*, 54, 57 *bottom*, 59 (nos. 6, 7, 8), 60, 74, 91 *bottom*, 94 *left, right*, 96, 97, 98, 100 *bottom*, 107, 108, 118 *left*, 133 *bottom left, bottom right*, 140, 143, 146, 147, 164 *top*, 181, 183 *top*, 194 *left*, 195 *left* (×4), 198 *bottom*.; Smith-Kline Beecham: 10, 11 *top*; Mary Smith Horticulture: 71 *top*; Tony Stone Images: 128; Unilever: 63; Bob Watkins: 100 *top*; Wellcome Trust/National Medical Slide Bank: 82 *top*, 106, 109, 137, 151 *top, bottom*; Wildflower & Wetlands Trust: 48 *right*; World Health Organisation: 195 *right*.

Certain material in this volume is taken from or based on already published sources as follows:

p25, Picture 3 *Urban Ecology*, David Gilman (MacDonald Educational).
p 35 *Vanishing Birds*, Tim Halliday (Sidgwick and Jackson).
p 80 , Picture 7 *Nutrition for Developing Countries*, Maurice King *et al.* by permission of Oxford University Press.
p 96, Picture 2 *Conception, Birth and Contraception*, RJ Demarest and JJ Sciarra (Hodder & Stoughton).
p 97, Picture 3 *Understanding the Human Body*, ER and EMcl Tudor (Pitman) by permission of Longman Group Ltd.
p 97, Picture 4 *Sex and Fertility*, C Wood (Thames and Hudson).
p 98, Picture 7 and p 126, Picture 5 from *Standard Grade Biology*, J. Torrance (Hodder & Stoughton)
p 123 *The Science of Life* , Gordon Rattray Taylor (Thames & Hudson). © Thames & Hudson.
p 127 *Reminiscences and Reflections*, Hans Krebs (1981) Oxford University Press.
p 128, Picture 2 *Principles of Human Anatomy*,GT Tortora (Canfield Press).
p 203 from *The Daily Telegraph* 12 July 1989.
p 187 *Farmers Weekly* 29 December 1995.

Certain questions have been adapted from past Standard Grade Biology examination papers (© Scottish Examination Board).

To the reader

This book is about biology. It is about the way living things work, particularly the human, and how our knowledge of living things can be used for the benefit of humankind. One of the most important problems in biology at the moment is how we can get the best out of our environment without damaging it. You will find a lot about that in this book.

You will also find a lot about how biology can be used in industry. This is an important aspect of the subject with an exciting future.

The book is split up into the seven Standard Grade Biology topics. In addition there is an introductory section about the basics of biology. Each topic includes questions (with a mauve background) – some of which are based on questions from the Standard Grade Biology examination. Most topics contain activities (blue background). These are things to do in the laboratory or at home and include some of the practical techniques you need to complete the course successfully. There are also extension exercises (green background) which take some ideas a bit further.

Alastair Hay and Michael Roberts

Many people helped to write this book, particularly John Holman, Ken Dobson, Stuart Elford and Dr Tim King. In addition we would like to thank the following for helping us with particular topics.

David Alford, formerly National Association of British and Irish Millers
Janet Alford, formerly Estate Office, Longford Castle
John Barker, King's College, London
Philip Bunyan, ASE Laboratory Safeguards Committee
Bill Butler, Ministry of Agriculture, Fisheries and Food
Dr Jonathan Cooper, Queen Mary's Hospital for Children, Carshalton
Dr Arthur Cruickshank, Open University
Dr P G Debenham, ICI Cellmark
Dr Nicholas Denny, Queen Elizabeth Hospital, King's Lynn
Craig Egner, Sea Fish Industry Authority, Edinburgh
John Finagin, Rhyl High School
Malcolm Hardstaff, formerly Marlborough College
Dr June Hassall, formerly Ministry of Education, Jamaica
Dr Neil Ingram, Clifton College
Roy Johnson, Alcohol Concern, London
Peng Tee Khaw, Moorfields Eye Hospital
Dr Patricia Kohn, University of Sheffield
Dr John Land, Marlborough College
B J R Mack, Unilever Plantation Group
Grace Monger, formerly The Holt School, Wokingham
Pamela Parker, formerly Amersham General Hospital
Dr James Parkyn, formerly Marlborough College
Dr Alan Radford, University of Leeds
The Rev Dr Michael Reiss, University of Cambridge
Dr Steve Smith, St Helier's Hospital, Carshalton
Bruce Tulloh, formerly Marlborough College

Contents

Section A Some basic principles	6 – 21
A1	How scientists work	6
A2	Studying biology	10
A3	The characteristics of living things	12
A4	Identifying, naming and classifying	14
A5	Who's who in the world of living things	16

Section B The biosphere	22 – 49
B1	Habitats and communities	22
B2	Finding out where organisms live	24
B3	Feeding relationships	28
B4	Food chains and humans	32
B5	Populations	36
B6	The wheel of life	40
B7	Pollution	42
B8	Management and conservation	46

Section C The world of plants	50 – 77
C1	Introducing plants	50
C2	Seeds and germination	52
C3	From flowers to fruits	56
C4	Reproduction without sex	60
C5	How plants feed	64
C6	The leaf, organ of photosynthesis	68
C7	Controlling photosynthesis	70
C8	To and from the leaf	74

Section D Animal survival	78 – 111
D1	Food and diet	78
D2	More about food and diet	82
D3	How we digest our food	86
D4	From egg and sperm to embryo	92
D5	Internal and external development	96
D6	Controlling human reproduction	100
D7	How do we get rid of unwanted substances?	104
D8	Responding to the environment	110

Section E Investigating cells	112 – 127
E1	Cells, the bricks of the body	112
E2	Diffusion and osmosis	116
E3	Cell division	118
E4	Enzymes	120
E5	Obtaining energy	124

Section F The body in action	**128 – 167**
F1 How we move	128
F2 Energy balance	134
F3 How we breathe	136
F4 The heart and circulation	140
F5 Blood, the living fluid	146
F6 The eye	150
F7 The ear and hearing	156
F8 The nervous system	160
F9 Exercise and fitness	164
F10 Staying fit for life	166

Section G Inheritance	**168 – 187**
G1 Variation	168
G2 Introducing inheritance	170
G3 More about heredity	174
G4 Genetics and society	182

Section H Biotechnology	**188 – 203**
H1 Living factories	188
H2 Working with microbes	192
H3 Dealing with waste	196
H4 Genetic engineering	200

| **Index** | **204** |

A1
How scientists work

Here we look at what science is and how scientists work.

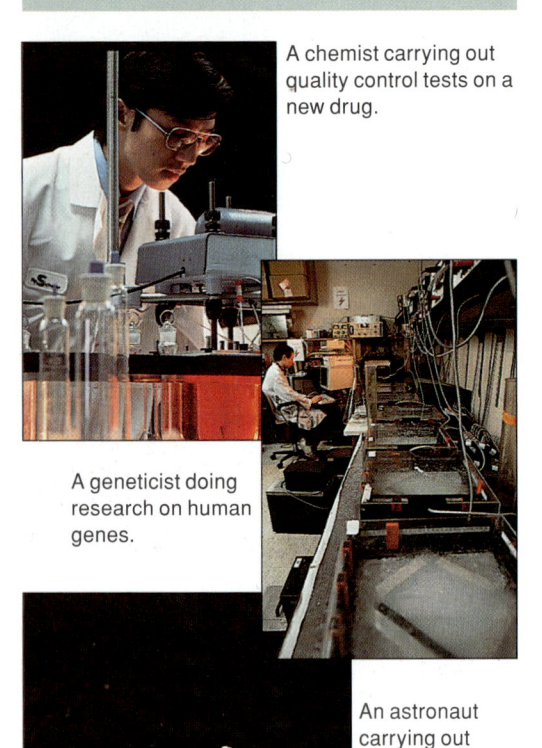

What's happened to my stereo?

Suppose you switch on your stereo and nothing happens. How do you go about finding what is wrong with it?

Well, first you think what the fault might be. Then you carry out a simple test to see if your idea is right. If the result of the test supports your idea, you then set about mending the machine in the right way. On the other hand, if the result of the test suggests that your idea is wrong, you give up that idea and think of another one.

This is exactly what scientists do when they tackle a problem. People call it the **scientific method.** The name makes it sound rather grand, but it is really what people usually do when wanting to find something out. For example, the same procedure is used by a doctor who wants to find what's wrong with you, a garage mechanic who has to mend your car, and a police detective who is trying to solve a crime.

So really the scientific method is just common sense. With that in mind, let's look at it in detail.

The scientific method

The scientific method starts off with an **observation**: you notice something interesting – it may be an object of some sort, or it may be something happening. You then ask questions about it: what is it, what is it doing, why is it there?

The next step is to think of a possible explanation for it. We call this an **hypothesis**. From the hypothesis, various **predictions** can be made. A prediction is simply a consequence which follows logically from the hypothesis.

You then test the predictions to find out if they are true. This is usually done by carrying out **experiments**. If your predictions turn out to be right, the hypothesis may well be true.

If your hypothesis appears to be true, you can make further predictions from it. These, too, can be tested by experiments. In this way, new discoveries are made, and new problems crop up.

Picture 2 describes an investigation in terms of the scientific method. Now let's look at the main steps in the scientific method more closely.

The main steps in the scientific method

Observing things

The natural world is full of interesting things. It may be the way clouds form, or the way substances react when mixed together, or the way animals move. Scientists are always on the look-out for interesting things to ask questions about.

To be useful, scientific observations must be accurate and carefully recorded. This is one reason why you will need to keep a notebook in your science course.

Making hypotheses

This involves thinking up explanations, and that means using your imagination. However, you must not let your imagination run away with you, otherwise your hypotheses may be just science fiction!

To be of any scientific use, a hypothesis must be testable. This means that you must be able to make predictions from it which can be tested by experiments.

Doing experiments

In picture 2 an experiment is done to find out if plants grow towards light. A potted plant is lit from one side, and you see if it grows towards the light.

However, there is something more that has to be done; we must obtain a second plant and light it from above. We need this second plant to provide a

A chemist carrying out quality control tests on a new drug.

A geneticist doing research on human genes.

An astronaut carrying out investigations in space.

A geologist examining a sample of rock.

Picture 1 Scientists at work.

standard with which to compare the first plant. The second plant in the experiment is called the **control**.

It is essential that the two plants are kept in exactly the same conditions, except for the light they receive. To put it in a general way, *we must keep all the variables constant except the one whose effect we are investigating*.

An experiment of this kind, in which the experimenter controls the conditions, is called a **controlled experiment**.

A control is not needed for all experiments. For example, suppose you do an experiment to find out if heavy objects fall faster than light ones. You don't need a control for this experiment. (Can you see why?) However, you do need to keep all variables the same when making your comparison. These variables include the shape and density of the objects and the height from which you drop them. The two objects should differ only in weight.

Drawing conclusions

Ideally, an experiment should be so well planned that only one conclusion can be drawn from the results. However, this is not always possible. Often two or more different conclusions may be drawn, though usually one is more likely than the others.

When you look at the results of your own experiments, it is a great temptation to draw only the conclusion that you want to draw. This is usually the one that supports your hypothesis. Always think of other possible conclusions, however unlikely they may seem to be.

Look again at picture 2. The conclusion from the experiment is that plants grow towards light. But at least two other conclusions are possible. Can you think what they are?

Repeating experiments

When you do an experiment at school, you probably do it only once. There is not usually time to do it more than once, even if you want to. But real science is not like that. In a proper scientific investigation, you do the experiment over and over again until consistent results are given every time. Only then can you be sure that you are doing the experiment correctly, so that valid conclusions may be drawn.

Even that is not the end of it. In real science experiments are repeated by other scientists, and they too should get the same results.

What are variables?

In any experiment you are faced with **variables**, that is, things which can change or vary. Suppose you want to find the effect of temperature on the rate of a chemical reaction. In this case the relevant variables are temperature and reaction rate. The reaction rate is called the **dependent variable** because it depends on other things (including temperature). Temperature, however, is an **independent variable** – so are other conditions such as pressure and light intensity.

In an experiment we alter (i.e. *manipulate*) one of the independent variables (in this case the temperature) and see what effect this has on the dependent variable (in this case the reaction rate). All other independent variables must be kept constant.

1. Which are the dependent and independent variables in the investigation summarised in picture 2? Which variable is manipulated, which one is measured and which ones should be kept constant?

2. Can you think of examples where temperature is the dependent variable?

Picture 2 An investigation presented in terms of the scientific method.

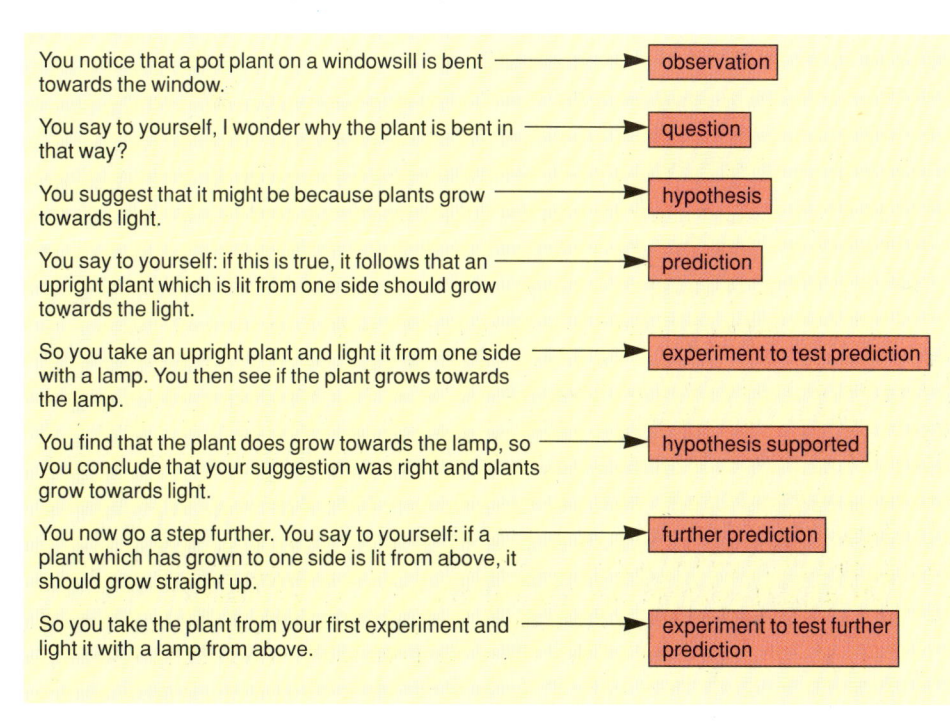

You notice that a pot plant on a windowsill is bent towards the window.	observation
You say to yourself, I wonder why the plant is bent in that way?	question
You suggest that it might be because plants grow towards light.	hypothesis
You say to yourself: if this is true, it follows that an upright plant which is lit from one side should grow towards the light.	prediction
So you take an upright plant and light it from one side with a lamp. You then see if the plant grows towards the lamp.	experiment to test prediction
You find that the plant does grow towards the lamp, so you conclude that your suggestion was right and plants grow towards light.	hypothesis supported
You now go a step further. You say to yourself: if a plant which has grown to one side is lit from above, it should grow straight up.	further prediction
So you take the plant from your first experiment and light it with a lamp from above.	experiment to test further prediction

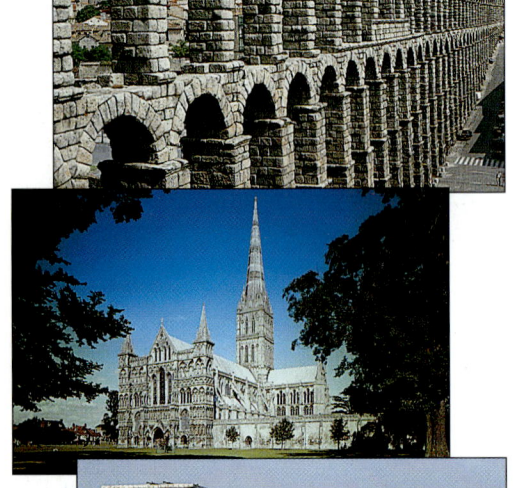

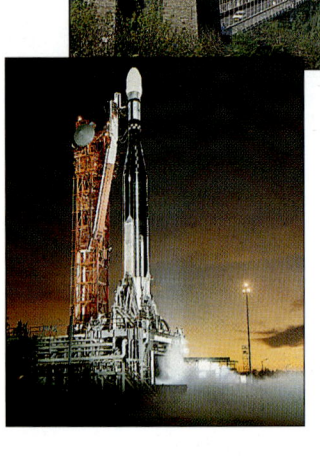

Playing fair

We can sum up what we have said so far like this: when you test a hypothesis, you must carry out the experiment in such a way that it really does test the hypothesis. This means that you must:
- include any necessary controls,
- keep all independent variables constant except the one which you are investigating,
- repeat the experiment until you get similar results every time.

If you test your hypothesis in this way, then it is a **fair test.** If, however, your test falls short in any way, then it is an unfair test. Unfair tests are useless in science, and the results can be very misleading.

Proving things

In picture 2 the plant that was lit from one side bent over towards the light. Does this *prove* that plants grow towards light? Surely the answer is no. The results of this experiment support the hypothesis, but they do not prove it. They provide **evidence**, not proof. To prove the hypothesis you would have to do some other experiments. What should they be?

Rarely is a hypothesis proved beyond all doubt. However, more and more evidence may be obtained to support it. When enough evidence has been found, we can call the hypothesis a **theory**. A theory is like a hypothesis, but much more certain.

Generalisations

The experiment in picture 2 has not been done on every species of plant in the world. However, it has been done on enough species for us to feel certain that plants in general grow towards light. A statement of this sort is called a **generalisation**.

Generalisations are useful because they help us to cut through the detail of the subject and see patterns. They also enable us to make predictions about things we do not yet know. For example, think of the generalisation that plants grow towards light. From this we can predict that plants have some way of sensing where the light is coming from. Having made this prediction we can test it by doing appropriate experiments.

Making use of science

For centuries the discoveries of science have been used to improve human life. Using science in this way is called **technology**.

We are all familiar with the way physics and chemistry affect our lives: electricity, transport, computers, medicines, dyes and so on. Your physics and chemistry books are full of examples. Some of the ways biology affects our lives are mentioned in the next topic.

All sorts of things have to be done before a scientific discovery can be turned into something useful. Take penicillin, for example (see page 203). Sir Alexander Fleming discovered penicillin in 1929, but it was ten years before it was put on the market. Why do you think there was such a long delay? In Britain we have a very good reputation for making scientific discoveries, but not such a good reputation for marketing them.

Technologists are concerned with making things work. Many of them are **inventors**, applying the discoveries of science to making things that people want. How many inventions can you think of which directly affect your life?

As with science itself, an invention often starts with an observation. James Watt watched a kettle boiling, and this led to his inventing the steam engine. But it took people with other talents to turn Watt's invention into a full-scale railway system with stations, tunnels, bridges, signals and so on. This is the world of technology for which science is only the beginning.

Picture 3 Technology over the centuries. Top to bottom: Cheops pyramid and temple in Egypt; a Roman aqueduct in Spain; Salisbury Cathedral, the tallest spire in England; Clifton suspension bridge in Bristol; Mariner IV rocket.

Activities

A Observing things and asking questions

On your way home from school, or the next time you go for a walk, look for interesting scientific things. They may be objects such as animals, plants or rocks, or they may be events such as birds feeding or leaves falling off a tree.

Make a list of ten such things. In each case write down one question relating to the observation, and say how it might be investigated further.

B Testing a hypothesis

Your teacher will give you some Plasticine, a tall measuring cylinder and a stopwatch. Use them to test the following hypothesis: a streamlined object moves through water faster than a non-streamlined object.

Write an account of your experiment, explaining your method and describing your results.

What predictions can you make from your results about the shapes of animals that live in water? In what way might the results be useful in industry?

What design problems did you encounter in your experiment, and how did you overcome them?

Questions

1. Someone has suggested that cows yield more milk if you play music to them. How could you test this hypothesis?

2. There is a large tree growing in the middle of my lawn. I have noticed that there are lots of daisies in the lawn, but none under the tree.
   a Suggest two hypotheses to explain why there are no daisies under the tree.
   b Choose one of your hypotheses and make a prediction from it which can be tested by an experiment.
   c Describe an experiment which could be done to find out if the prediction is correct.
   d Assuming that your hypothesis turns out to be true, make a further prediction which could be tested by an experiment.

3. When carrying out an experiment you must keep all variables constant except the one you are investigating.
   a Explain the meaning of the word variable. Give an example so as to make the meaning clear.
   b Why is it necessary to keep all variables constant except the one you are investigating?

4. The experiment in picture 2 on page 7 is not, as described, a fair test of the hypothesis. In what way or ways is it not a fair test? Rewrite the experiment in your own words so that it is a fair test.

5. The picture shows a body louse which feeds by sucking human blood through the skin.
   a Write down *two* observations from the picture.
   b Ask a question about *one* of the observations and put forward an hypothesis to answer it.
   c How would you test the hypothesis?

Thinking scientifically

In studying science one of the things you have to do is to learn to think scientifically. What does this mean? Well, it can best be understood by knowing the difference between a scientific statement and an unscientific statement.

A scientific statement is one which can be disproved by investigation. An example of a scientific statement is 'potatoes contain starch'. We can test this statement by carrying out a simple chemical test on a potato.

Here is an example of an unscientific statement: 'Britain is better under the Conservatives.' This is an unscientific statement because it cannot be tested by investigation and therefore cannot be disproved. It's a statement not of science but of opinion.

This exercise is about unscientific statements which manufacturers sometimes make about their products. Here is an example. It is written on the side of bottles containing a certain type of bleach which is used as a powerful disinfectant in the home:

"THE FRESH SMELL TELLS YOU IT KEEPS ON KILLING GERMS"

1. Explain why it would be impossible to test this statement scientifically.

   Suggest a *scientific* statement which the manufacturer might make about this particular product.

2. Visit a supermarket and look at the labels on the various items. Find five statements which you think are scientific and five which are unscientific.

Choose one of the unscientific statements and write a letter to the manufacturer criticising this kind of advertising. (There's no need to post it!)

A2
Studying biology

In this topic you will find out what biology is and why we study it.

What is biology?

Biology is the study of living things. Living things are called **organisms**. Organisms include animals and plants. Some organisms are so small that they cannot be seen with the unaided eye; we call them **microorganisms**, or **microbes** for short. Microbes are very important to us as we shall see later; studying them is therefore an important part of biology.

The different branches of biology

Zoology:	the study of animals
Botany:	the study of plants
Human biology:	the study of humans
Microbiology:	the study of microorganisms (microbes)
Anatomy:	the study of the structure of living things
Physiology:	the study of how the body works
Nutrition:	the study of food and how living things feed
Heredity (genetics):	the study of how characteristics are passed from parents to offspring
Ecology:	the study of where organisms live.

Biology as a science

Biologists investigate organisms and make discoveries about them. Biology is a scientific subject, just like chemistry and physics. We can therefore study organisms using the methods of science, as described in the last topic. This involves making careful observations and carrying out experiments.

Drawings

As you study biology you will find that you need to make a record of your observations. Often the best way of doing this is to make a **drawing**. The aim is to produce an accurate record of what you see, so the drawing must look like the real thing. Of course, if you are drawing a fly you need not put every hair in the right place. However, the general impression must be as realistic as possible.

A useful biological drawing is shown in picture 2. It was done by a pupil in a school. Notice that she has given her drawing a title and has labelled the various parts.

When you make a drawing always write down how many times larger, or smaller, your drawing is than the real thing. This is called the **scale**. If your drawing is twice as large as the specimen, the scale is ×2. If you draw it life-size, the scale is ×1. And if you draw it half the natural size, the scale is ×0.5.

Diagrams

We often make diagrams in biology. A biological diagram shows how things relate to each other, not what they actually look like. Look, for example, at the diagram of the human blood system on page 140. It shows the general plan of the circulation, but not the individual blood vessels and where each one goes. Note that arrows have been put in to show the direction in which the blood flows, and colour has been used to distinguish between the different types of blood. As with drawings, a diagram must always have a title and be fully labelled. Think how useless a London Underground map would be if the stations had no names!

Jobs involving biology

Not all biologists spend their time doing experiments and making drawings! Some apply their knowledge of biology to other things. Doctors, nurses, physiotherapists, vets, farmers and foresters are all biologists in different ways.

Picture 1 A biologist at work in the laboratory.

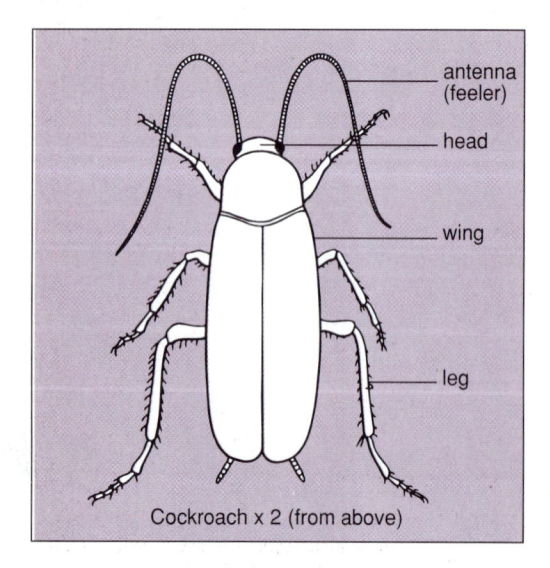

Picture 2 A biological drawing should be realistic but simple. There is no need to shade it.

They all study biology in their training, and biology comes into everything they do (picture 3).

Can you think of any other jobs which involve biology?

Biology and industry

For thousands of years humans have used yeast, a tiny microorganism, for making bread and alcoholic drinks such as beer and wine (see page 188). These processes are now major industries. They are examples of how biology can be applied to making commercially useful products.

Today microorganisms are used in many other production processes. Bacteria and fungi are particularly useful in this respect. In some cases the organism's genes are first changed to make it produce the thing we want. This is called **genetic engineering**. Microorganisms reproduce very quickly, so vast numbers of them can be used for mass production in large-scale industrial plants (picture 4).

The application of the science of biology to the manufacturing industry is known as **biotechnology**. Large amounts of money have been invested in this new type of industry.

Biology and the environment

Our environment is threatened by pollution – not just our own local surroundings but the environment of the whole world.

The most important part of the environment which is under threat is the atmosphere. Biology comes into this because the gases in our atmosphere are controlled by the natural activities of living organisms, notably respiration and photosynthesis.

Over the last two centuries humans have changed the composition of the atmosphere. This in turn has brought about other changes, for example an increase in the world's temperature. If nothing is done about this, life itself could be threatened.

Safeguarding our environment is one of the greatest challenges facing scientists today. We shall return to this later.

Biology and everyday life

Biology comes into our lives all the time. The food we eat, our health and our environment are just three ways in which biology affects us personally.

Many hobbies and outdoor pursuits also involve biology. Gardening, fishing and bird-watching are three examples (picture 5). Can you think of others?

Picture 3 This vet uses her knowledge of biology to care for the health of animals.

Picture 4 Inside a biotechnology plant. The technician is adjusting a fermentation unit in which millions of microorganisms produce a particular type of protein for human use.

Picture 5 Fishing, gardening and bird-watching are all hobbies involving biology.

A3 The characteristics of living things

Certain features are common to all living things.

Living things move

Movement is obvious in the case of an animal like the human. We move our arms and legs by means of **muscles**. Most organisms can move by one means or another, at least at some period in their life cycle.

Movement is usually less obvious in plants. To see movement in a plant you must look inside it, under a microscope (activity A).

Living things are sensitive

If you sit on a drawing pin, you jump up quickly. You are **sensitive** to the sharp point. The pricking of your bottom is called the **stimulus** (plural: **stimuli**). Your jumping is called the **response**.

Living things respond to different kinds of stimuli. The main ones are touch, chemicals, heat, light and sound.

At first sight you might think that plants are an exception to the rule that all organisms respond to stimuli. After all, if you hit a tree, it does not move away. However, plants *do* respond to certain stimuli, but much more slowly than animals. They do not have muscles. Instead they respond by *growing* in a particular direction. For example, most plants grow towards light.

An interesting case of a plant responding quickly to touch is investigated in activity B.

Living things grow

As an animal or plant develops, it gets larger and heavier. In other words, it **grows**. In this process its volume and mass increase.

Growth takes place by substances being taken into the organism from outside. These substances are then built up into the structures of the body: they become part of the organism. This is called **assimilation**.

Living things feed

We have just seen that, in order to grow, an organism must take substances into its body. This is achieved by **feeding (nutrition)**.

Animals and plants feed in quite different ways. Animals feed on complex organic substances (**heterotrophic nutrition**). These substances are often solid and have to be broken down into a soluble form: this process is called **digestion**.

In contrast to animals, plants make their own food (**autotrophic nutrition**). They take in simple things like carbon dioxide and water and build them up into complex organic substances. Energy is needed for this: it comes from sunlight. The green pigment **chlorophyll** enables the plant to use sunlight in this way: this is why plants are usually green. The process by which plants make food is called **photosynthesis**.

Living things transfer energy

Living things need energy to move, grow, replace worn-out structures, and so on. They obtain this energy from their food. The food is broken down into carbon dioxide and water, and energy is transferred. This process is known as **respiration**.

Respiration normally requires oxygen. Organisms get this vital gas from the air or water around them.

Living things get rid of poisonous waste

In many ways an organism is like a chemical factory. Substances are constantly being broken down to release energy, or built up to make things.

Some of the by-products of these chemical reactions are poisonous. They

Picture 1 The gymnast is showing one of the basic features of life, movement.

Picture 2 All organisms feed. This lizard, known as a bearded dragon, is eating a grasshopper.

must not be allowed to accumulate inside the organisms or they will kill it. So the body must get rid of them. This is called **excretion**.

Living things produce offspring

Organisms produce offspring. This is known as **reproduction**. Usually it involves the union of two individuals, a male and a female. This of course is **sexual reproduction**.

Some organisms can reproduce on their own without the help of another individual. This is called **asexual reproduction**. At its simplest, the organism merely splits in two. In good conditions asexual reproduction may take place very quickly and sometimes a very large number of offspring are produced.

When organisms reproduce, instructions in the form of **genes** get passed from the parents to the offspring. Genes are made of a substance called **DNA**. This stands for **deoxyribonucleic acid**. DNA belongs to a group of substances called **nucleic acids**.

DNA occurs in the cells of all organisms from bacteria to humans. It gives every individual organism its unique characteristics and has been aptly described as the molecule of life.

Picture 3 Reproduction is one of the basic features of living things. Here, a labrador bitch is suckling her young.

Activities

A Detecting movement in a plant

Movement is difficult to see in most plants, but here is an exception.

1 Obtain a sprig of the water plant Canadian pondweed (*Elodea*) which has been kept in the light for several hours.
2 Cut off one of the leaves and put it in a drop of water on a microscope slide.
3 Cover the leaf with a coverslip.
4 Look at the leaf under the low power of your microscope.
   Can you see lots of small green objects inside the leaf? These are called chloroplasts and they contain chlorophyll. If they are moving, describe their movement as fully as you can. What use do you think these movements are to the plant?

B Observing a plant responding to touch

Few plants respond quickly when you touch them, but certain sensitive plants do, for example *Mimosa pudica*.

1 Obtain a potted specimen of a sensitive plant.
2 Gently touch the top side of a leaf with a needle. What happens?
3 Gently touch other parts of the plant, including the lower side of the leaves, and the stem.
   Describe what happens in each case.
4 Pipette a drop of water onto one of the leaves. What happens?
   What use do you think this response might be to the plant? How do you think the response might be brought about? How would a similar response be brought about in an animal?
   Can you think of any other plants that respond to touch? Why is it useful to them to respond to touch?

C Recognising the characteristics of living organisms

1 Make a list of the characteristics of living things given in this topic, starting with 'living things move' and finishing with 'living things produce offspring'.
2 Examine various organisms or pictures of organisms, provided by your teacher.
   They might include the following: an earthworm, a locust, a frog or toad, a green plant, a clam, a snail, a mould, a lichen, yeast, and yourself.
3 For each organism write down the particular characteristics which you can *see* it possesses. Do not write down the characteristic unless you can actually see it.
   After doing this, you will realise that some of the characteristics of life are difficult to see in organisms.
   How could you find out if an organism possesses a characteristic of life which you cannot actually see?

Questions

1 Of all the characteristics of living things mentioned in this topic, which ones are most important in each of the following?
   The number of characteristics which you should mention in each case is given in brackets.
   a A person watching television (1),
   b a footballer kicking a ball (2),
   c a lion stalking a zebra (2),
   d germs spreading through your body when you are ill (1),
   e a plant bending towards the light (1),
   f a person panting after a race (1),
   g a bean plant climbing up a bamboo cane (2).
2 If you blow up a balloon and then hold it in front of the fire, it increases in size.
   Is the balloon growing in a biological sense? Give reasons for your answer.
3 A visitor to our planet from outer space thinks motor cars are alive.
   In order to straighten the matter out for our extra-terrestrial friend, make a list of ways in which a motor car is similar to living organisms, and a list of ways in which it is different.

A4 Identifying, naming and classifying

About one and a half million kinds of organisms have been discovered. How do we identify, name and classify them?

Picture 1 Five flowering plants which you might see on a walk.

Picture 2 The sea mouse *Aphrodite*. It is not a mouse at all, but a relative of the earthworm.

Picture 3 The marsh marigold, *Caltha palustris*. Its many common names include King cup, golden cup, brave celandine, horse blob, May blob, Mary bud, soldier's button and publicans and sinners!

How do we identify living things?

Suppose you go for a walk and you see one of the plants shown in picture 1. How can you find out its name? One way might be to compare it with pictures in a book. This is all right if it is a short book, but if it is a long one it can be tedious and it is difficult to know where to start.

It is better to use a **key**. Keys are used by biologists to identify organisms quickly and accurately.

A key for identifying the plants in picture 1 is shown below.

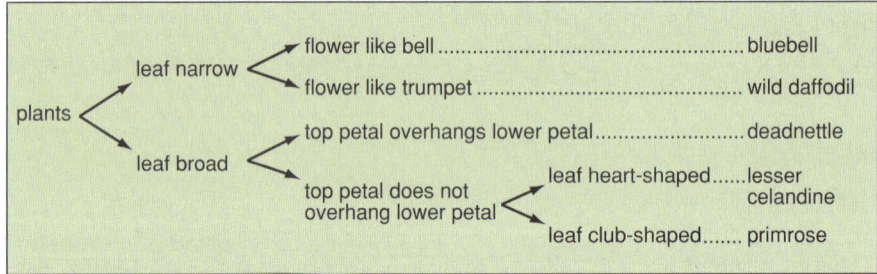

```
                    ┌─ flower like bell .................... bluebell
         ┌ leaf narrow ┤
         │          └─ flower like trumpet ................. wild daffodil
plants ──┤
         │          ┌─ top petal overhangs lower petal ...... deadnettle
         └ leaf broad ┤                    ┌ leaf heart-shaped ...... lesser celandine
                    └─ top petal does not ┤
                       overhang lower petal└ leaf club-shaped ....... primrose
```

Because of its shape, this is called a **spider key** or **tree key**. The trouble with keys of this kind is that they take up a lot of room. So usually we use a **numbered key**. A numbered key for the plants in picture 1 is shown below. Use it to identify each of the plants.

1	leaves narrow	go to 2
	leaves broad	go to 3
2	flower like bell	bluebell
	flower like trumpet	wild daffodil
3	top petal overhangs lower petal	deadnettle
	top petal does not overhang lower petal	go to 4
4	leaf heart-shaped	lesser celandine
	leaf club-shaped	primrose

What's in a name?

The names of the plants given in the key which you have just used are **common names**. They are the names which we use in everyday language like cat, dog, lion and so on.

The trouble with common names is that they can be misleading. One reason is that they are often based on superficial appearance. Look at the animal in picture 2, for example. It is called a 'sea mouse'. But it isn't a mouse at all. It's a relative of the earthworm. It got its name because it looks hairy and reminded someone of a mouse!

Another problem is that an organism may have more than one common name. Take the plant in picture 3, for example. Most people would probably call this plant a marsh marigold. However, it is known by hundreds of other names. Some of them are given in the caption underneath the picture. To make matters worse, in parts of America it is called a cowslip, a name which in Britain is given to a completely different plant.

A better way of naming organisms

Biologists use a standard international system. Each type of organism is given two names. This is called the **binomial system**. For example, the lesser celandine in picture 1 is called *Ranunculus ficaria*.

The first name, *Ranunculus*, is the name of the **genus** to which the plant belongs. The lesser celandine shares this name with other closely related plants such as buttercup and crowfoot.

The second name, *ficaria*, is the name of the **species** to which the plant belongs. This name is possessed only by the lesser celandine; no other plant in the genus has this name.

All organisms are given two names in this way. Thus the family dog is *Canis familiaris*, the cat is *Felis catus*, and you are *Homo sapiens*. These are called **proper names** or **scientific names**. They are written in Latin or have Latin endings. It is usual to start the genus name with a capital letter, and the species name with a small letter, and to print both in italics.

The trouble with scientific names is that they are often long and difficult to remember. For example, there is a certain type of worm which is called *Haploscoloplos bustorus*! So, to make things easier we often call organisms by their simpler common names. This is all right so long as we can be sure that there will be no confusion.

How do we classify organisms?

Classification means puttings things into groups. The smallest group that an organism belongs to is the species. As we have seen, related species are placed in the same genus (plural: genera). Now we can put similar genera into larger groups, and these groups can in turn be lumped together into even larger groups.

If we go on doing this, we finish up with five very large groups called **kingdoms**. Each kingdom contains many different organisms, but they all have certain basic features in common. In the next topic we shall look at the kingdoms and see something of the variety that exists within them.

Questions

1 Write down the common names of five well-known organisms other than the ones mentioned in this topic, then use books to find out their proper names.

2 It is particularly important that organisms should be given their proper names in medicine, agriculture and industry. Why?

3 The following questions are about the key to the plants in picture 1.
  a Why were bluebells distinguished from daffodils by their flowers rather than by their leaves?
  b If you were to distinguish between the lesser celandine and primrose by their flowers rather than by their leaves, what would you say about them?

4 A scientist visits an uninhabited island and discovers the insects shown in the illustration below. Make up a name for each insect, and devise a key which would enable another visitor to the island to identify them.

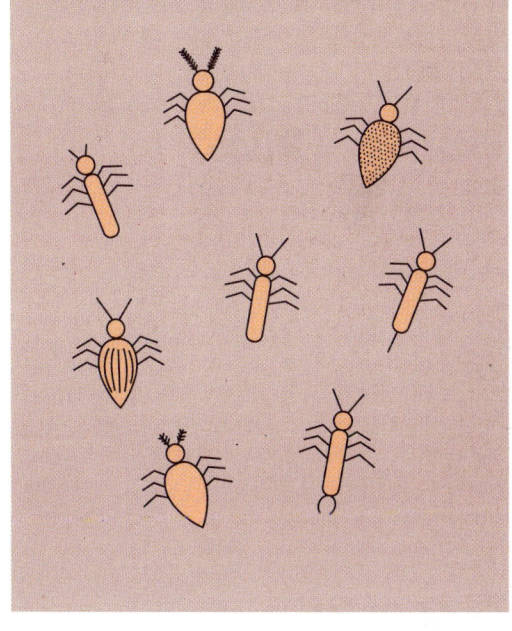

Activities

A Using a key (Practical technique 4)
Your teacher will give you a collection of organisms or pictures of organisms labelled A, B, C, etc. You will also be given a key for identifying them. Use the key to identify each organism. Make a table showing which features enabled you to carry out your identifications.

B Making your own key

1 Your teacher will give you a collection of organisms, or pictures of organisms, together with their names.

2 Make a key, similar to the one on page 14, which would enable a person to find out the name of each organism. To do this, write out a spider key first, and then make a numbered key from the spider key.

3 Ask a friend to identify the organisms using your key.

4 If your friend runs into any difficulties, improve the wording of the key to make it clearer.

Why is a numbered key better than an spider key?

A5
Who's who in the world of living things

Here we shall look at the main groups of living things, and get a glimpse of the variety that is found amongst organisms.

Introduction

There are several different ways of classifying living things. In this book we shall divide them into five kingdoms:

Bacteria Kingdom,
Protoctist Kingdom,
Fungus Kingdom,
Plant Kingdom,
Animal Kingdom.

Most living things belong to the plant and animal kingdoms. It is here that we find the greatest number of species and the widest variety of form. In the lightning tour that follows we can only touch on the tremendous variety that really exists.

The sizes which are given with the pictures are approximate. The smallest organisms consist of only one cell (**unicellular**). The larger ones are made up of many cells (**multicellular**). Those that can only be seen properly by using a microscope are **microorganisms** (**microbes**).

Bacteria kingdom

Can only be seen with the high power of the light microscope. Consist of a single cell with a wall but no proper nucleus. Varied methods of feeding. Some, e.g. blue-green bacteria, feed by photosynthesis. Occur in air, water, soil or inside other organisms. Many of them cause diseases.

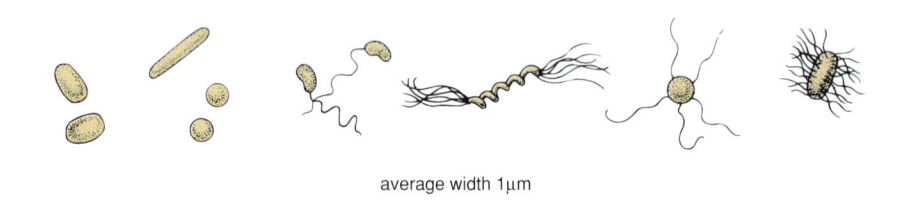

average width 1μm

Protoctist kingdom

A wide range of single-celled and simple many-celled organisms.

The single-celled ones have a proper nucleus and can usually be seen with the low power of the microscope. Some feed by taking in organic substances, others by photosynthesis. The photosynthetic ones are called **algae**. Most algae are many-celled but do not have roots, stems or leaves. They are usually green, but sometimes brown or red. Protoctists live mainly in water and soil; some of the single-celled ones are parasites.

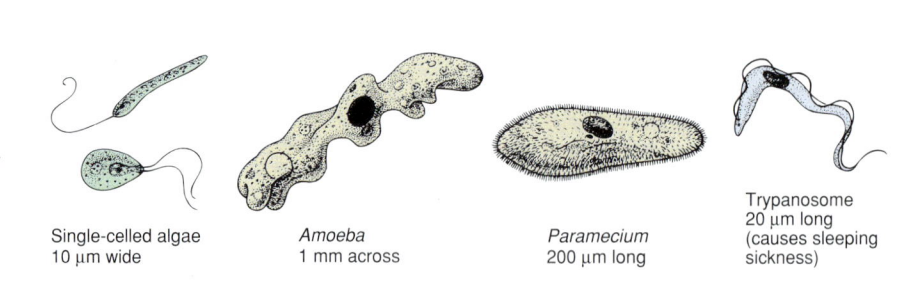

Single-celled algae 10 μm wide

Amoeba 1 mm across

Paramecium 200 μm long

Trypanosome 20 μm long (causes sleeping sickness)

Fungus kingdom

Most are many-celled, consisting of a network (**mycelium**) of fine threads (**hyphae**). The threads may be densely interwoven to form mushrooms and toadstools. Feed by absorbing organic substances from dead or living material. Latter are parasites, especially of plants.

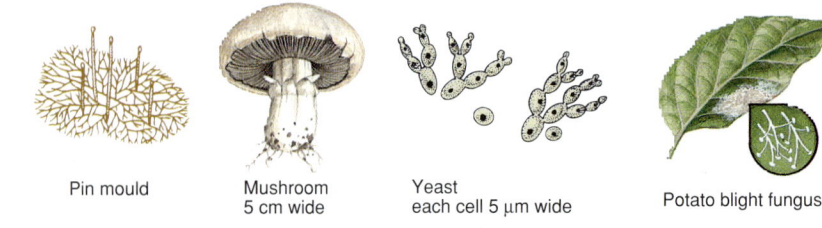

Pin mould

Mushroom 5 cm wide

Yeast each cell 5 μm wide

Potato blight fungus

Who's who in the world of living things 17

Lichens
Consist of a fungus and a plant-like protoctist combined together. Grow on rocks and tree trunks. Very resistant to drying.

Shrubby lichen
10 mm high

Leafy lichen
(flat)

Plant kingdom

Many-celled organisms which contain the green substance chlorophyll and make their own food by photosynthesis.

Mosses and liverworts (Bryophytes)
Have simple leaves or leaf-like form but no proper roots or stems, and no vascular tissue. Found mainly in damp places. Reproductive spores are formed in **capsule**.

Moss
10 mm high

Liverwort
5 mm wide

Ferns
Have proper roots and stems, and leaf-like fronds with vascular tissue. Young fronds are coiled into a bud (called a 'fiddlehead'). Found mainly in damp places. Reproductive spores are formed on the undersides of the fronds. The spore bodies are in clusters called **sori** (singular: **sorus**).

Common fern has unbranched fronds
40 cm high

Bracken
(has branched fronds)

Conifers
Mainly large plants with seed-bearing **cones** for reproduction. Most of them keep their leaves throughout the year (evergreen).

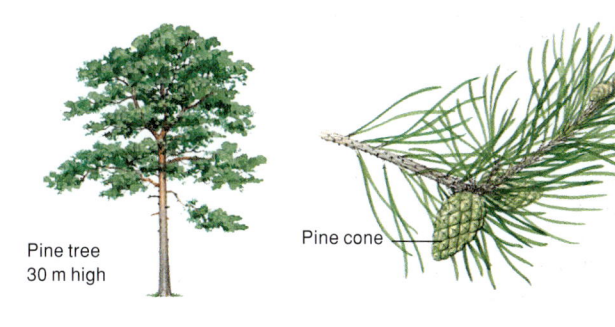

Pine tree
30 m high

Pine cone

Flowering plants
Wide range of plants with seed-bearing **flowers** for reproduction. Seeds protected inside fruits. Range from small herbs to massive trees. Some are evergreen, others drop their leaves in winter (deciduous).

Foxglove
45 cm high

Oak tree
25 m high

Grass
30 cm high

Iris
45 cm high

Palm tree
10 m high

Animal kingdom

Many-celled organisms that feed on other organisms. They all have a nervous system and usually move around.

Animals without backbones (invertebrates)

Cnidarians
Simple sac-like body with tentacles and **stinging cells**. Live singly or in colonies, either attached or floating. May produce a hard external coating (e.g. corals). Most live in the sea, a few in fresh water.

Hydra (lives in ponds) 10 mm long

Jellyfish 10 cm wide

Sea anenome 5 cm tall

Coral

Flatworms
Body elongated and flat. Some live in fresh water, but most are parasites of animals. For example, the liver fluke lives in the livers of sheep and other mammals.

Fresh-water flatworm 10 mm long

Tapeworm 5 m long

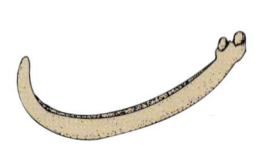

Blood fluke 15 mm long

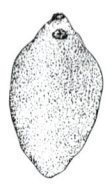

Liver fluke 2 cm long

Roundworms
Body elongated and thread-like, round in cross-section. Some live in soil but most are parasites of plants or animals.

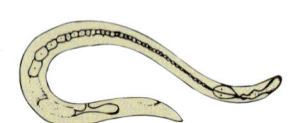

Ascaris 30 cm long (human roundworm)

Threadworms 1 cm long (live in rectum of humans)

Annelids (segmented worms)
Body long and divided by rings into a series of **segments** (annelid means 'ringed'). Lack legs but have bristle-like **chaetae** which may assist in locomotion. Most are aquatic (live in water), but some live in the soil. Some are external parasites.

Earthworm 15 cm long (burrows in soil)

Leach 5 cm long (sucks blood)

Ragworm 15 cm long (swims in the sea)

Tube worm 10 cm lohg (lives in a tube in the sea)

Who's who in the world of living things 19

Molluscs
Body soft and unsegmented, usually covered by a **shell**. Most are aquatic, some live on the seashore and on land.

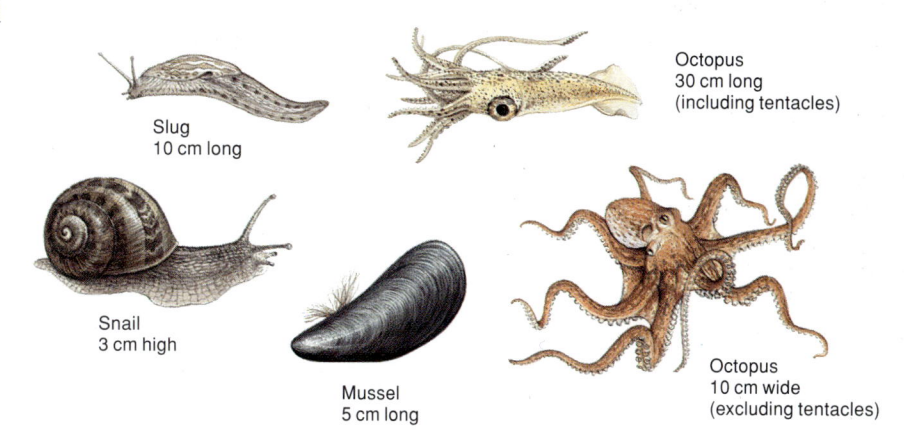

Slug
10 cm long

Octopus
30 cm long
(including tentacles)

Snail
3 cm high

Mussel
5 cm long

Octopus
10 cm wide
(excluding tentacles)

Echinoderms
Body based on a pattern of five parts which typically radiate out like a star. Have a tough skin, often with **spines** (echinoderm means 'spiny skin'). All live in the sea.

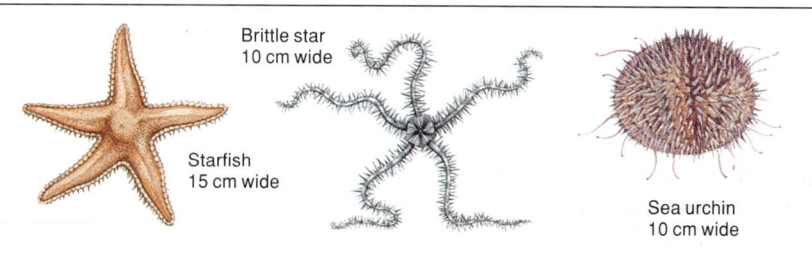

Starfish
15 cm wide

Brittle star
10 cm wide

Sea urchin
10 cm wide

Arthropods
Segmented animals with a hard cuticle (**exoskeleton**) and jointed appendages on at least some of their segments (arthropod means 'jointed foot'). Most have feelers (**antennae**) and **compound eyes**. (Compound eye is made up of many little eyes packed together.) Some, e.g. insects, have air holes (**spiracles**) for breathing.

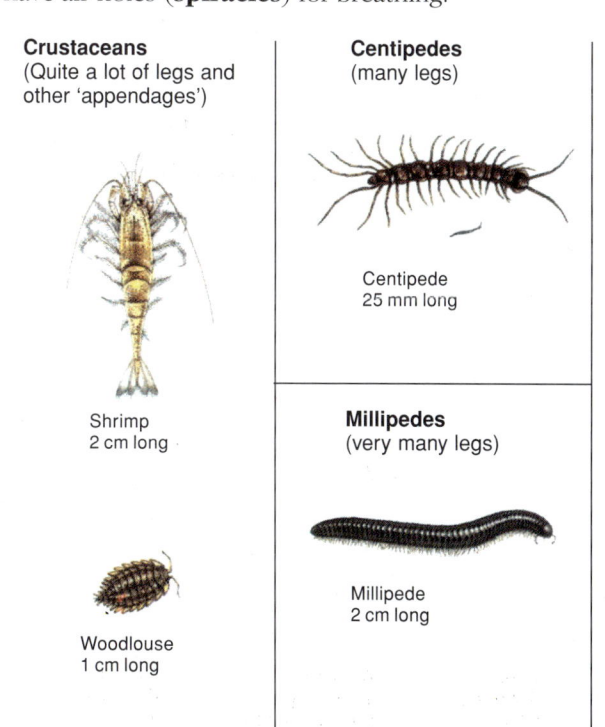

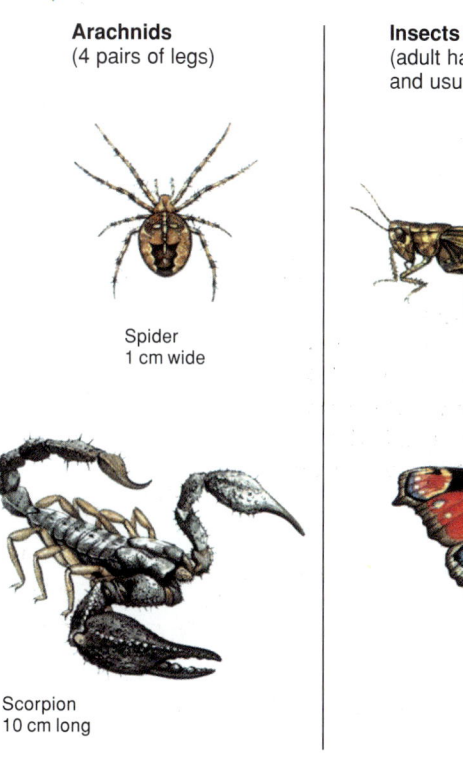

Crustaceans
(Quite a lot of legs and other 'appendages')

Shrimp
2 cm long

Woodlouse
1 cm long

Centipedes
(many legs)

Centipede
25 mm long

Millipedes
(very many legs)

Millipede
2 cm long

Arachnids
(4 pairs of legs)

Spider
1 cm wide

Scorpion
10 cm long

Insects
(adult has 3 pairs of legs and usually 2 pairs of wings)

Locust
5 cm long

Butterfly
15 mm long

Animals with backbones (vertebrates)

Fish
Skin covered with **scales**. Live in water. Have **gills** for breathing and fins for movement.

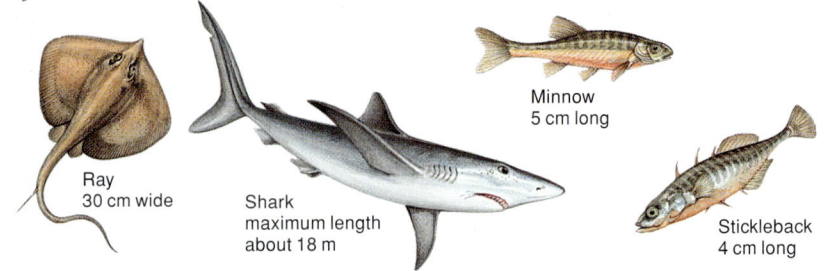

Ray 30 cm wide
Shark maximum length about 18 m
Minnow 5 cm long
Stickleback 4 cm long

Amphibians
Have soft skin without scales. Live on land but lay eggs in water. Have **tadpole** (larva) which changes into the adult. Tadpole is aquatic with gills, adult is usually terrestrial (land-living) with lungs.

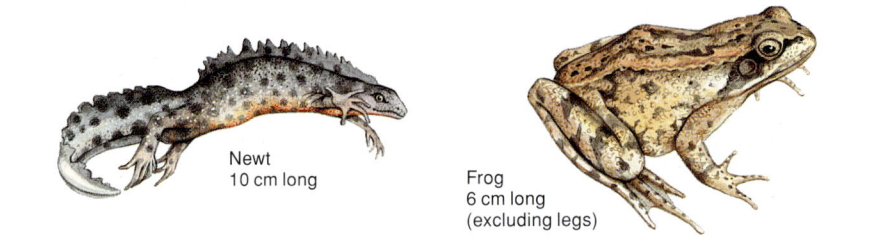

Newt 10 cm long
Frog 6 cm long (excluding legs)

Reptiles
Have hard, tough skin with **scales**. Eggs have a soft shell and are laid on land. Lungs for breathing.

Common lizard 12 cm long
Crocodile about 9 m long
Tortoise 20 cm wide
Snake about 10 m (python etc.)

Birds
Have skin with **feathers**. Eggs have hard shells. Wings for flying, and a beak for feeding. Have lungs and are 'warm-blooded'.

Sparrow 15 cm long
Owl 30 cm high
Vulture wingspan 1 m
Ostrich 2.5 m tall (does not fly)

Mammals
Have skin with **hair**. The young develop inside the mother and after birth are fed on milk from her **mammary glands**. Have lungs and are 'warm-blooded'.

Kangaroo 2 m high
Lion 2 m long
Whale about 33 km long
Human 2 m high

Activities

A Putting some familiar animals and plants into groups

1 Examine various organisms, or pictures of organisms, provided by your teacher. All of them are featured in the classification on pages 16–20.

2 Write down the name of the group to which each organism belongs. Use the classification to help you.

3 Look carefully at each organism.

Which particular feature or features enabled you to place each organism in its group?

From its structure, what can you say about the sort of place where it lives, and the kind of life it leads?

B Putting some unfamiliar animals and plants into groups

1 Examine various organisms which are not illustrated in the classification on pages 16–20.

2 Write down the name of the group to which you think each organism belongs. Do this by relating the characteristics of the organism to the information given on pages 16–20.

3 Look carefully at each organism.

Which specific illustration on pages 16–20 does each organism resemble most closely?

In what ways do they resemble each other?

Give the results of this investigation as a table. Devise the table yourself so as to present all the information in the clearest possible way.

What special features does each organism have?

Do you have difficulty in placing some of the organisms? If so, why?

Present the results of this activity as a table so as to show all the information clearly.

C Collecting and naming organisms

1 Collect organisms from a habitat near your school or home. Your teacher will show you how to collect the organisms.

2 Examine each organism, using a hand lens or microscope if necessary.

3 Use the classification on pages 16–20 to find out what group each organism belongs to.

4 Return all living organisms to their habitat afterwards.

Questions

1 What group does each of these organisms belong to: moss, jellyfish, turtle, tapeworm, whale, mushroom, pin mould, tube worm, seaweed, newt?

2 What would be the easiest way of telling the difference between:
 a an arthropod and a vertebrate,
 b an insect and an arachnid,
 c an amphibian and a reptile,
 d an alga and a fungus,
 e a conifer and a flowering plant?

3 From books, try to find out the largest member of each of the following groups: algae, ferns, conifers, flowering plants.

In each case give the proper name and common names of the organism, and state its approximate size.

4 Give the name of an animal which:
 a is shaped like an umbrella and has stinging cells,
 b lays eggs with a soft shell,
 c has a pouch in which the young develop,
 d is shaped like a star,
 e has two pairs of wings,
 f lives on land but lays its eggs in water,
 g has long tentacles and belongs to the same group as snails,
 h has mammary glands,
 i has four pairs of legs,
 j has scales and gills.

5 Give the name of an organism which:
 a reproduces by means of flowers,
 b has frond-like leaves,
 c consists of only one cell and is coloured green,
 d causes a disease,
 e has no chlorophyll.

6 Which of the following features are possessed only by insects, and which ones belong to other arthropods too:
 a hard cuticle,
 b joints,
 c six legs,
 d feelers,
 e two pairs of wings?

7 The picture below is of a small insect which lives in the soil. Name two important structures, typical of most insects, which it lacks. Why do you think this insect does not need these particular structures?

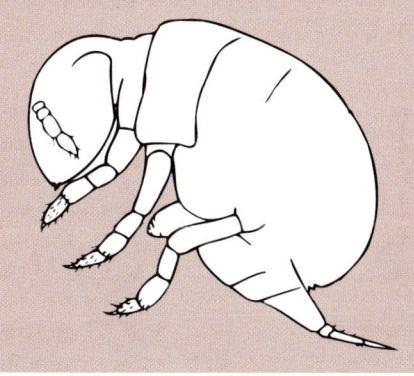

Tops, bottoms, fronts and backs

Most animals move with one end of the body in the lead. This is the front or **anterior** end. The other end is called the **posterior** end. In most animals there is some kind of head at the anterior end. This is where we expect to find the mouth and the main sense organs.

The lower side of the body, the side that's usually closest to the ground, is called the **ventral** side. The upper side is called the **dorsal** side. Humans stand and walk on two legs – we are **bipedal**. In this case the ventral side faces the front.

1 Why is it useful for an animal to have its mouth and main sense organs at the anterior end?

2 Do plants have an anterior and posterior end? If not, why?

3 What are the advantages and disadvantages of being bipedal?

B1 Habitats and communities

Usually lots of different species are found living together in particular places.

Picture 1 A freshwater pond in Scotland.

Picture 2 A Scottish wood in autumn.

Picture 3 A grassland in East Africa.

Picture 4 Desert plants in the Californian desert.

Where do living things occur?

Living things are found almost everywhere: on land and in the air, in water and underground. They occur in the soil, under logs and stones, in grass and in trees. Various pests may share our homes with us, and some live as parasites inside us.

The place where an organism lives is called its **habitat**. Examples of habitats are shown in pictures 1 to 4. Within a habitat organisms may live in a particular place such as under a stone or log. These are called **microhabitats**.

Communities and ecosystems

In a habitat such as a pond or wood, the various organisms can be divided up into producers, consumers and decomposers. Each type of animal or plant forms a **population**. Together these populations make up a **community**. Every habitat has its own typical community.

Within the community each species feeds on, or is eaten by, other species. In other words each species occupies a particular feeding position in the habitat. This is called its **ecological niche**. We will come back to these ideas on page 28.

All the organisms of the community are therefore affected by the other organisms within the community, directly or indirectly. For example, bees get nectar and pollen from flowers and so the flowering plants are an essential part of the bees' environment. It works the other way round too; the plants depend on the bees for pollination, so the bees are part of the plants' environment. Organisms which make up part of another organism's environment are called **biotic factors** of the environment.

The organisms in a community are influenced by environmental factors such as temperature, humidity and light intensity. Since these factors are non-living, they are called **abiotic factors**.

The organisms interact with each other (biotic factors) and the environmental conditions (abiotic factors) to make an **ecosystem**.

Measuring abiotic factors

Abiotic factors are non-living factors in an ecosystem. They include light intensity, soil pH, soil moisture content, rainfall and temperature. Whether or not an organism may be able to live in a habitat will depend a lot on the abiotic factors present.

Measuring abiotic factors is important if we are to understand what sort of conditions organisms require to live. The Activity section below shows how some abiotic factors can be measured.

However, as in all scientific activities involving measuring, errors may occur. For example, when measuring light intensity, the measurer must be sure to keep his or her shadow away from the light intensity meter. Since cloud cover can vary so much, the measurer must be sure to take the meter reading at more or less the same time when comparing two habitats. Alternatively, the habitats should be compared when the cloud cover is approximately the same.

When measuring soil moisture content, it would be a good idea if several measurements were taken from the same spot and an average value calculated. This rules out the possibility of a single particularly wet or particularly dry sample being taken which does not fairly represent the whole area.

Questions

1. Name as many organisms as you can think of which form the biotic environment of the following:
   a. a lion,
   b. a tadpole of the common frog,
   c. a mosquito,
   d. a cabbage white butterfly.(adult and larva),
   e. you.

2. The tapeworm, *Taenia solium*, lives in the small intestine of the human. What can you say about its physical environment? What problems does it face?

3. Look at pictures 1 to 4 on page 22. For each habitat shown, suggest some examples of populations of animals and plants that are, or may be, present. Why do you find these populations in one, but not all, of the habitats?

4. A brick wall runs east–west. There are mosses on the north side, but not on the south side. Suggest two possible reasons for this. Describe experiments which you could do to test your suggestions.

Activities

Measuring abiotic factors
(Practical techniques 2 and 3)

Choose two contrasting land habitats, e.g. a dense wood and an open meadow. Compare the physical environments of the two habitats. Measure the physical features as follows:

- **Water**. Place a **rain gauge** (picture 1) in each habitat, and measure the height of the water after a period of time.

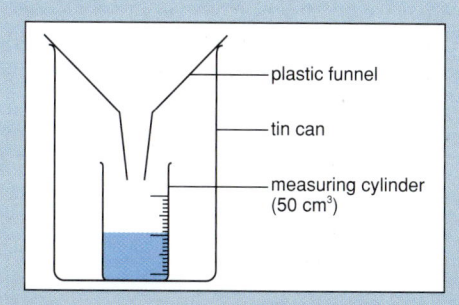

- **Humidity**. Use **cobalt chloride paper**. This is blue when dry and pink when moist. Time how long it takes for a piece of the paper to change from blue to pink in each habitat.

- **Air movement**. Compare the wind speed in the two habitats with an **anemometer** (picture 2). Count the number of times the arms swing round in a certain time.

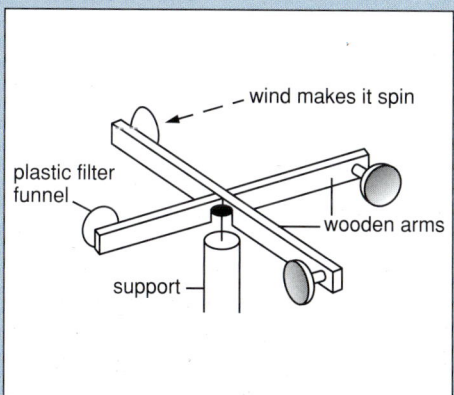

- **Temperature**. Use a **thermometer** to measure the temperature at different times of the day, and/or leave a **maximum–minimum thermometer** in each habitat for 24 hours to obtain the temperature range.

- **Light**. Use a **light meter** to measure the light intensity in each habitat.

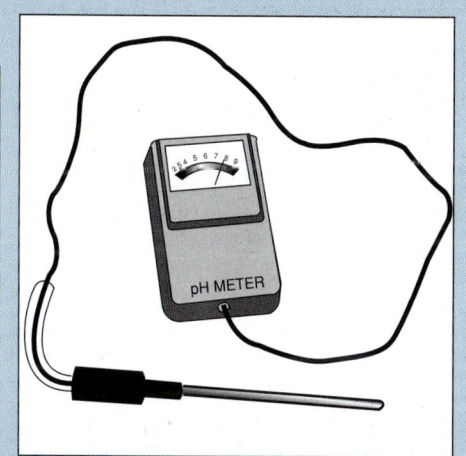

Picture 1 A rain gauge for comparing the rainfall in different habitats.

Picture 2 An anemometer for comparing wind speeds in different habitats.

Picture 3 A soil pH meter for measuring acidity/alkalinity.

- **Soil features**. Use a **soil pH meter** (picture 3) to measure acidity/alkalinity or a **moisture probe** to measure soil water content.

B2
Finding out where organisms live

The places where a species occurs make up its distribution. How can we investigate distribution?

Picture 1 These students are using a quadrat to estimate the number of plants of a particular species in a meadow.

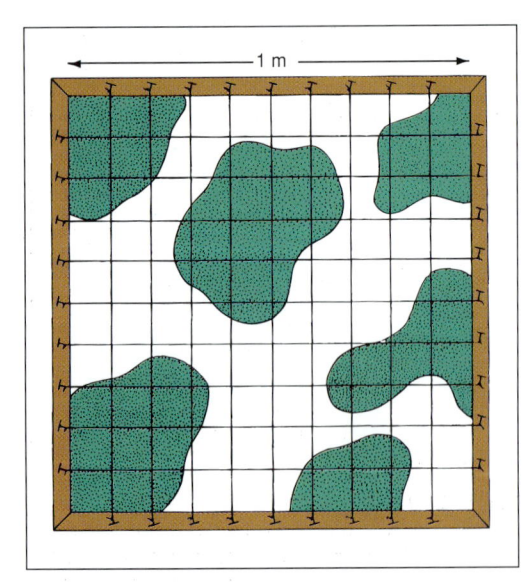

Picture 2 A grid made by dividing a one-metre quadrat into 100 smaller squares. The green areas represent patches of grass. You estimate the percentage of the quadrat which is occupied by grass.

Investigating distribution

To study a species' distribution we need to find out roughly how many individuals occur in different places.

The simplest way of doing this is to look at the habitat and describe in words what occurs where. Each species is given one of these descriptions:
- **Dominant**. The species that has the greatest effect on the environment, e.g. a tree.
- **Abundant**. Species that are hardly ever out of sight, e.g. grass.
- **Frequent**. Species that are constantly found but are fairly spread out, e.g. thistles in a field.
- **Occasional**. Species that are seldom found.
- **Rare**. Species that are hardly ever found.

This is not an accurate way of assessing distribution, but it may enable you to spot something which you can then investigate more carefully if you want to.

Sampling

Suppose you suspect that there are more thistles in one field than in another field of the same size. What can you do to make sure? One way would be to count all the thistles in each field. However, this would probably drive you mad. So you count the number of thistles in, say, ten squares, chosen at random. Then you work out the average. We call this process **sampling**.

Sampling is often carried out in biology, not just in studying habitats but in other situations as well. For example, the number of blood cells in a person's circulation can be estimated in the same kind of way.

Quadrats and grids

One of the commonest ways of sampling a habitat is to use a **quadrat**. This is a square metal or wooden frame, laid randomly on the ground. The measurer counts the individual plants inside it. The total number of plants in the quadrat is known as the **plant density**.

A quadrat can be adapted for estimating ground coverage by a plant. This is good for grass or moss where counting individual plants is impossible. The quadrat is divided up into 100 smaller squares, known as a **grid**, and the measurer counts how many squares the plant is in. This represents the **percentage cover**.

Look at picture 2. What is the percentage cover of the grass? By randomly choosing the areas to be sampled and doing as many quadrats as possible, errors may be reduced.

Transects

You may have noticed that in some places the types of organisms gradually change as you go across a habitat. In such cases it is useful to record where each type of organism occurs. You can do this by making a **line transect**. A length of tape, marked at regular intervals, is stretched across the habitat. You then record the positions of all the plants that are touching the tape (picture 3).

The trouble with a line transect is that it only gives you the organisms that are right on the line. A better method is to lay out two parallel tapes a metre apart and record the plants between them. We call this a **belt transect**. If you lay a grid between the two tapes, it will help you to put the different plants in their right positions.

You may want to see how the numbers of a particular species change as you go across a habitat. To do this you lay a quadrat or grid at regular intervals in a straight line across the habitat. You then count the number of plants, or estimate the area occupied by them, in each square. What would be the best way of presenting your results?

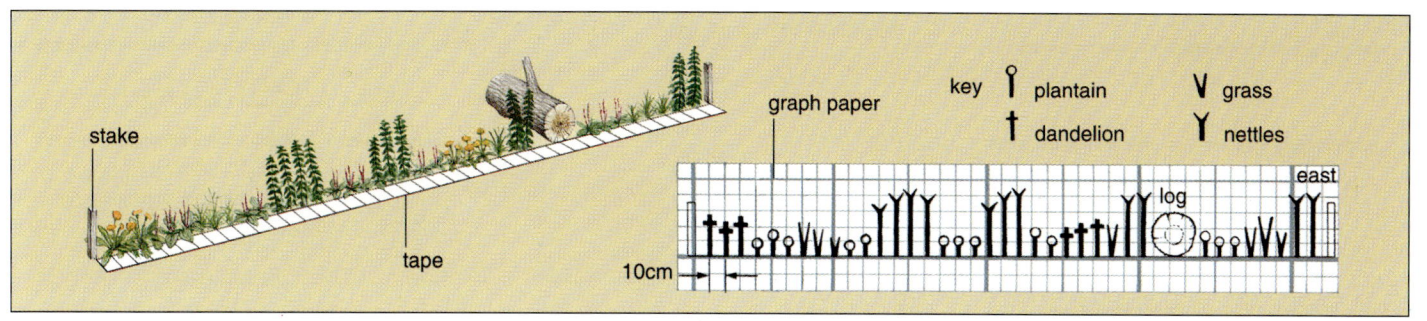

Picture 3 How to make a line transect. On the left are the plants which might be touching a tape that you have attached to the ground. On the right is the way you should record the positions of the various types of plant.

Collecting and trapping

For collecting small organisms, without harming them, simple traps can be used like the one shown in picture 4. Drain holes in the bottom of the jar make sure that rain water does not collect there and drown the trapped animals.

Errors can also occur in this method of sampling. To avoid these, set up several traps in different areas and make sure that the jar is level with the soil surface and the opening is covered. Carry out the collections at the same time of day and check the traps regularly. Some trapped animals may eat the others.

If you want to estimate the total number of individuals in a habitat, you can use a special technique called the **capture-recapture method**. This is explained on the next page.

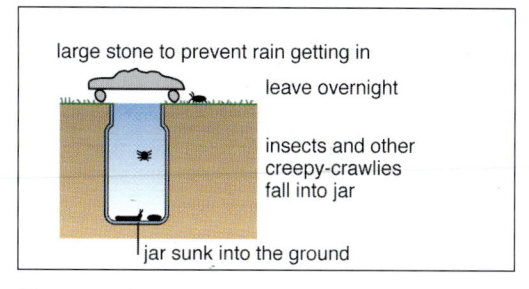

Picture 4 A pitfall trap, an example of a random trapping device. It is pure chance as to whether or not an animal falls into the jar.

Relating an organism's distribution to the environment

There is a large beech tree in the middle of my lawn. I have noticed that the number of daisy plants increases as one goes further from the trunk. Why is this?

The most obvious reason that springs to mind is that there is more light further from the trunk. To test this idea you estimate the number of daisy plants per square metre at different distances from the trunk, using a quadrat. You also find the average light intensity at each position, using a light meter of the kind that photographers use.

You then plot graphs of the number of daisies and the average light intensities against the distance from the trunk, as shown in picture 5. You can see at once that the two curves are very similar. This suggests that they are related in some way. In mathematician's language, there is a **positive correlation** between them.

Biologists often look for relationships, particularly when investigating the environment. But remember: an apparent relationship between two things does not prove that they are connected. For example, the change in the number of daisies on my lawn might be caused by some factor other than the light intensity, or by several factors acting together. The only way of proving that light intensity is involved is to rule out all the other possibilities.

It's often difficult to find out why organisms are distributed in a particular way simply by making measurements in their natural habitats. Sometimes you have to do **controlled experiments** indoors as well. You put the organism in different conditions and find out which one suits it best.

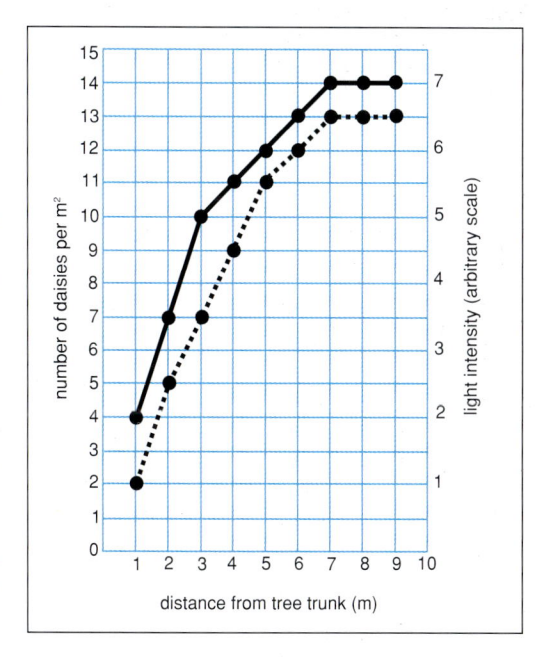

Picture 5 This graph shows the number of daisy plants, and the average light intensities, at different distances from a tree trunk. The number of daisy plants is represented by the solid curve, the light meter readings by the dotted curve. Notice that the two curves follow each other exactly. This suggests that they *may* be related in some way.

Activities

A Estimating the size of a population
(Practical technique 1)

1 Obtain a quadrat, one metre square.

2 Select a field, and decide what particular weed you wish to investigate.

3 Lay the quadrat on the ground, and count the number of weeds inside it.

If a weed is touching the frame, include it in your count if more than half of it is inside the quadrat.

4 Repeat the above procedure with the quadrat in at least five different places, chosen at random.

5 Work out the average number of weeds per square metre in the field. This is the **density** of weeds.

Do you think this is a good method of finding out how many weeds there are in the field? If not, why not?

What are the main reasons for any inaccuracies in the results?

What could be done to improve the method?

B Estimating the area of ground occupied by grass

1 Obtain a grid. This should be a one-metre quadrat that has been divided into 100 squares.

2 Find a suitable area of ground that has patches of grass.

3 Lay the grid on the ground, and estimate the number of squares which contain grass. If a square is only partly filled with grass, take this into account in making your estimate. For example, four squares that are each a quarter full count as one square.

The final figure you arrive at is the **percentage cover**.

4 Repeat the above procedure with the grid in at least five different places, chosen at random.

5 Work out the average percentage cover of grass in the area.

Do you think this is a good method of finding out how much grass there is in an area. If not, why not?

C Investigating distribution

Look around your local countryside, a park or the grounds of your school and find a wild plant whose distribution looks interesting. If you're stumped your teacher will help you.

Choose one of the methods described in this topic and use it to investigate the plant's distribution.

Do your results show anything interesting about the plant's distribution? If they do, what further investigations might you carry out?

Questions

1 When using a quadrat to investigate the number of plants in a field, you should place the quadrat on the ground randomly. Why is this important, and how can it best be achieved?

2 Look at picture 2 on page 24. Work out the percentage cover of the grass in this illustration.

3 Your friend maintains that there are more minnows in his pond than in yours. What could you do to find out if he is right?

4 A student counted the number of daisy plants in thirteen one-metre quadrats on a lawn. Here is a summary of her results:

Number of daisies	4 5 6 7 8 9
Number of quadrats in which the above number of daisies occurred	1 2 4 3 2 1

a Plot these results on graph paper.
b Calculate the average number of daisy plants per square metre.
c What sort of graph have you drawn? Why is it the best way to present the results?

Capture–recapture method

Suppose you want to estimate the total population of animals in a particular area. You can do this using the **capture–recapture method**.

First you capture a sample of individuals, and count them. You then mark them in some way that does not harm them. With beetles, for example, a small dab of non-toxic paint on the back will do.

You now release all these marked individuals back into the habitat, and give them time to mix with the rest of the population. Then you capture another sample of individuals. You count the individuals in this second sample; you also count the marked individuals in the sample.

To find out the total population, you use this neat little formula:

$$\text{population size} = \frac{n_1 \times n_2}{n_m}$$

where:

n_1 is the number of individuals captured in the first sample (the ones that were marked and released),

n_2 is the number of individuals in the second sample,

n_m is the number of marked individuals in the second sample.

Using this method, you can compare the total populations in different areas, or you can compare the populations in the same area at different times – day and night, for example, or different times of the year.

Suppose you want to estimate the size of the population of ground beetles in a particular habitat using the capture–recapture method. Explain *in detail* how you would do this. What precautions would you take to ensure that your estimation is as accurate as possible?

Two examples of adaptation

Here we look at the main features of two animals that live in very different environments. We shall see how the features of these animals help to adapt them to their environments.

The camel

Look at the Arabian camel in picture 1. Although there were wild camels at one time, the camel is now a domestic animal. It lives in the desert areas of north Africa and the Middle East where temperatures are generally high and rainfall low. Although the desert can be extremely hot, the temperature may vary greatly between night and day and between winter and summer. Camels are herbivorous, feeding on desert plants.

Here are the main features of camels which enable them to live in the hot, dry desert:

- The nostrils are narrow slits and are lined with hair. They can be almost completely closed. They filter dust from the air during sand storms.
- The long thick eyelashes protect the eyes from sand and grit.
- The feet, instead of having hooves, are splayed out and have leathery soles for walking on soft shifting sand.
- Camels can go for a long time without eating or drinking. Water is stored in the stomach. The hump contains fat, which serves as a food store from which water can be made by metabolism. When a camel does drink, it drinks a lot (as much as 40 litres in ten minutes!).
- The tissues can tolerate large temperature swings. The body temperature may vary from 34°C at night to 41°C during the day.
- The tissues can tolerate dehydration. As more and more water is lost, the body fluids become more and more concentrated.
- The body is cooled by sweating. However, the camel sweats only when the body temperature is high and there is a reasonable amount of water in the body.
- Being large, camels have a relatively small surface–volume ratio. This reduces heat energy loss.
- The skin has a covering of fur which insulates the body against the loss or gain of heat energy.

The polar bear

There is only one species of polar bear. It lives in the Arctic, in areas where the temperature is below freezing for most of the year. Polar bears spend much of their time walking on floating ice, and swimming in the water (picture 2). They are carnivorous, and feed mainly on fish, seals and walruses.

Here are the main features of the polar bear which help it to live in the Arctic:

- The fur is white, like the surroundings.
- The forelimbs have enormous claws and are very powerful.
- The feet have hairy pads which assist movement over ice.
- Eyesight is good, and so is the sense of smell.
- The animal is an excellent swimmer, propelling itself through the water with its powerful forelimbs.
- The thick fur insulates the body against heat energy loss when the animal is on land.
- A thick layer of fat (blubber) beneath the skin insulates the body against heat energy loss when the animal is in the water.
- Although carnivorous, polar bears will eat plant food if necessary.

Picture 2 Polar bears are good at walking on slippery surfaces such as ice. They are also good at swimming.

Picture 1 The Arabian camel, also known as a dromedary, has a single hump and long legs. It is a fast runner and is used for riding. An Arabian camel has been known to cover 150 miles in 11 hours.

1. Why is it helpful for the polar bear to eat plant food as well as animal food?
2. Polar bears are white. What might be the advantage of this? Can you think of any possible disadvantages?
3. The polar bear's fur is a good insulator on land, but not in the water. Why the difference?
4. The polar bear is so well adapted to living in the cold that it does not need to hibernate. Why is hibernation useful to a cold-dwelling animal?
5. Why is it useful to a camel to be able to tolerate wide fluctuations in its body temperature?
6. Desert mammals face a conflict: they need to save water but they also need to lose it (by sweating, for example) to cool themselves. How does the camel resolve this conflict?
7. Do you think camels would survive in the Arctic and polar bears in the desert? Give reasons for your answer.

B3 Feeding relationships

In the natural world, animals feed on plants and on other animals. This is an essential part of the balance of nature.

Picture 1 The larva of the great diving beetle, *Dytiscus marginalis*, is an aggressive predator found in ponds. It sinks its fangs into the prey and sucks up its juices. It may get through as many as 20 tadpoles in an hour. The adult beetle is equally voracious.

A food chain

Suppose we put some water weeds, tadpoles and a couple of great diving beetles into a jar of pond water, and watch what happens. We find that the tadpoles nibble at the weeds, and the beetles eat the tadpoles. We can sum up the feeding relationship between the three organisms like this:

weeds → tadpoles → beetles

We call this a **food chain**. Tadpoles eat only plants: they are **herbivores**. In contrast, the great diving beetle feeds only on animals: it is a **carnivore** (picture 1).

There are only three organisms in the food chain shown above. However, in a lake there might be some pike. These fish eat water beetles, amongst other things. So in the lake the food chain would be:

weeds → tadpoles → beetles → pike

The pike has been called a 'water wolf'. It is one of the most savage predators found in fresh water. The animal that comes at the end of a food chain like this is called the **top carnivore**.

Producers and consumers

Let's think about this food chain in a bit more detail. The weeds make their own food by photosynthesis; they get the energy for doing this from sunlight. Because they make food, we call them **producers**.

In contrast, the animals in the chain get their food by eating other organisms. For this reason we call them **consumers**.

In this particular chain there are three consumers. The tadpoles are the first consumers, the beetles are the second consumers, and the pike is the third consumer. They are known as the **primary**, **secondary** and **tertiary consumers** respectively (picture 2).

The stages in a food chain are called **feeding levels** or **trophic levels**.

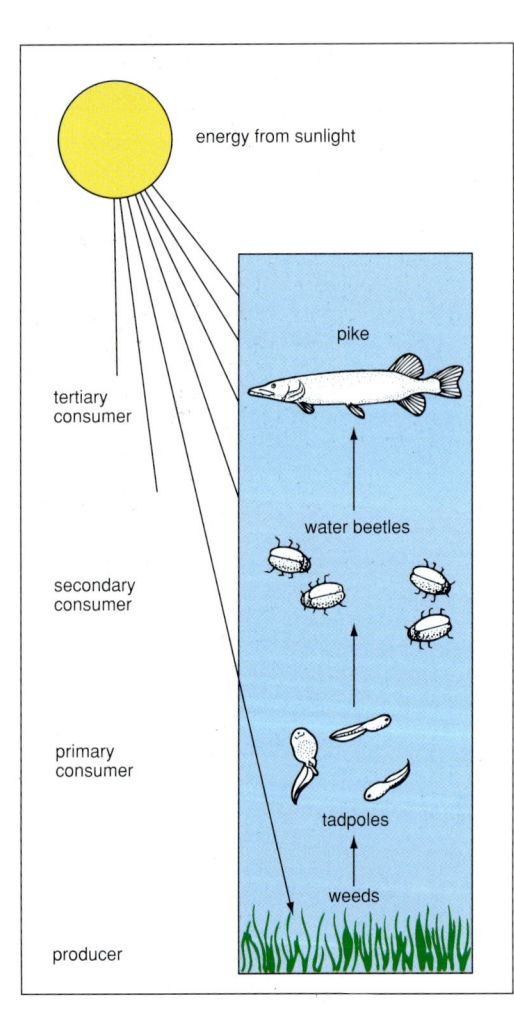

Picture 2 A food chain is made up of a series of feeding levels, also called trophic levels. In the food chain shown here the weeds are at the first feeding level, the tadpoles at the second, the beetles at the third, and the pike at the fourth. The arrows show the direction of energy flow.

Pyramid of energy

In picture 2 only a very small fraction of the Sun's energy that falls on the weeds is transferred to the plants' tissues and food stores. And when a tadpole eats a weed only about one tenth of the energy in the plant is transferred to the body of the tadpole. The rest is lost in the tadpole's waste matter (excreta) or in its respiration. The same thing happens when the tadpoles are eaten by the beetles, and again when the beetles are eaten by the pike.

In other words, at each step of the food chain, a lot of energy is lost. Picture 3 shows this as a diagram: it is called a **pyramid of energy**.

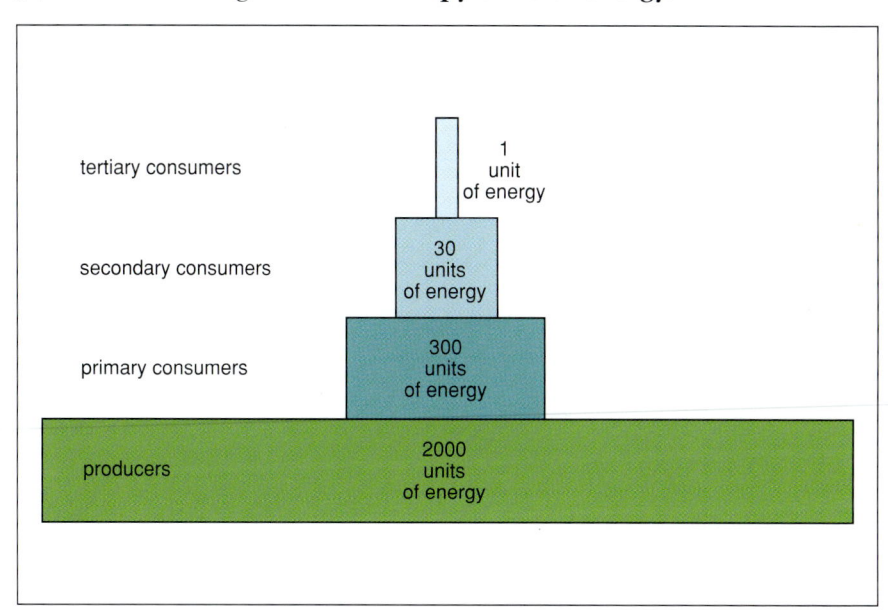

Picture 3 This diagram shows the decrease in energy that occurs at each level in a food chain. The diagram is called a pyramid of energy. The figures are typical of a food chain in fresh water such as a lake.

Pyramids of numbers and biomass

The energy loss just described means that, as you go along the food chain, the number of organisms which can be supported at each level gets less and less. Thus a given number of tadpoles will feed a smaller number of beetles, and these beetles will feed an even smaller number of fish. This drop in numbers at each level in a food chain gives what we call a **pyramid of numbers**.

For the same reason there is also a drop in the total mass of living material at each level of a food chain. This is called the **pyramid of biomass**.

Food webs

In a natural habitat such as a lake or pond, it would be unusual for the organisms to be linked together in a simple chain. Many more species will be present than the ones in picture 2, and each may have several sources of food.

By observing all the organisms in a habitat, you can build up a diagram summarising who feeds on what. This is called a **food web**. A simple food web is shown in picture 4.

In a habitat which contains a large number of different species, the food web may be very complex. A complex food web is shown in picture 5. Food webs can be divided up into a series of feeding (trophic) levels, just as food chains can. Can you recognise the different feeding levels in pictures 4 and 5? As with food chains, there is a drop in energy, numbers and biomass at each level.

Questions

1 In picture 2 which organisms are
   a herbivores,
   b carnivores,
   c predators,
   d prey?

2 Fill in the missing organism in each of the following food chains:
   a grass → ? → human
   b grass → deer → ?
   c lettuce → ? → fox
   d aphid (greenfly) → ladybird → ?

3 The following is a food chain that ends with the human:

   plant → bee → human

   Explain precisely how plants provide food for bees, and how bees provide food for humans.

   How does this food chain differ from the ones in question 2?

   Do you think it should be regarded as a food chain? Explain your answer.

4 This question is about the food web in picture 4.
   a How many food chains can you see in this picture? Write them out separately.
   b What would happen to the numbers of the other organisms in the web if all the fish were destroyed?
   c A food chain is more easily destroyed than a food web. Why? Use picture 4 to illustrate your answer.

5 Food chains rarely have more than four trophic levels. Why do you think this is?

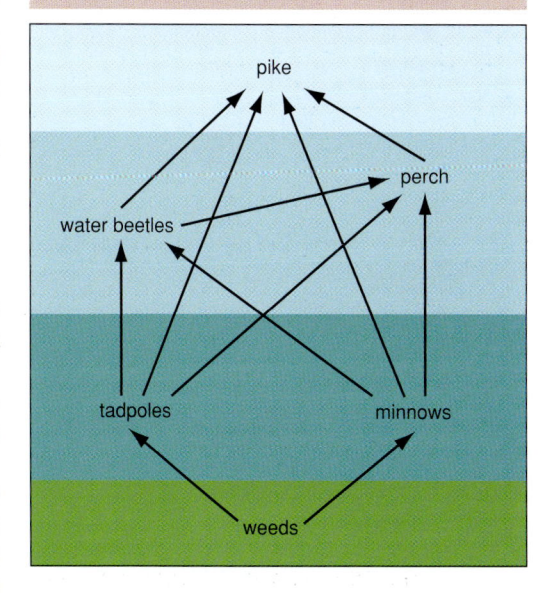

Picture 4 A simple food web in a pond. The colours are different trophic levels.

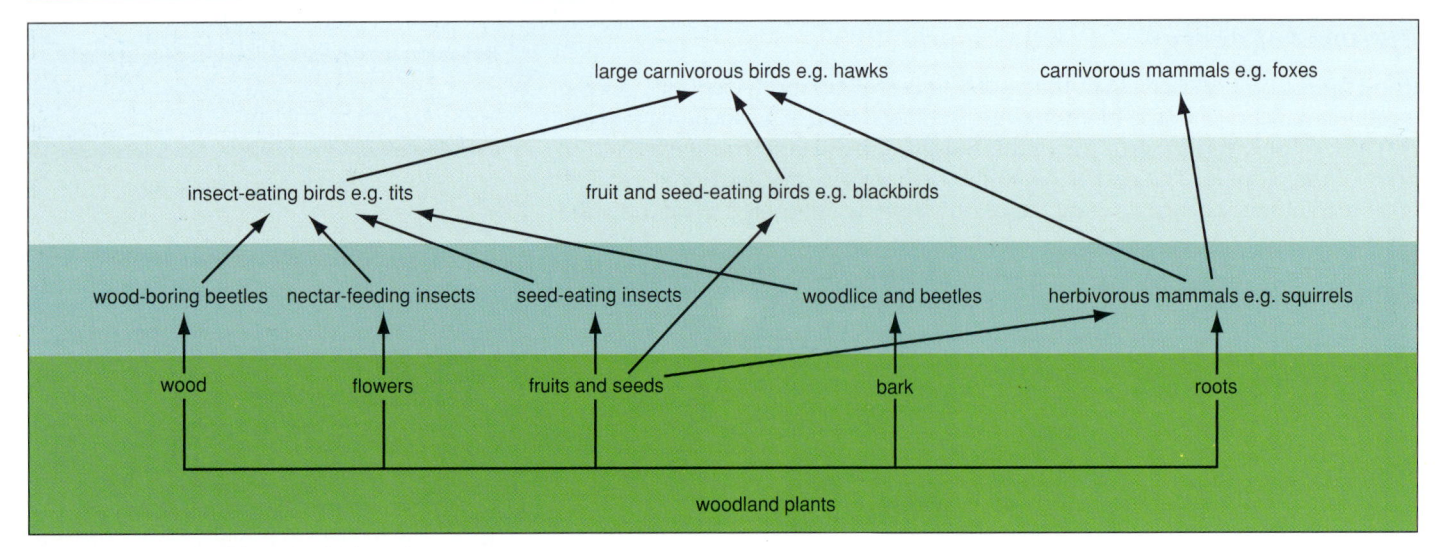

Picture 5 A food web in a wood. The colours are different trophic levels.

Picture 6 Humans are at the end of many food chains.

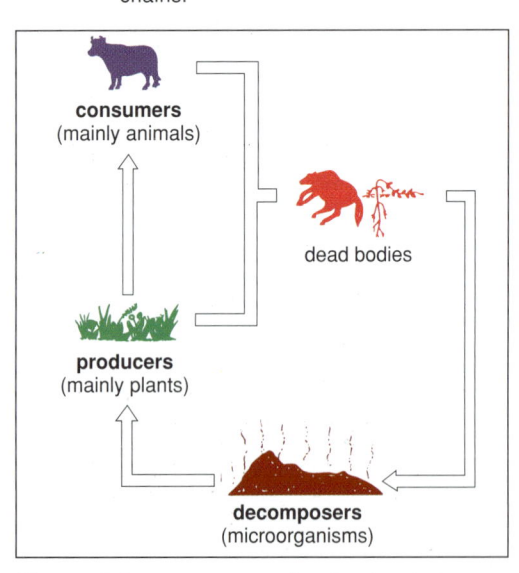

Picture 7 Decomposers enable the chemical elements in the bodies of the producers and consumers to be used again. The arrows show the flow of materials from one organism to another.

Food chains in the service of humans

Look at picture 2 again. The pike that ate the beetles that ate the tadpoles that ate the weeds might be caught by a fisherman for his supper. The food chain would then be:

weeds → tadpoles → beetles → pike → human

So food chains can provide us with food.

Some of the most important food chains occur in the sea. In the surface water where light can penetrate, there are millions of microscopic organisms called **plankton**. Some of these organisms are like plants and feed by photosynthesis. Others are like animals and feed on the plant-like ones. The animal plankton, in turn, is eaten by fish such as the herring, giving us the following food chain:

plant plankton → animal plankton → herring → human

Our fishing industry depends on this and other similar food chains. On land, farming involves several important food chains such as:

grass → sheep → human
grass → cattle → human

Of course humans eat plants as well as animals: we are **omnivores**. When we eat such things as bread or cornflakes, we are the primary (and only) consumers in this very simple food chain:

wheat → human

The decrease in energy which occurs at each level of a food chain is a very important consideration in growing crops and raising livestock. This is dealt with in the next topic.

Decomposers

When animals and plants die their bodies **decay**. This is because they are fed upon by bacteria and other microorganisms which break them down.

The organisms which bring about decay are called **decomposers** or **saprobionts**. As a result of their activities, simple substances are released from the dead bodies. These substances are absorbed by plants, and can go through the food chain all over again (picture 7).

Decomposers thus enable chemicals to be re-cycled and used again. They play an important part in the cycling of elements such as carbon and nitrogen (page 40).

Feeding relationships

Removing an organism from a food web

The complex feeding relationships in a food web are delicately balanced. Look at picture 4 again. Suppose we remove the pike. The result would be a huge increase in the population of the perch and water beetles since their predator has been removed. In time, the numbers of tadpoles and minnows would decrease as they are eaten by the greater number of water beetles and perch. The water weeds would then be able to grow and eventually they would fill the entire pond, and the perch and water beetles would die of starvation. The food web would have broken down completely.

Simple food webs like this are easily disrupted. More complicated webs may be able to withstand the removal of one species.

Humans must be very careful not to disturb and harm ecosystems through their actions. How could the pike have been removed from a pond ecosystem?

In Scotland, the red deer population has risen greatly. One of the reasons has been the removal of the wolf. This carnivorous animal was the red deer's only natural predator. How was the wolf removed from Scottish habitats?

Picture 8 Red deer. The wolf would have kept their numbers down naturally.

Questions

1 Study the food web in picture 5, then answer these questions:
   a Give one example of a predator in the food web, and write down the name of an animal which it preys on.
   b The food web does not include the leaves of the woodland plants. Write down a food chain which might lead from the leaves.
   c A chemical substance, poisonous to animals but not to plants, leaks onto the ground in the wood. Explain how this might affect the food web.
   d What might happen to the wood eventually if all the foxes were destroyed? Explain your answer.

2 As one proceeds along a good chain, each organism tends to be larger than the one before.
   a Give an example of a food chain which illustrates this.
   b Why do you think this is true?
   c Give an example of a food chain which is an exception to this.

3 The loss of energy at each level of a food chain or web can be shown as a pyramid of numbers, a pyramid of biomass or a pyramid of energy.
   Which do you think is the best way of showing the energy loss, and why?

4 The diagram below shows the total number of organisms per square metre at each level of a food web in a river.

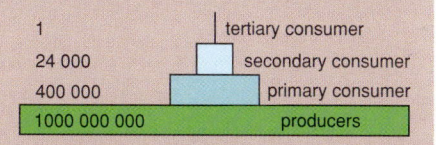

1	tertiary consumer
24 000	secondary consumer
400 000	primary consumer
1000 000 000	producers

   a What process enables the producers to provide food for the primary consumers?
   b Why are there fewer secondary consumers than primary consumers?
   c What can you say about the kinds of organism that comprise the producers and primary consumers?
   d Suggest one change in the environment that might greatly increase the number of producers in this pyramid.

5 The following figures show the total mass of body material, excluding water, formed in one square metre of grassland during one year:

   plants   470.0 g
   herbivores   0.6 g
   carnivores   0.1 g

   a Why does the total mass of body material decrease at each step of the chain?
   b These figures were obtained by measuring the 'dry mass': that is the mass after all traces of water have been removed by drying. Why is this better than measuring the 'wet mass'?

Funny pyramids

If we construct pyramids of numbers for various food chains, we find that some of them have unusual shapes so that they are not really pyramids. Here are three examples of 'funny pyramids':

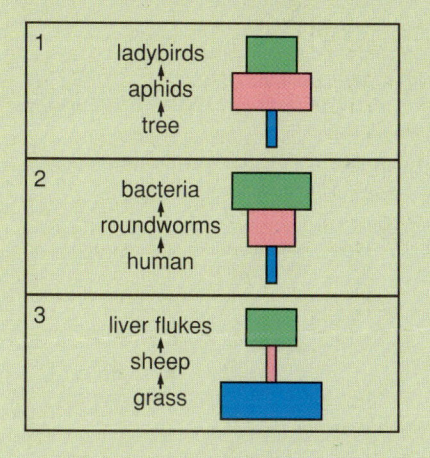

1 ladybirds
   ↑
   aphids
   ↑
   tree

2 bacteria
   ↑
   roundworms
   ↑
   human

3 liver flukes
   ↑
   sheep
   ↑
   grass

1 Explain in your own words why each of these food chains gives a funny pyramid. (Hint: the first pyramid is easy to explain. To help you explain the second and third pyramids, find out about the organisms involved by looking up pages 16 and 18.)

2 For each food chain, draw what you would expect to get if you constructed (a) a pyramid of biomass and (b) a pyramid of energy.

B4
Food chains and humans

Food chains play a vital part in our lives, as we shall see here.

Picture 1 Wheat, one of our most widely grown crops. From its seeds (grain) we get flour for making bread, cakes and breakfast cereals.

Energy from plants

Think of a crop plant such as wheat (picture 1). It captures light energy from the Sun and transfers the energy to starch and other organic substances by photosynthesis. However, only a small proportion of the light energy that strikes the plant is transferred in this way. Most of it is reflected, or passes straight through the leaves, or is used up in various chemical reactions inside the plant. The rest of the energy gets transferred to sugar, but most of this is used in respiration and only a small proportion gets into the starch and tissues of the plant. This is summed up in picture 2.

In picture 2, only five per cent of the total light energy that strikes the leaf finishes up in the starch and tissues. We call this the **energy conversion efficiency**. An energy conversion efficiency of five per cent is the best that can be achieved by a crop plant growing in really good soil in an ideal climate. In practice the average figure for a crop plant like wheat is about one per cent. Even sugar cane, grown in the best possible conditions in the tropics, rarely exceeds two and a half per cent.

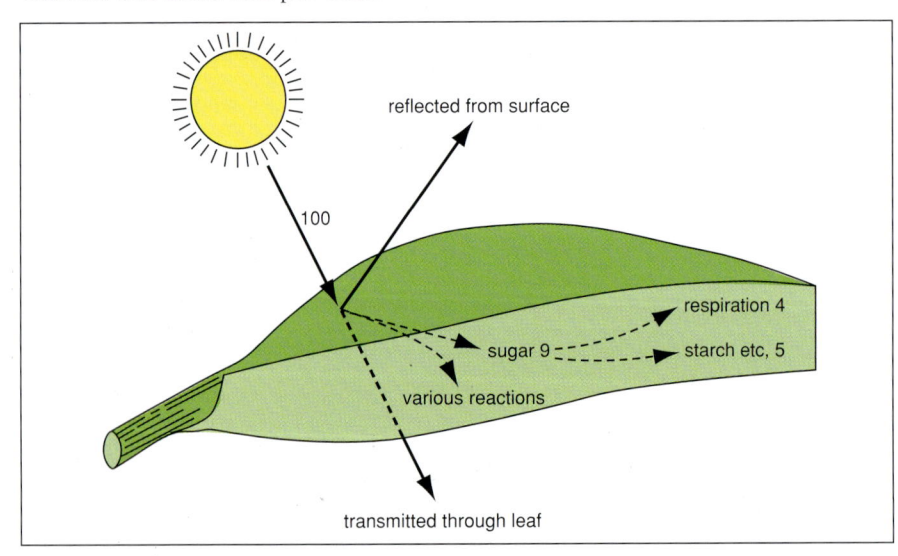

Picture 2 This diagram shows what happens to the energy in the light that strikes a plant. Suppose 100 units of energy strike the leaf. Only nine units get into the sugar that the leaf makes by photosynthesis. Of this, only five units get into the starch and tissues of the leaf.

Growing plants for human use

The aim is to transfer the maximum amount of energy from the Sun into the part of the plant you want to harvest. This is what **plant farming** (**plant husbandry**) tries to achieve.

Agriculture is growing crop plants such as wheat, barley and oats.

Horticulture is growing mainly garden plants out of doors or in glasshouses.

Both involve:
- **Soil management**. The soil must contain the right nutrients, if necessary by adding a **fertiliser**, and it must be adequately watered by rain and/or irrigation.
- Making sure the plants get enough **light** and **warmth**, by natural or artificial means.
- **Controlling pests** so that they do not harm the plants or reduce their yield.
- **Breeding plants** so as to ensure a supply of new ones for future use. Plant breeding aims to produce improved varieties.

All these aspects of growing plants are dealt with in detail in other parts of the book.

Food chains and humans 33

Picture 3 Cattle transfer energy from plants such as grass to their tissues.

Energy from meat

Think of a cow eating grass in a lush meadow (picture 3). The grass contains energy in its starch and tissues. These are eaten by the cow. However, only a small fraction of the energy in the grass is transferred to the cow's tissues.

Picture 4 shows what happens to the rest of the energy. Most of it passes straight through the gut without being absorbed and is lost in cowpats, or in methane gas given off by microbes in the cow's stomach. Someone has worked out that there is enough energy in the gas given out by a cow to light a small house! Further energy is lost in urine, or used up in respiration.

Altogether only four per cent of the energy taken in by the cow gets into its tissues. Still more energy is lost when the cow is eaten by humans, because we only eat the meat. Non-edible structures like the bones, horns and skin get left behind.

Plant or animal food, which is better?

Humans are **omnivores** – that is, we eat animals *and* plants. From the energy point of view, it is more economical to eat plants than animals. This is because so much energy is lost as it passes from plants to animals in the food chains.

For this reason, plant crops like wheat, maize and rice will feed more people than livestock such as cattle and sheep. This is particularly important in densely populated countries: an area of land with crops can support more people than the same area of land with cattle.

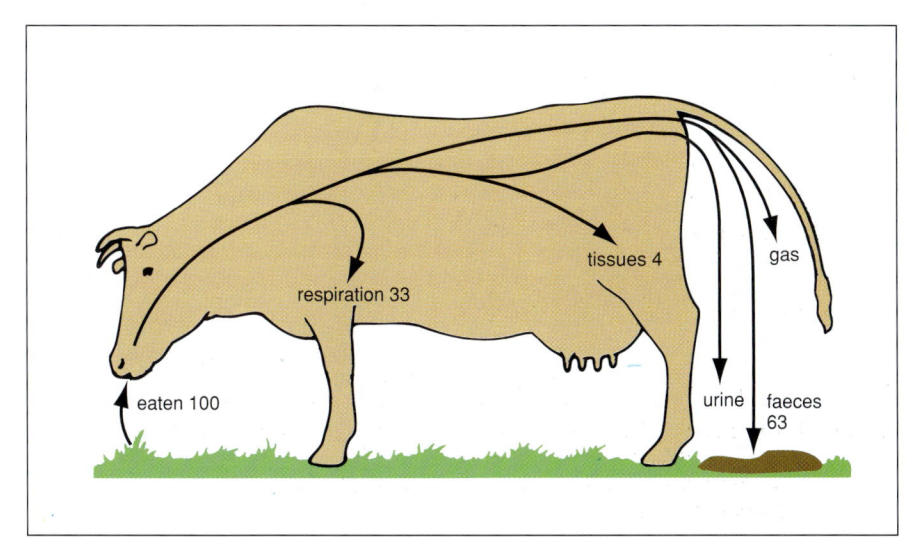

Picture 4 Here we see what happens to the energy in the grass eaten by a cow. Suppose 100 units of energy are ingested. Only four units get into the cow's tissues. The rest is lost in respiration, urine, faeces and gas.

Raising animals for human use

The aim is to transfer the maximum amount of energy from plants into the tissues of the animals. This is what **animal farming (animal husbandry)** tries to achieve.

Cattle are farmed for beef and milk, sheep for meat and wool, pigs for meat, and poultry for meat and eggs.

Animal farming involves:

- Providing the animals with the **right environment**, either out of doors or, when necessary, under cover. Areas of land which are unsuitable for growing crops, e.g. moorland and steep hillsides, may be suitable for grazing animals such as sheep and deer.

- Giving the animals the **right kind of diet** of natural food, e.g. grass, and/or artificial food containing the right combination of nutrients.

- **Keeping the animals healthy** by good hygiene and having them immunised against infectious diseases.

- **Breeding animals** so as to ensure a supply of new stock. Animal breeding, like plant breeding, aims to produce improved varieties.

These topics are dealt with in detail in other parts of the book.

The demand for food is huge. This is well illustrated by egg production from hens. Think how many eggs the average person eats in a week. Now multiply that by the entire population. You can see why we need poultry farmers.

Free-range hens roost in small huts and are allowed to wander about freely in an enclosure. **Battery hens** are housed indoors in rows of boxes where their diet and environment are carefully controlled. In Ohio, USA, there is a poultry farm where 4.8 million hens lay 3.7 million eggs every day!

Some people object to the intensive way battery hens are kept, but it is difficult to see an alternative when the demand for eggs is so great.

34 The biosphere

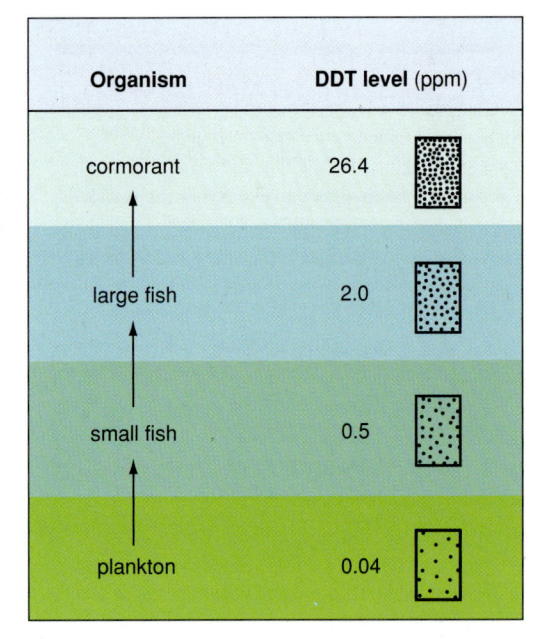

Organism	DDT level (ppm)
cormorant	26.4
large fish	2.0
small fish	0.5
plankton	0.04

Picture 5 This diagram shows the amounts of DDT in four organisms in a food chain. The amounts of DDT are expressed in parts per million (ppm). Notice how the DDT gets more and more concentrated as it goes from one level of the food chain to the next. This is because it is held in the organisms' bodies instead of being excreted.

Getting other things from food chains

We don't just get energy from food chains. In addition we get all sorts of chemical substances needed for life.

Some of these substances get more and more concentrated as they pass along the food chains. Take vitamin D, for example. This is made by plant plankton in the sea. Then it gets into the animal plankton. Eventually it gets into the fish that eat the plankton. The fish store and concentrate it in their livers. This is why cod liver oil is such a good source of vitamin D.

Food chains and poisons

Unfortunately it is not always useful substances that get into food chains. Sometimes poisons do so too. Such is the case with the insecticide DDT.

DDT keeps its poisonous properties for a long time after it has been released into the environment. If it gets into a river or lake, it is taken up by the plankton. It then passes along the food chains, becoming more and more concentrated as it does so (picture 5). DDT damages animal tissues. It may also be a danger to humans. For this reason it has been banned in many countries, including Britain.

Unfortunately DDT isn't the only poisonous substance to get into food chains. Some years ago over sixty people died in Japan from eating fish whose bodies contained mercury. The mercury had been discharged into the sea from a factory and had passed right through the food chains.

Germs, too, may pass along food chains. For example, if *Salmonella* bacteria are present in the food given to hens, the hens and their eggs may become infected. The bacteria may then get into humans, causing Salmonella poisoning. Matters are made worse if the excreta and/or remains of dead hens are fed to the hens. This closes the food chain and results in repeated infection of the hens.

Activities

A What food chains do you enter into?

Make a list of all the foods you can think of which you eat during a typical day. For each one write down the food chain which it is part of, putting yourself as the final consumer.

B Comparing the cost of meat and vegetables

Visit a supermarket and find out the cost of a selection of:

1 meats, e.g. beef, lamb, pork and chicken,
2 vegetables, e.g. cabbage, cauliflower, carrots, potatoes.

Express each cost as price per gram. Calculate the average price of meats and vegetables.

Can you relate the difference in the prices of meats and vegetables to the food chains involved? Bear in mind that other factors besides food chains help to set the prices of specific foods. Can you suggest what these factors are?

Which are the cheapest and the most expensive meats? Suggest reasons for the difference. Which are the cheapest and most expensive vegetables? Again, suggest reasons for the difference.

C The economics of human food chains

Think about these two food chains:

wheat → cow → human

wheat → human

1 You have been asked by Her Majesty's Government to compare the cost to society of these two food chains. Make a list of all the information which you would need in order to carry out this task. In each case suggest where the information might be obtained. Say how you would present your comparison.

2 Cost does not just mean money. It also means cost to personal health and cost to the environment. Compare the two food chains from these points of view.

Fish farming

The aim in fish farming is to cultivate fish so that they breed rapidly enough to produce populations that can be harvested profitably.

Fish farming is becoming more and more important. In 1993 there were nearly two thousand fish farms in Britain. About one third of the total value of all fish produced or landed in Britain comes from fish farms.

Two main types of fish are farmed in Britain, salmon and trout. The eggs are hatched in special hatcheries where the temperature and water flow are controlled so that the embryos have an adequate oxygen supply and develop at the optimum rate.

When the young fish are large enough they are transferred to ponds, tanks or cages. Diet is very important. Trout and salmon are carnivorous, and natural food (small fish, etc) may be supplemented by scientifically formulated pellets.

Disease can spread quickly through the fish population, particularly if the fish are overcrowded. All sorts of precautions are taken to prevent this.

Questions

1. Imagine you are a wheat farmer. You are determined to grow wheat so efficiently that you achieve the maximum yield of energy per hectare. how could you do this?

2. The cow in picture 4 has an energy conversion efficiency of only 4 per cent. However, the perch, a fresh water fish, has an energy conversion efficiency of 22.5 per cent.
   a. What is meant by the term energy conversion efficiency?
   b. Suggest reasons why the perch is a better energy converter than the cow.

3. Suppose the leaf in picture 2 is eaten by the cow in picture 4. What proportion of the Sun's energy that strikes the leaf will get into the cow's tissues? Show your reasoning.

4. It is better for people in densely populated countries to concentrate their efforts on growing crops rather than raising livestock. Why? What might make it difficult?

5. Some types of chicken-feed include the ground-up remains of dead hens.
   a. What are the advantages of using dead hens for making chicken feed?
   b. Some health officials think that it is a bad practice. Why?
   c. If the practice was discontinued, suggest an alternative use for the dead hens.

6. You are faced with having to choose between a beefburger and a vegeburger.
   a. Sketch the probable pyramid of energy for each, with you at the top.
   b. Which is more likely to be the more expensive, and why?
   c. What are the advantages of being a vegetarian from the point of view of the environment?

7. The following figures show the concentration of mercury in sea water and in various organisms in a particular area. The measurements are in parts per million (ppm).

sea water	0.00003 ppm
algae	0.03 ppm
fish	0.3 ppm
water birds	2.0 ppm

   a. How many times more concentrated is the mercury in the fish than in sea water?
   b. Suggest an explanation for these figures.
   c. Eating fish with a mercury level higher than 0.5 ppm is potentially dangerous to humans. A level of 0.2 ppm in the human body causes symptoms of mercury poisoning which, in extreme cases, may lead to kidney damage, paralysis and death. Use this information to explain why the figures given above are important to us.

The case of the Peregrine falcon

The Peregrine falcon is a swift, deadly predator – one of the most beautiful of all birds of prey. It nests on cliff ledges and rocky crags and is frequently found in coastal areas where it feeds mainly on sea birds.

After the end of the Second World War, a dramatic decline in the number of Peregrine falcons was noticed in both America and Europe. No reason for this decline could be seen, until in 1958 a British ornithologist, Derek Ratcliffe, observed that many of their nests contained broken eggs and that the parents often ate their eggs.

Ratcliffe noted that the decline in the number of Peregrines had begun at about the time that DDT and other pesticides were being used a lot. At first he thought that egg-eating by the parents was a behavioural disorder caused by the pesticides attacking the nervous system. But later he showed that the eggs were not deliberately broken by the parents, but were crushed during incubation because they had abnormally thin shells. They were eaten as a natural response to the fact that they were broken.

Since then a great deal of research has been done into the way that DDT affects birds. It has been found that it interferes with the hormones that control the deposit of calcium in eggshells. This results in the eggs being thin-shelled and fragile. DDT also causes a reduction in the amount of the sex hormone oestrogen, with the result that the bird lays fewer eggs than usual.

(Adapted from Tim Halliday, '*Vanishing Birds*', Sidgwick and Jackson)

1. DDT is particularly harmful to birds of prey, that is birds which eat other animals. Why do you think this is?

2. Although DDT in food chains harms birds, there is no evidence that it has ever harmed humans. Suggest a reason why humans have not been harmed by it.

3. DDT has been banned in Britain but is still used in certain developing countries. Why do you think developing countries still want to use it?

4. How do you think new pesticides should be tested to see if they are safe?

Picture 1 A peregrine falcon.

B5 Populations

People, people everywhere! This topic is about populations: how they grow and what happens when they get too big.

Picture 1 Oxford Street, London, on a busy day.

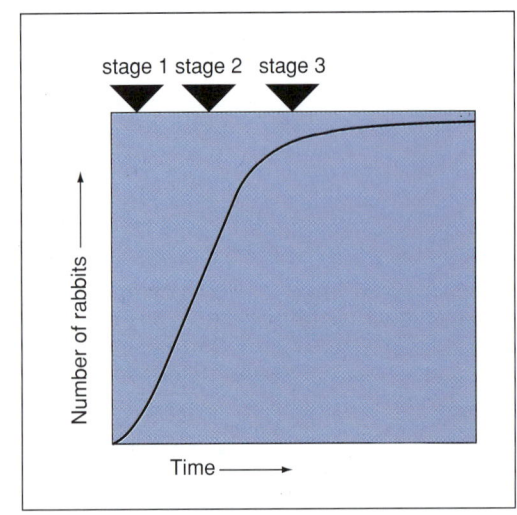

Picture 2 This graph shows how a population of rabbits may grow. In stage 1 the population grows slowly at first and then gradually gets faster. In stage 2 the population grows exponentially at the maximum rate. In stage 3 the population growth gradually slows down, and eventually the population stops growing altogether.

How do populations grow?

Suppose you put 100 rabbits onto an unpopulated island. The rabbits reproduce and the population increases. If you counted the rabbits at intervals and plotted their numbers against time, you would find that the population rises as shown in picture 2.

One of the most noticeable things about populations is that they increase very quickly. This is because the numbers go up by *multiplication*, like this:

$$100 \xrightarrow{\times 2} 200 \xrightarrow{\times 2} 400 \xrightarrow{\times 2} 800 \xrightarrow{\times 2} 1600 \xrightarrow{\times 2} 3200 \text{ etc.}$$

In other words, the total number *doubles* at regular intervals. This type of increase is described as **exponential**. It is how populations tend to grow, whether they are rabbits, flies or humans – unless something happens to stop the natural increase.

Why do populations grow?

In any community new individuals are born and older ones die. The rate at which individuals are born is called the **birth rate**, and the rate at which individuals die is called the **death rate**. Birth rate and death rate are explained in more detail in the box at the foot of this page.

Populations increase because new individuals are born at a faster rate than older ones die. In other words, the birth rate is greater than the death rate.

Populations are also affected by individuals entering or leaving the community, that is **immigration** and **emigration**.

What stops populations growing?

Look again at the graph in picture 2. Notice that eventually the curve flattens out. In other words, the population growth slows down and the numbers level off.

Why does this happen? In the case of our rabbits there are a number of possibilities. Here are some of them:

1 The food (grass and so on) begins to run out, so some of the rabbits starve.
2 There are so many rabbits that there is no room for any more burrows.
3 The rabbits are so overcrowded that diseases spread rapidly and many die.
4 Being overcrowded, the rabbits suffer from stress and this interferes with their reproduction.
5 Predators such as foxes and birds of prey eat more of the rabbits because, being commoner, they are easier to catch.

How to work out population growth from the birth rate and death rate

The birth rate and death rate are expressed as yearly percentages.

If the birth rate is 10 per cent, it means that for every 100 individuals at the beginning of the year, there are 10 more (i.e. 110) at the end.

If the death rate is 3 per cent, it means that for every 100 individuals at the beginning of the year, there are 3 less (i.e. 97) at the end.

The whole population therefore shows a net increase of 10 − 3 = 7 per cent.

This means that for every 100 individuals at the beginning of the year, the actual number at the end is 107.

These are the kinds of checks which stop populations growing for ever. The first two involve **competition**: the rabbits compete with each other for scarce resources such as food and living space. There may also be competition between the rabbits and other species. Which other species might compete with rabbits, and for what?

If there are no predators, humans may step in and take control. At one time Australia had no rabbits, but in 1859 some domestic rabbits escaped from their pen when it was swept away by a flood. These rabbits ran wild and bred at such a rate that parts of Australia were soon overrun with them. They did a lot of damage to crops and gardens. Unfortunately there were no predators to keep them under control. Eventually the virus disease myxomatosis was deliberately introduced to destroy them – an example of **biological control**. The disease swept through the rabbit population, and their numbers fell.

The human population

Picture 4 shows the population of Britain over the last 7000 years. Notice how it has increased. In fact the graph looks rather like the one in picture 2. In particular, notice that the population has grown more during the last 200 years than in the whole of the previous 5000 years.

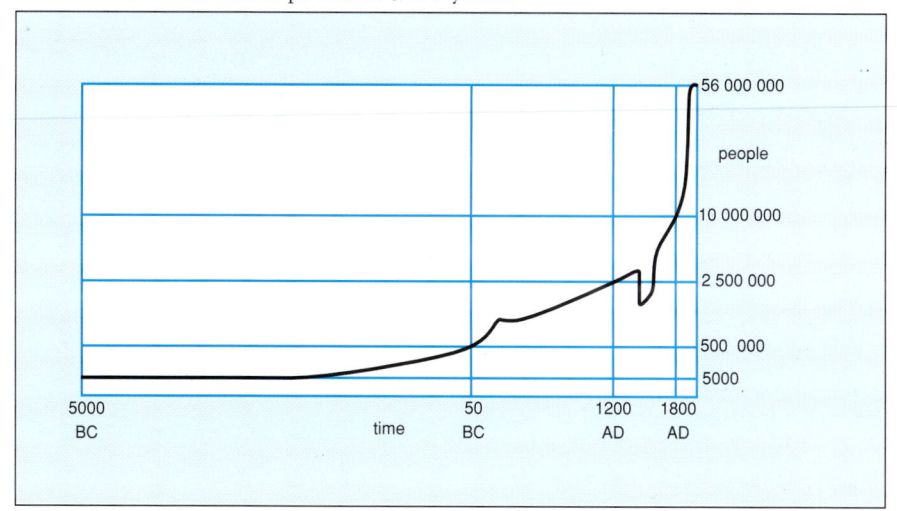

Picture 3 Foxes feed on rabbits and help to keep their numbers down.

Picture 4 The graph shows how the population of Britain has grown since 5000 BC.

What has caused this recent increase? It's mainly because the death rate has fallen due to better health. Fewer infants die and old people live longer.

Obviously this increase can't go on for ever. One way of stopping it is by **birth control** (see page 100). Birth control certainly seems to be having an effect in Britain because the population is now showing signs of levelling off. But this is not true of many developing countries where the populations are continuing to rise rapidly.

In the world as a whole the population is increasing by about 80 million people each year (picture 5): that's 9000 an hour, or 150 a minute. Someone has worked out that if the human population were to go on rising uncontrollably, the whole of the Earth's surface would be covered with people standing shoulder to shoulder within 600 years!

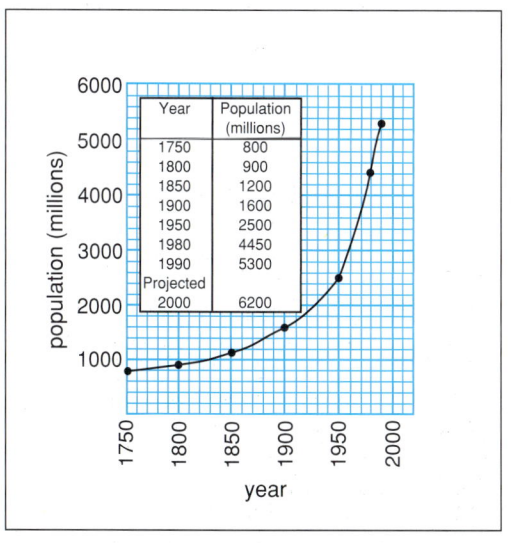

Populations under control

In a natural community of organisms, such as a pond or wood, the population sizes of the various species stay more or less constant. Numbers are kept under control by all sorts of checks, and there is a natural balance between predators and prey. Uncontrolled growth of the sort that we see in the human population is the exception rather than the rule.

Year	Population (millions)
1750	800
1800	900
1850	1200
1900	1600
1950	2500
1980	4450
1990	5300
Projected 2000	6200

Picture 5 World population growth from 1750 to 1990.

Questions

1. Study picture 2, then suggest two reasons why the rise in population is slow to begin with and then speeds up.
2. If all its offspring survived, a single greenfly could produce 600 000 000 000 offspring in one season, with a mass of over 600 000 kg – roughly equivalent to 10 000 men. What prevents this happening?
3. Study the graph in picture 4 and then answer these questions.
   a How can we say what the population of Britain was in 5000 BC?
   b Suggest a possible reason why the population was rising around 50 BC.
   c What do you think caused the sudden fall in the population between AD 1200 and 1800?
   d Why has the population risen so quickly since AD 1800?
   e Suggest two reasons why the population appears to be levelling off now.
4. The table shows the birth and death rates for four countries.

Country	Birth rate %	Death rate %
UK	1.71	1.19
USA	1.76	0.96
China	2.9	1.3
India	4.2	1.7

Calculate the percentage yearly increase in the population of each country. Suggest reasons why the population is increasing at different rates in the four countries.

5. 'Most of the ecological and social problems facing the human race are caused by over-population.' Think about this statement and discuss it with your friends. Start by making a list of the problems in order of urgency.
6. Population growth is kept under control by competition for scarce resources. Illustrate this with reference to (a) rabbits and (b) humans.

What other forces besides competition keep population growth under control?

The environment under strain

Suppose you are a parent of a large family. What would be your main concern? Surely it would be to make sure that your family is well fed, clothed and housed. This means spending your money wisely, and making certain that you don't spend more than you earn.

The same thing applies to a whole country. It's part of **economics**. One of the main tasks of a country's government is to look after the economy. The government tries to do this in such a way that everyone enjoys a high standard of living.

With a large population, goods – including food – have to be produced on a massive scale. This requires **industry** and **farming**, and that in turn requires energy and raw materials. The larger the population, the greater the strain on our natural resources. Between 1924 and 1985 the number of new houses built in England and Wales since 1919 rose from less than half a million to over 14 million. In one year the British Sunday newspapers alone swallow up paper from about five million trees.

No wonder there is not much natural countryside left. No wonder so much of our land is covered with houses, factories and farms.

Since the Second World War the number of licensed vehicles in the United Kingdom has increased from less than 4 million to over 24 million (see picture 1). No wonder there is so much **pollution**.

To satisfy the needs of a rapidly growing population that wants more and more, we have changed our world.

What exactly has changed? Not just the surface of the Earth where people live, but the whole of that part of the Earth and its atmosphere where there is life. This is called the **biosphere**.

Here are two particularly important ways in which the biosphere has changed:

- We have increased the amount of carbon dioxide in the air. This is raising the temperature of the world as a result of the **greenhouse effect.**

- We have released chlorofluorocarbons (CFCs) which destroy the **ozone layer** in the upper atmosphere. The ozone layer protects us from harmful ultraviolet rays which can cause skin cancer.

These are both aspects of pollution. You will find more about them on pages 42–43. All we shall say here is that they are made much worse by the size of the human population. When you squirt an aerosol can, the amount of CFCs that you put into the air is tiny. But millions of people using CFCs all over the world can have a tremendous effect on the atmosphere.

It's only relatively recently that these momentous changes have started taking place on our planet. That's because only in recent times has the world had to support such a huge and demanding population.

Humans have been on Earth for about a million years; we have started ruining it in less than two hundred. It could take thousands of years to put right the harm that we have already done.

1. Do you think it would be possible to solve our environmental problems without reducing the population?
2. Refrigerators are now manufactured on a large scale in many developing countries. These refrigerators release CFCs but the countries concerned say that they cannot afford to change their factories to produce non-CFC refrigerators. They say to the developed countries: 'For years you've been producing refrigerators that give out CFCs, and now you tell us not to!' How would you answer this?
3. To what extent does greed add to our environmental problems?

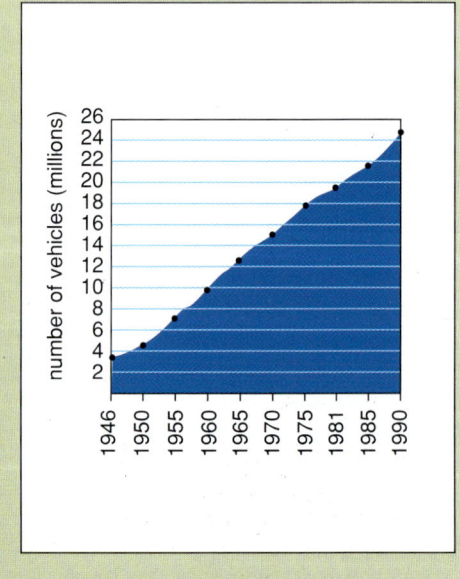

Picture 1 Growth of licensed vehicles 1946–1990. From Guiness UK Data Book 1992.

Population structure

Look at the picture below. These diagrams are called **population pyramids**. They show the population for different age groups in Great Britain at various intervals of time from 1891 to 1980.

In 1891 the most numerous people were the youngest ones. However, by 1947 the proportion of people in the 35 to 39 age group had increased, due to better health, but the proportion of teenagers had decreased. Notice the increase in the number of children in the nought to four age group: this was caused by an increase in the birth rate just after the second world war. It is known as the **post-war bulge**.

You can see the post-war bulge again in the 1956 and 1980 pyramids. These later pyramids also show a marked increase in the proportion of elderly people compared with the 1891 pyramid.

Population pyramids are useful because they enable us to forecast the population structure in the future. This is important in planning things like schools, housing needs and medical services.

Examine the 1980 population pyramid below.

a In what age group is the post-war bulge evident?

b How would you account for the post-war bulge?

c Why do you think the proportion of teenagers was so high in 1980?

d Why do you think the proportion of under tens was relatively low?

What do you think the population pyramid for Great Britain will look like in the year 2000? Try drawing it, and give reasons for your prediction.

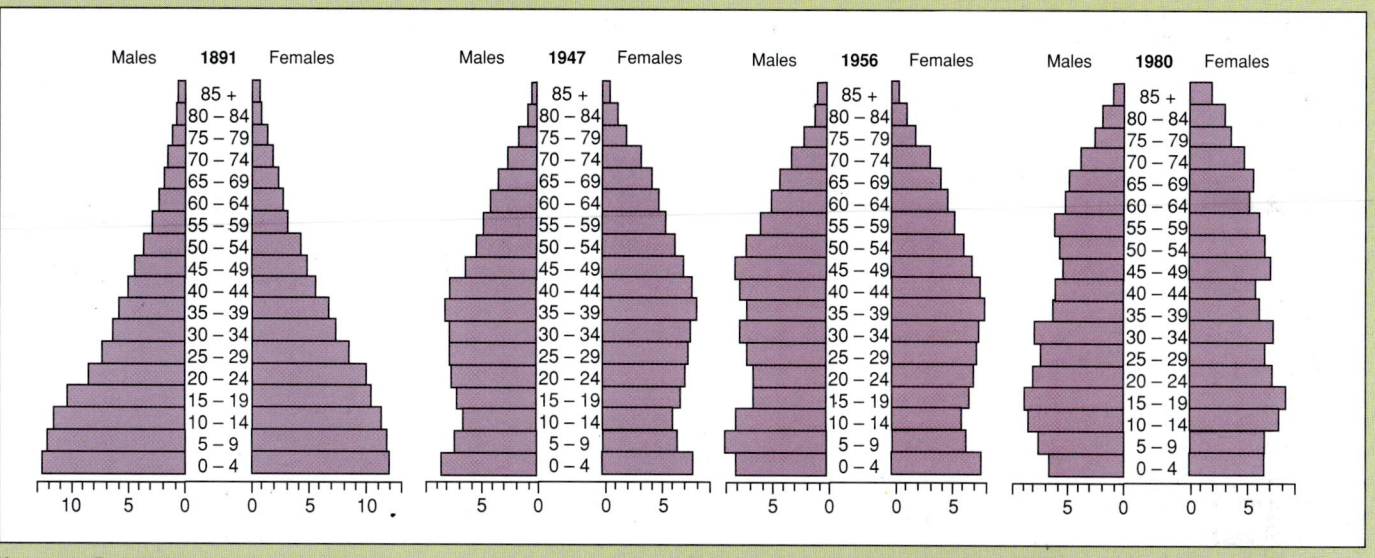

Picture 1 Population pyramids for Great Britain. The length of each horizontal bar represents the percentage of people, male or female, in a particular age group in the population.

Competition

We have seen in an earlier section that animals and plants live in habitats. In these habitats, each species has a particular feeding niche. This means that it eats only a certain combination of other organisms. In all ecosystems no two niches can be exactly the same. In other words, different species cannot share the same niche. This is because of **competition**.

Competition occurs between animals not only for food but for water, mates and nesting sites or space for rearing offspring. Plants also compete with each other for water, light and soil minerals.

A plant, for example, that has longer roots than the plant growing beside it, will more likely survive a hot dry spell when water is in short supply. An animal that is dominant over others when fighting will have first choice of mates. Weaker ones may fail to breed at all.

Competition is particularly severe between members of the same species (intraspecific competition) because their needs are virtually the same. Even between different species (interspecific competition) it can be severe.

The graph shows the growth of two populations of *Paramecium*, a unicellular organism. When reared separately they grow in a typical way (red lines), as we have seen on page 36. When reared together, one species has the upper hand and in the course of 16 days, the other becomes extinct (black lines). The two species have competed for the same food supplies but only one has been successful.

Most animals are adapted in their behaviour to feed on slightly different food sources, or at different times of the day, in order to avoid competition.

1 Why do caterpillars have different food requirements from the butterflies they become?

2 Do humans compete for space, mates and food? How is competition for these resources different in humans compared with other animals?

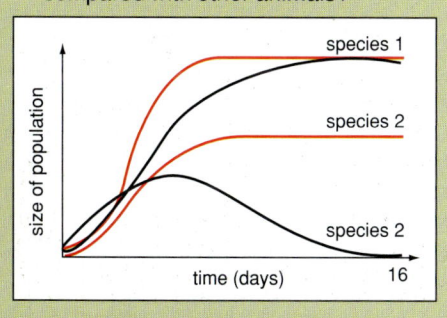

Picture 1 Populations of *Paramecium* reared separately (red) and together (black).

B6
The wheel of life

Chemical elements circulate in nature and can be used over and over again. Here we see how this applies to carbon and nitrogen.

The cycling of carbon

The air around us contains a small amount of carbon dioxide. This is constantly being absorbed by plants and turned into sugar and other complex carbon compounds (**photosynthesis**).

Now after a plant has been eaten by an animal, the carbon compounds get into the animal's cells. Here they are broken down into carbon dioxide and water (**respiration**). The carbon dioxide is breathed out. As a result, carbon dioxide is put back into the air. Plants also put carbon dioxide back into the air, but not all the time.

When the animals and plants die, they decay. Bacteria and other decomposers feed on them. They too respire, and so once again carbon dioxide is put back into the air.

So we see that carbon goes round and round in nature. This is known as the **carbon cycle** (picture 1).

Plants do not always decay after they have died. In certain circumstances they form peat which becomes fossilised into coal. When coal and other fossil fuels are burned, carbon dioxide is released (**combustion**). This too is part of the carbon cycle.

The cycling of nitrogen

In the soil there are inorganic nitrogen compounds called **nitrates**. They are dissolved in the soil water. The nitrates are absorbed by the roots of plants, and the plants then turn them into amino acids which are used to build up **proteins**.

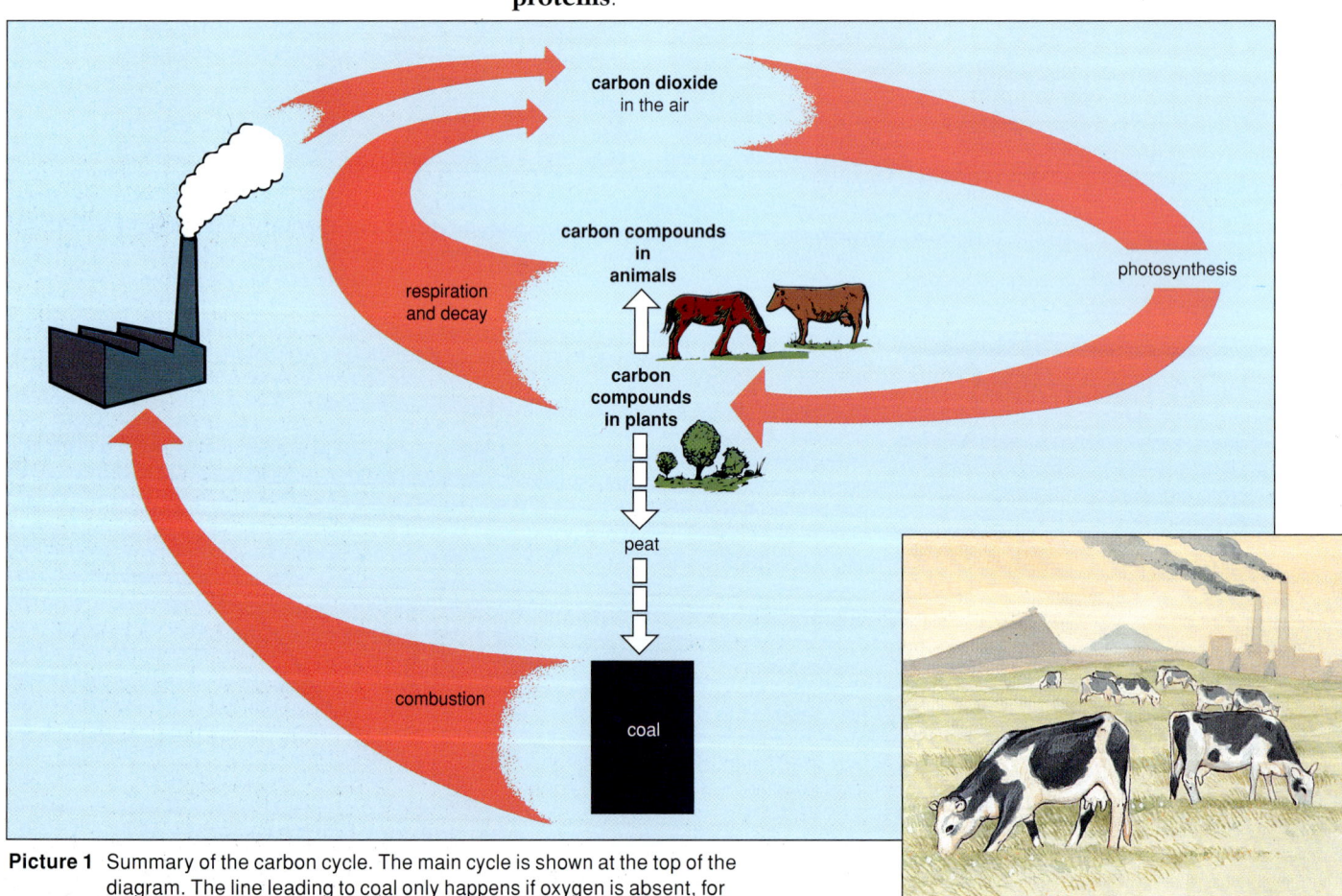

Picture 1 Summary of the carbon cycle. The main cycle is shown at the top of the diagram. The line leading to coal only happens if oxygen is absent, for example in bogs and swamps: the bacteria that cause decay cannot live without oxygen, and so the dead plants pile up, forming soft, black peat. In the course of time the peat gets buried and hardens to form coal.

Picture 2 This scene contains some of the main participants of the carbon cycle.

The wheel of life **41**

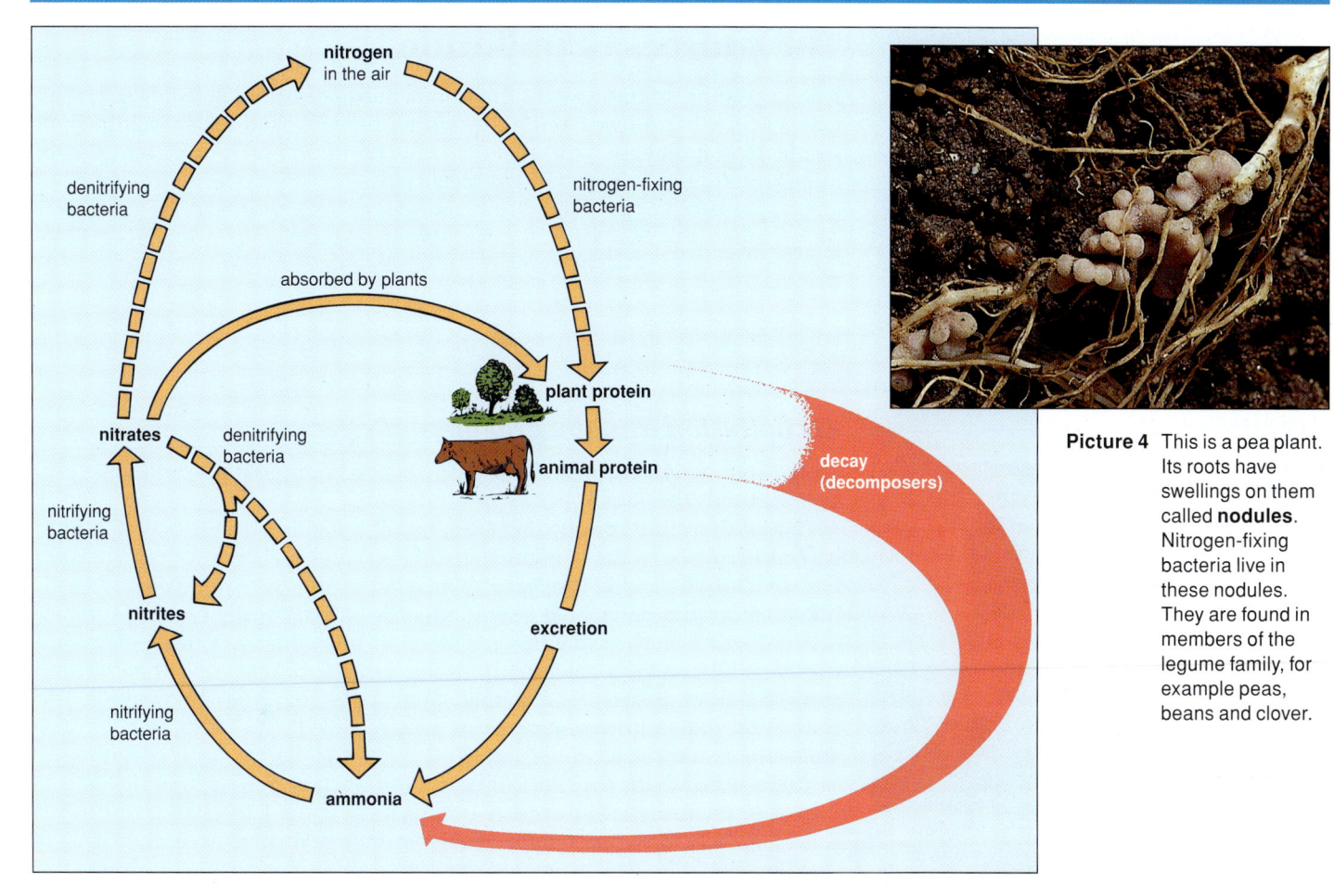

Picture 3 Summary of the nitrogen cycle. The diagram shows how nitrates can be formed by the action of bacteria on animal and plant protein. Some nitrates can also be made by the action of lightning on the nitrogen in the air.

Picture 4 This is a pea plant. Its roots have swellings on them called **nodules**. Nitrogen-fixing bacteria live in these nodules. They are found in members of the legume family, for example peas, beans and clover.

Now think what happens when a plant is eaten by an animal. The nitrogen in the plant protein gets into the animal's body and becomes part of its protein.

When the animals and plants die, they decay. Bacteria and other decomposers break down the proteins into ammonia. Ammonia is also formed from the animals' excreta.

Now in the soil there are bacteria which turn ammonia into nitrites, and others which turn nitrites into nitrates. The effect is to put nitrates back into the soil, where they can be used again by plants. These bacteria enrich the soil in nitrates and make it good for plants to grow in. Because of this, they are called **nitrifiers**.

The circulation of nitrogen is known as the **nitrogen cycle** (picture 3). In picture 3 notice that certain bacteria turn nitrates into nitrites, ammonia and even nitrogen. These bacteria lower the nitrate content of the soil and make it less good for plant growth – in fact nitrites are poisonous to most plants. For this reason, we call these bacteria **denitrifiers**.

Plants cannot make use of the element nitrogen. However, certain bacteria can absorb it from the air and use it for making protein. These bacteria are called **nitrogen-fixers**. Some of them are found free in the soil. Others live in the roots of plants belonging to the legume family, for example peas, beans and clover (picture 4). When these plants decay, the nitrogen which the bacteria have fixed goes into the soil where it can be used by plants. Nitrogen-fixing bacteria are therefore very useful because they increase the amount of useful nitrogen compounds in the soil.

Questions

1 Study the carbon cycle in picture 1, then answer these questions:
   a What is photosynthesis and how does it remove carbon dioxide from the air?
   b What is respiration and how does it add carbon dioxide to the air?
   c What is decay and how does it add carbon dioxide to the air?
   d What happens chemically when coal is burned, and how does it affect the carbon cycle?

2 Construct a diagram to show how oxygen circulates in nature. Why is this important to humans?

3 Farmers often plough plants such as clover or lucerne into the soil. Why is this a good thing to do? Explain your answer.

4 The bacteria responsible for decay, nitrification and nitrogen-fixation all require oxygen. However, denitrifying bacteria do not need oxygen. Bearing this in mind, what advice would you give to farmers about how to look after their soil?

B7 Pollution

Here we look at the effects of pollutants released by humans and how they may be controlled.

The sources of pollution

Pollution is the addition to the environment of poisonous substances (pollutants) which harm living things, including humans, and may result in their death. Most pollutants are added to the environment by the activities of humans and can be divided into three groups:

- domestic, e.g. sewage,
- agricultural, e.g. fertilisers and pesticides,
- industrial, e.g. chemicals, gases and radioactive waste.

Pollution occurs on land, in the sea, in the air and in fresh water environments such as ponds and streams.

Air pollution and the greenhouse effect

Table 1 summarises the main substances that cause air pollution and some possible methods of control.

One of the more serious problems facing humans is the threat of **global warming** caused by the continued use of fossil fuels. Whenever these fuels are burned, carbon dioxide is released. Once in the atmosphere this gas helps to trap some of the Sun's heat energy which would normally escape. A greenhouse does much the same thing as the glass traps the Sun's heat energy and prevents it getting out (picture 2). In the past the balance of carbon dioxide gas with other gases has remained quite constant. Nowadays people are concerned that, with so much extra carbon dioxide gas being put into the atmosphere, the Earth could overheat.

There is no doubt that the concentration of carbon dioxide in the air *has* increased (picture 3). The average temperature of the Earth has also shown a small increase. In the past 100 years the average temperature in the USA has risen by about 2°C. It is estimated that if the amount of carbon dioxide in the atmosphere doubles, the average temperature of the Earth will rise by about 3°C. This may not sound a lot, but it will make a big difference to the climate.

Some of the effects may be welcome. In places with good rainfall, farmers would be able to grow bumper crops. But there would be more droughts, wetlands would dry up and more land would be turned into deserts. The level of the sea would rise. This is because water expands when heated, and some of

Picture 1 Industry is one source of air pollution. This smoke is coming from an asphalt plant in Colorado.

Table 1 The main air pollutants.

Air pollutant	Source	Effects	Possible methods of control
Sulphur dioxide (SO_2)	Burning fossil fuels	Causes acid rain	Remove sulphur from fuels before burning. Remove sulphur dioxide from chimney gases of power stations
Nitrogen oxides (NO, NO_2, N_2O)	Vehicle exhausts, burning fuels	Help cause acid rain and photochemical smog	Fit catalytic converters to vehicle exhausts. Modify engines to run on a weaker mixture of fuel and air
Carbon dioxide (CO_2)	Burning fuels	Causes greenhouse effect, affecting Earth's climate	Burn less fossil fuels
Carbon monoxide (CO)	Burning fuels, vehicle exhaust, cigarette smoke	Poisonous to animals, including humans	Ensure vehicle engines are well maintained. Prevent cigarette smoking
Hydrocarbons	Vehicle exhausts, burning fuels	Help cause acid rain and photochemical smog	Fit catalytic converters to vehicle exhausts. Modify engines to run on a weaker mixture of fuel and air
Smoke	Burning fuels	Damages lungs; reduces photosynthesis of plants	Use smokeless fuels. Make sure engines and burners have plenty of air to burn fuel efficiently
Lead compounds	Car exhausts	Damage nervous system of humans	Use unleaded petrol
Chlorofluorocarbons (CFCs)	Aerosol propellants, refrigerators	Destroy ozone in the ozone layer which protects Earth from ultra-violet radiation. Also contribute to the greenhouse effect	Use different substances as aerosol propellants and refrigerants

the ice at the Poles would melt. This would bring floods to low-lying areas, including parts of Britain.

Carbon dioxide is not the only 'greenhouse gas', but it is the most serious one because there is so much of it. So much that there is no chance of removing it from all vehicle exhausts and other places it comes from. The best way to reduce it is to burn less fossil fuel. But it will take time to put things right. Even if we cut back on using fossil fuels today, global warming would still continue for many years. This is because so much carbon dioxide has already been added to the atmosphere from fuel we have burned in the past.

It is not good enough either to simply start using nuclear energy. Radioactive waste from the fuel used in nuclear power stations produces dangerous radiation. It is well known that radiation can cause some forms of cancer like leukaemia and, in addition to accidental leaks from nuclear power stations, large scale disasters have contaminated ecosystems in various parts of the world. The waste remains dangerous for many years and has to be stored in sealed vaults very carefully. This is not without risk. The containers could leak and, unless detected, the waste could then contaminate the surrounding environment.

Destroying the ozone layer

Ozone is an unstable form of oxygen. A very thin layer of ozone about 20–40 kilometres above the Earth acts as a natural sun screen and filters out some harmful ultraviolet light from the sun. If this form of radiation reaches Earth, it can cause sunburn and skin cancer.

Damage to the ozone layer has occurred due to the use of chemicals called **chlorofluorocarbons (CFCs)**. They are used in refrigerators and as the propellants in aerosols. The chemicals slowly move upwards to the ozone and destroy it.

Many countries have now agreed to stop using CFCs by substituting 'ozone friendly' products. However, the damage to the ozone layer is expected to continue for some time yet and humans are advised to 'cover up' in sunny weather and use a good sun-block cream.

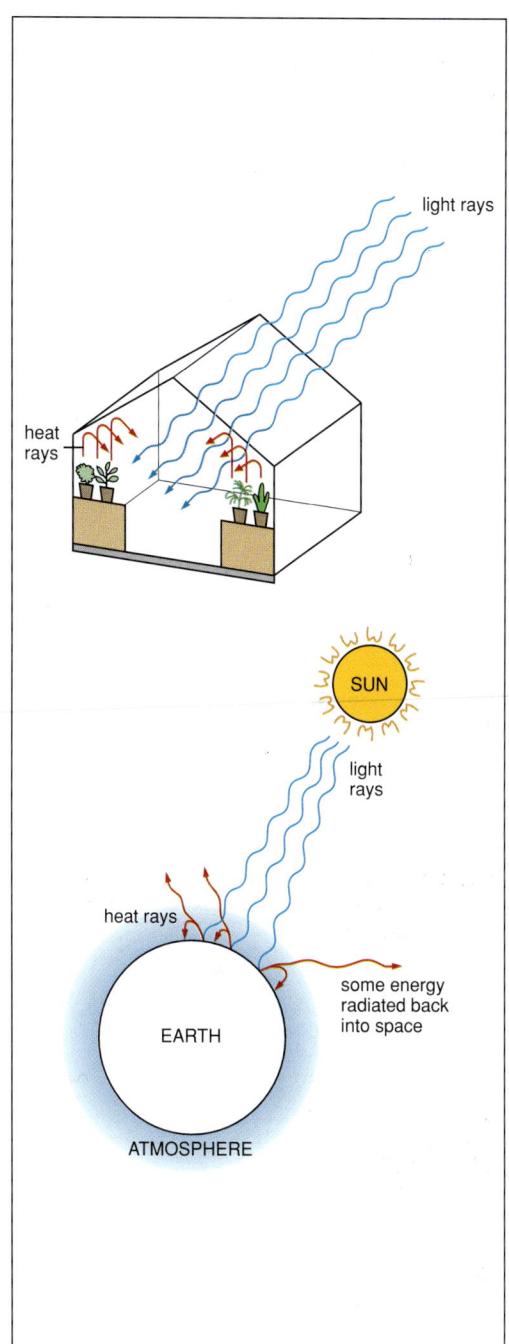

Picture 2 The greenhouse effect. The Sun gives out light rays (electromagnetic radiation of short wavelength) which pass through the glass into the greenhouse. They strike objects in the greenhouse, warming them. These objects give out heat rays (electromagnetic radiation of long wavelength) which cannot get through the glass. So heat energy is trapped inside the greenhouse. In the same kind of way, light rays from the Sun heat up the Earth's surface. Some of the heat energy which the Earth gives out is trapped by carbon dioxide and other gases in the atmosphere. These gases hold heat energy in, just as glass does in a greenhouse.

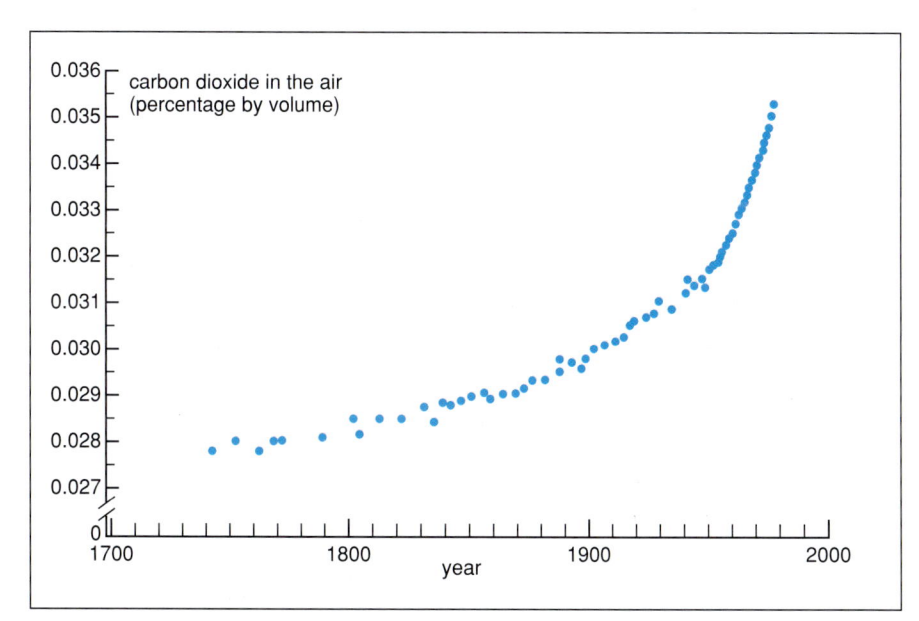

Picture 3 This graph shows how the concentration of carbon dioxide in the air has increased since 1700.

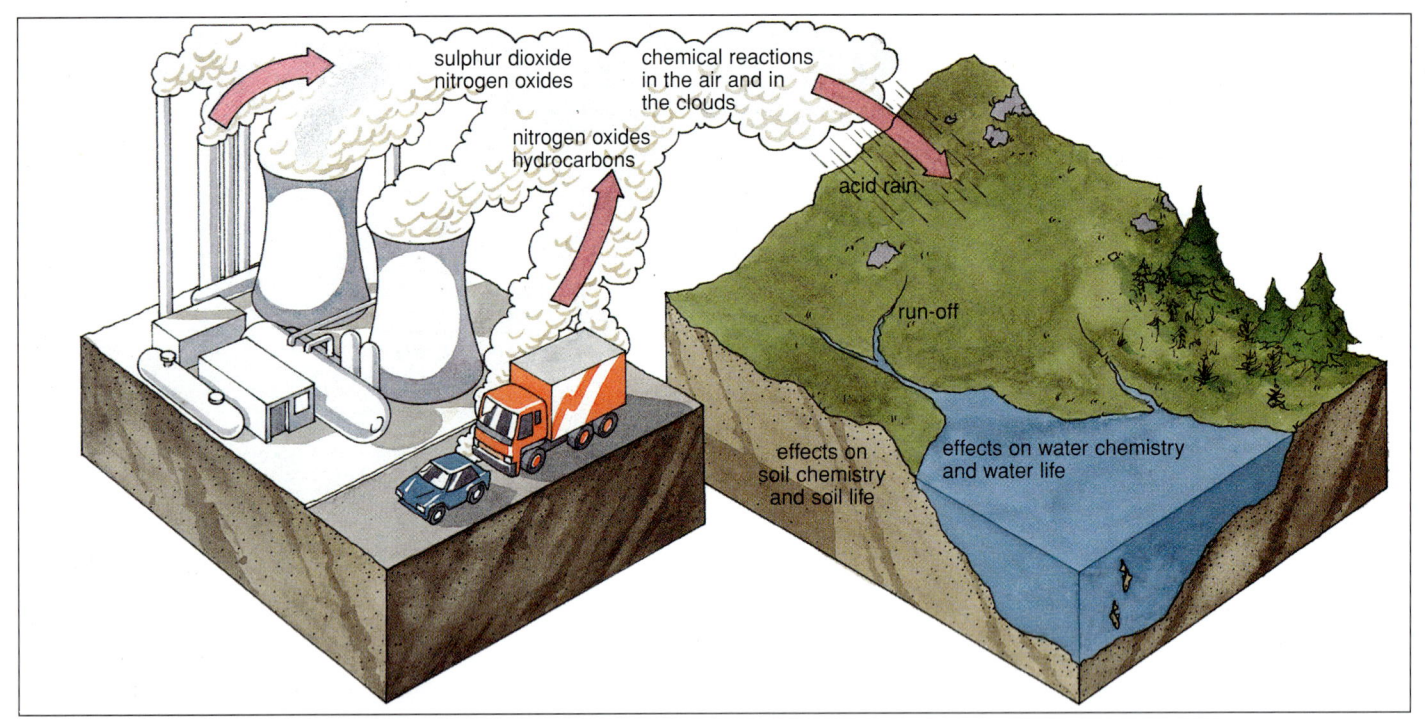

Picture 4 This diagram summarises the formation of acid rain.

Acid rain

Two of the gases released when fuels are burned, especially in vehicle engines and power stations, are sulphur dioxide and nitrogen dioxide. After they have been released, these gases undergo chemical reactions in the air to form acids. For example, sulphur dioxide reacts with oxygen to form sulphur trioxide. The sulphur trioxide then reacts with water to form sulphuric acid.

Reactions like this make rain water acidic, resulting in **acid rain**. Acid rain generally has a pH of between 5 and 2. In extreme cases it may be as acidic as vinegar. Picture 4 summarises how acid rain is formed.

When acid rain falls into streams and lakes, it makes them acidic. This may kill fish and other water life. Fish have been dying in lakes in Scandinavia, probably because of acid rain. Some of the acid gases there come mainly from Germany and Britain, carried hundreds of miles on the prevailing wind.

Acid rain also affects the soil. It may have helped kill pine and fir trees in Europe, particularly Germany. It also damages buildings and other structures by corroding metals and wearing away stonework.

Acid rain kills lichens. In fact the number of species of lichens growing on tree trunks and other exposed surfaces in an area is an indication of the concentration of sulphur dioxide in the atmosphere. This has been used as a measure of the amount of pollution in different parts of the country. More species occur in rural parts of Britain, particularly in the west, than in industrial regions. In badly polluted areas there are no lichens at all. Lichens are known as **indicator species** (see page 45).

It is not easy to control acid rain because scientists do not yet fully understand what causes it and what its effects are. Sulphur dioxide is certainly involved. The chimneys of coal-burning power stations can be fitted with units which remove sulphur dioxide from the chimney gases, but this is very expensive. Nitrogen oxides in car exhaust can be controlled by fitting cars with catalytic converters which remove the gases, or by careful engine design.

Questions

1 In large American cities drivers are encouraged to offer seats in their cars to other people ('pool riding'). The fast lane of highways is reserved for such drivers, and heavy fines are given to drivers of single-occupant cars that use the fast lane. Consider the case for and against such a scheme.

2 The figures below give the estimated total amounts of carbon involved in four processes per year for the whole world.

Process	Amount of carbon (gigatonnes)
Photosynthesis	142
Respiration	136
Burning fossil fuels	5
Deforestation	2

(One gigatonne = 1 000 000 000 tonnes)

Comment on these figures.

3 Here are three ways of slowing down the greenhouse effect and global warming:
 a Use energy sources that do not produce carbon dioxide.
 b Save more energy than we do at present.
 c Speed up the rate at which carbon dioxide is removed from the atmosphere.

How might each of these approaches be achieved?

Water pollution

All living things need water. Humans require large quantities of clean water for many reasons. However, human activities can lead to water pollution.

One of the most common is the pollution of the sea, and sometimes fresh water, by oil. When a tanker or oil rig leaks, a thin slick of oil may form on the surface of the water. The slick may then be carried by water currents and deposited on the shore. This not only ruins the beach for local residents and holiday-makers but also kills fish and sea birds (picture 5).

One remedy is to spray the oil slick with detergents which break up the oil into droplets. This makes it easier for the sea to disperse the oil. Oil booms may also be used to contain a spillage in a small area and special ships can be used to scoop the oil from the surface of the sea into storage vessels. Careful management of tankers and oil installations would avoid the need for costly clean-up operations and prevent habitat destruction.

Another serious form of water pollution is the discharge of untreated sewage into rivers. Sewage, a form of organic waste, provides a good food supply for bacteria in the river and as a result their population greatly increases. Unfortunately, as this large number of bacteria breaks down the sewage, they use up all the oxygen in the river. This makes it difficult for any other organisms, like fish, to survive. Eventually the river becomes so low in oxygen that all organisms die except those that can survive in habitats with little or no oxygen. These are invertebrate animals such as rat-tailed maggots and *Tubifex* worms (picture 6).

However, as the sewage is gradually broken down the number of bacteria decreases and the oxygen level rises (picture 7). This happens downstream from the sewage inflow.

A greater variety of animal life now exists. For example, the nymphs of the mayfly and stonefly can only survive in water that has a very high oxygen concentration (picture 8). Biologists can use the presence or absence of these animals to measure the level of pollution in the water. Like lichens, they are indicator species.

Full treatment of sewage must be carried out if the problems described are to be avoided (see page 198).

Picture 5 This cormorant was the victim of a spillage of oil from a damaged oil tanker.

Picture 6 Rat-tailed maggots and *Tubifex* worms indicate areas of high pollution.

Picture 8 Nymphs of stonefly and mayfly indicate areas of low pollution.

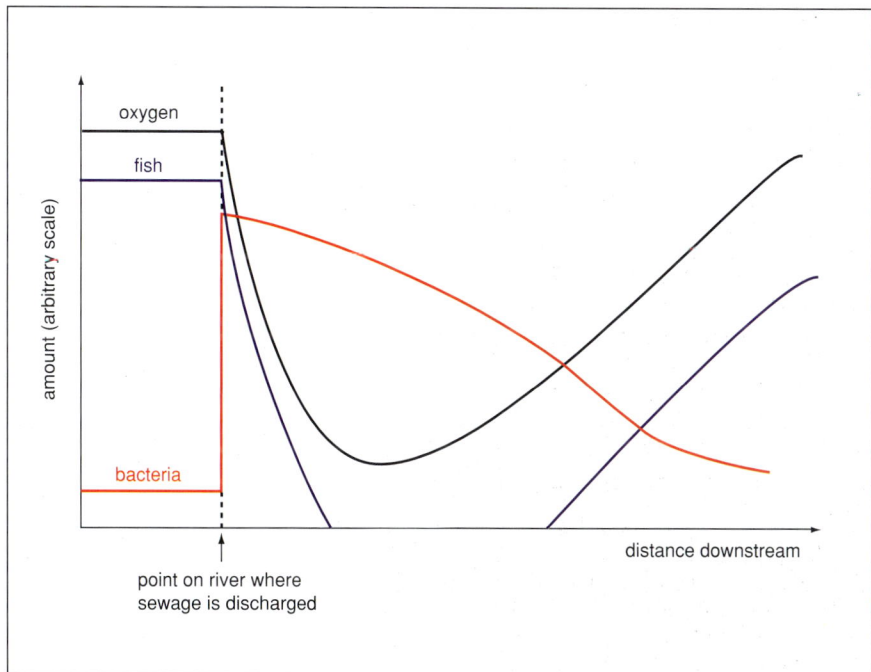

Picture 7 Graph showing the changes in oxygen content, bacteria numbers and fish numbers in a river.

B8 Management and conservation

We can control the environment to serve our needs, but we must be careful how we go about it.

Modern farming

Nowadays farmers usually fill their fields with just one type of crop, wheat for instance, which they grow year after year. This is called **monoculture**. Fertilisers enrich the soil with nutrients, and herbicides ensure that no weeds are present to compete with the crop. With plenty of food and no competition, the crop plants can be grown very close together. All this has the effect of increasing the yield. Modern machinery for ploughing, sowing the seeds and harvesting means that fields can be enormous (picture 1).

The disadvantages of monoculture

Monoculture enables the land to be used intensively. This means more food for more people. However, when carried out on a large scale it involves cutting down trees and removing hedges. This destroys the natural environment, kills wildlife and makes the countryside look dull. What's more, with repeated ploughing and the use of artificial fertilisers, the soil crumbs break up and the soil becomes fine and dusty. It then gets blown about by the wind, causing **erosion**. The structure of the soil can be regained by leaving it fallow for a year, or by growing grass on it, or by adding manure to it.

There is another drawback too. Suppose a pest happens to get into the crop. Any natural predators that might control it will have been killed by pesticides. For example, if greenflies get into the crop, there will be no ladybirds to control them. With the plants so close together, the pest will spread quickly through the crop. To some extent the risk of this happening can be reduced by rotating crops; different types of crop are attacked by different pests, and rotation may prevent a pest completing its life cycle. The same thing may be achieved by varying the times when particular crops are sown.

The control of components of an ecosystem

A wheat field is an **artificial ecosystem**. It is created and managed by farmers for the sole purpose of producing a crop plant. The ecosystem has been deliberately changed by the farmers to maintain the ecosystem in this way.

In an attempt to increase the productivity of the field, trees and hedges are removed (picture 2). This makes the field larger and allows heavy machinery to move efficiently. However, because the trees and hedges provided shelter, their removal means that the soil can be easily blown away. This results in **soil erosion**.

Clearing weeds ensures that the crop plants have no competition for resources. Sadly, it also deprives the environment of plant variety and reduces the habitats available to animals.

Farmers add fertilisers to the soil. These can be artificial, like nitrates and phosphates, or natural, like animal manure. Applying too much fertiliser can lead to the pollution of lakes and ponds as it is washed from the field by heavy rain. This leads to the unchecked growth of pond algae and the death of other living organisms.

The use of crop sprayers and irrigators, the erection of fences and the repeated ploughing of fields, all alter the environment. Humans must therefore be very careful with the management of such activities.

Picture 1 Harvesting wheat on a large scale in North America. In Canada there is a single fenced wheat field with an area of 140 km². That's larger than the city of Sheffield!

Picture 2 Since 1947 over 100 000 miles of hedges have been ripped up in Britain – enough to go round the Earth four times.

What does good management involve?

All sorts of things can be done to improve the management of farmland so as to conserve or restore the natural environment. Trees and hedges can be replanted. Marshy areas, once drained to increase farming land, can be left undrained and natural. Care can be taken to regulate the addition of chemicals, like fertilisers, pesticides and weed killers, to the environment. With the careful use of selective pesticides and biological control agents, it is possible to get rid of pests but leave other species unharmed.

Sensible, sympathetic management not only results in excellent crop yields, but greatly contributes to saving our dwindling wildlife (picture 3). It also provides pleasure for hikers and tourists.

When management is lacking

There are places in the world where ecosystems are not managed properly. An example is the tropical rain forest. Here vast numbers of trees have been felled for timber, or burned to clear the forest for growing crops, raising livestock or industrial development (picture 4). In the Amazon alone, an area the size of France has been destroyed in a single year.

Not only does this kill the wildlife on a massive scale, but it also changes the pattern of rainfall and ruins the soil.

It's a matter of need

It is easy to condemn governments and developers in tropical countries for ruining the rain forests, but they are only doing what we in Britain have done – though more slowly – for centuries. At one time Britain was a land of forests. Gradually the trees were cleared to provide fuel, timber for building, and space for growing crops.

Today Britain has very little natural woodland, let alone forests. This is not just because wicked people have destroyed them. There is a real conflict between our desire to have unspoiled places, and the needs of a modern industrial society. The problem is made worse by the fact that our country is small and densely populated (picture 5).

This makes it even more important that the land should be managed properly. In practice this means reaching a compromise between conservation on the one hand, and food-production, industry and housing on the other. To reach a compromise, there has to be cooperation between government, local authorities and individual people.

The place where you live

Think about the place where you live. Has the environment been spoiled or is it cared for? Is there any natural countryside and wild life, and if so is it under threat? What sort of development has taken place in your area, and has it all been necessary? Have attempts been made to improve the environment, and if so by whom? How could you improve it?

Answering these questions helps to bring home the conflict between the opposing forces of urbanisation and conservation. To understand this more fully we need to know exactly what conservation involves.

Picture 3 The copse in the centre of this wheat field is a haven for wildlife.

Picture 4 Part of a tropical rain forest being cleared.

Picture 5 A small, densely populated country like Britain needs land for urban development.

48 *The biosphere*

Picture 6 Wildebeest and zebra in Serengeti National Park in East Africa. The numbers of these herbivores are kept at the right level by natural processes, including predation by lions. The ecosystem as a whole is carefully managed by game wardens. But even in game parks poachers threaten animals like the gorilla and elephant.

Picture 7 Slimbridge Wildfowl Trust Centre in Gloucestershire is a sanctuary for many species of migratory birds.

What is conservation?

To conserve something means to protect it and keep it in a healthy state. Applied to our environment, it means protecting ecosystems so that the organisms in them can flourish. Perhaps the most successful, and certainly the largest, examples of conservation are seen in some of the game parks of Africa (picture 6).

Sometimes special steps have to be taken to help endangered species to survive. Such was the case with the Hawaiian goose. This unfortunate bird was shot by hunters and its chicks were preyed on by animals introduced by humans. By 1950 it was almost extinct. Then a few were brought to the Wildfowl Trust Centre at Slimbridge in Gloucestershire. Here, in one of the best-managed semi-natural ecosystems in the world, they bred successfully (picture 7).

Soon there were more Hawaiian geese at Slimbridge than there had been in Hawaii! In the early 1960s some of them were taken back to Hawaii and released. Since then their numbers have gradually increased. This is a success story in conservation, but sadly there are not many like it.

Conserving food resources

One reason for conserving ecosystems is that they may contain animals we (and future generations) need for food. Such is the case with sea fish such as herring and cod.

One of the main ways of catching fish is by **trawling** (picture 8). The modern trawler is a very efficient vessel. The nets are large and special echo-sounding equipment is used for locating large shoals of fish. In **factory trawlers** there are machines for gutting, skinning, filleting and freezing the fish on board.

This looks like a success story in technology. However, we have to make sure that we do not take so many fish out of the sea that their numbers begin to fall. This means that *we must not remove them faster than they can be replaced by their natural processes of reproduction*.

In the European Union there are agreed quotas regulating the number of tonnes of the various types of sea fish that may be caught by each member country each year. The quotas are set annually by negotiation, and are based on scientific advice from bodies concerned with fisheries management.

We must also make sure that no damage is done to the food chains which fish depend on. These food chains start off with **plankton**, and so it is particularly important that no harm comes to the organisms that make up the plankton.

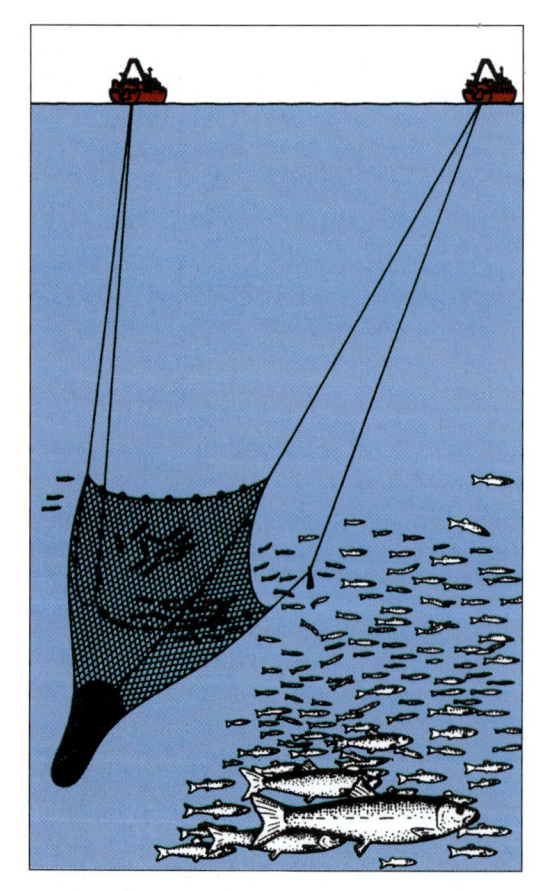

Picture 8 Many of the fish we eat are caught by trawling. The net here is one of several different kinds that are commonly used. To prevent over-fishing, various regulations limit the sizes of nets and their mesh.

Activities

A Finding out about a market garden

A market garden is a place where plants such as lettuces and tomatoes are grown for selling. This is called horticulture, and it is a good example of an artificial ecosystem.

Visit a market garden. Find out what sort of crops are grown, and who the main customers are.

Choose one crop, and try to find answers to these questions:

1. How is the crop protected from unsuitable weather conditions?
2. What sort of pests have to be controlled, and how is this done?
3. What kind of fertilisers are used, and how are they applied?
4. In what form are the plants sold? What steps are taken to ensure that they are free of disease and do not present a health hazard?

Write an account of the way the crop is grown, concentrating on the extent to which it forms part of a managed ecosystem.

B Finding out about a farm

1. Choose a particular type of farm, e.g. one that grows cereal crops such as wheat or barley, or one that rears livestock such as cattle, sheep or pigs.
2. From books, find out as much as possible about this type of farm. Try to get interested in one particular aspect – such as how the farmer achieves maximum productivity without damaging the local environment.
3. If possible, talk to a farmer or, better still, visit a farm. Write down a list of questions beforehand which you would like to ask the farmer.
4. Write a report on your farm, concentrating on the aspects that interest you most.

C The pros and cons of monoculture

Hold a debate. The motion is as follows: *Monocultural crop-growing on a large scale damages the environment unacceptably and should be stopped.*

D Conservation in your area

1. Try to find one example of a conservation project which has been carried out in your area. Find out as much about it as you can, in particular how it is looked after and managed. Write an account of it, and say how it has benefited (a) wildlife and (b) people.
2. Suggest a conservation scheme which has not been carried out in your area but which, in your opinion, should be. Outline what might be done, and give reasons for your suggestions.

Questions

1. You have been appointed Minister of Conservation. Write down ten laws you would like to introduce, in order of priority. Give reasons for each one, and say what problems you might have in getting it through Parliament.
2. An area of natural woodland in Britain is destroyed and replaced by a very productive wheat field. As a result, the ecosystem of the area is changed.
   a. What is meant by the word ecosystem?
   b. In what ways does the ecosystem of the wheat field differ from that of the woodland?
3. Why don't the wild flowers on the downs get eaten by the grazers? Suggest two possible hypotheses and describe how each could be tested.
4. Why do you think clearing the tropical rain forest:
   a. alters the pattern of the rainfall,
   b. ruins the soil?
   What other effects might it have?
5. Even the best run farms are at the mercy of the climate. Illustrate this with reference to a wheat farm. Suggest two events which can ruin a harvest.
6. The figures show the agreed fishing quotas in tonnes for cod and herring in 1994 for the United Kingdom and the whole of the European Union.

	UK	EU
Cod	56 700	205 720
Herring	106 360	833 200

   a. What sort of information is needed to set the quotas?
   b. Why do you think the quota for herring is much larger than the quota for cod?
   c. The quotas for herring and cod could be quite different in a few years time. Suggest a reason for this.
   d. How do you think the UK keeps to its quota? (Hint: the Ministry of Agriculture, Fisheries and Food (MAFF) publishes statistics every month on UK fish catches.)
   e. Can you suggest ways of managing fisheries other than by setting quotas?

Killer worm threatens farms

Read the newspaper extract on the right, then answer these questions.

1. What lesson does this story teach us about conservation?
2. Does it matter if earthworms get eaten? What use are they?

AN UNWELCOME visitor from New Zealand has colonised Northern Ireland and is killing off the native earthworms that are essential to soil fertility.

The visitor is a flatworm called *Artioposthia triangulata*, which can grow up to six inches long and weigh two grams. It can eat a whole earthworm in 30 minutes.

The killer worm has been found in every Ulster county and, according to the Department of Agriculture, the only check to its increasing numbers appears to be the availability of food. 'The potential impact on local populations of earthworms cannot be overestimated,' said a department spokesman.

By Godfrey Brown
Agriculture Correspondent

C1 Introducing plants

In this section we will learn why plants are important.

Picture 1 Rice plants. Rice feeds one third of the world's population.

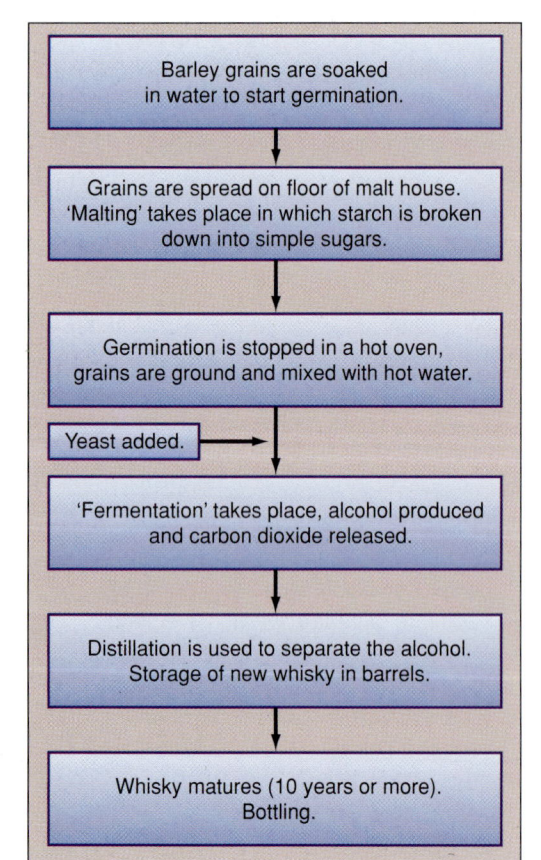

Barley grains are soaked in water to start germination.
↓
Grains are spread on floor of malt house. 'Malting' takes place in which starch is broken down into simple sugars.
↓
Germination is stopped in a hot oven, grains are ground and mixed with hot water.
↓
Yeast added.
↓
'Fermentation' takes place, alcohol produced and carbon dioxide released.
↓
Distillation is used to separate the alcohol. Storage of new whisky in barrels.
↓
Whisky matures (10 years or more). Bottling.

Picture 2 A summary of Scotch whisky making.

Plants – the basics

There is a huge variety of plants in the world. They live in almost every habitat and can survive in some of the harshest environments (including our homes, if we forget to water them). They can give humans some of their best artistic moments and yet go unnoticed by most of us. They appear to be unimportant and often are seen as weeds, growing where we do not want them.

Yet plants are the crucial link between the sun and all other living things on the planet. They transfer the sun's light energy to chemical energy which all animals depend on for food. This process is called **photosynthesis** which you will read more about on page 64.

Plants maintain the balance of atmospheric gases by taking in carbon dioxide and releasing oxygen. They also regulate the level of water in the soil, removing large quantities by evaporation.

Plants are also the homes or habitats for many organisms, and the huge variety of plants ensures that there is a wide range of habitats for every possible sort of animal.

Humans and plants

There are three main ways that humans use plants:

■ As a food supply. For example, rice, maize and wheat form the staple foods of many countries (picture 1). All sorts of vegetables and fruits add variety to our diet. Herbs, spices, sugar, nuts, coffee, tea and cocoa are all plant products. In addition, barley is used for the manufacture of whisky, one of Scotland's most important exports.

■ As a source of raw materials, for example, timber, paper, rubber, rope and string. Perfumes, textile fibres such as cotton, and the dyes and inks to colour them, are all obtained from plant sources.

■ As a source of medicines. A famous example is the drug digitalis which is obtained from the foxglove. It can be used to strengthen the muscle tissue in the wall of the heart. Quinine (an anti-malarial drug) is obtained from the Cinchona tree, and curare (a muscle relaxant) comes from the bark of trees such as *Strychnos*. Herbal cures were first written down by Babylonians in about 2000 BC and simple herbal cures are still common today. Camomile tea soothes upset stomachs and indigestion.

Three specialised uses of plants

Making Scotch whisky

Barley, not just from Scotland, is harvested and transported to the distillery. Once cleaned and weighed, the grains are soaked in large tanks and then spread on the floor of the malting house where they germinate and convert the stored starch into simple sugars. This process is called 'malting' and takes between 8 to 12 days. You shall read more about malting later.

The grain is then dried in a special oven, ground and added to hot water. Yeast is added and the process of fermentation takes place where sugar is converted into alcohol and carbon dioxide gas is released. This takes about 48 hours.

The next stage, distillation, separates the water and yeast from the alcohol. The resulting alcoholic liquid is collected and stored in old sherry barrels. This gives the distinctive colour to malt whisky.

Bottling takes place some years later, after the whisky has matured. Scottish malt whiskies are famous all over the world. Picture 2 summarises the process.

Introducing plants

The use of plants in dyeing

Another famous Scottish export is tartan cloth. The close weave of the material makes it midge-proof and reasonably waterproof – perfect for Scotland! In the past, the wool was first soaked in human urine to remove the grease, then washed and dried. After spinning, the wool was placed in boiling water with the dye and simmered gently until the required colour was obtained.

Various plants were used to give the traditional reds, yellows, blues and browns. Table 1 summarises some of the plants that were, and sometimes still are, used in the dyeing process.

Nowadays, modern chemistry has produced artificial dyes which have replaced most of the traditional plant-based ones.

The jute industry

Jute is a fibre from stems of plants still grown in Bangladesh. The plants (*Corchorus capsularis* and *C. olitorius*) can stand up to 5 metres high and have stems about 2 cm thick (picture 3). The stems from the plant are first rotted in water (traditionally in rivers and ponds), enabling the bark to be pulled off the underlying fibre. The fibres are then softened by passing them through heavy rollers and soaking them in oil and water for 24 hours. They are dried, carded (combed) and finally drawn into a yarn.

The yellow-brown jute can be dyed and is used in the manufacture of the backing fibres of carpets and linoleum flooring.

Dundee is well known for the manufacture of jute-based products.

The importance of plant conservation

The plant kingdom makes a huge contribution to our lives. Therefore the removal of plants from our environment is often very noticeable and may make our surroundings poorer.

As is said on page 47, large areas of tropical rain forest are being cleared every year for activities such as farming, timber production and mining. The loss of these habitats may have serious consequences for the future. Not only does it threaten animal life with extinction, but many plants whose properties have yet to be discovered could disappear. New food crops or plants with special medicinal properties could be destroyed and lost forever.

Many farmers hope that wild crops will contain characteristics which can be bred into the modern-day varieties. These characteristics could improve the yield or make the crop more able to resist disease. Currently, a wild variety of maize (*Zea diploperennis*) could make seed-sowing a thing of the past. It produces underground stems, called rhizomes, which make the plant perennial.

There are many more potential uses of plants. The development of new medicines, such as drugs for the treatment of cancer, is one example. The use of plant material as a source of fermentable sugars to produce alcohol is another. The alcohol can be mixed with petrol (in a ratio of 2:8) and used as a fuel for motor engines. Known as 'Gasohol', it is used particularly in Brazil.

Plant	Dye colour obtained
Heather	Yellow
Nettle	Green
Sorrel roots	Red
Dandelion root	Purple
Dulse (seaweed)	Brown
Meadow sweet	Black
Elder berries	Blue
Bramble berries	Grey-blue
Alder bark	Black
Lichens	Reds, yellows and browns

Table 1 Plants and the colours that can be extracted from them.

Picture 3 Jute drying, after the bark has been removed, in Bangladesh.

Questions

1 It is estimated that twenty million hectares of tropical rain forest are cleared every year. Write a short paragraph (perhaps in the form of a letter to a newspaper) explaining the importance of conserving rain forest areas.

2 Humans are always looking for new products which can be obtained from plants. However, sometimes it is difficult to develop a new plant product efficiently. Describe some of the problems that a drug company could face, if it were trying to develop a new medicine from a newly discovered plant source in Malaysia.

C2
Seeds and germination

Here we look at seeds and what happens to them after they have been dispersed.

Picture 1 A selection of seeds, all used in cooking.

Inside a seed

If you have broad beans with your lunch, they will be soft. But in their natural state, they are hard and dry. This is true of seeds in general. In this state they survive the winter, or the dry season in the tropics.

Picture 2 shows a broad bean seed. It is surrounded by the **seed coat** or **testa**. This is a tough fibrous layer which protects the internal structures of the seed. If you want to see inside the seed, you need to soften it first. This can be done by soaking the seed in water for a day or so. You can then slice it down the middle. Inside is the embryo made up of two parts:
- a young shoot (called the **plumule**),
- a young root (called the **radicle**).

These will eventually develop into the new plant. There is also a pair of thick seed leaves (called **cotyledons**). These are the food store of the seed. The energy provided by the starchy food in the seed leaves will be used for germination.

The seed develops into a new plant

When spring arrives, the seed bursts open and a new plant grows out. This process is called **germination**.

Picture 3 shows stages in the germination of the broad bean. First the seed takes up water, mainly through the little hole in its wall (picture 2). This makes it swell. As a result, the seed coat splits, and the new plant starts growing out – the root first, then the shoot. The root grows downwards, and the shoot upwards. The shoot is bent back on itself, like a hook. This protects its delicate tip as it pushes up through the soil.

The tip of the root is protected by a slimy mass of loosely packed cells called the **root cap**. This prevents it being damaged as it grows down into the soil. As it grows, the root gives off side branches which help to anchor the young plant and absorb water and mineral salts from the soil (picture 4). Slender root hairs increase the surface area for absorption.

The shoot eventually breaks through the surface of the soil. It then straightens, and the first leaves open out and turn green. Germination is complete, and we now have a young plant or **seedling**.

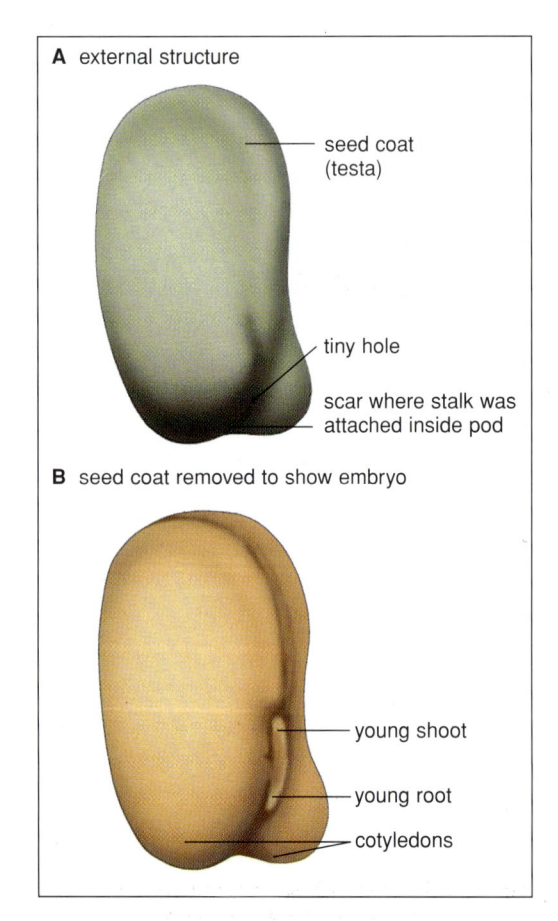

A external structure
- seed coat (testa)
- tiny hole
- scar where stalk was attached inside pod

B seed coat removed to show embryo
- young shoot
- young root
- cotyledons

Picture 2 The structure of a broad bean seed.

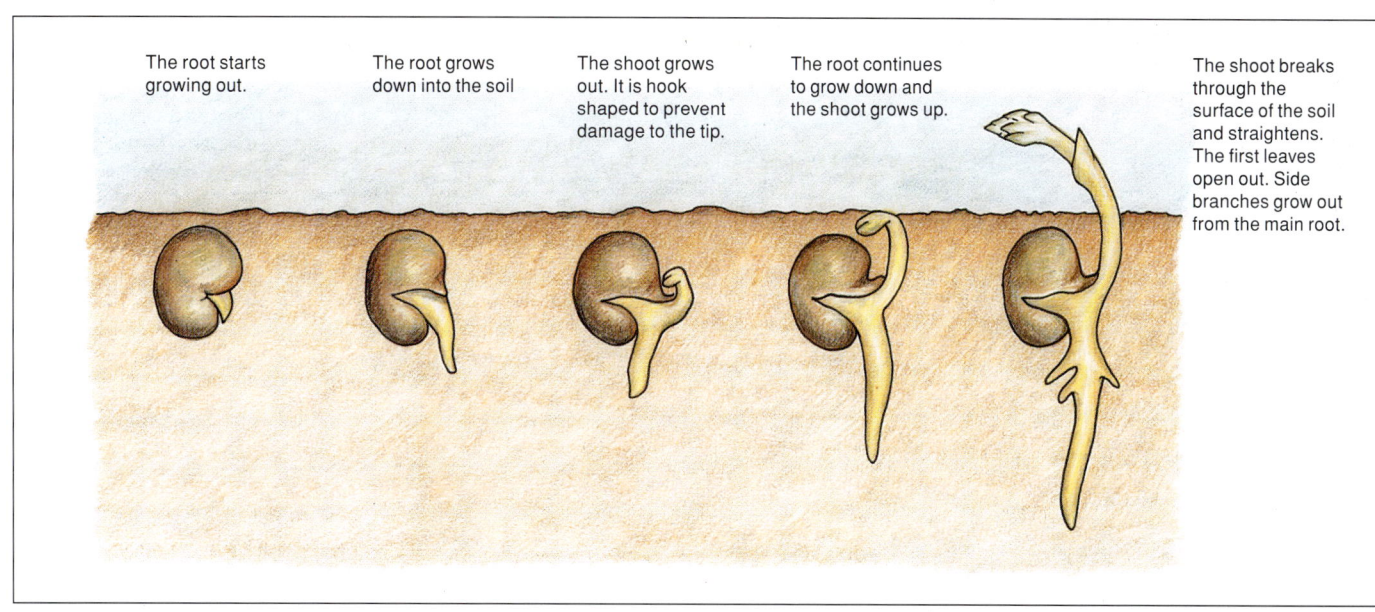

Seeds and germination

The root starts growing out.

The root grows down into the soil.

The shoot grows out. It is hook shaped to prevent damage to the tip.

The root continues to grow down and the shoot grows up.

The shoot breaks through the surface of the soil and straightens. The first leaves open out. Side branches grow out from the main root.

Picture 3 Germination of a broad bean seed. It takes about 12–14 days to reach the stage shown on the far right.

Not all plants germinate like the broad bean, but it is typical of many. Wheat germinates like the broad bean but the shoot, instead of being hooked, points straight up (picture 5). Its delicate tip is protected by a sheath called the **coleoptile**. When the leaves open out, they break through the coleoptile. Wheat is a type of grass, and all grasses have a coleoptile.

Where does the germinating seed get its food from?

For the embryo to grow, food is needed. In the broad bean, the food comes from the cotyledons. They remain inside the seed coat beneath the soil. The insoluble starch in the cotyledons is turned into soluble sugar. This is then transported to the tips of the shoot and root where growth takes place.

Once the seedling has formed its first green leaves, it can make its own food by photosynthesis. It is then self-supporting. The cotyledons are no longer needed; their food store has been used up, and they wither away.

Picture 4 In this picture of young broad bean seedlings notice the side roots.

What conditions are needed for germination?

It is very annoying when you plant seeds in the garden and they don't grow. This is usually because the seeds lack the conditions they need in order to germinate.

What are these conditions? We can find out by trying to germinate seeds in different conditions – you can do this for yourself in the activity on page 55.

From experiments of this sort we can say that these three conditions are needed for germination:

- **Water** is needed for the seed to swell and burst open. It is also needed for the stored food to be made soluble and moved to the growing embryo.
- **Oxygen** is needed for the embryo to respire. Respiration supplies energy for the embryo to grow and develop.
- **Warmth** is needed by most seeds. This is why seeds do not normally germinate till the spring or summer. The degree of warmth varies from one type of plant to another.

What about **light**? Most seeds will germinate in the light or dark. However, some germinate only in the dark. Others require light. The amount of light needed may be very small – one quick flash is enough in some cases.

All plants need light once the young shoot breaks through the surface of the soil. This is because light is needed for the leaves to open out and make chlorophyll. Only then will they start photosynthesising and feeding the plant.

Picture 5 The shoot of this wheat seedling is covered by a sheath-like coleoptile from which the first leaf can be seen emerging.

54 *The world of plants*

Picture 6 Wheat grain store, Iowa, USA.

Food from seeds

Seeds contain a store of food for feeding the new plants until they can support themselves. This makes them a good source of food for humans. In peas and beans the food is in the **cotyledons**. In cereals like wheat the food is in the **endosperm** (see page 57). Some seeds contain oil which is used for various purposes. Such is the case with rape, the bright yellow crop that adds splashes of colour to the British countryside in the spring. We also get oil from the seed (and fruit) of the oil palm. Its story is told on page 63.

Wheat and rice seeds are particularly useful because they form the main part of the diet of so many people. Starch, protein and a number of other useful nutrients are packed into the ripe seeds (the **grain**). From the grain all sorts of foods are made, including bread.

Wheat and rice seeds are a more concentrated source of food than, say, potatoes. This is because seeds contain so little water. In fact one kilogram of wheat has more food in it than three kilograms of potatoes. A grain store, like the one in picture 6, is a concentrated source of naturally dehydrated food.

Wheat seeds and bread-making

The picture shows the inside of a wheat seed or **grain**. It is surrounded by a coat called the **bran**. Inside is the embryo and a mass of tissue called the **endosperm**.

Wheat grain is used for making flour from which, of course, bread is made. For making white bread the bran and the embryo are removed first, leaving only the endosperm. This consists mainly of starch. It is ground up (milled) into **white flour**.

For making wholemeal bread the entire grain, including the bran, is ground up. This gives **brown flour**. The brown colour is caused by a pigment in the bran. You have probably been told that wholemeal bread is good for you. It is. The reason is that the whole wheat grain contains not only starch, but other useful substances such as cellulose and vitamins. The cellulose makes wholemeal bread coarser than white bread, and provides fibre in the diet.

Nowadays white flour has some of the missing nutrients added to it after milling. So it's good for you too. But it doesn't contain as much fibre.

Wheat grain contains a protein called **gluten**. This is present in flour, and it makes dough sticky. When you make a loaf and the dough rises, the gluten holds it together and stops the gas escaping (see page 188). Gluten is therefore important in baking bread. Wheat is the only cereal that contains gluten, which is why wheat is so good for making bread. However, some people are allergic to gluten, and it can make them very ill. They have to eat gluten-free bread, e.g. bread made from rye.

Wheat grown in Europe doesn't contain as much gluten as wheat grown in North America. English bakers use a mixture of home-grown and imported wheat.

However, in France they use only homegrown wheat, so their bread doesn't hold together so firmly. French bakers get round this by making their loaves long and thin.

1 Why is it a good idea to include fibre in our diet?

2 Name the gas that is given off in dough. Where does it come from?

3 Do you think bread could be made from broad beans? Explain your answer.

4 You can buy 'French loaves' in Britain, but people say that they are not as good as the bread you buy in France. Why the difference?

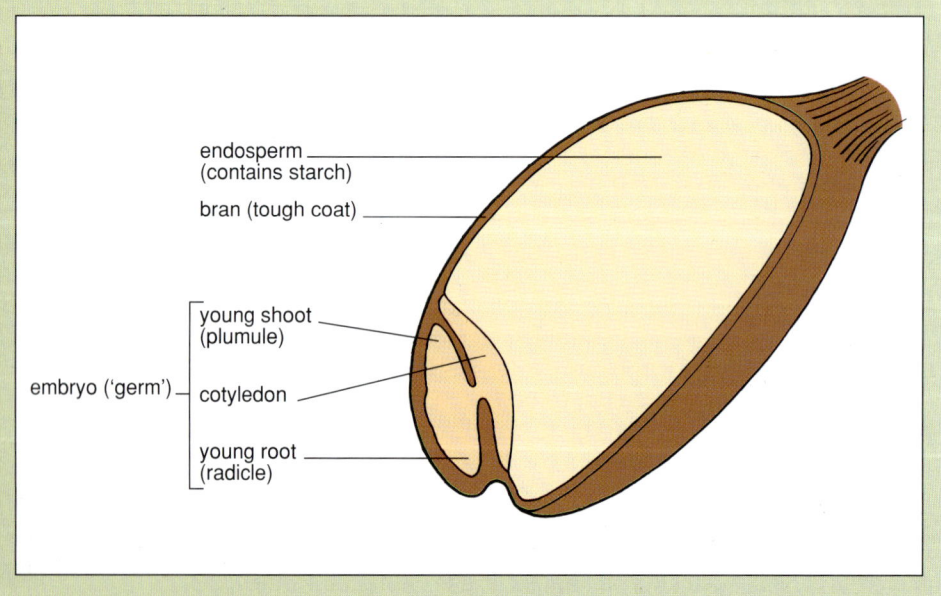

Picture 1 The inside of a wheat seed.

What conditions are needed for germination?

Look at the test tubes in the diagram below. You may even wish to set them up yourself.

In which test tubes will the seeds germinate? What is the purpose of the control tube?

Five days later, the results of this investigation would show that water, oxygen and warmth are required for successful germination. Light is not required for germination but it is needed by the plant for normal growth. Without light the plant becomes tall, thin and has yellow leaves. This is known as **etiolation**.

The same sort of apparatus can be used to investigate the effect of temperature on germination. Several tubes are set up like tube A, but are then placed in different locations with differing temperatures. The table shows six of these areas. After five days the number of seeds that have germinated in each tube can be counted. The results are also in the table.

Location	Temperature	% Germination
Freezer	−10°C	0
Fridge	4°C	5
Room	16°C	55
Incubator 1	28°C	85
Incubator 2	40°C	0

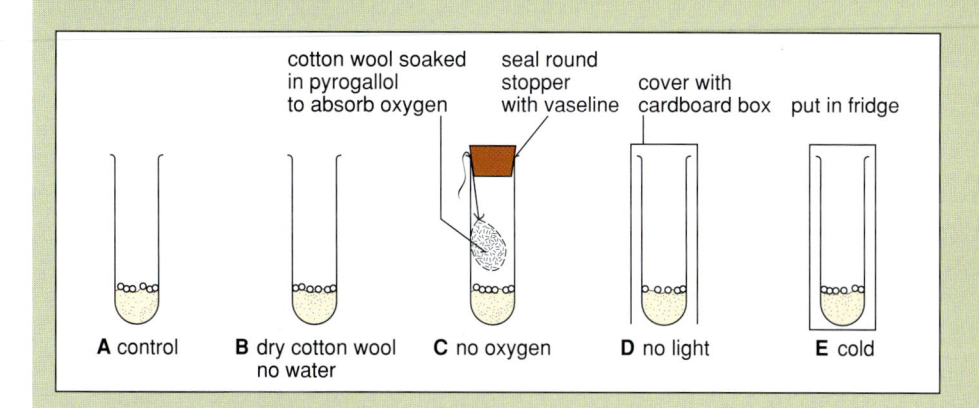

1. Plot a line graph of these results.
2. Which variable was altered in this investigation? Which variables have to remain constant during the investigation?
3. At which temperature do seeds germinate best? This is known as the **optimum** temperature for germination.
4. Is this experiment a fair test? How could the accuracy of this investigation be improved?

Diagram showing test tubes:
- **A** control
- **B** dry cotton wool, no water
- **C** no oxygen (cotton wool soaked in pyrogallol to absorb oxygen; seal round stopper with vaseline)
- **D** no light (cover with cardboard box)
- **E** cold (put in fridge)

Questions

1. Look at picture 1 on page 52. Name as many of the seeds as possible. How many have you eaten?

   Now think of as many foods as you can that are made from seeds. Bread, for example, is made from wheat. What others are there?

2. Seeds which are planted too deep in the soil will not germinate. Suggest *two* possible reasons for this. Describe an experiment which you would carry out to test one of your suggestions.

3. The graph shows how the dry mass of a germinating seed (and seedling) changes from the moment germination starts. (The dry mass is estimated by getting rid of all traces of water from the plant and then weighing it.)

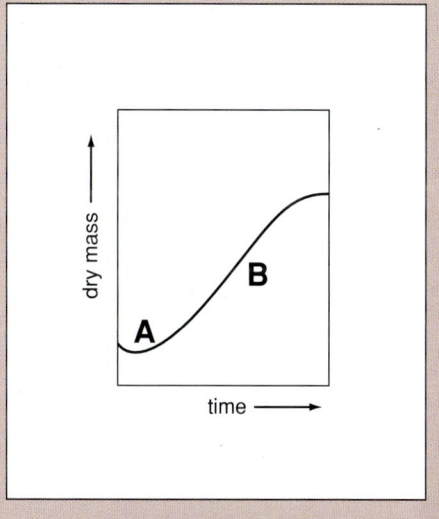

   a. How do you think this experiment was actually carried out?
   b. Explain what is happening at points A and B on the graph.

4. From a previous section of work on page 44, we know that rain can be acidic. Will this fact change how well seeds germinate?

   a. Design an investigation to find out how changing the pH of the soil affects germination. Which factors are you going to have to keep constant during this investigation?
   b. What do you think will be the optimum pH for seed germination? How could you investigate whether or not the optimum pH is the same for all seeds?

C3
From flowers to fruits

In flowering plants the part of the plant responsible for sexual reproduction is the flower.

Picture 1 This flower has been sectioned down the middle to show the inside.

Picture 3 There is an infinite variety of flowers. This orchid attracts insects by looking like a potential mate.

The ins and outs of a flower

The main parts of a flower can be seen very easily in plants like cherry, plum and hawthorn. This kind of flower is shown in the pictures below.

The flower is made up of a series of rings of structures. The outermost ring consists of several small leaf-like **sepals**. These protect the flower in bud. Then come the **petals** which are often brightly coloured and strongly scented. These attract insects. Next come the **stamens** which look rather like pins. And finally in the centre there is a club-shaped **carpel**.

At the base of each petal you can see an area which is slightly thicker than the rest. This is called the **nectary**, and it produces a sugary liquid called **nectar**.

The stamens are the male part of the flower. Each one consists of a slender **filament** with a knob at the top called the **anther**. The anther contains four **pollen sacs** in which **pollen grains** are formed. The pollen grains are equivalent to an animal's sperm.

The carpel is the female part of the flower. It consists of three parts: a slightly swollen **stigma** at the top, then a slender stalk called the **style**, and a swollen **ovary** at the bottom. Inside the ovary there is a small body called an **ovule** which is attached to the wall of the ovary by a short stalk. There is a small hole in the wall of the ovule, leading to the inside. In the middle of the ovule, surrounded by a little bag, is an **egg cell**. This is equivalent to an animal's egg.

Variations on the theme

Not all flowers are like the one just described, though they all follow the same basic plan. In particular their shapes and symmetry differ (picture 3). So do the numbers of the parts. For example, the buttercup has many carpels, each containing one ovule, whereas the sweet pea has one carpel containing a row of ovules.

Flowers differ in other ways too. For example, in a daffodil the petals may be joined to form a 'trumpet', and in tulips the sepals are missing.

Picture 2 The structure of a typical flower.

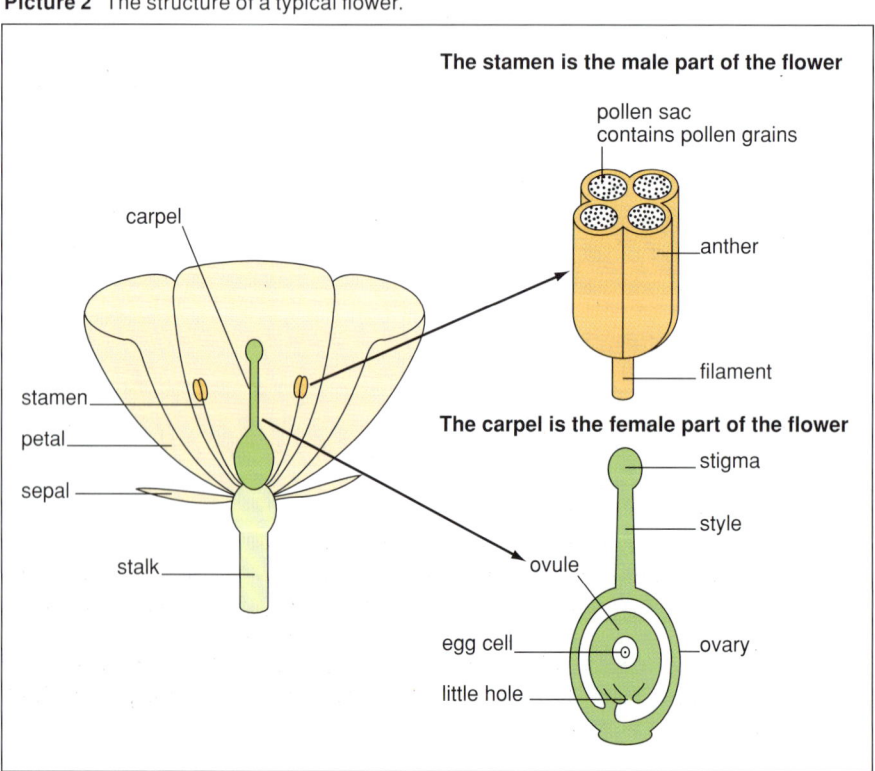

Pollen and pollination

Pollen grains are very small, like little specks of dust. Their job is to see that the egg cells become fertilised.

The pollen grains develop inside the anthers. When the anther is mature, it splits open down each side and the pollen grains are set free. They are then carried to another flower, and if one of them gets onto a stigma it sticks to it. The process by which the pollen grains reach the stigma is called **pollination** (picture 4).

Why is the pollen carried to another flower? Why not let it fall onto the stigma of the same flower? Actually this does sometimes happen – it is called **self-pollination**. But it isn't good for the species. It is much better if the pollen is transferred to another flower on a different plant of the same species. This is called **cross-pollination**.

The pollen grains are usually transferred by wind or insects. In the tropics some flowers are pollinated by humming birds and bats. Of course, pollination can also be carried out artificially by humans.

An example of a **wind-pollinated plant** is hazel. The familiar hazel catkin is a clump of very small male flowers. The catkin hangs down and is shaken by even the slightest gust of wind. This ensures that the pollen is scattered over a wide area. The pollen grains themselves are small and light.

An example of an **insect-pollinated plant** is the rose. Insects such as bees visit the flowers to feed on the nectar. As the insect pokes its head into the flower, its hairy body gets covered with pollen (picture 5). When the insect visits another flower, some of the pollen gets onto the stigmas, pollinating them. The pollen grains often have sculptured or spiky walls which help them to stick to the insect (picture 6).

Experiments have shown that insects such as bees are attracted to flowers by their colour, shape and smell. Some flowers are wonderfully adapted to attract insects and to make it easier for them to collect the pollen. For example, many flowers have lines or spots on the inner side of their petals. These markings show bees where to enter the flower and reach the nectar.

Fertilisation

Once a pollen grain has landed on a stigma, it sends out a snake-like outgrowth called a **pollen tube**. This grows into the stigma and down the style. The course that it normally takes is shown by the arrow in picture 4. Towards the tip of the pollen tube there is a nucleus. This is equivalent to the nucleus in the head of an animal's sperm.

When the pollen tube reaches the ovary it pushes its way into the ovule, usually through the little hole in the wall. It now grows towards the egg cell in the centre. Then the pollen nucleus fuses with the egg cell nucleus. This is **fertilisation**, and it is equivalent to the fertilisation of an egg by a sperm.

What happens next?

The fertilised egg now divides into a little ball of cells which becomes an **embryo**. This remains in the centre of the ovule where it becomes surrounded by a special tissue called the **endosperm**. The endosperm supplies the embryo with food. Humans have a particular interest in the endosperm – you probably ate it for breakfast (see page 54).

Meanwhile the ovule itself becomes the **seed**, and the tissue round it forms a protective **seed coat** (**testa**). As this happens, water is drawn out of the seed, with the result that it becomes very dry. In this state the embryo becomes dormant, and can survive bad conditions such as drought or cold.

While the seed is forming, the ovary expands into a **fruit**. So the seed becomes surrounded by a fruit. If you cut fruits open, you can expect to find seeds inside.

Picture 4 In pollination pollen grains are transferred from an anther to a stigma. A pollen tube then grows down the style to the ovary, as indicated by the arrow.

Picture 5 A bee collecting pollen from a flower.

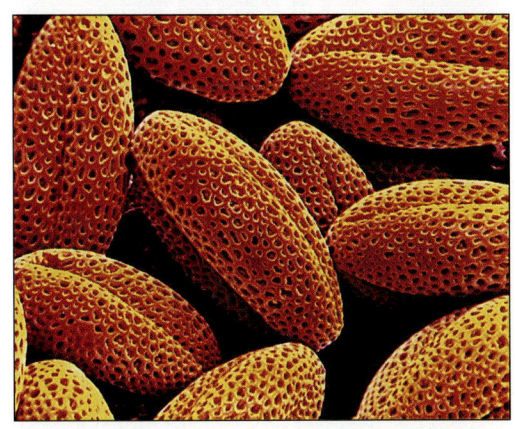

Picture 6 Pollen grains of the rape plant *Brassica napus* as seen greatly magnified by the scanning electron microscope. Notice the sculptured walls. They help the pollen to stick to insects.

58 *The world of plants*

Picture 8 The fruits of the sycamore tree have 'wings' which enable them to whirl through the air.

Picture 7 Some edible fruits

Picture 9 Dandelion fruits are like little parachutes and float through the air.

Fruits and dispersal

The job of the fruit is to help spread the seeds. This is called **dispersal**. Efficient dispersal is important to all organisms, not just plants. It ensures that the species is distributed over a wide area. This helps to avoid overcrowding, and increases the chances of survival.

Fruits disperse their seeds in many different ways. Some are eaten by animals, particularly birds. The soft part of the fruit is digested but the seeds are protected from the action of the animal's digestive juices. Eventually they pass out with the faeces, probably a long way from where the fruit was eaten. These sorts of fruit are often highly coloured, and this attracts animals. Think of bright red cherries, for example. They also taste good – which is why humans are interested in them (picture 7).

Other fruits disperse their seeds by floating through the air, clinging to the fur of animals or floating in water. These fruits are usually dry and hard, and they release their seeds by splitting open. In some cases the fruit splits open with such force that the seeds are thrown out quite a long way. In other cases the seeds may be shaken out of the fruit, like pepper from a pepper pot. Examples of fruits, and the way they disperse their seeds, are given in pictures 8 to 12.

Picture 10 The fruits of burdock, called burs, have hooks which cling to the fur of animals and to people's clothes.

Picture 11 The fruit of the coco-de-mer palm from the Seychelles contains air spaces which enable it to float in the sea.

Picture 12 The fruit of a poppy, called a capsule, scatters its seeds when it is shaken by the wind.

From flowers to fruits **59**

Activities

A Making a drawing of the structure of a typical flower
(Practical technique 7)

1 Your teacher will give you a flower – a tulip or something similar.
2 Identify its parts using picture 2 to help you.
3 Cut it in half with a scalpel or razor blade. Make an accurate drawing of the half flower, labelling the important parts (anther, filament, ovary, stigma, style, petal, sepal).
4 Pull off the sepals, petals, stamens and stigma and style. Slice open the ovary and look for the ovules inside. Place two or three ovules on a microscope slide and view with a lens or microscope.
5 Similarly, open an anther and sprinkle some pollen onto a microscope slide. Again, view and draw.

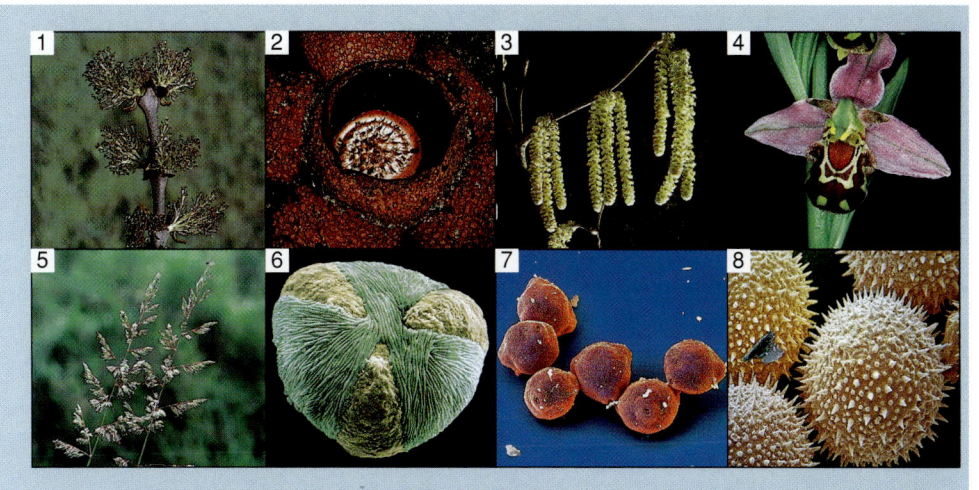

B Comparing wind- and insect-pollinated flowers

Look at the pictures of flowers or pollen grains in the photographs above.
Use the table below to decide whether they are pollinated by insects or wind.

Wind-pollinated flowers	Insect-pollinated flowers
Generally small	Generally large
Petals green or dull coloured	Petals often brightly coloured
Do not produce nectar	Petals produce nectar
Flower hangs down for easy shaking	Flower faces upwards
Stamens and stigma hang out of petals	Stamens and stigma inside petals
Large number of pollen grains produced	Smaller number of pollen grains produced
Pollen grains are light and smooth	Pollen grains are heavier with spikes for sticking to insects
Stigma has feathery branches for catching pollen	Stigma is like pinhead and lacks branches

Questions

1 Each of the words in the left-hand column is related to one of the words in the right-hand column. Write them down in the correct pairs.

sepal	colour
petal	egg cell
pollen	sugar
nectary	sperm
ovule	leaflet

2 Explain the difference between pollination and fertilisation.

Why do plants generally produce very large numbers of pollen grains?

3 'One year's seeding, seven years' weeding'.

What do you think this saying means, and what should gardeners do about it?

4 The flower shown diagrammatically below is pollinated by wind.

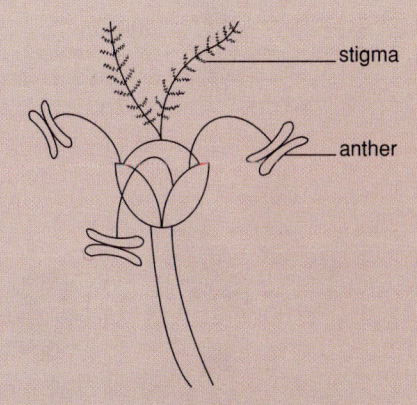

How might this arrangement of flower parts favour cross-pollination rather than self-pollination?

5 The fruit of the coco-de-mer palm (picture 11) can weigh over 20 kg but a dandelion fruit only weighs about a milligram. Why does the dandelion fruit have to be so light, when the coco-de-mer fruit can be so heavy?

6 The flowers of primroses are of two kinds. Some flowers have their anthers high up and their stigmas low down, whilst others have their stigmas high up and their anthers low down, as shown in the illustration below. They are pollinated by bees.

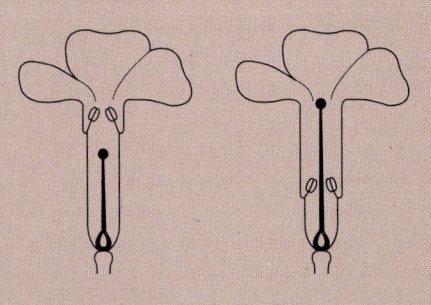

How might this arrangement of flower parts favour cross-pollination?

C4 Reproduction without sex

Some organisms can reproduce on their own without the help of another individual.

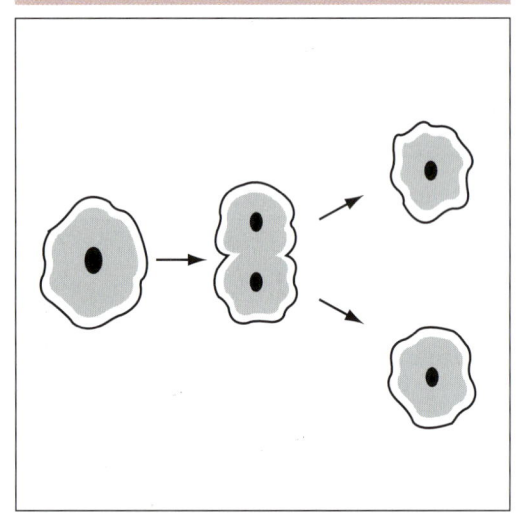

Asexual reproduction

Can you imagine your arm dropping off and develping into a new you! This may seem a weird idea, but it is the kind of thing that happens with some organisms. It is called **asexual reproduction** – reproduction without sex.

At its simplest, asexual reproduction takes place by the organism splitting in two (**binary fission**). Many single-celled organisms do this, for example *Amoeba* (picture 1). Bacteria do it too. In suitable conditions bacteria can split once every twenty minutes or so. This may not seem very fast, but try working out how many bacteria would be formed from one original cell after 24 hours. No wonder bacterial diseases can spread so quickly.

Another quick way of reproducing is by **budding**. This is what yeast does. Yeast is a single-celled fungus. When it buds, it sends out a small outgrowth which gets steadily larger and then breaks away as a new cell (picture 2).

Many organisms produce **spores**. Mosses, ferns and fungi all do this. It is a very fast way of reproducing. For example, a single mushroom can produce millions of spores in a very short time. Fungus spores are very light, and can be carried over long distances by the wind. This makes fungal diseases like potato blight difficult to get rid of.

Plants reproduce sexually – that's what flowers are for. However, many of them reproduce asexually as well. This is called **vegetative propagation**.

Vegetative propagation

You may have noticed that many garden plants die down in the autumn, but the following spring they grow up again in the same place. During the summer they form underground **storage organs** which fill up with food substances such as starch. The organ remains dormant in the soil during the winter, and next year a new plant grows out of it (picture 3). Some well-known storage organs are shown in picture 4.

These organs enable plants to carry on from one year to the next. For this reason, they are called **perennating organs**. But they are also a way of reproducing. This is because a plant may produce not just one but several storage organs. Each then gives rise to a new plant. A potato plant, for example, may produce a whole bunch of potato tubers (picture 5).

These storage organs are very important for humans, because we use them as food. Go into any large supermarket and you will see hundreds of them.

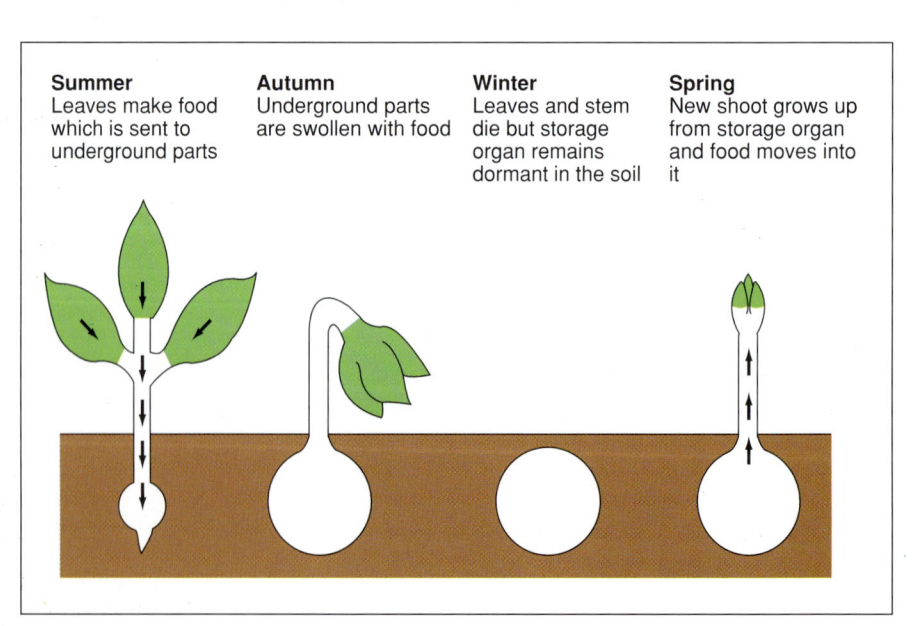

Picture 1 An amoeba reproducing by binary fission. The organism rounds off like a ball. Then the nucleus (black blob) splits in two, followed by the cytoplasm. The two small amoebas then feed and grow to full size.

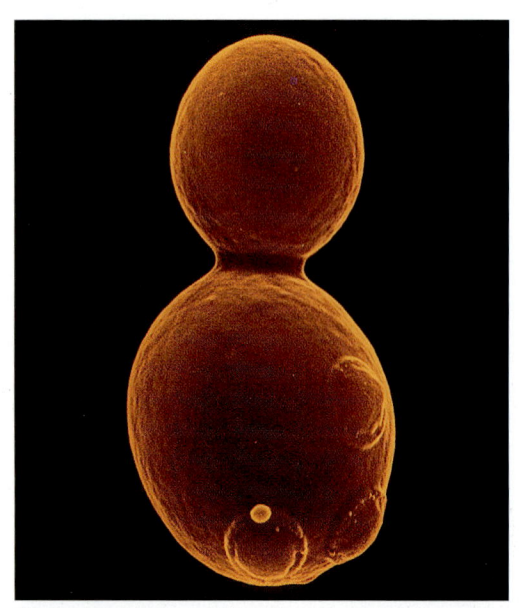

Picture 2 A yeast cell budding. Sometimes a cell produces several buds at once or a bud starts budding before it has broken off.

Summer Leaves make food which is sent to underground parts

Autumn Underground parts are swollen with food

Winter Leaves and stem die but storage organ remains dormant in the soil

Spring New shoot grows up from storage organ and food moves into it

Picture 3 How a storage organ enables a plant to survive the winter and come up again in the spring. Many herbaceous perennials behave like this.

Reproduction without sex **61**

Picture 4 A selection of plant storage organs. These particular ones are all used by humans for food.

Other methods of vegetative propagation

Vegetative propagation does not always involve forming a storage organ. Many plants do it in other ways. For example, part of a plant – a leaf perhaps – may drop off and take root in the soil.

Some plants send out, from the base of the stem, a side branch which grows along the surface of the soil. This is called a **runner**. Roots grow down from it at the nodes and new plants develop at these points, as shown in picture 6. Strawberry plants spread this way. So, unfortunately, do certain weeds – which makes them very difficult to get rid of.

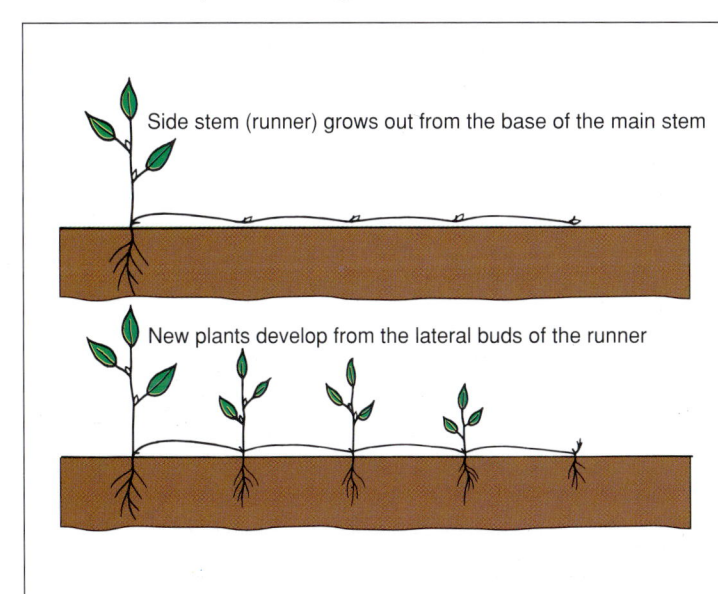

Picture 5 A single potato plant with tubers. The tubers are 'new' potatoes.

Side stem (runner) grows out from the base of the main stem

New plants develop from the lateral buds of the runner

Picture 6 How a plant produces a runner. The photograph shows a young strawberry plant growing from a runner.

Picture 7 A spider plant. Notice the new plants developing from the ends of the hanging side branches.

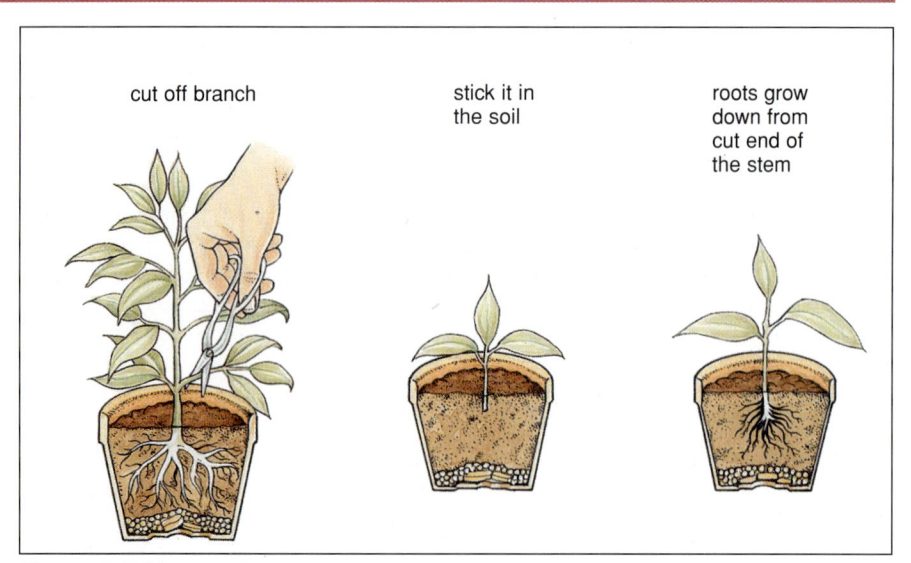

Picture 8 Taking a cutting.

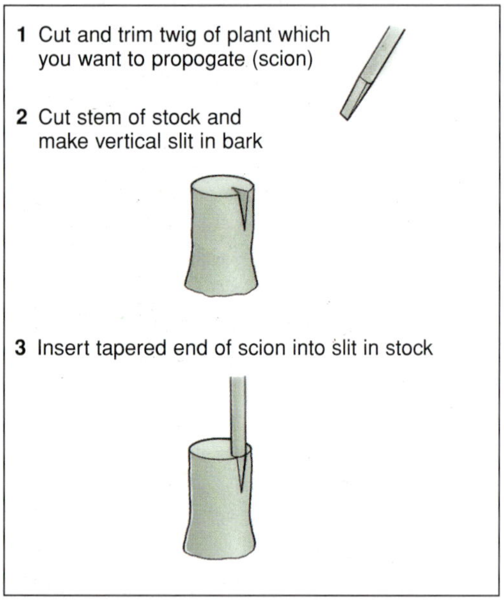

1. Cut and trim twig of plant which you want to propogate (scion)
2. Cut stem of stock and make vertical slit in bark
3. Insert tapered end of scion into slit in stock

Picture 9 Grafting one plant onto another. This is just one of a number of methods that can be used.

Picture 10 Grafting young trees.

You have probably seen the plant in picture 7 in someone's house. Perhaps you even have one in your house. It is called a spider plant. This plant sends out shoots which hang down and produce new plants at the ends. These are also runners, since roots eventually grow from each new plant on the hanging branches.

Artificial propagation

Humans can reproduce some plants without the need for flowers and seeds. Here are two common ways of doing this.

Taking cuttings

People often reproduce their favourite plants by taking cuttings. A healthy young branch is cut off from the parent plant. A slanting cut is used since this increases the surface area for water absorption. Any flowers are removed along with some of the lower leaves and the cutting is placed in good moist soil. Removing the lower leaves prevents the cutting from losing too much water. Roots grow out, and the cutting becomes established as a new plant.

Grafting

Suppose you have an apple tree in your garden, and you want to have another one exactly like it. How could you produce a second apple tree just like the first one? One way would be to cut a young twig off the apple tree and join it to the trunk or branch of another similar tree. This is called **grafting**.

If the two plants are to join properly, the cut surfaces must be in close contact with each other. Picture 9 shows one way of doing this. The two plants are bound together with tape or raffia, and the joint is covered with wax. This prevents evaporation, and stops microbes getting in (picture 10).

The aim in grafting is to get the living tissues of the two plants to grow together. Once this happens, water and nutrients will pass freely from one to the other.

Grafting is carried out a lot by gardeners and growers of trees and shrubs. The plant you want to propagate is called the **scion**, and the one you join it to is called the **stock**. The stock is chosen for its good roots and resistance to disease. The scion is chosen for its good flowers or fruits. The new plant combines the best qualities of both.

Reproduction without sex

Producing offspring without involving sex cells or fertilisation is called **cloning**. A clone is a group of identical organisms produced by asexual reproduction. Taking cuttings and grafting are examples of cloning.

Sexual versus asexual reproduction

The most important advantage of sexual reproduction is that the offspring are different from each other. This is called **natural variation** and enables the species of plant to survive changing environmental conditions. For example, a change over the years in rainfall may mean that the plants require to be more tolerant of dry conditions. The variety of plants, resulting from sexual reproduction, ensures that there will be a good chance of a plant of this type in the population. The dispersal of seeds also means that plants are less likely to have to compete with each other for light, water and minerals.

Asexual reproduction, on the other hand, produces offspring identical to each other. This means that the plants are able to grow well in the habitat which already suits the parent plant. This allows the plant population to become dominant in the habitat. In addition, asexual reproduction avoids the vulnerable stages of pollination, seed dispersal and germination.

Advantages of artificial propagation to humans

Artificial propagation has a number of advantages over those mentioned already.

It guarantees a particular type of product, e.g. all Bramley apples with the same flavour, or a particular variety of rose with the same colour of petals.

Rare plants, perhaps on the verge of extinction, can be maintained in the greenhouse and later reintroduced to their natural habitat. Their genes are saved for possible future use.

Large numbers of identical plants can be produced for landscaping purposes in towns and newly built areas.

Cloning for the benefit of humans: oil palms

The oil palm is a very important plant. The seed and the fruit both contain oil which is used for cooking and for making soap. When properly cultivated, the oil palm gives higher yields of oil per hectare than any other oil-producing crop.

The trees can be grown from seeds, but there is a lot of variation in the new plants. Some are good, others poor. This is the trouble with growing plants from seed — you cannot always be sure what you are going to get. So it was decided to try and clone the oil palms.

After ten years of painstaking research at Unilever's Colworth Laboratory in England, successful clones were made from small pieces of root. In 1976 the first fields of cloned oil palms were set up in Kluang, Malaysia. The parent trees were carefully selected for their good qualities. As expected, the new trees turned out to be just as good.

Today plantations of cloned oil palms can be seen in many tropical countries. It's a sure way of growing exactly the sort of plants you want.

1 What problems do you think the scientists at Unilever came up against in trying to clone the oil palm?

2 If you were cloning oil palms, what qualities would you want the parent plants to have?

3 What are the possible disadvantages of cloning oil palms on a large scale?

4 Does cloning mean that oil palms need never again be grown from seeds? Explain your answer.

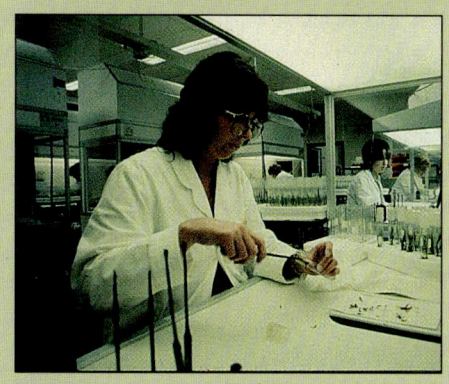

Picture 1 Cloning oil palms in the laboratory.

Questions

1 In good conditions a bacterial cell splits every twenty minutes. How many would be formed from one original cell after ten hours?

2 One mushroom can produce ten thousand million spores in a few days. Why does it need to produce so many?

3 A storage organ such as a potato tuber is also called a perennating organ. Why?

4 What are the advantages to a gardener of propagating a plant by vegetative means?

5 When taking a cutting, it is advisable:
a not to take a branch which has a flower on it,
b to cut the branch just below a node,
c to remove some of the leaves from the branch.
Suggest a reason for each of the above.

6 In choosing an individual for propagation, what features should the gardener look for and what precautions should be taken?

7 In theory it would be possible to produce dozens of genetically identical humans by cloning.
a How might this be done?
b What would be the main difficulties?
c Do you think it would be a good idea? Give reasons.
d Would you expect cloned humans to behave the same? Explain your answer.

C5
How plants feed

You and I feed by taking in organic food. Plants feed quite differently, as we shall see.

Picture 1 This plant is full of food substances. How did they get there?

Picture 2 Mount Everest, the highest mountain in the world. Its peak is well over 8000 metres above sea level. Imagine a pile of sugar that high!

Photosynthesis

Look at the plant in picture 1. It has no mouth and no gut, and yet it is full of food such as sugar. Where does it get its food from? There are only two possible places: the soil and the air. But there's no sugar in soil or air, only simple substances like carbon dioxide and water. What the plant does is to absorb these simple substances from its surroundings and build them up into sugar and other complex substances.

Making complex substances from simpler ones is called *synthesis*, and plants need light for doing this. So the process by which plants make food is called **photosynthesis**.

What happens in photosynthesis?

The simple substances which the plant uses for photosynthesis are carbon dioxide and water. A land plant like the one in the picture gets **carbon dioxide** from the air, and **water** from the soil. These two substances are turned into **sugar**, and **oxygen gas** is given off as a by-product. The reaction requires energy, and this normally comes from **sunlight**. The green substance **chlorophyll** enables the plant to transfer energy from sunlight to sugar. It is therefore an essential helper in the process.

Photosynthesis is not a single reaction, but takes place in a series of small steps. However, it is usually summed up by this simple equation:

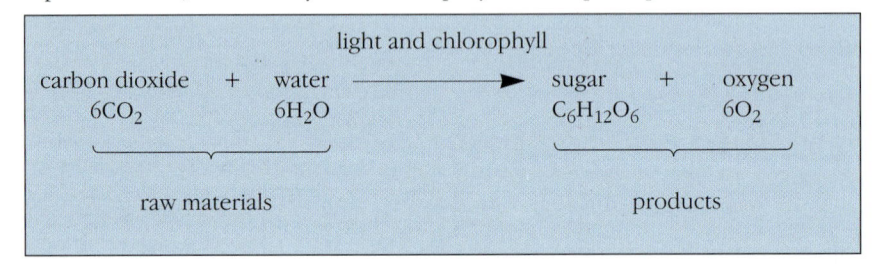

$$\underbrace{\text{carbon dioxide} + \text{water}}_{\text{raw materials}} \xrightarrow{\text{light and chlorophyll}} \underbrace{\text{sugar} + \text{oxygen}}_{\text{products}}$$
$$\underbrace{6CO_2 \quad\quad\quad 6H_2O} \quad\quad\quad\quad\quad\quad \underbrace{C_6H_{12}O_6 \quad\quad 6O_2}$$

Some of the sugar formed by photosynthesis is turned into **starch** for storage. Light is needed for making sugar, but not for turning the sugar into starch.

Chemical tests can be carried out to see if plants contain sugar or starch. If they do, it shows that photosynthesis has been taking place.

Why is photosynthesis important?

Animals can't make organic food substances for themselves. The only way an animal can get these substances is by eating plants, or by eating animals which have eaten the plants (or by eating animals which have eaten the animals which have eaten the plants!)

So animals depend on plants for food. When you eat a beefburger, you are able to do so only because the cow ate grass. We can sum this up by saying that plants produce food which can then be consumed by animals. This is the basis of **food chains**. You will find more about this on pages 28–30.

To give you some idea of the importance of photosynthesis, here are some figures. A hectare of maize – that's a field about the size of two football pitches – can produce more than 20 000 kg of sugar in a year. This is enough to sweeten over one million cups of tea.

Here is another way of looking at it: if all the sugar made by the world's plants in three years was piled up, it would form a heap the size of Mount Everest!

And there's another reason why photosynthesis is important. The oxygen in our atmosphere has been put there by plants over millions of years as a result of photosynthesis. This is the oxygen on which we depend for respiration. Without it animals could not exist.

Activity

Testing a leaf for starch
(Practical technique 8)

EYE PROTECTION MUST BE WORN

1. Put the leaf (or leaf part) into a beaker of boiling water for about 1 minute. This will kill the leaf cells.
2. Turn off the bunsen burner and put the leaf into a test tube containing a little ethanol. Take care, ethanol is flammable. Return this tube to the beaker of hot water.
3. Let the ethanol boil for about 5 minutes. This removes the chlorophyll from the leaf.
4. Rinse the leaf in water. This removes the ethanol and softens the leaf.
5. Put the leaf on a tile and cover with iodine solution. A blue-black colour shows that starch is present.

Picture 3 A starch print on a geranium leaf. The top picture shows the mask on the leaf. The bottom picture shows the print.

What do plants need for photosynthesis?

Look at the equation for photosynthesis on page 64. From it we can say that for photosynthesis a plant needs **light**, **carbon dioxide**, **chlorophyll** and **water**.

We can do experiments to show that these things really are needed for photosynthesis. The experiments can be done on potted plants such as geraniums. We take the presence of starch in the leaves as an indication that photosynthesis has been taking place.

The principle behind the experiments is quite simple. First we make the plant use up all its stores of starch. This is called **de-starching**. It can be done by putting the plant in the dark for a few days. To make sure that the plant has been completely de-starched, we do an iodine test on one of its leaves.

We then give the plant everything it needs for photosynthesis except the one thing we want to investigate. After several days, we again do an iodine test on one of the leaves to see if the plant has been making starch. If it has not made any starch, we conclude that the missing factor is needed for photosynthesis.

As in other biological experiments, we must have a **control** with which to compare the result. The control plant is given everything it needs, including the factor being investigated.

With these principles in mind, let's look at the experiments in detail. We shall use the method for testing a leaf for starch which is shown in the activity alongside.

Do plants need light for photosynthesis?

We put one de-starched plant in the dark. We put a second de-starched plant in the light, to serve as a control. After a few days we test each plant for starch. We find that only the plant in the light has made starch. This suggests that light is needed for photosynthesis.

Here's another method which is fun to do. We take a de-starched plant and cover part of one leaf with a piece of foil or black paper which does not let light through. We then leave the plant in the light. After a day or two we test the leaf with iodine. As you might expect, starch is absent from the covered part of the leaf. In fact the characteristic blue-black colour develops only where the leaf was uncovered. This is called a **starch print** and it is a striking way of showing that light is needed for photosynthesis (picture 3).

Do plants need carbon dioxide for photosynthesis?

We set up two de-starched plants side by side. One of them is given air from which all the carbon dioxide has been removed. The other one is given air containing plenty of carbon dioxide – this is the control. The details of the experiment are shown in picture 4 on page 66.

After several days a leaf from each plant is tested with iodine to see if it has made any starch. It turns out that the plant without carbon dioxide has not made starch. This suggests that carbon dioxide is needed for photosynthesis.

Do plants need chlorophyll for photosynthesis?

The ideal way to investigate this would be to take all the chlorophyll out of a leaf, and see if this stops it making starch. However, it is impossible to remove the chlorophyll without killing the leaf.

So what can we do? Luckily nature comes to our aid. It so happens that the leaves of some plants (including certain varieties of geranium) are green in some places but white or yellow in others. Chlorophyll is present in the green areas, but absent from the non-green areas. Such leaves are described as **variegated** (picture 5).

Picture 4 An experiment to find out if plants need carbon dioxide for photosynthesis. The top plant was given air with no carbon dioxide. The bottom plant was given air with carbon dioxide.

To find out if chlorophyll is needed for photosynthesis, all we have to do is to de-starch a variegated plant and then put it in the light.

After a few days we do the iodine test on one of its leaves. The blue-black colour develops only in the parts of the leaf that were green. This suggests that photosynthesis takes place only where chlorophyll is present.

Do plants need water for photosynthesis?

There is no *simple* experiment that can be done to answer this question. You can't do it by taking all the water out of a plant, because that would kill the plant. The only way is to find out what happens to the water which a plant takes up into its cells. Scientists have done this by giving plants a special form of water called **heavy water** and then tracing what happens to it. The results show that water is definitely needed for photosynthesis.

Can you say what the water is needed for? (Hint: look at the equation on page 64.)

What does photosynthesis produce?

We have seen that plants make substances such as sugar and starch. However, they will only do this in the light. This strongly suggests that these substances are produced by photosynthesis.

Plants also produce oxygen. This can be shown quite easily by using a water plant such as Canadian pondweed. Canadian pondweed gives off bubbles of gas when put in the light. Picture 6 shows an experiment which can be done with this plant. The bubbles of gas are collected in an upturned test tube, and then tested for oxygen.

We now know that all green plants give off oxygen. They will only do so in the light, and this suggests that oxygen is a product of photosynthesis.

Picture 5 A plant with variegated leaves.

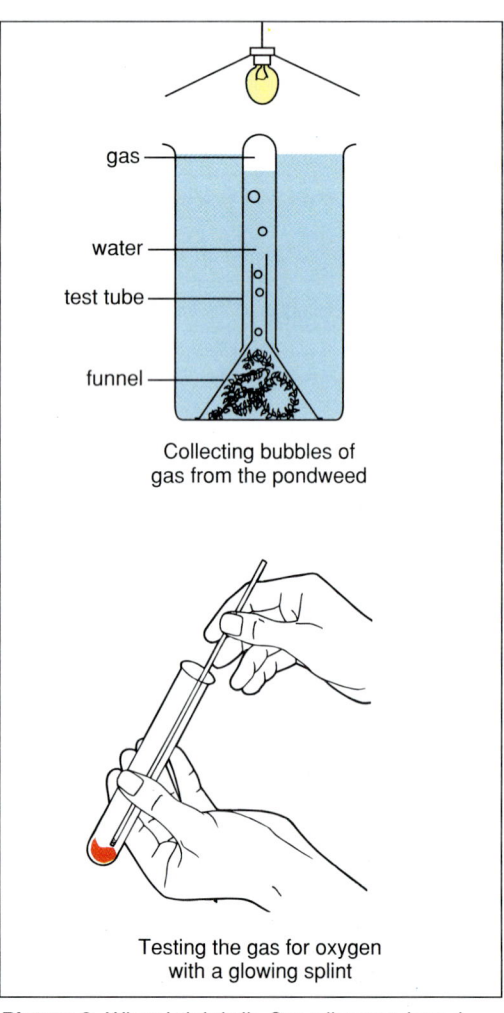

Picture 6 When brightly lit, Canadian pondweed (*Elodea*) gives off bubbles of gas. Here you see the bubbles being collected in an upturned test tube, and then tested for oxygen with a glowing splint.

What happens to the sugar made by photosynthesis?

Scientists have given plants radioactive carbon dioxide. Soon afterwards the radioactivity was detected in the sugar made by the plant. Later on, other substances inside the plant became radioactive. We now know that plants make sugars first and then convert them into these other substances.

One of these substances is **cellulose** which is needed for cell walls. **Amino acids** are also formed from the products of photosynthesis. They are the building blocks of **proteins** which are needed for growth and as enzymes.

To make proteins a plant needs nitrogen and sulphur as well as carbon, hydrogen and oxygen. Land plants obtain these extra elements from the soil in the form of **mineral salts**. Water plants get them from the surrounding water.

Some of the sugar made by photosynthesis is used for respiration or converted into starch for storage. Certain plants form other storage substances such as fats and oils. These, and all other substances which plants contain, come from photosynthesis (picture 8).

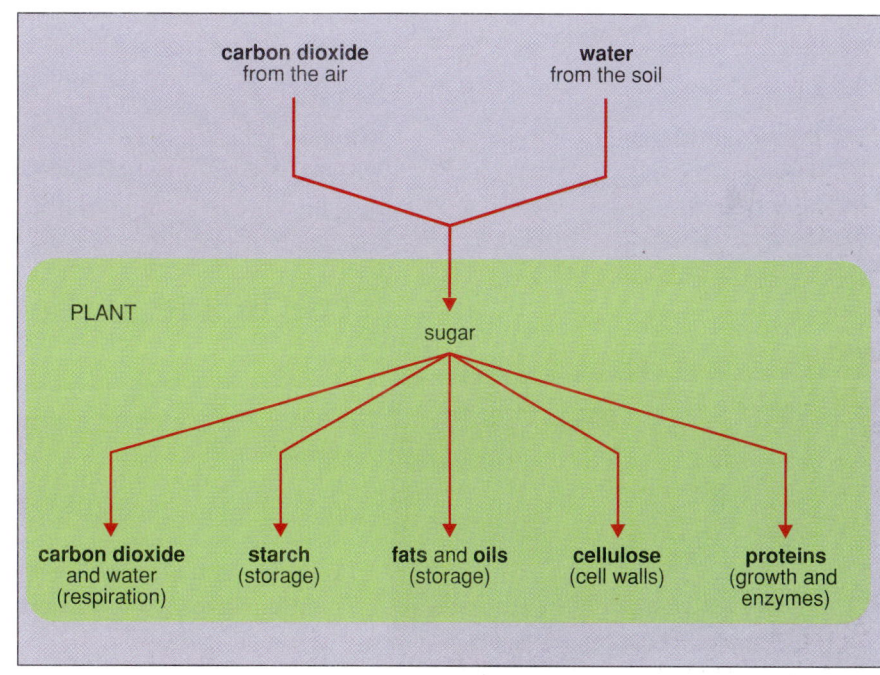

Picture 7 A scientist, wearing protective gloves, is giving a simple plant-like organism carbon dioxide containing radioactive carbon atoms.

Picture 8 The diagram shows what can happen to the sugar which a plant makes by photosynthesis.

Questions

1 One of the first experiments which led to the discovery of photosynthesis was done by a Dutchman called Van Helmont in 1692.

Van Helmont weighed a young willow tree. Then he filled a pot with soil, and weighed that. He then planted the tree in the soil.

He carefully covered the soil and then left the tree to grow, giving it nothing but water. After five years he weighed the tree and the soil, again. He found that the tree had gained 74 g in mass, but the soil had lost only 56 g. The tree seemed to have gained 18 g from somewhere other than the soil.

a Why did van Helmont cover the soil, and what may he have used for this?
b How had the tree gained 18 g?
c If you were to repeat Van Helmont's experiment today, what precautions would you take to make sure that your results were accurate?

2 Suppose there was a great disaster and all plant life was suddenly wiped out. What effect might this have on humans, and why?

3 When finding out if a particular condition is needed for photosynthesis the plants should be de-starched first.

a How are they de-starched?
b Why is this necessary?
c How could you make sure they have been completely de-starched before you begin the experiment?

4 Elizabeth wants to find out if a potted plant needs carbon dioxide in order to make starch. She is not satisfied with the method given in picture 4 on page 66 so she tries a different way. She selects two leaves on the plant and, without cutting them off, she encloses each one in a small polythene bag. In one bag she puts some soda lime, and in the other bag she puts some saturated sodium hydrogencarbonate solution.

Make a diagram of the set-up. Do you think Elizabeth's method is as good as the one in picture 4? Give reasons for your answer.

5 'When you eat a beefburger, you are able to do so only because the cow ate grass.' Explain this statement.

C6
The leaf, organ of photosynthesis

This topic is about leaves, and how their structure suits them for carrying out photosynthesis.

The outside of the leaf

Look at picture 1. In this photograph you can see the main features of a typical leaf. Picture 2 will help you to identify its parts.

Each leaf is attached to the stem or branch by a **leaf stalk**. This leads to the **veins** in the leaf. The leaves of this particular plant have a **main vein** running down the middle, with **side veins** branching out on either side. The veins carry substances to and from the leaf. They also strengthen it.

You may have noticed that leaves are often shiny, particularly on the upper side. This is because they are covered by a layer of waxy material. This is called the **cuticle** and, if thick enough, it is waterproof. It protects the leaf from losing too much water in hot, dry weather.

Immediately under the cuticle is a layer of cells, the **epidermis**, which forms the 'skin' of the leaf. The epidermis may be pierced by lots of tiny holes called **stomata** (singular **stoma**) (picture 3). The stomata are mainly on the lower side of the leaf. They allow gases to diffuse in and out of the leaf, and water vapour to escape. Each stoma is flanked by a pair of **guard cells** which can open and close rather like doors. They close in hot, dry weather to prevent too much water evaporating from the leaves.

Leaves are generally flat, sometimes large and often numerous. The result is that they have a large surface area for absorbing carbon dioxide and light. The veins help to support the leaf and hold it out flat, so that it can catch the maximum amount of light. In many plants the leaves are positioned in such a way that they don't shade each other (picture 4).

The inside of the leaf

You can see the inside of a leaf by looking at thin slices (sections) of it under the microscope. The sections can be cut in various planes so as to give a three-dimensional picture of the leaf (picture 5).

Between the upper and lower epidermis are lots of cells which together make up the **mesophyll**. These cells contain **chloroplasts**, and this is where photosynthesis takes place – it is the 'business part' of the leaf.

The mesophyll towards the upper side of the leaf consists of cells shaped like bricks and arranged neatly side by side. They are called **palisade cells**. The other mesophyll cells are rounded and more irregular in their arrangement.

Between the mesophyll cells are **air spaces** into which the stomata open. When photosynthesis is taking place, carbon dioxide diffuses through the open stomata into the air spaces. It then diffuses into the cells.

Photosynthesis takes place mainly in the palisade cells. They contain most of the chloroplasts, and they are near the surface of the leaf that gets most light.

Picture 1 Leaves are the main place where photosynthesis takes place.

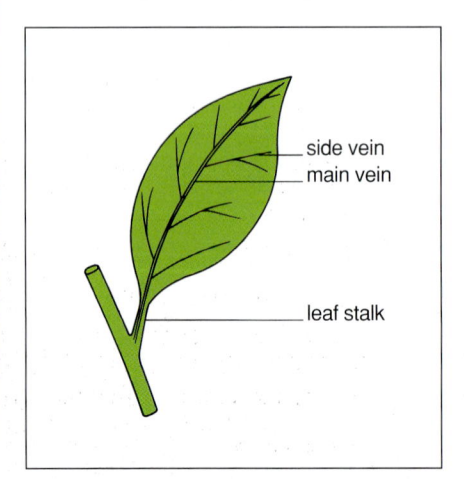

Picture 2 The parts of a typical leaf.

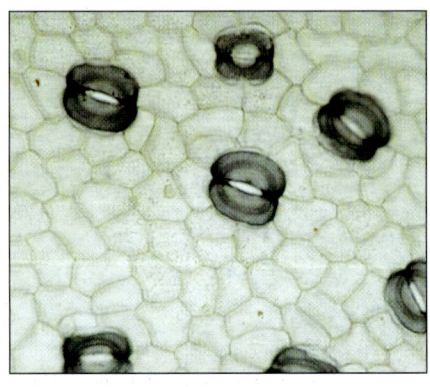

Picture 3 Photograph of the epidermis on the lower side of a leaf, showing the stomata. The photograph was taken down a microscope.

The chloroplasts are often clustered towards the tops of the cells, in the best position for catching light.

You can see a vein in picture 5. This is made up of two parts: the xylem towards the top, and the phloem below. The **xylem** brings water and mineral salts to the leaf. The **phloem** takes soluble sugar and other products of photosynthesis away from the leaf. We shall have more to say about these **vascular tissues** on pages 74–76.

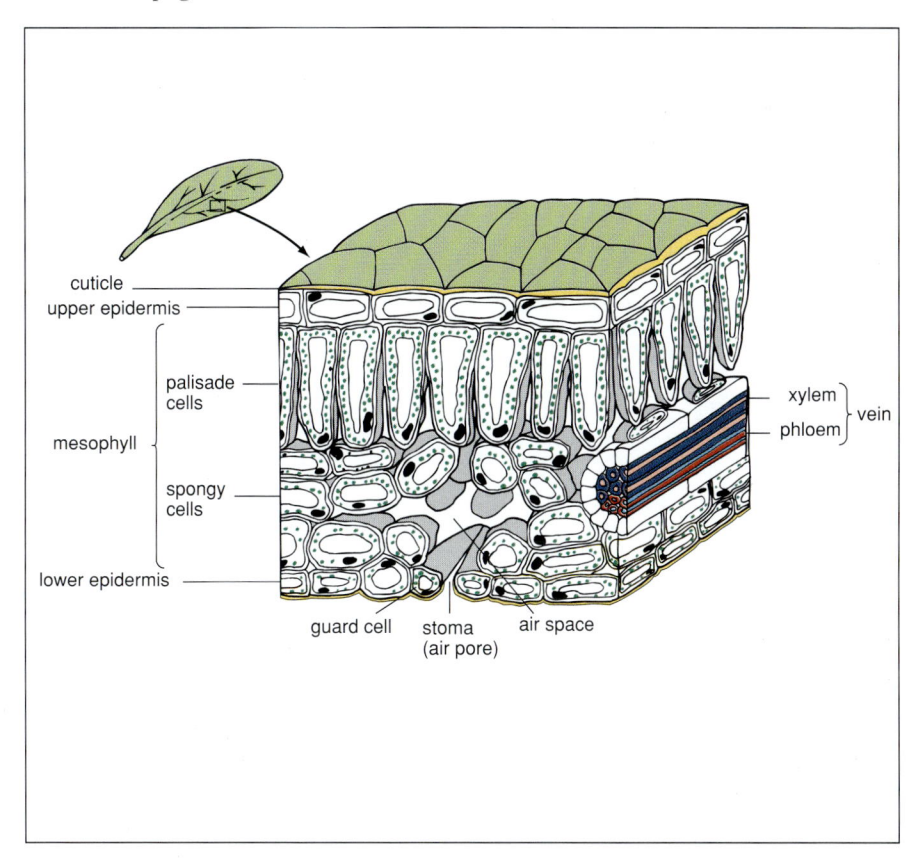

Picture 5 A small part of a leaf, greatly enlarged, to show the structures inside it. The green dots in the cells are chloroplasts.

Picture 4 In many plants the leaves are arranged so as not to shade each other. Two arrangements are shown here.

Questions

1. Each word in column A matches one or more words in column B.

A	B
air space	carbon dioxide
chloroplast	chlorophyll
stoma	light
xylem	water

   a Against each word in column A write down the matching word or words from column B.
   b What do the words in column A have in common?
   c What do the words in column B have in common?

2. Why are the leaves of most plants (a) numerous and (b) thin?

3. Suggest a reason why:
   a there are normally more stomata on the lower side of a leaf than on the upper side,
   b the cuticle is usually thicker on the upper side of a leaf than on the lower side.

4. Make a list of all the internal features of a green leaf which help it to carry out photosynthesis efficiently.

5. The photograph on the right shows the end of a branch of a chestnut tree.
   a In what way might the positioning of the leaves help the tree with photosynthesis?
   b How do the tree's trunk and branches help the leaves to photosynthesise?

C7
Controlling photosynthesis

Photosynthesis can occur rapidly or slowly, depending on circumstances.

Picture 1 The lights in this commercial greenhouse enable the plants to photosynthesise even when it is dark or gloomy outside.

Picture 2 Primroses can photosynthesise efficiently in shady places such as woods.

Picture 3 The lettuces in the right-hand box were grown in an atmosphere containing extra carbon dioxide. The lettuces in the left-hand box were grown in a normal atmosphere. The lettuces that were given extra carbon dioxide are larger than the other ones, and fewer of them can be fitted into the box.

Getting a good yield

Think of a wheat field. The faster the wheat plants photosynthesise, the more food they produce. In other words, the yield is greater.

Four main things affect the rate of photosynthesis and therefore the yield. They are: **light**, **carbon dioxide**, **temperature** and **water**. Let's look at each in turn.

Light

Up to a point, the brighter the light, the faster is the rate of photosynthesis. On a sunny day plants photosynthesise faster than on a dull day, and plants growing in an open field photosynthesise faster than plants growing in the shade.

This is important to gardeners and farmers. If you want your crops to do well, you must grow them in a place that gets plenty of sunlight. Sometimes artificial lights are shone on greenhouse plants to increase productivity (picture 1). However, certain wild plants are adapted to living in shady places such as a wood. They can photosynthesise even in dim light (picture 2).

As with many other things in life, it is possible to have too much of a good thing: in very bright sunshine photosynthesis actually slows down. This is because bright sunshine contains a lot of ultraviolet light which can damage plants.

Which is the best type of light for photosynthesis?

Ordinary white light, such as sunlight, is made up of different colours or wavelengths. These make up the **spectrum**.

Not all the colours of the spectrum are used by plants for photosynthesis, only **blue** and **red**. In fact chlorophyll only absorbs these two colours. Other colours, particularly green, pass straight through chlorophyll or are reflected from it. The reason why leaves look green is that green light is reflected from the chlorophyll inside them. Green is the colour they do *not* use.

A plant which is deprived of red or blue light cannot photosynthesise properly and it will not make much food. Sunlight provides these colours in the right proportions. People who use artificial light in greenhouses must make sure that it contains these colours. Light manufacturers produce special lamps for this purpose.

Carbon dioxide

The more carbon dioxide there is in the air surrounding a plant, the faster the plant photosynthesises. The amount of carbon dioxide in the atmosphere is about 0.03 per cent, and it doesn't vary much. Even so, there are slight differences from place to place which may affect the rate of photosynthesis. For example, the concentration of carbon dioxide close to the ground in a dense forest is higher than in an open field. Why do you think this is?

Extra carbon dioxide is sometimes pumped into greenhouses, or produced by a 'burner', so as to increase the rate of photosynthesis. Picture 3 shows how helpful this can be.

Temperature

Up to a point, the warmer it is, the faster is the rate of photosynthesis. Normally an increase in temperature of 10°C roughly doubles the rate. This is true of chemical reactions in general, including photosynthesis.

In the natural world there are tremendous variations in temperature, both from place to place and at different times of the year. One of the reasons why plants do so well in greenhouses is because of the warmth (picture 4).

But there is a limit. If the temperature gets much above 40°C, photosynthesis slows down rapidly and then stops altogether. This is because heating destroys the enzymes which are responsible for making the chemical reactions work.

Water

A plant which is beginning to wilt through lack of water may photosynthesise at only half the normal rate. This is not because it hasn't got enough water for photosynthesis – even a wilted plant has enough water for that. It's because lack of water produces other effects, and these then slow down photosynthesis. Can you think what these other effects might be?

Which places are best for photosynthesis?

One of the best natural places for photosynthesis is the tropical rain forest. Long hours of sunshine, warmth and a high rainfall ensure a high rate of photosynthesis and good growth. The tropical rain forest has been described as a vegetative frenzy (picture 5)!

Crop plants grown in the tropics make particularly large amounts of food. This is true of sugar cane, for example, which gives a higher yield of organic matter than any other crop plant (picture 6).

Sugar cane needs a hot, moist climate with temperatures averaging around 25°C and an annual rainfall of about 150 cm. It gets this in places such as the Caribbean and South East Asia. When it is grown in drier regions like North America and southern Africa, water must be supplied by irrigation.

In parts of the world where conditions are less favourable for photosynthesis, plants may be grown in special air conditioned greenhouses. Here all the conditions affecting the rate of photosynthesis are carefully controlled. There is more about this on page 73.

Which parts of the world do you think are *worst* for photosynthesis, and why? What sort of plants can grow in such places, and how do they survive?

Picture 4 Britain is too cold for melons to be grown out of doors. However, the warm conditions inside a greenhouse enable these excellent melons to be produced.

Picture 5 The conditions in this jungle in Malaysia are just right for a high rate of photosynthesis.

Picture 6 Sugar cane growing in Malaysia. Sugar cane can photosynthesise more efficiently than any other crop plant. It provides most of the world's sugar.

Activities

A Does raising the light intensity increase the rate of photosynthesis?

For this experiment use *Elodea* (Canadian pondweed)

1. Darken the room so that the light from the windows does not vary and upset your results.
2. Cut off a piece of the weed about 5 cm long.
3. Attach a paper clip to the uncut end of the weed to weigh it down.
4. Put it in a beaker or jam jar of water as shown in the picture. The cut end should point upwards.
5. Blow bubbles through the water with a straw: this will ensure that the pondweed has a good supply of carbon dioxide.
6. Place a lamp to one side of the jar.
7. Fill a narrow aquarium tank with water and place it between the jar and the lamp. This will serve as a heat shield and prevent the pondweed heating up.
8. Illuminate the weed with the lamp placed a long way away (say 50 cm).
9. Wait a few minutes, then count the number of bubbles given off during a one minute period. Do this three times and work out the average.
10. Now bring the lamp closer (say 20 cm), wait a few minutes, then count the number of bubbles again. Do this three times and work out the average.

How many bubbles are given off per minute (i) with the lamp a long way away, and (ii) with the lamp close?

Do you find that the closer the lamp, the greater the rate at which bubbles are given off?

Does raising the light intensity increase the rate of photosynthesis?

B Does raising the carbon dioxide concentration increase the rate of photosynthesis?

You can raise the concentration of carbon dioxide in a body of water by adding sodium hydrogencarbonate (bicarbonate of soda). When this is added to the water, carbon dioxide is quickly formed. (Can you explain the chemical reaction?)

Plan an experiment to find out if raising the carbon dioxide concentration increases the rate of photosynthesis of Canadian pondweed.

You could use the same technique as in activity A, i.e. count the number of bubbles given off by the plant in a certain time. Or you might be able to think of a better way. For example, instead of counting bubbles, might it be possible to *collect* the gas given off in a certain time, and measure its volume? Think about, and if possible design, an apparatus that could be used for doing this.

Discuss your plan with your teacher, then try out the experiment.

To think about

Think of the plants in a typical pond: water lilies, pondweed and so on. These plants get their carbon dioxide from the surrounding water. The carbon dioxide is in solution, and it diffuses into the plants' cells. However, carbon dioxide diffuses more slowly in water than in air. How might this affect the plants in a pond, and what could be done about it?

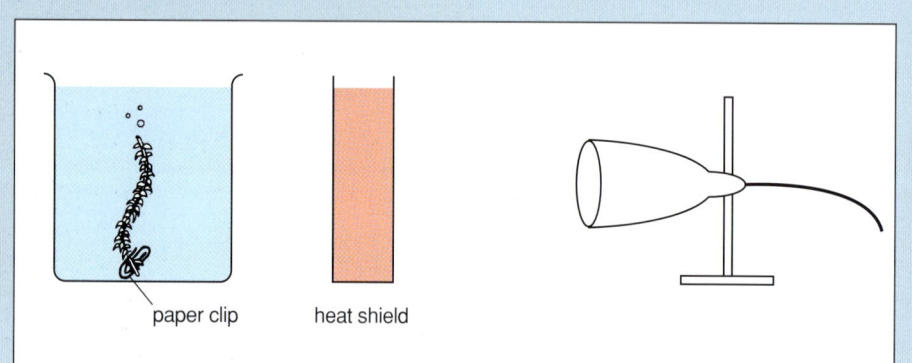

Questions

1. Mr Smith plants his onions in a shady place whereas Mrs Jones plants hers in the sun. Whose onions would you expect to do best, and why?
2. Someone observed that wheat grows taller, and gives a higher yield of grain, close to a certain coal-burning factory than further away.
   a. Suggest a reason for this.
   b. What investigations would you carry out to find if your suggestion is right?
3. Describe an experiment which you could do to find out which colours of the spectrum are used by a potted plant for photosynthesis.
4. The following figures give the total annual amounts of organic matter produced per hectare by plants in different parts of the world:

Sugar cane, Java	87 tonnes
Tropical rain forest	59 tonnes
Pine forest, Britain	16 tonnes

   Account for the differences. Approximately how much organic matter would you expect wheat to produce in Britain? Give a reason for your answer.
5. A scientist grew some cereal plants in a field. During the course of one day he took several plants every four hours and measured the amount of sugar in the leaves. The sugar concentrations, expressed as a percentage of the dry mass of the leaves, are given in the table at the top of the next column.

Time of day	Sugar concentration
4 am	0.45
8 am	0.60
12 noon	1.75
4 pm	2.00
8 pm	1.4
12 midnight	0.5
4 am	0.45

   a. Plot the data on graph paper, putting sugar concentration on the vertical axis.
   b. What is the probable concentration of sugar in the leaves at 10 am and 2 am?
   c. At what time of the day is sugar probably at a maximum in the leaf, and why?
   d. Explain why the sugar concentration changes over the 24 hour period.

Getting the best out of a greenhouse

Here are some of the things you need to bear in mind if you have a greenhouse:

- It must not get too hot, and the light must not be too bright. Too much heating and light can make plants produce less food, not more.
- The air must be fairly moist (humid). If it is too dry, a lot of water may evaporate from the plants and they may wilt. But if it is too moist, fungal pests may flourish.
- The plants must have a good supply of all the chemicals they need, including carbon dioxide, water and mineral salts.

Now look at the picture. This shows how a modern greenhouse meets these requirements. Of course, you want the running costs to be as low as possible. This means turning off energy-consuming devices such as the heater and lights when they are not needed. In large greenhouses used by market gardeners, the lights, heating, carbon dioxide and humidity are all regulated automatically.

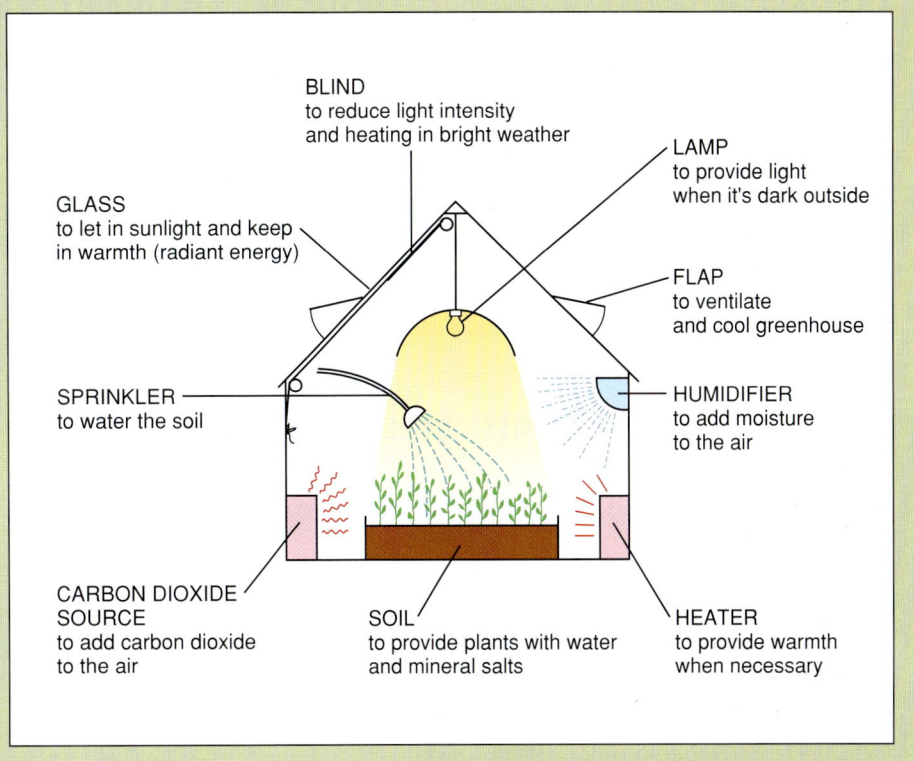

Picture 1 A greenhouse should provide everything plants need for photosynthesis and growth. In a modern commercial greenhouse the conditions are regulated by computer-controlled feedback mechanisms. For example, suppose the concentration of carbon dioxide falls too low. This is detected by special sensors that feed the information into a microcomputer, which then instructs the carbon dioxide source to release more carbon dioxide.

Labels: BLIND to reduce light intensity and heating in bright weather; LAMP to provide light when it's dark outside; GLASS to let in sunlight and keep in warmth (radiant energy); FLAP to ventilate and cool greenhouse; SPRINKLER to water the soil; HUMIDIFIER to add moisture to the air; CARBON DIOXIDE SOURCE to add carbon dioxide to the air; SOIL to provide plants with water and mineral salts; HEATER to provide warmth when necessary.

When several things control the same process

Look at the graph below. It shows the results of an experiment to find the effect of raising the light intensity on the rate of photosynthesis – like the activity on page 72.

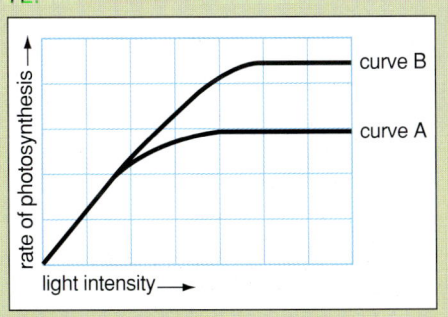

First look at curve A. As the light intensity is gradually raised, the curve rises, i.e. the rate of photosynthesis increases.

However, there comes a point when the curve flattens out – the rate of photosynthesis does not increase any more, however much you raise the light intensity.

Why do you think the rate of photosynthesis stops increasing at this point? Well, it could be that photosynthesis is going at its maximum possible speed. But it could be that something other than light is preventing the process going any faster.

What might this 'something' be? One possibility is carbon dioxide. How could we find out if it is carbon dioxide? One way would be to raise the concentration of carbon dioxide in the atmosphere surrounding the plant and repeat the experiment.

The result of doing this is shown in curve B. This time a much higher rate of photosynthesis is achieved. This tells us that carbon dioxide must have been controlling the rate of photosynthesis when the curve flattened out in the first experiment. We say that carbon dioxide was the **limiting factor** controlling the process – it was setting the pace.

What do we learn from this experiment? Well, here's one thing: in a greenhouse there is no point in giving plants extra light if the concentration of carbon dioxide is too low. It simply won't make any difference. This is an example of how an experiment done by scientists in a laboratory can be useful to people who grow plants for sale.

1. The three main conditions which affect the rate of photosynthesis are light, temperature and carbon dioxide. Which condition is likely to limit the rate of photosynthesis of wheat plants in a field in Britain on a cloudless day at:

   a noon in mid-summer,
   b dusk in mid-summer,
   c noon in mid-winter,
   d dusk in mid-winter?

   What effect do you think clouds have on the rate of photosynthesis?

2. A market gardener who is thinking of installing artificial lights in a greenhouse might benefit from reading the passage above. Why?

C8
To and from the leaf

Plants have a transport system for taking things to and from the leaf.

Picture 1 The root hairs of wheat seedlings.

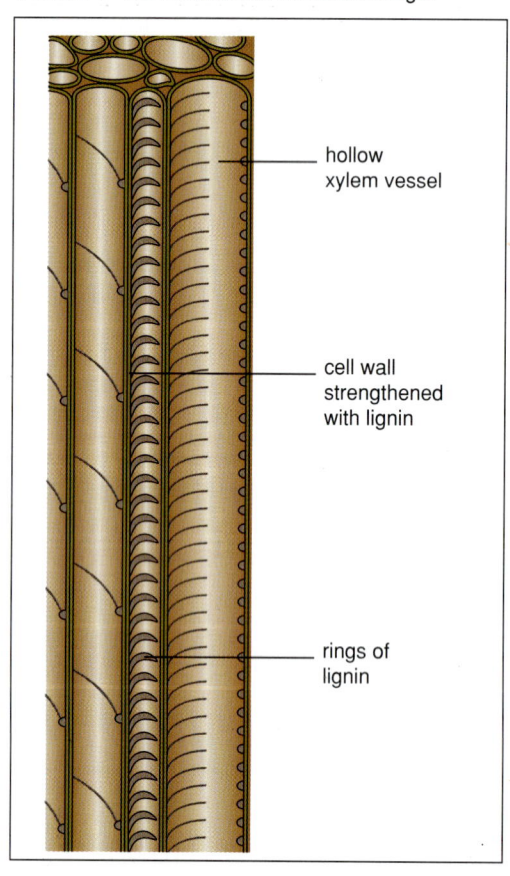

Picture 2 Xylem tubes (vessels).

Why do plants need a transport system?

Water and food are basic needs for all living organisms. The cells of the plant, whether in the root or in the leaves, require them too.

Plants obtain water from the soil. This must be transported from the soil to the leaves, where it will be used for photosynthesis. Water is also required to help support the plant and hold the leaves out flat. If a plant runs short of water, the cells lose water and go flabby. The plant then droops. This is called **wilting** (see page 117). Plants are adapted in various ways to prevent this happening.

Likewise, the sugars manufactured by photosynthesis must be transported to the root and shoot tips to provide energy for growth, or to underground food stores to keep the plant through the winter. Sugars may also be transported to the growing fruit. This makes them sweet which encourages animals to eat them and ensures the dispersal of the seeds.

How does water get to the leaves?

Water evaporates from the leaves and other parts of the plant above the ground. The evaporation of water from the plant is called **transpiration**. It occurs mainly through the stomata. However, as quickly as water is lost from the leaves, more water enters the roots and flows up the stem. The water flows up the plant in narrow pipes, rather like capillary tubes. These tubes are called the **xylem**.

The water rises up the stem mainly by being 'pulled' from above. The 'pull' is created by the evaporation of water from the leaves. If you stop this by, for example, cutting off the leaves or blocking the stomata, the flow of water up the stem slows down or stops.

The roots anchor a plant to the soil. They also provide a link with the soil water. The ends of the roots, except for the tip, are covered with delicate **root hairs** (picture 1). They increase the surface area for absorption.

The structure of the xylem

Picture 2 shows the structure of some xylem cells. They are hollow and do not contain any living material. They are, therefore, dead. The walls of the tubes are made of lignin, which is a hard, waterproof material. The **lignin** is often thickened into rings or spirals on the inside of the xylem tubes.

In trees and shrubs the xylem tubes are one of the main components of wood.

How do sugars travel around the plant?

Sugar and other soluble food substances made in the leaves are transported to where they are needed or can be stored. They move along special tubes called **phloem**. The movement of food substances in the phloem is called **translocation** and it requires energy.

The importance of the phloem in transporting food can be seen in trees. In a tree trunk, the phloem is in the soft inner part of the bark. If a ring of bark is cut from a tree trunk, food substances cannot get down to the roots. As a result, the roots starve and the tree dies.

Grey squirrels damage trees by gnawing their bark and damaging the phloem, and in Africa elephants sometimes kill trees by stripping off the bark with their tusks.

Insects such as greenflies get their food from the phloem of plants. The insect sticks the tip of its needle-like proboscis into one of the tubes and feeds on the sugars which are flowing along it. The insect does not even have to suck. The pressure in the phloem tubes is sufficient to drive the sugar solution up the proboscis and into the insect's gut.

The structure of the phloem

Unlike the xylem, phloem is a living tissue. It is made up of numerous cells called **sieve tubes**. Each tube is connected to the next by a perforated wall (the **sieve plate**) and contains cytoplasm but no nucleus. However, alongside each sieve tube is a **companion cell** which has a large nucleus. It is not fully understood how sugars are moved through the phloem. Picture 3 shows the internal structure of a phloem tube and its companion cell.

Other functions of the transport system

The xylem tubes not only transport water but also essential minerals. These are dissolved in the water that the roots absorb. They include nitrates, vital for the formation of plant protein, and magnesium, a vital component of chlorophyll.

The lignified xylem also gives support to the plant, allowing it to grow tall and straight. Giant redwood trees can be 100 metres high. They are held up with the help of lignified tissue.

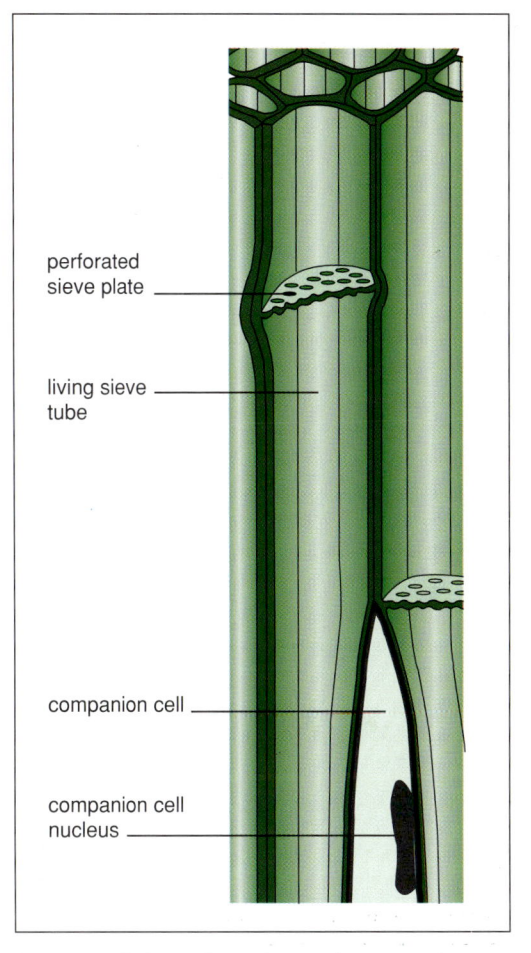

Picture 3 Phloem sieve tubes and a companion cell.

Questions

1 Suggest a reason for the following:
  a It is better to water plants in the evening than in the middle of the day.
  b Before transplanting a plant it is a good idea to remove some of its leaves.
  c Water moves up a stem more quickly on a dry day than on a humid day.
  d In very humid conditions water may drip from leaves.

2 If a tree is felled, a watery liquid may ooze out of the stump for a while. Comment on this observation.

3 The following features are found in different species of plants that live in hot, dry places. In each case explain how the feature helps the plant to cope with a shortage of water in its environment.
  a Thick cuticle covering the leaves.
  b Small leaves.
  c Stomata sunk down into pits in the epidermis.
  d Very deep roots.
  e Roots just beneath the surface of the soil.

4 A scientist investigated the uptake of mineral salts by the roots of young barley plants. This is what she found:
  a Salts were taken up even when they were more dilute in the soil water than inside the root.
  b The rate of uptake was increased by raising the temperature, so long as it did not exceed 40°C.
  c Uptake stopped if the roots were treated with a poison that stopped respiration.
  d Uptake was much slower if the soil was waterlogged.

What conclusions can be drawn from these findings? How might they help farmers?

The vascular tissue of a plant

Together, the xylem and phloem make up a plant's **vascular tissue**. Picture 1 shows how this tissue is arranged in a typical non-woody flowering plant such as a buttercup or sunflower. The xylem carries water and mineral salts upwards. The phloem carries soluble food substances downwards.

In shrubs and trees the vascular tissue is arranged as in picture 2. The xylem forms the wood in the trunk and branches. The part of the wood in the centre (**heartwood**) is extemely dense and hard; its job is to support the plant. The part further out (**sapwood**) is less dense and therefore softer; it too supports the plant, but it also carries water and mineral salts upwards.

The phloem is the soft inner part of the bark. It carries soluble food substances from leaves to roots.

The hard outer part of the bark is made of **cork** which is a dead tissue. Cork is impervious to gases, but here and there the corky cells are more loosely packed, forming pimple-like **lenticels**. These serve as 'breathing pores'. Through the lenticels oxygen diffuses to the living tissues beneath, and carbon dioxide diffuses out.

1 Which sort of wood is more suitable for timber, heartwood or sapwood? Give a reason for your choice.
2 How could a five-year-old child kill a tree with a penknife? Explain your answer.

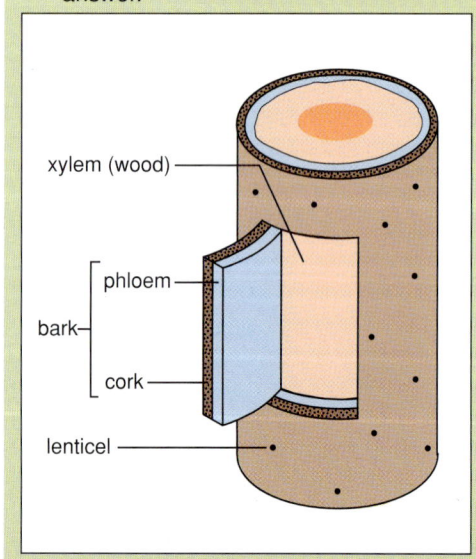

Picture 1 The vascular tissue inside the leaf, stem and root of an herbaceous flowering plant. Xylem red, phloem blue.

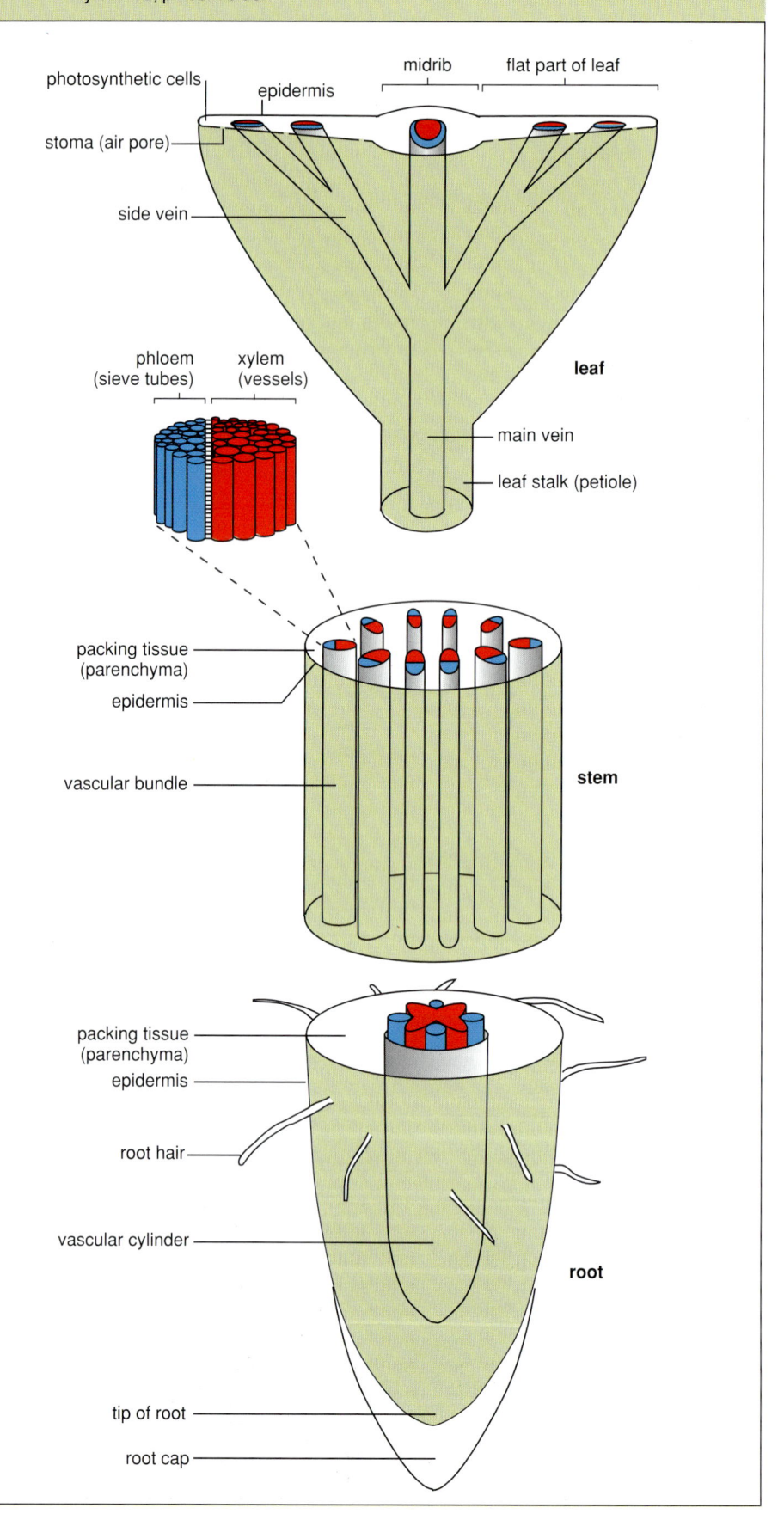

Picture 2 How the vascular tissue is arranged in the trunks and branches of trees and shrubs.

The flow of water through a plant

Look at the root hair in picture 1. It is a long extension of a single cell which sticks out from the outer layer of the root. It lies between the soil particles, which are normally surrounded by water.

The cell surface membrane of the root hair is partially permeable (see page 117). The concentration of water molecules inside the root hair is normally lower than in the soil water. The result is that water flows into the root hair by osmosis.

The water then diffuses from the root hair to the next layer of cells in the root, and then to the next layer – and so on. Eventually the water reaches the xylem tubes in the centre of the root.

Not all the water enters the root hair by osmosis. Much of the water simply diffuses into the cellulose wall of the root hair. The cell wall is like a sponge, and is normally saturated with water. The water then flows along the walls of the root cells until it reaches the centre of the root.

Once the water enters the xylem tubes, it flows from the roots to the stem and so to the leaves. The columns of water in the xylem tubes are prevented from breaking by strong cohesive forces that exist between the water molecules.

Water passes out of the xylem tubes in the leaves. It then flows from one leaf cell to the next mainly via the cell walls. The water then evaporates from the cell walls into the air spaces within the leaf (picture 2).

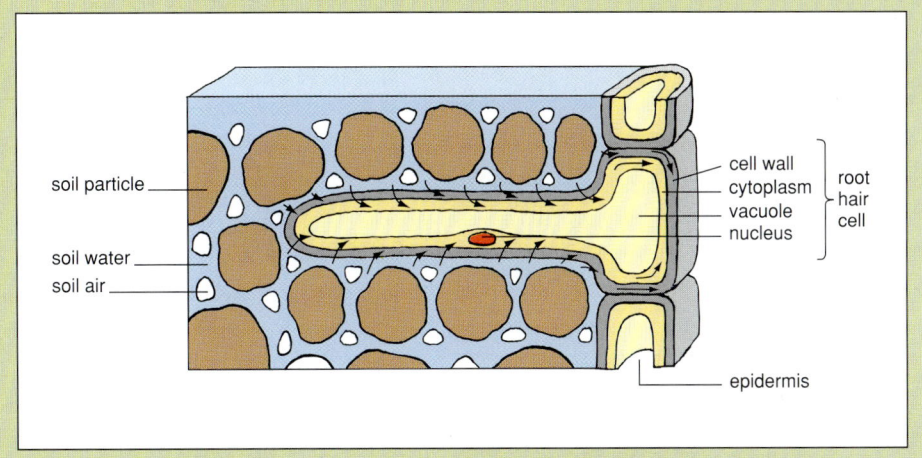

Picture 1 A root hair. The arrows indicate the absorption of water into the root hair cell.

Finally, the water vapour diffuses through the open stomata to the outside of the leaf. This is **transpiration**.

The greater the rate of transpiration, the faster water flows from roots to leaves – provided there is enough water in the soil. The rate of transpiration depends on a number of things. In general, it is speeded up by high temperature, a dry atmosphere (low humidity) and air currents.

The flow of water through the plant is called the **transpiration stream**. Mineral salts absorbed by the root hairs are swept along in the transpiration stream. This is how essential elements needed by the plant reach the leaves.

1. Suggest two ways in which transpiration is useful to a plant.
2. In what circumstances would you expect transpiration to be very slow?

   Think of as many circumstances as you can.
3. A giant sequoia tree may be over 80 metres tall. Are you surprised that water in a tree can reach such a great height? Scientists are! What is surprising about it?

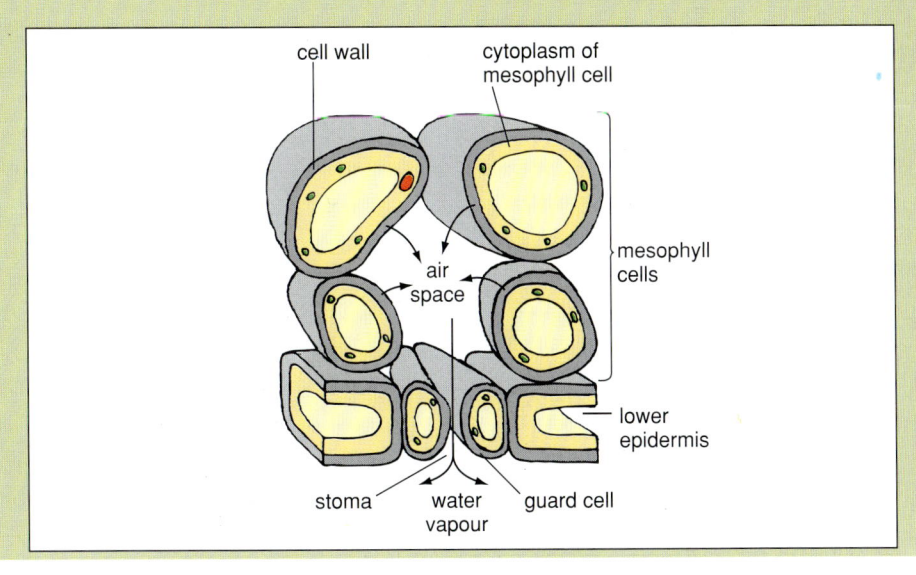

Picture 2 The internal structure of the lower part of a leaf, just inside a stoma. The arrows indicate the evaporation of water from the cells and the diffusion of water vapour to the outside.

D1
Food and diet

The study of food is called nutrition. The next two topics are about nutrition.

Picture 1 In the course of a lifetime a person may eat 100 tonnes of food.

Picture 2 A balanced diet is a *varied* diet. By eating lots of different kinds of food, you are likely to get all the substances you need.

Why do we need food?

We need food for four main reasons:
- It serves as a fuel, giving us energy and warmth.
- It provides materials for growth.
- It enables us to repair and replace tissues.
- It keeps us healthy and helps us to fight disease.

Our diet

The food we eat each day makes up our **diet**. Whatever we choose to eat, our diet must include the following substances: **carbohydrates, fats, proteins, water, minerals** and **vitamins**.

A diet which contains all the necessary substances, but not too much of any of them, is called a **balanced diet** (picture 2). The food substances themselves are called **nutrients**.

The chemistry of these substances is dealt with on page 81. Here we shall concentrate on the part they play in our diet. We shall deal with the substances that we need in bulk in this topic, and those that we need in only small amounts in the next one.

Carbohydrates

■ **Sugar**

Sugar gives us energy, so we call it an energy food. Different foods contain different kinds of sugar. For example, the sugar in fruit is **fructose** or **glucose**, and in milk it is **lactose**. Ordinary table sugar is **sucrose**.

Most of the world's sugar comes from sugar cane. This is a giant grass, rather like bamboo, which may reach a height of six metres. It is grown in hot countries. Sugar, in the form of sucrose, is stored in its thick stem. The juice is extracted from the stem, and then purified (refined). After that, water is evaporated from it, so sugar crystals are formed. This is **white sugar**.

Brown sugar is less refined than white sugar. It contains various impurities which give it its brown colour and make it slightly sticky. These impurities do us no harm – in fact, when used in cooking, they add flavour to things like cakes and biscuits.

Another source of sugar is sugar beet which is grown in temperate countries including Britain. Sugar beet stores sugar in thick swollen roots.

■ **Starch**

Starch is found particularly in bread, potatoes and cereals. Like sugar, starch gives us energy.

Starch occurs in plant cells as **starch grains**. Each grain contains many tightly packed starch molecules, and each starch molecule consists of a chain of sugar molecules. So starch is a concentrated store of energy.

Each starch grain is surrounded by a membrane, rather like a little envelope. When you cook a starchy food such as a potato, the starch grains swell up and burst. This releases the starch molecules, which can then be easily digested.

■ **Cellulose**

Cellulose is the substance which plant cell walls are made of. It is tough and rubbery. The cellulose walls of neighbouring cells are stuck together by a sort of glue. This is why raw plants are often difficult to chew. Cooking dissolves the glue, with the result that the cells come apart. This makes the plant softer and easier to eat. The same sort of thing happens when fruits ripen.

Humans cannot digest cellulose – we don't have the necessary enzyme in our gut for breaking it down. This means that we cannot get energy from it. However, it still has a useful function: it is our main source of **dietary fibre** (**roughage**). This keeps food moving along the gut, and helps to prevent con-

Food and diet 79

stipation and cancer of the colon (bowel) (see page 91).

Unrefined foods such as wholemeal bread, bran cereals and fresh fruit and vegetables contain plenty of fibre. This is one reason why such foods are good for us.

Fats

Fats occur in both animal and plant foods. Butter, dripping and lard are animal fats obtained from cattle and pigs. These fats are solid at room temperature, though if you heat them they become liquid.

Plant fats, on the other hand, are normally liquids at room temperature – we call them **oils**. Two well known examples are corn oil and olive oil. Both are used in cooking.

Margarine, unlike butter, consists mainly of plant oils. These are obtained from peanuts, soya beans and so on, and are then turned into solid fat by chemical treatment.

Fats give us energy, so – like carbohydrates – they are energy foods. In humans and other mammals, fat is stored under the skin; this helps to keep the body warm, as well as serving as an energy store.

There are many kinds of fat. Each contains particular **fatty acids** (see page 81). Now some fatty acids are **saturated**, whereas others are **unsaturated**. (An unsaturated fatty acid is one which contains less than the maximum amount of hydrogen possible.) Fatty acids which are very unsaturated are called **polyunsaturates**.

In general animal fats contain a high proportion of saturated fatty acids, whereas plant oils contain a high proportion of polyunsaturated fatty acids. For good health we should eat mainly polyunsaturates. The reason is that polyunsaturates reduce the amount of another substance in the body: **cholesterol**.

What is cholesterol?

Cholesterol is a fat-like substance which the body needs for a number of purposes. So basically cholesterol is a useful substance. We get it from various foods, particularly egg yolk. The trouble is that if we take in too much, it can cause **heart disease** (see page 144).

Now scientists have found that saturated fats raise the concentration of cholesterol in the body, whereas polyunsaturates lower it. So for good health it makes sense to eat foods that are high in polyunsaturates and low in saturates. Most plant foods are of this kind. Table margarines and spreads with a high polyunsaturate content are generally better for us than butter (picture 3).

The harmful effects of saturated fats and cholesterol start early in life. So children should have a diet with not too much animal fat.

Proteins

A certain amount of protein is present in most foods, but it is particularly plentiful in milk, eggs and meat. In milk and eggs the protein is in liquid form. In meat it consists of solid thread-like fibres – the animal's muscle.

Proteins form the main structures of the body like muscles and skin. So we need proteins for growth and body-building, and for repairing tissues. We also need proteins to make enzymes. In addition, we can get energy from proteins.

How much protein do we need each day? Picture 4 shows what doctors recommend. In practice most people could manage with a lot less than this. In rich countries people tend to eat much more protein than they need. On the other hand, in poor countries many people get very little. A growing child who does not get enough protein may develop **protein deficiency disease** (**kwashiorkor**) (picture 5).

Getting the right kinds of proteins

Proteins are composed of amino acids (see page 81). We can make some of these for ourselves, so we do not need them in our food. Others we cannot

Picture 3 Table margarines usually contain a high proportion of polyunsaturated fat.

Picture 4 Doctors recommend us to eat about 70 grams of protein each day for a healthy life. This amount of protein is present in the piece of meat and glass of milk in this picture.

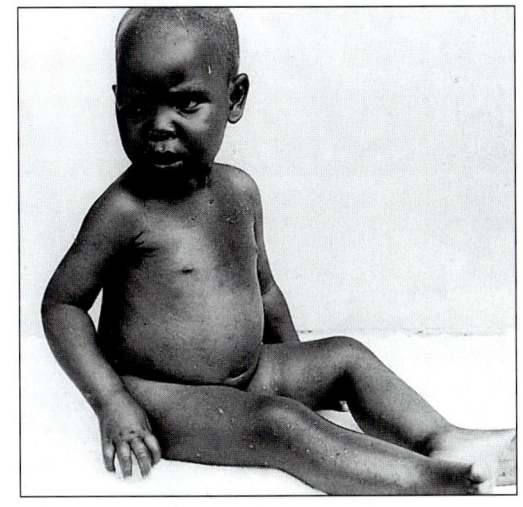

Picture 5 This child is suffering from lack of protein in the diet. The child is weak and listless. He looks fat because fluid has collected in the tissues. This is one of the commonest types of malnutrition in poor countries. It is often seen in babies who are being breast-fed by an undernourished mother, particularly if she is carrying another child.

Table 1 In this table, each food is given marks out of ten, depending on how good it is at giving us all the amino acids we need. A high mark means that the protein in the food contains all the essential amino acids in the right proportions for humans. A low mark means that it is short of certain essential amino acids.

Type of protein	Marks out of 10
Mother's milk	10
Eggs	10
Fish	8
Meat	8
Cow's milk	7½
Potatoes	7
Liver (beef)	6½
Rice	5½
Soya beans	5½
Maize	5½
Wheat (white flour)	5
Peas	4½
Beans	4½

Picture 6 Drought like this may lead to famine.

Picture 7 This bar chart shows the relative amounts of different substances in some well-known foods. The numbers alongside each bar are the percentages.

make, so they must be included in our diet. These **essential amino acids** are vital for good health, and absence of just one of them can have serious consequences.

Now look at table 1. This shows how good different proteins are at giving us the amino acids that we need. As you can see, animal proteins come out on top. Plant proteins come lower down. This does not mean that plant proteins are no use. They are, provided that a mixture of different ones is eaten. Different plant proteins contain different essential amino acids, so eating the right mixture of plants can give you all the amino acids you need. By doing this you are also avoiding animal fats which may be harmful. Wheat protein and bean protein provide a good balance of amino acids, so beans on toast can be a nutritious meal.

Notice that one of the best plant proteins is soya bean protein. What's more, the total amount of protein in soya beans is greater than in most plants. Soya beans are therefore used for manufacturing artificial meat. It is called **textured vegetable protein**.

Artificial meat is also made from bacteria and fungi. The protein is textured and flavoured to make it taste and feel like chicken or ham (see page 199).

Water

Water is essential for life (see page 81). It must therefore be included in our diet. A person can go without food for several weeks, but would die in a few days from lack of water.

We take in water mainly by drinking. However, there is plenty of water in most solid foods. A lettuce or cabbage is 90 per cent water, and even bread contains about 40 per cent. Some animals get all their water from solid food and never drink, but humans normally need to drink about a litre of liquid every day.

Shortage of water in our environment (drought) is one of the main causes of famine. It kills livestock, and causes crops to fail.

Finding out what's in our food

Experiments can be done to find out how much of each substance is found in different foods (picture 7). This information is particularly useful to people who plan meals for schools and hospitals, because it tells us what each kind of food is useful for. For example, maize contains mainly carbohydrate and is therefore a good energy food. On the other hand, meat contains mainly protein, which makes it good for growth and body-building.

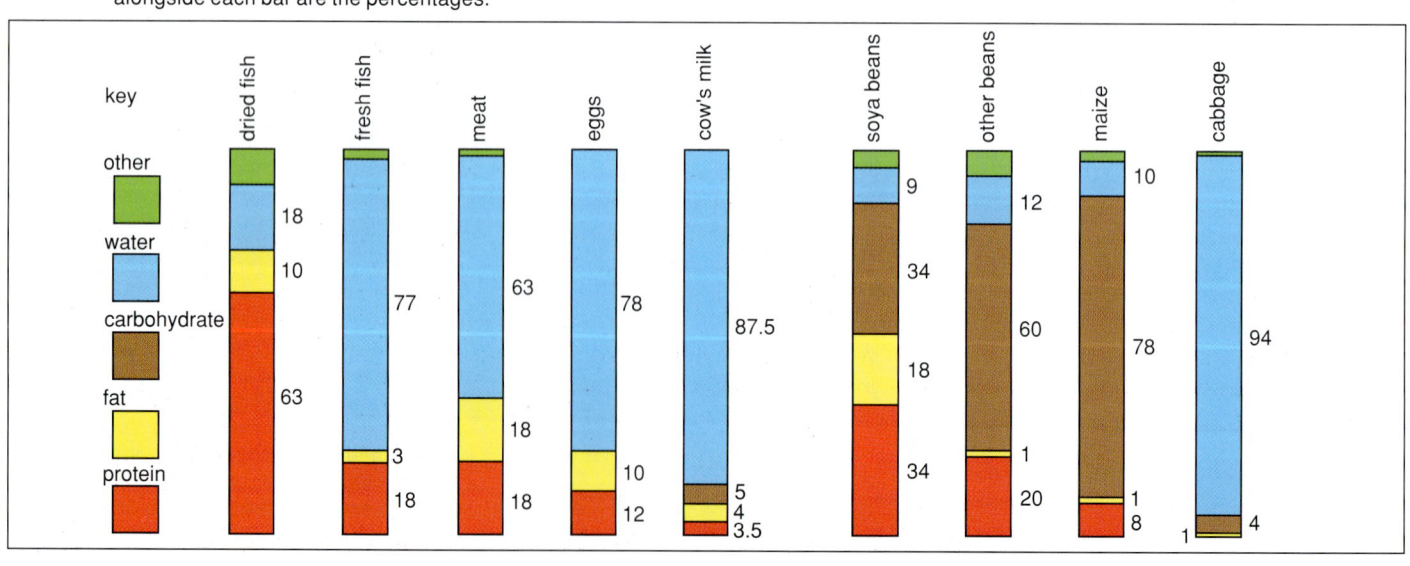

What are living things made of?

All living things, including humans, are made of chemical substances. Here is a summary of the main substances found in the body:

Organic substances:	Carbohydrates
	Fats and oils (lipids)
	Proteins
Inorganic substances:	Salts
	Water

Picture 1 shows the proportions of each of these substances in the human body. You may be surprised to see that our bodies contain far more water than any other substance. The fact is that we are really very wet.

What are the functions of these substances?

Each substance has certain jobs to do. These are their main jobs:

Carbohydrates give us energy; one of the best known carbohydrates is sugar of which there are several different types.

Fats and **oils** (**lipids**) also give us energy; there is a lot of fat under the skin where it helps to keep us warm, and oils on the surface can help to make the body waterproof. Fat also occurs in cell membranes.

Proteins help to build up the body; they form important structures like muscles and tendons, and are also important as enzymes as we shall see in a moment.

Salts help to make the tissues and organs in the body work properly.

Water provides a fluid in which other substances can move about the body and react together within the cells.

How are the substances constructed?

All carbohydrates contain carbon, hydrogen and oxygen. One of the simplest is **glucose** which is a type of sugar. Its formula is $C_6H_{12}O_6$: this shows that a molecule of it contains six carbon atoms, twelve hydrogen atoms, and six oxygen atoms.

Glucose molecules can be linked together to form more complex carbohydrates, for example **starch** and **glycogen**. Their function is to store energy for use when it is needed.

One of the most complex carbohydrates is **cellulose**, the material of which plant cell walls are made. Like other carbohydrates, it consists of lots of glucose molecules linked together.

Fats and oils are complex substances too. Their molecules are made up of two parts: **glycerol** and **fatty acids**. Like carbohydrates, fats and oils contain carbon, hydrogen and oxygen.

Proteins are amongst the most complex substances found in living things. They contain nitrogen as well as carbon, hydrogen and oxygen. Sulphur, too, is usually present. A protein molecule consists of one or more chains of chemical building blocks called **amino acids**. Sulphur helps to cross-link the amino acid chains. Some proteins are solid, others are in solution. Muscle is a solid protein, whereas egg white is a soluble protein.

Proteins may combine with other molecules to form even more complex substances. For example, they combine with nucleic acids such as DNA to form **nucleoproteins**.

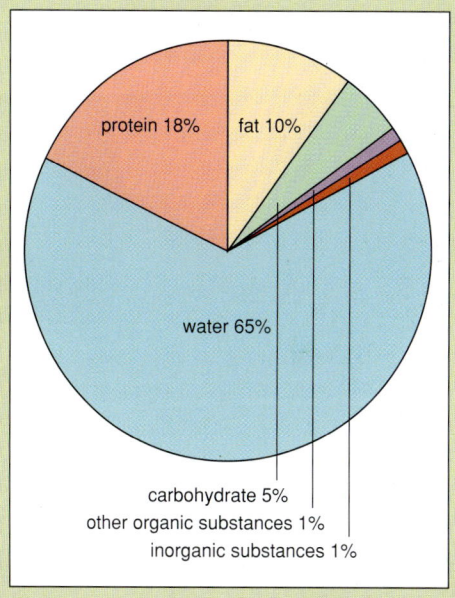

Picture 1 This pie chart shows the relative amounts of the main substances which make up the human body.

- protein 18%
- fat 10%
- water 65%
- carbohydrate 5%
- other organic substances 1%
- inorganic substances 1%

Questions

1. Give four reasons why we need food.

2. Give one example of a food which contains:
    a. lactose,
    b. sucrose,
    c. cellulose,
    d. sunflower oil,
    e. liquid protein.

3. What effect does cooking have on each of the following:
    a. potatoes,
    b. eggs,
    c. cabbage,
    d. beef?

    Explain your answers.

4. Explain each of the following statements.
    a. Children suffering from shortage of protein do not grow as quickly as they should.
    b. Eggs are better for body-building than bread.

5. Look at picture 7 then answer these questions.
    a. Which food contains most protein?
    b. Which food contains most carbohydrate?
    c. Which food contains most water?
    d. Which food would you recommend for a person who wants to avoid heart disease?
    e. Which plant food would be best for a vegetarian, and why?

6. Each of the foods in the left-hand list is closely related to one of the words in the right-hand list. Write them down in the correct pairs.

    | wholemeal bread | protein |
    | sugar | insulation |
    | butter | artificial meat |
    | eggs | roughage |
    | soya beans | energy |

7. The amount of protein present in a particular food, and how good that protein is for body-building, are two quite different things.

    Explain what this statement means.

D2
More about food and diet

This topic is mainly about substances that we need in only small amounts.

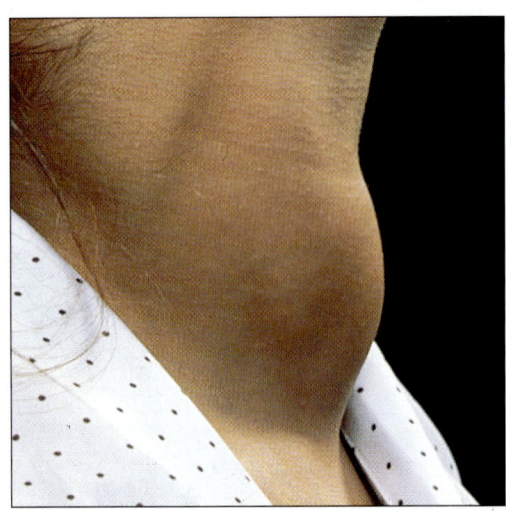

Picture 1 This person is suffering from goitre, caused by lack of iodine in the diet.

Picture 2 Portrait of a man drawn by the Italian artist Leonardo da Vinci in the fifteenth century. Notice his swollen neck. He may have lived in an area where there was no iodine in the water.

Mineral salts

Mineral salts contain certain chemical elements. All these elements have particular jobs to do in the body. Here are some of the more important ones:

■ Sodium

We take in sodium when we eat salt, for common salt is sodium chloride. Salt is present in most foods, though of course some are saltier than others.

Our blood must contain the right amount of salt. It helps our nerves to transmit messages and our muscles to contract. If you run short of it, you get cramp. We lose salt when we sweat. Miners, and other people who work in hot places, eat salt tablets to make up for the salt they lose in sweating.

It is important not to eat too much salt. It can cause high blood pressure, and may be linked with heart disease.

■ Calcium

When a baby is born, its bones are soft. For the bones to harden, they must take up calcium compounds. These compounds are calcium phosphate and calcium carbonate. The process is called **calcification**. A similar process makes the teeth hard.

Calcium occurs particularly in milk, cheese and fish. If a child does not get enough calcium, its bones remain soft and become deformed. This is called **rickets**. Calcium is also needed for making muscles contract, and it helps blood to clot when you cut yourself.

■ Iron

Iron is needed for our blood. It is present in haemoglobin, the red pigment which carries oxygen.

Iron is particularly plentiful in liver and kidneys. Small amounts occur in most drinking water, and we get quite a lot of it from metal utensils used in cooking. The amount of iron in a piece of beef can be doubled by mincing it in an iron mincer.

Shortage of iron results in the blood containing too little haemoglobin. This is a type of **anaemia**. The oxygen-carrying ability of the blood is reduced, resulting in tiredness and lack of energy. People who are anaemic are often recommended to take iron tablets.

■ Iodine

Some elements are needed in only tiny quantities. They are known as **trace elements** (**micronutrients**). One such element is **iodine**.

Iodine is present in most drinking water, and in sea foods. We need it for making a hormone called **thyroxine**. This is produced by the **thyroid gland**, situated close to the 'Adam's apple' in the neck.

Thyroxine speeds up chemical reactions in the body, making us more active. If we do not get enough iodine, the thyroid gland cannot produce thyroxine. As a result, the gland enlarges, causing the neck to swell. This condition is called **goitre** (picture 1).

There are some places where the drinking water lacks iodine. One such place is Derbyshire in the middle of England. In the old days it was common for people in that area to have enlarged thyroid glands, so the condition was called 'Derbyshire neck'. Nowadays, iodine is added to salt, so the condition no longer occurs. Before reading on, look at picture 2 and see what you make of it.

Vitamins

In the early 1900s an English scientist, Frederick Gowland Hopkins, discovered something interesting. He fed some rats on a special food mixture containing purified carbohydrates, fats, proteins and minerals – all the substances known to be necessary for healthy life. After a few weeks the rats were dead.

However, a second group of rats was given exactly the same food mixture, plus a very small amount of milk. They flourished. Apparently the milk contained something extra which the rats needed. We now know that this extra 'something' was **vitamins** (picture 3).

Vitamins are organic substances needed in the diet. Each has a specific job to do. If any of them is missing from the diet, we become ill and may die. They are needed in only small amounts and are therefore called micronutrients.

Vitamins are known by letters: A, B, C, etc. This way of naming them was introduced before their chemical structure was known. It is still used, though we can now give them proper chemical names as well.

For vitamins to do their jobs they must be in solution. Some of them dissolve in water, others in fat. This is one of many reasons why we need water and fat in our diet.

Now let's look at some of the more important vitamins in detail.

■ **Vitamin A** (*fat soluble*)

Vitamin A (retinol) is important for our eyes. It protects their surface, and helps us to see in dim light.

The best source of this vitamin is fish liver oil. We can also get it by eating carrots. The orange substance in carrots (called **carotene**) is turned into vitamin A inside our bodies.

Shortage of vitamin A makes it hard to see in dim light. This is known as **night blindness**. Severe lack of it causes the cornea to become thick and dry, a condition called **xerophthalmia**. In extreme cases this can lead to total blindness.

■ **The B vitamins** (*water soluble*)

This group of vitamins helps our cells to transfer energy in respiration.

The first B vitamin to be discovered was **nicotinic acid**, or **niacin** for short. There is plenty of it in liver, meat and fish. Lack of it results in a disease called **pellagra** (picture 4).

One of the most important B vitamins is **vitamin B1 (thiamine)**. It occurs in yeast and cereals. Lack of it causes a disease called **beri-beri**. This is an African word meaning 'I cannot'. The muscles become very weak, and in the end the person becomes paralysed and dies.

There is a lot of vitamin B1 in rice; it is in the husk, the tough coat surrounding the grain. When rice is prepared, the husk is usually stripped off and the grain is polished. This removes the vitamin. Beri-beri is therefore common in parts of the world where people live on polished rice.

Another important B vitamin is **vitamin B2 (riboflavin)**. It is found particularly in leafy vegetables, eggs and fish. Lack of it causes sores round the mouth, and poor growth.

■ **Vitamin C** (*water soluble*)

In the 1740s Admiral Anson led a fleet into the Pacific to fight the Spanish. During the voyage, 626 of his 961 men died of a disease called **scurvy**. In this disease, bleeding occurs in various parts of the body, particularly the gums (picture 5 on next page).

Scurvy is caused by lack of **vitamin C (ascorbic acid)**. This vitamin keeps the delicate lining of the mouth cavity and other body surfaces in a healthy state. It is abundant in green vegetables such as spinach, and citrus fruits such as lemons and limes. If people eat this kind of food, they will not get scurvy. In the 1800s British naval ships always carried a supply of lemons or limes to combat scurvy. This is why British sailors were called 'limeys'.

One snag about vitamin C is that it is destroyed by heating. As a result, a lot of it can be lost during cooking, and while the food is being kept hot afterwards. In restaurants and canteens, where food is kept hot for a long time, over ninety per cent of the vitamin may be lost.

Picture 3 The two rats at the top were fed on a full diet including vitamins. The two rats at the bottom were given a full diet minus vitamins.

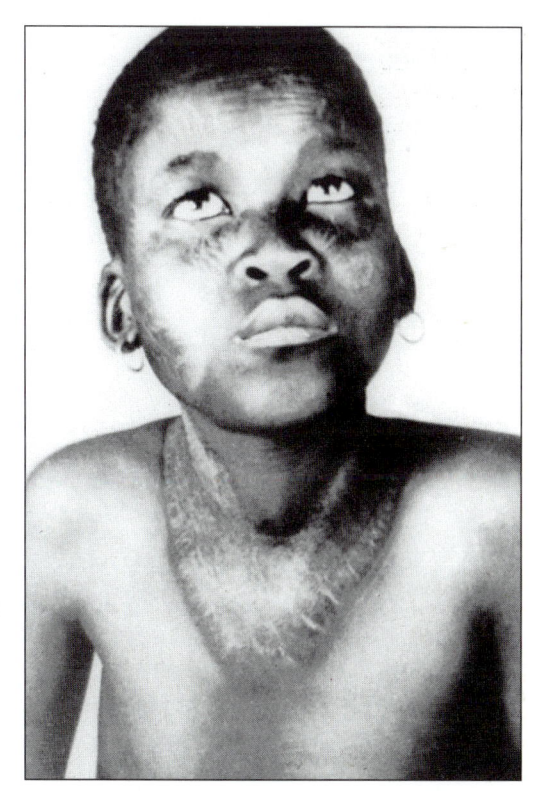

Picture 4 This boy is suffering from pellagra, caused by lack of the vitamin niacin (nicotinic acid). Notice the marks on his neck, shaped like a necklace. This is a characteristic feature of the disease.

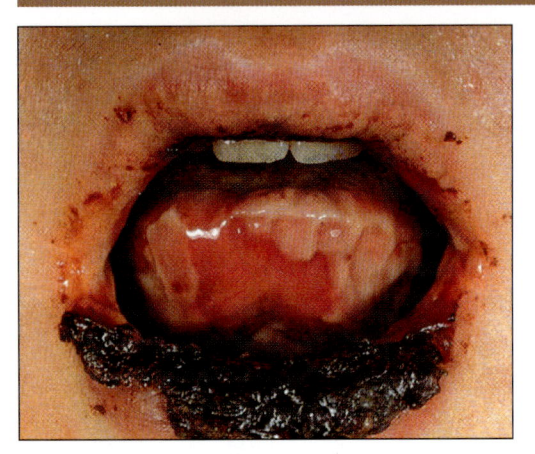

Picture 5 Lack of vitamin C causes scurvy, which is characterised by bleeding gums. Vitamin C helps our cells to stick together. When we don't get enough of it, the cells come apart.

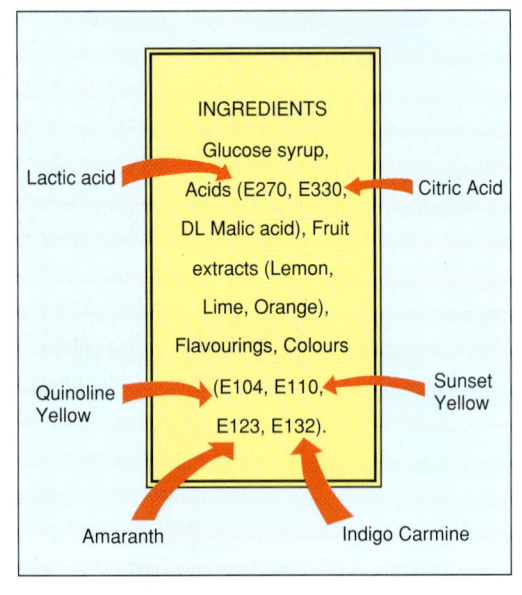

Picture 6 The additives in a packet of boiled sweets. Lactic acid and citric acid are both naturally occurring substances which are produced commercially by fermentation with microbes. They help to preserve food. In addition, citric acid enhances flavour and provides Vitamin C which is an anti-oxidant. Quinoline Yellow, Sunset Yellow, Amaranth and Indigo Carmine are all synthetic dyes which colour food in various ways. Certain people are allergic to these dyes, and some dyes may trigger hyperactivity in children.

■ **Vitamin D** (*fat soluble*)

We saw earlier that as a child grows, its bones become hard by taking up calcium salts. For this to happen **vitamin D** (**calciferol**) is needed. A child who does not get enough vitamin D will develop rickets, the same disease that occurs if there is not enough calcium in the diet.

Vitamin D occurs in fish liver oil. A certain amount of vitamin D can be made by the body itself. It is made in the skin provided sunlight is present. In a sunny climate an adult can get all the necessary vitamin D this way.

Vitamin deficiency in the modern world

Years ago vitamin deficiency diseases were very common, even in countries like Britain. Nowadays they are common only in poorer parts of the world. But even in rich countries they occur from time to time. Those at risk include pregnant women, old people living alone, and people who prefer not to eat certain kinds of food. It is a good idea for such people to take **vitamin tablets**.

Can you have too much of a vitamin? The answer is yes in some cases. However, it is unlikely to result from our food. It is more likely to result from taking too many vitamin tablets. For example, large doses of vitamin D can cause tissues other than the bones to become calcified – the liver for instance.

Vegetarians

Vegetarians eat plant food, but not meat. Their diet includes animal products such as milk and eggs, but not the animals themselves. Strict vegetarians, known as **vegans**, don't even eat animal products.

A vegetarian diet that includes dairy products can provide everything needed for a healthy life. Plants can provide lots of fibre, vitamins and polyunsaturated fat, so a vegetarian diet is good in that respect.

Vegans have to make sure that their food gives them all the substances they need. In general their diet needs to be bulky and varied. This will ensure that they get enough carbohydrate and protein, together with the full range of vitamins and essential amino acids.

Food additives

Nowadays all sorts of food additives, natural and synthetic, are added to food by the manufacturers. Some sweeten, flavour or colour the food. Others (**preservatives**) increase its shelf life by checking the growth of microbes. **Emulsifiers** and **stabilisers** give the food the right consistency, perhaps thickening it or making it into a jelly. **Anti-oxidants** prevent oxidation of substances in the food when exposed to air; oxidation makes fats and oils go rancid, and fruit such as apples and bananas turn brown when cut.

Some people are allergic to certain additives, and in rare cases children may become over-active because of them. Such additives include the colourings tartrazine and sunset yellow. Another additive which may cause problems is monosodium glutamate. This occurs naturally in a Japanese seaweed, but is made commercially from sugar beet and wheat gluten. It is used to flavour meat products. It gives some people headaches and nausea. More serious are artificial sweeteners called cyclamates. They can damage our chromosomes, and have now been banned.

Food additives have had bad publicity, and more and more foods are appearing in the shops that are additive-free. However, it is only fair to point out that some people are allergic to *natural* foods too (see page 149). If the public wants foods that look and taste nice, and can be kept for a reasonable time, then additives have to be used. It is the manufacturers' responsibility to carry out all the necessary safety tests beforehand.

All packaged foods and drinks in European Union countries are required to display a full list of additives, either by name or 'E number'. This enables shoppers to know exactly what they are buying (picture 6).

Activities

A Testing foods for glucose
(Practical technique 9)

You can do this by carrying out the following test. Try it on orange juice, banana, bread, milk, egg white, butter or margarine, a breakfast cereal, baby food and other foods of your own choice.

1. If the food is not already in liquid form, mash it up with a pestle and mortar, and add a little water to make a suspension.
2. Pour about 2 cm³ of the food into a test tube.
3. Add about 2 cm³ of Benedict's solution to the test tube, and shake.
4. *Wear eye protection.* Boil some water in a beaker over a bunsen burner.

EYE PROTECTION MUST BE WORN

5. Put the test tube in the beaker of boiling water, and leave it there for a minute or two.

If a precipitate develops, glucose is present. (The precipitate is usually orange.)

B Testing food for vitamin C

1. Obtain a lemon, and squeeze some of its juice into a beaker.
2. Pipette one drop of blue DCPIP solution onto a white tile. (DCPIP is short for 2,6-dichlorophenol indophenol.)
3. With a pipette or syringe add lemon juice to the DCPIP solution, drop by drop, and stir with a needle.

Count how many drops of lemon are needed to make the DCPIP solution turn colourless.

The disappearance of the blue colour tells us that vitamin C is present in the lemon juice.

4. Use this test to compare the vitamin C content of different foods. In each case get some juice out of the food. Then find out how many drops of the juice are needed to decolourise one drop of DCPIP solution.

Do you think this is an accurate way of comparing the vitamin C content of different foods?

How could you make the experiment more accurate?

Why can't this test be done with blackcurrant juice?

5. *Wear eye protection.* Boil some lemon juice in a test tube. Then test it for vitamin C with DCPIP solution.

EYE PROTECTION MUST BE WORN

What effect does boiling have on vitamin C?

6. Investigate other factors that may affect the vitamin C content of juice.

Different types of carbohydrates

- **Monosaccharides** consist of single glucose (or glucose-like) molecules on their own. Glucose itself is an example. So is fructose (fruit sugar).
- **Disaccharides** consist of two glucose (or glucose-like) molecules linked together, e.g. sucrose (cane sugar), maltose (malt sugar) and lactose (milk sugar).
- **Polysaccharides** consist of many glucose molecules linked together, e.g. starch, glycogen and cellulose.

Questions

1. Each of the diseases in the left-hand column is caused by lack of one or more of the substances in the right-hand column. Which causes which?

night blindness	iron
rickets	vitamin A
anaemia	calcium
goitre	vitamin D
xerophthalmia	iodine

2. Explain the reasons for each of the following statements.
   a. Carrots are good for you.
   b. A person who has been sun-bathing all day eats a salt tablet.
   c. Old people who live alone tend to get scurvy towards the end of the winter.

3. This question is about the diet of a growing child.
   a. Suggest *four* particularly important nutrients which should be included in the diet. In each case give an example of a food which contains a lot of the nutrient, and explain why the nutrient is so important.
   b. Suggest *two* nutrients which should be left out of the diet. In each case give an example of a food which contains a lot of the nutrient, and explain why it should be avoided.

4. Describe an experiment which could be done to find out if the husk surrounding the rice seed contains a substance which prevents beri-beri.

5. Scientists carried out an experiment to find the effect of cooking a finely shredded cabbage on the amount of vitamin C in it. They put the cabbage in boiling water and boiled it for 10 minutes. They found the vitamin C content at intervals, expressing it as a percentage of the amount in the uncooked cabbage.

   Here are the results.

Time after putting the cabbage in the water	Vitamin C content
0 min	100%
1/2 min	66%
1 min	55%
4 min	49%
7 min	43%
10 min	37%

   a. Plot these results on graph paper.
   b. Suggest reasons why the vitamin C content of the cabbage falls.
   c. What experiments could you do to test your suggestions?
   d. What advice would you give to a chef about cooking vegetables?

6. Make a list of all the advantages of being a vegetarian that you can think of. Include advantages to society as well as to the individual. What precautions should you take if you are a vegan, and why?

D3
How we digest our food

What will happen to this hamburger after Rachel has put it in her mouth?

Picture 1 Taking the Big Bite, the start of digestion.

Some facts and figures about the gut

The human gut is about 9 metres long altogether, over four times a person's height. This is short compared with a cow, whose gut may exceed 50 metres.

The human small intestine is about 6 metres long, and the large intestine 1.5 metres. The small intestine is narrower than the large intestine, which is why it is described as 'small'.

The human stomach has a volume of 1 to 1.5 litres. However, the stomach wall is very elastic, allowing its volume to increase by three times or more during a large meal. Compare this with the rumen of a cow which has a volume of 20 litres.

A person produces 1 to 1.5 litres of saliva daily. This is small compared with a cow which can produce as much as 190 litres in a day.

The gut

The mouth leads into the **gut**. The gut is really a tube which runs from the mouth to the anus. It is between eight and nine metres long – that's about four times Rachel's height. Being so long, most of it is coiled up. This enables it to fit neatly into the **abdomen**.

The gut isn't a simple tube. It consists of a series of parts, each with a particular job to do. The parts of the gut are shown in picture 2.

What happens in the gut?

Let's look at the basic principles before we get down to details. A hamburger contains starch, fat and protein. The protein and fat are mainly in the meat, and the starch is in the bun.

After the hamburger has been taken into the mouth (**ingested**), it is chewed and swallowed. As the bits of hamburger pass along the gut, the large insoluble molecules, like starch, fat and protein, are broken down into small soluble molecules. This process is called **digestion**. The soluble substances are then **absorbed** through the lining of the gut into the bloodstream. They are then carried round the body to where they are needed.

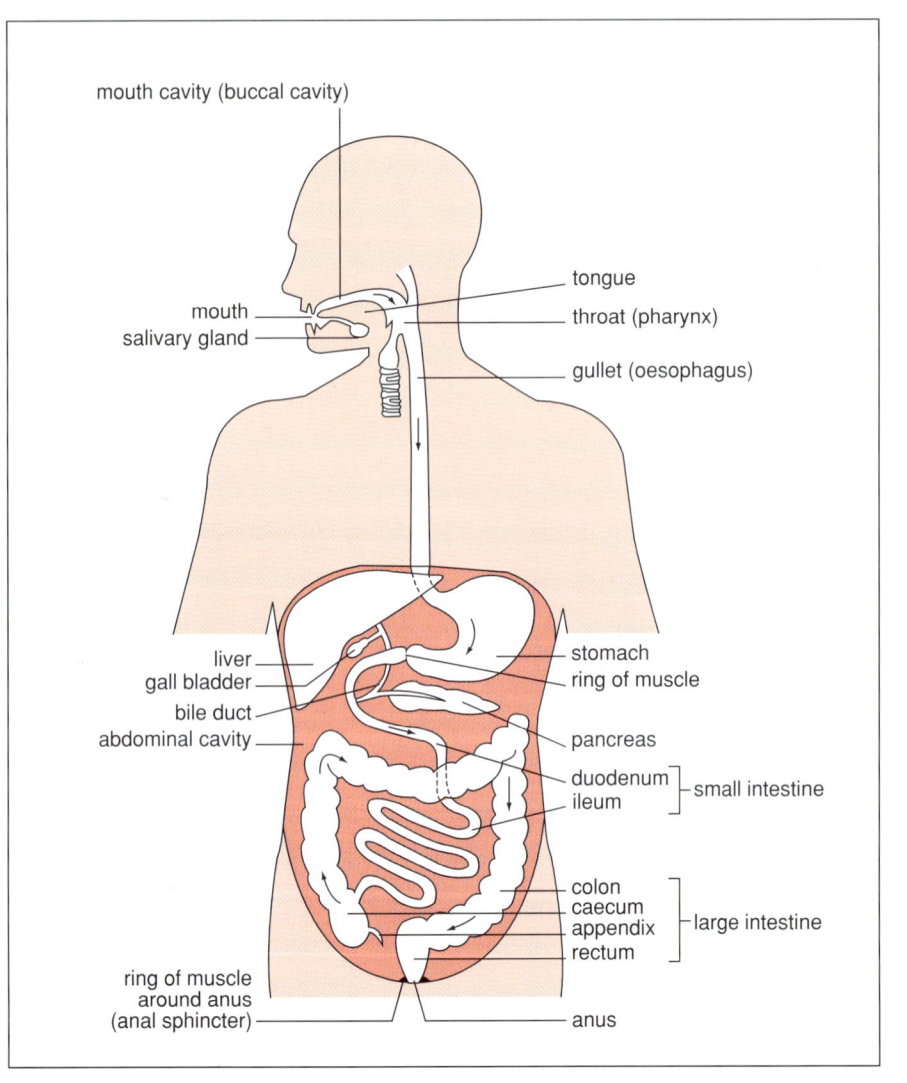

Picture 2 This diagram shows the main parts of the human gut and the organs connected to it. The arrows show the course taken by the food as it moves along the gut.

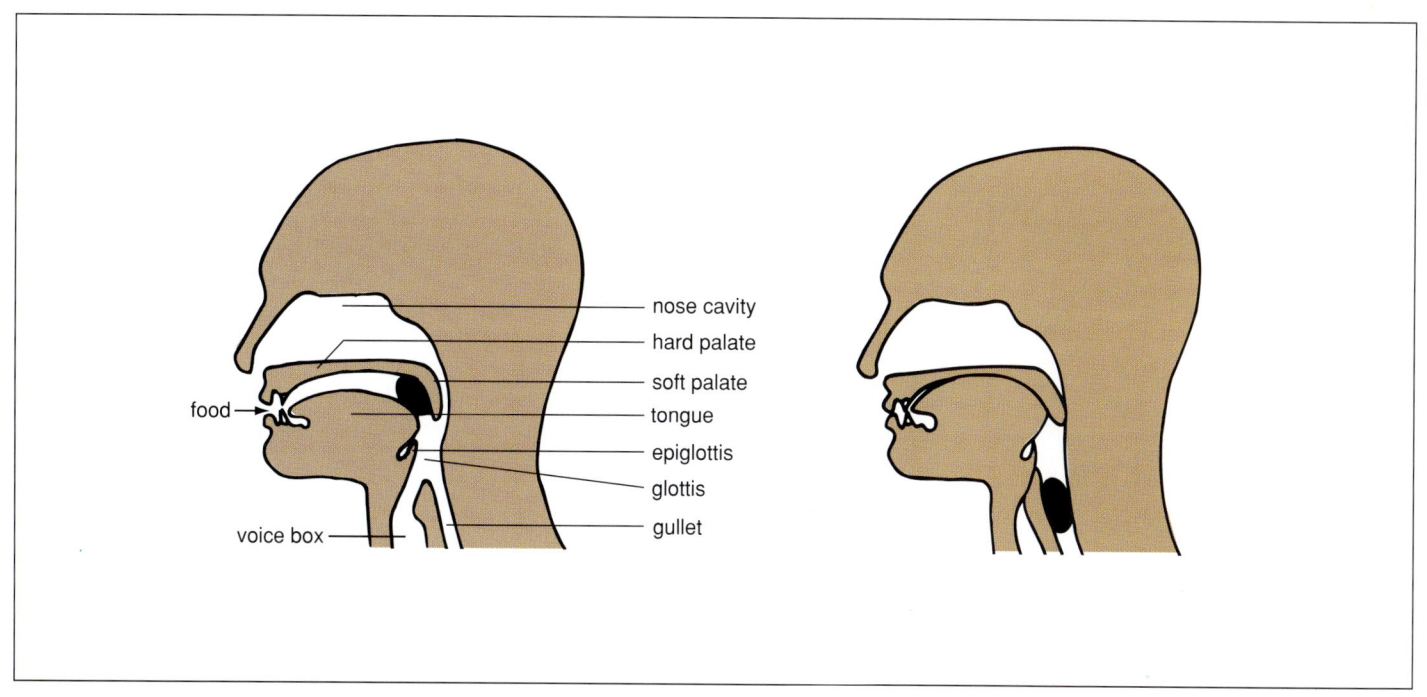

How does digestion take place?

Digestion is brought about by **digestive enzymes** (see page 120). There are several types, and each acts on a particular substance in the food. Thus **carbohydrases** act on carbohydrates such as starch, **lipases** on fat and **proteases** on proteins.

Digestion is helped by **chewing**. Chewing breaks the food into small pieces, increasing the surface area over which the enzymes can act.

Now let's look in more detail at what happens in each part of the gut. The enzymes are summarised in table 1 on the next page.

In the mouth cavity

When you take some food into your mouth, your mouth waters – it becomes full of **saliva**. Saliva is produced by **salivary glands** which are connected to the mouth cavity by ducts.

Actually your mouth starts watering before you eat. Salivating is a reflex which is triggered by the sight, smell and even the thought of food. (Reflexes are explained on page 160.)

Saliva contains an enzyme called **amylase**. This acts on starch, breaking it down into malt sugar (maltose).

Saliva also contains a slimy substance called **mucus**. This serves as a lubricant, enabling the food to slip easily through the throat when it's swallowed.

Saliva also contains an enzyme called **lysozyme** which kills bacteria.

Through the throat and down the gullet

Swallowing is a reflex which happens without you having to think about it. When you swallow, the food is pushed down your throat by the back of your tongue. At the same time the glottis is closed off, so the food is prevented from going down the wrong way (picture 3).

If food does try to enter the glottis, you cough and this dislodges it. Coughing is a reflex, triggered by irritation of the sensitive epithelium in that region.

Once swallowed, the food passes down the gullet to the stomach. The gullet has muscle tissue in its wall. A ring of muscular contraction moves slowly downwards, pushing the food in front of it. This process is called **peristalsis** (picture 4). Mucus acts as a lubricant, enabling the food to slip down easily.

Picture 3 How swallowing takes place. The black blob is a lump of food. Swallowing is a reflex. When you swallow, the nose cavity and glottis are closed off, as shown in the right-hand diagram, so food is prevented from going the wrong way. Notice how this closing off takes place. The soft palate moves back and presses against the back of the throat, and the front of the gullet moves up and presses against the epiglottis.

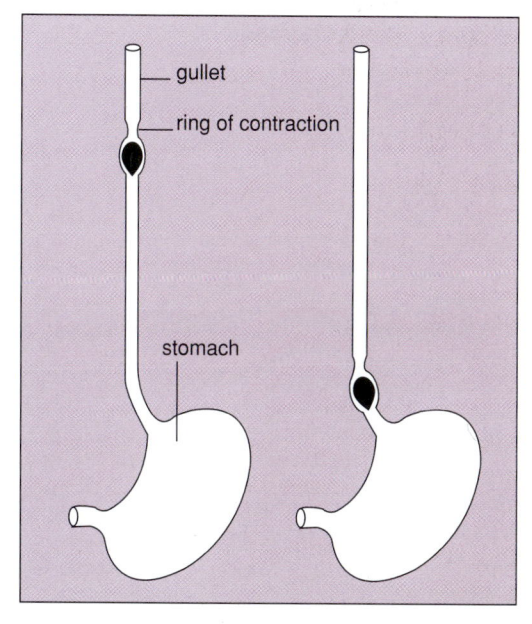

Picture 4 Food passes down the gullet by a ring of contraction which moves downwards sweeping the food before it. This is called peristalsis.

In the stomach

The wall of the stomach is thick and muscular, and it contains lots of tiny **gastric glands**, about 35 million altogether. The gastric glands produce a fluid called **gastric juice**. This contains an enzyme called **pepsin** which breaks down protein into simpler substances called polypeptides.

Pepsin works best in acid conditions. For this reason gastric juice contains **hydrochloric acid**. The acid also helps to kill germs that happen to get into the stomach. The wall of the stomach produces lots of mucus which protects the stomach lining from being damaged by the acid.

Food spends three or four hours in the stomach. Every now and again the stomach wall contracts, churning up the food and turning it into a mushy fluid. This mixes together the food with the digestive juices.

Between the stomach and small intestine there is a ring of muscle. This is tightly shut most of the time, but every now and again it opens. At the same time a wave of contraction passes along the stomach and sweeps some of the food into the small intestine. If there is anything wrong with the food, violent contractions occur in the other direction. As a result the contents of the stomach are shot up the gullet and out through the mouth. This is **vomiting** and it is a useful way of getting rid of germs and poisons.

The stomach of calves contains an enzyme called **rennin**. Rennin solidifies milk protein, which is then broken down by pepsin. If it was not solidified first, milk would pass through the stomach so quickly that digestion would not have time to take place.

In the small intestine

Despite its name, the small intestine is the longest part of the gut – it may be over six metres in length.

The small intestine has enzymes which continue the work already started in the stomach. There is more amylase to break down starch, and an enzyme called **trypsin** acts on protein. Other enzymes then complete the digestion of the hamburger: **maltase** turns maltose into glucose, **lipase** turns fat into fatty acids and glycerol, and **peptidases** turn polypeptides into amino acids. And if Rachel had been daft enough to sprinkle sugar on her hamburger, this would have been broken down in her small intestine by an enzyme called **sucrase**.

All the new substances formed by the action of these enzymes are soluble and can be absorbed through the lining of the intestine into the bloodstream. More about this in a moment.

Some of these enzymes are produced by the wall of the small intestine itself. Others are produced by the **pancreas** from which they flow down a duct into the small intestine. The pancreas also produces sodium hydrogencarbonate which neutralises the acid from the stomach. This is necessary because the enzymes in the small intestine will only work properly in alkaline conditions.

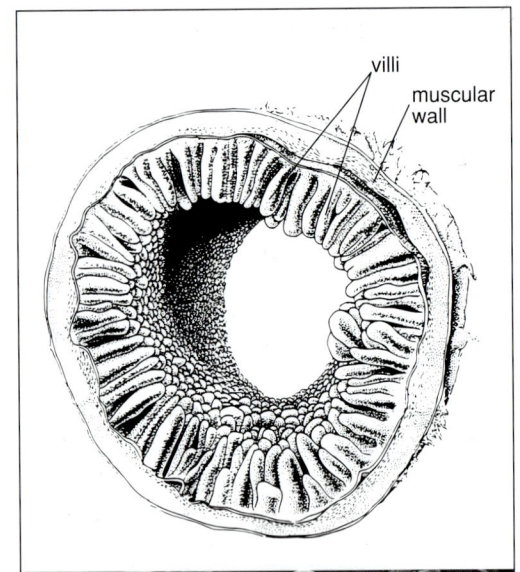

Picture 5 Looking into the small intestine. Notice the finger-like villi projecting into the cavity. The bottom picture, taken with a scanning electron microscope, shows the villi in surface view. There are 4–5 million villi in the human gut.

Table 1 The main enzymes found in the human gut. Bile salts are also included although they are not enzymes and don't alter the food chemically. In the case of some substances, digestion starts in the small intestine and is finished off inside the surface layer of cells.

Where it comes from	Where it works	Name of enzyme	Food acted on (substrate)	Substances produced (product)
salivary glands	mouth cavity	amylase	starch	maltose
stomach wall	stomach	pepsin	protein	polypeptides
liver	small intestine	bile salts (not enzymes)	fat	fat droplets
pancreas	small intestine	amylase trypsin lipase	starch protein fat	maltose polypeptides fatty acids and glycerol	can be absorbed into blood
wall of small intestine	small intestine	maltase sucrase peptidases	maltose sucrose polypeptides	glucose glucose and fructose amino acids

The part played by the liver

The liver produces a fluid called **bile**. Bile is stored in the gall bladder and after a meal it is squirted, bit by bit, into the small intestine.

Bile contains substances called **bile salts**. These act on fat, breaking it up into very small droplets. The same thing happens when washing-up liquid comes into contact with fat – the process is called **emulsification**. Emulsification helps the digestion of fat by increasing the surface area on which the enzyme lipase can act.

The hamburger is now more or less completely digested and the soluble products are ready to be absorbed.

Absorption

The inner surface of the small intestine has many finger-like projections called **villi** (singular **villus**). The villi greatly increase the surface area for absorption (picture 5).

The wall of the small intestine has a very good blood supply (pictures 6 and 7). The villi contain blood and lymph capillaries into which the digested food substances are absorbed. Muscle tissue in the wall enables the intestine to contract, squeezing the contents this way and that, and strands of muscle in the villi enable them to wave about. As a result the contents of the small intestine are constantly brought into contact with the lining.

Recent research suggests that the final step in the digestion of carbohydrates and proteins takes place inside the cells lining the villi.

Every now and again a ring of contraction passes along the small intestine, sweeping the contents towards the large intestine.

In the large intestine

The hamburger came with a piece of lettuce which contains cellulose. Humans don't have an enzyme for breaking down cellulose, so it can't be digested. Along with any other indigestible matter (**fibre**), it passes on to the colon, the first part of the large intestine.

As material moves along the colon, water is absorbed from it. As a result it becomes more and more solid. The solid matter moves on to the rectum where it is stored as **faeces**. The lining of the rectum produces mucus which acts as a lubricant and eases the passage of the faeces.

Eventually the faeces are eliminated through the anus. This is a reflex, triggered by the build-up of pressure in the rectum. The ring of muscle surrounding the anus opens up, and the wall of the rectum contracts forcing the faeces out. The polite word for this is **defaecation**.

Normally it takes between 24 and 48 hours from when the food is eaten to when the faeces are ready to be expelled through the anus. To keep up this sort of time scale, it is a good idea to eat plenty of fibre (see page 78). This stretches the wall of the large intestine, inducing it to contract. In this way the contents are kept on the move.

The caecum and appendix

The caecum and appendix are an offshoot from the large intestine, a kind of cul-de-sac or blind alley. They have no function in the human, but in grass-eating mammals such as rabbits they contain large numbers of helpful bacteria which can digest cellulose and break it down into glucose.

In humans the appendix sometimes gets infected with harmful bacteria. As the appendix sticks out from the intestine, the bacteria don't get flushed out by the normal passage of material along the gut. So they multiply there, and may cause severe inflammation leading to **appendicitis**. Normally appendicitis is cured by removing the appendix in an operation.

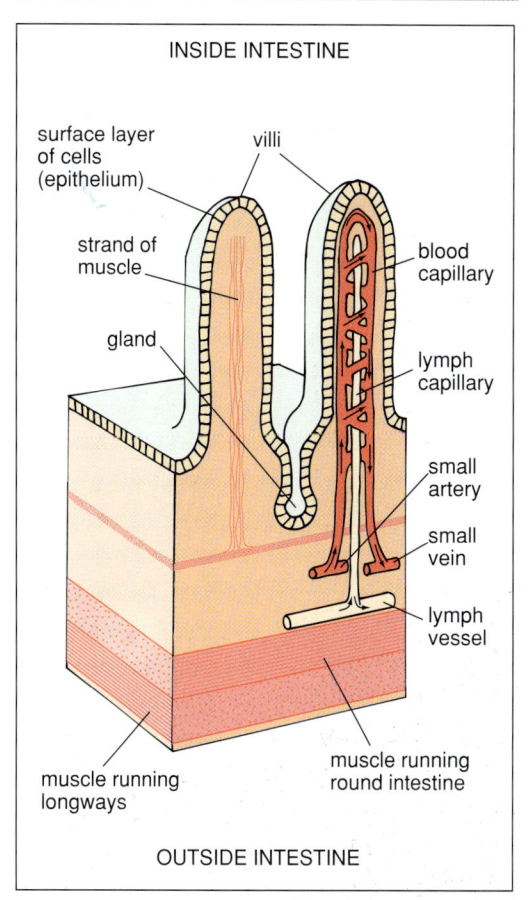

Picture 6 Diagram of the wall of the small intestine showing two villi in detail. Some of the fat we eat is absorbed into the lymph capillaries. Other digestive products are absorbed into the blood capillaries. The capillaries have been omitted from the left-hand villus so as to show the muscle.

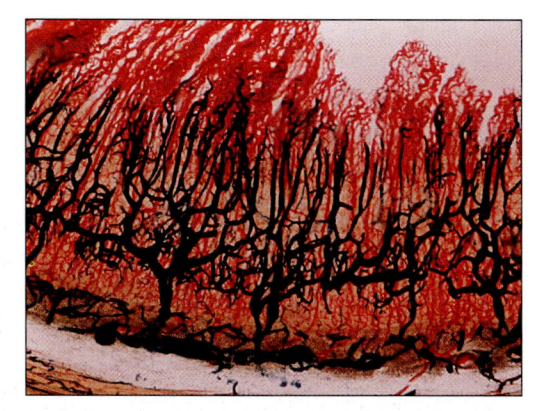

Picture 7 Part of the wall of the small intestine as seen under the microscope. The blood vessels have been injected with a dye so as to show them up. The arteries are red and the veins black.

90 Animal survival

Different teeth for different jobs

As we have seen on page 87, chewing starts the digestion process by breaking up the food into smaller lumps. This helps animals to swallow their food and also allows the digestive enzymes to get at the food more easily. However, the shape, number and arrangement of the teeth of different animals depends on what they eat.

Carnivores, like lions and tigers, have teeth which are designed to kill prey like zebra, and then tear it apart. Once caught, strong jaw muscles ensure a firm grip over the prey's windpipe. The zebra is suffocated.

Picture 1 shows the structure of a carnivore's jaw. The large **canine teeth** are the most obvious feature. They are like large daggers and are used to kill prey and rip flesh. The large **premolars** and **molars** can slide past each other and are able to slice and scrape flesh off bones, and the teeth at the back of the jaw can crush hard material such as bone. The small **incisors** grip and pull off small bits of food.

Herbivores like sheep have blunt incisors for cropping grass. Picture 2 shows the structure of a herbivore's jaw. There is a hard pad on the upper jaw which acts like a chopping board.

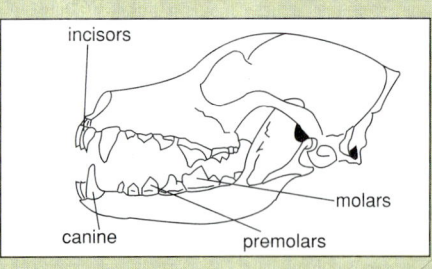

Picture 1 A carnivore's jaw.

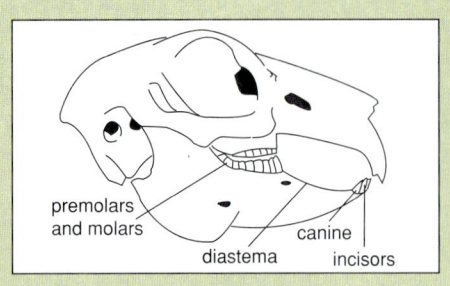

Picture 2 A herbivore's jaw.

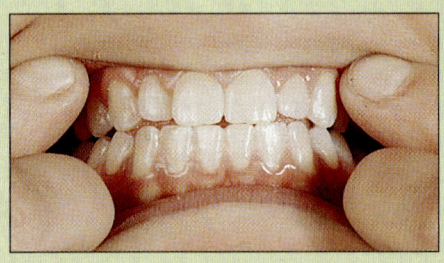

Picture 3 Human teeth.

In rabbits the incisor teeth are sharper for cutting grass. A gap in the mouth cavity provides a space for the tongue to move the food from the back to the front. The gap is called the **diastema**.

The remainder of the teeth in herbivores are generally flattened but with hard enamel ridges. As the jaw moves from side to side, as well as up and down, the grass is ground down on the ridges before being swallowed. However, the ridges on the teeth of some herbivores, such as the rhinoceros, mean that the jaw must move backwards and forwards to obtain the best grinding action.

Humans are omnivores, eating both plant and animal material. Picture 3 shows the arrangement of teeth in a human mouth.

Incisors are chisel shaped and are used to cut food. Canines are like small daggers and are also used to cut food. Premolars and molars have broad tops with bumpy surfaces and are used for grinding. The teeth are not specialised for either a carnivorous or a herbivorous diet. Because of our varied diet our teeth are required to cope with a large range of food types. Cooking food helps to make it less tough and therefore more easily broken down by our non-specialised teeth.

Questions

1 Why is the human intestine coiled rather than straight?

2 Which part of the human gut:
   a absorbs water from indigestible material,
   b contains the enzyme pepsin,
   c is normally acidic,
   d receives bile from the bile duct?

3 Explain each of the following:
   a If you chew a piece of bread for long enough, it eventually begins to taste sweet.
   b When you swallow a piece of food, the food normally does not go up into the nose cavity.

4 There is a disease of cattle in which the villi in the small intestine are destroyed and the inner lining of the small intestine becomes smooth. As a result the animal gets weak and wastes away. Why do you think the disease has this effect?

5 It has been suggested that saliva produced during a meal digests starch faster than saliva produced before the meal. Describe an experiment which could be done to find out if this is true.

6 The diagram on the right shows an experiment which is intended to show what happens in the human gut.

After being set up, glucose, but not starch, passes out of the bag into the surrounding water.

   a How could you show that glucose has leaked out, but starch has not?
   b How would you explain this result?
   c To what extent is this similar to what happens in the human gut?

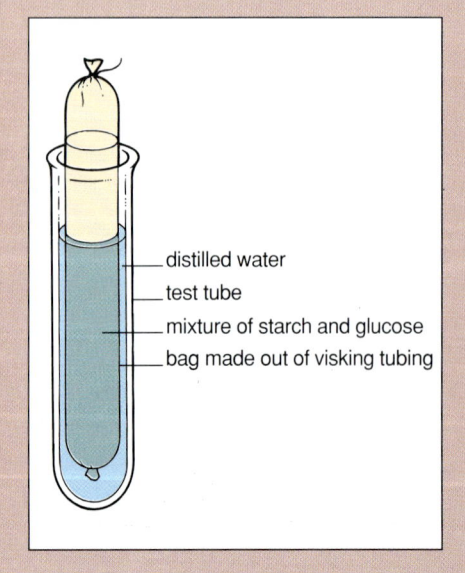

Constipation

The record time for constipation is claimed to be 102 days! Most people suffer from constipation at one time or another, but not for that long. It is caused by indigestible matter moving too slowly along the large intestine. The result is that more water is absorbed than usual, and the faeces become hard and dry.

Constipation can be caused by bad bowel habits. People usually feel the urge to defaecate after a meal, generally breakfast: this is a natural reflex arising from the stretching of the gut wall. If you keep suppressing this reflex, the faeces are held in the intestine and you may become constipated.

We can help to prevent constipation by eating foods which contain plenty of fibre, such as wholemeal bread and fresh fruit (see page 78). Fibre can't be digested so it adds to the bulk of material in the large intestine, stretching its wall. This stimulates the muscle tissue in the wall to contract, pushing the faeces along and keeping them moving.

1 Some people think that you should get into the habit of defaecating at a regular time each day. Others feel that you should defaecate only when you need to. What do you think?

2 People who have a mainly vegetarian diet defaecate more often than people who eat a lot of animal food. Why do you think this is?

3 A person who is constipated a lot is more likely to get cancer of the bowel than a person who defaecates regularly. Suggest reasons for this.

Seeing your own gut

Spread out your hands and place them on your abdomen. Immediately beneath your hands is your stomach and intestine, approximately eight metres of it. So near, and yet you can't see any of it. Is there any way a doctor can see it without cutting you open?

Yes there is, and it's done with **X-rays**. As you know X-rays are used to take pictures of our bones. A machine sends a beam of X-rays through the body; the X-rays do not pass easily through the solid bones. On the other side of the person there is a photographic film which, when exposed to the X-rays, goes dark everywhere except where the bones are.

Unlike bones, the gut lets X-rays through so it doesn't show up in X-ray pictures. How, then, can we see it? The answer is to get the person to drink a fluid which won't let X-rays through. The fluid fills the stomach and intestine, so when the person is X-rayed these parts of the gut show up clearly. The substance used is barium sulphate. It is taken as a thick suspension and is called a **barium meal** (picture 1).

A doctor may use this technique to find out if there's something wrong with a patient's gut. For example, a stomach ulcer will show up in an X-ray picture as an irregularity in the lining of the stomach. In hospitals X-ray pictures are taken by a specially trained person called a **radiographer**. Nowadays, continuous pictures are obtained on a television screen.

Another way of seeing the gut is to push a flexible tube, and a light, down the patient's throat into the stomach or small intestine. The doctor then looks through the tube at the lining of the gut (picture 2). This can help to confirm a diagnosis which has been made from X-ray pictures.

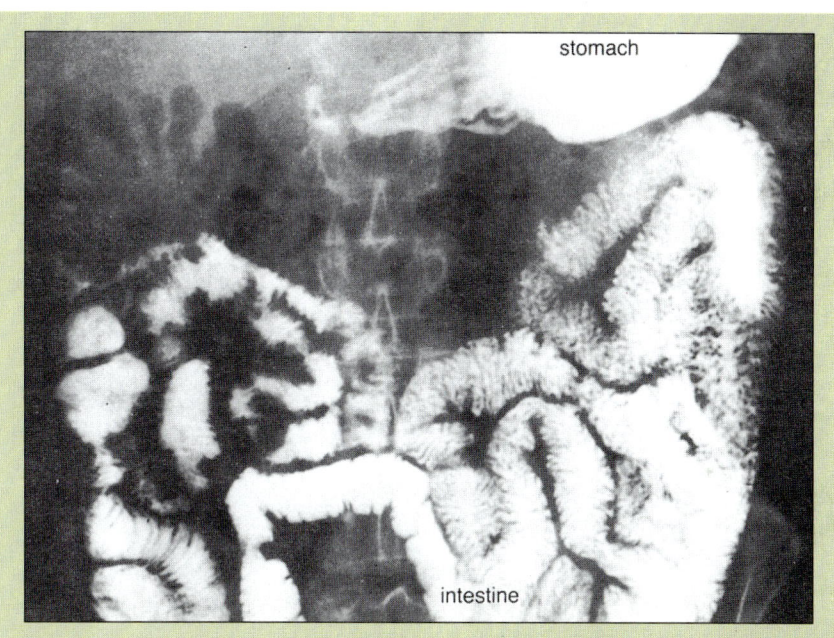

Picture 1 An X-ray photograph of the human gut taken after the patient had been given a barium meal.

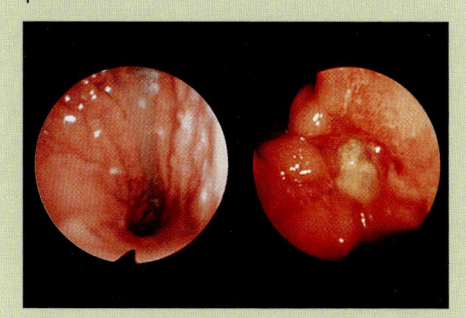

Picture 2 The lining of the stomach seen through a tube. Left: a healthy stomach. Right: a stomach ulcer.

1 Explain the meanings of the following words used in the passage:

(a) small intestine, (b) suspension, (c) irregularity, (d) radiographer.

2 Patients who are to have a barium meal are usually asked not to eat anything for about six hours beforehand. Why?

3 In picture 1 there appears to be no connection between the stomach and intestine. Suggest two possible reasons for this.

4 The tube which is used for examining a patient's stomach enables the doctor to actually see the lining of the stomach. How do you think it works?

D4
From egg and sperm to embryo

Here we shall look at the way an embryo is formed in the human.

Picture 1 Human reproduction brings delight to parents and it keeps the species going.

Picture 2 The reproductive system of the human female. The bladder is not shown.

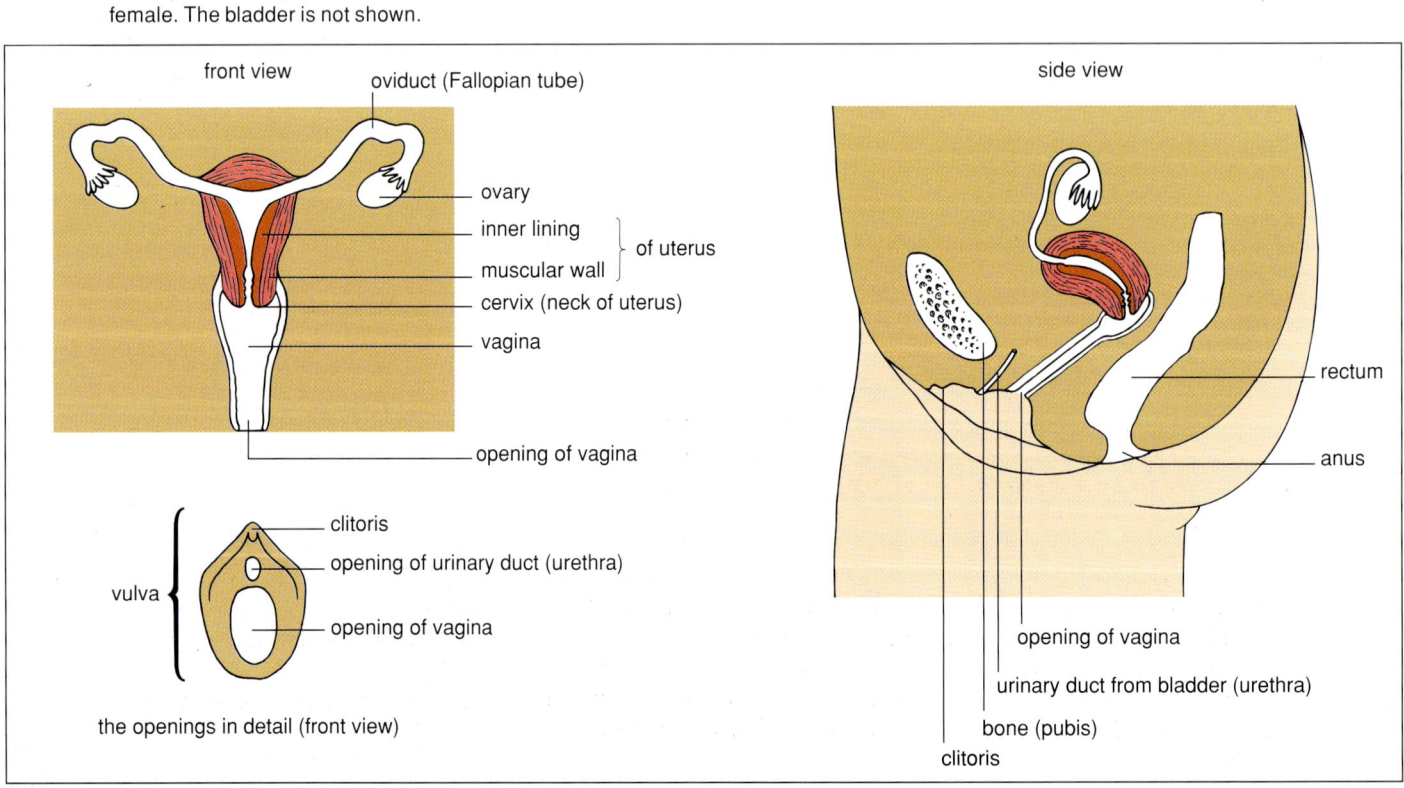

The human reproductive system

The organs which enable us to reproduce make up the **reproductive system**. The reproductive system does three things:

- It manufactures eggs and sperm. These are our 'sex cells' or **gametes**. The eggs are produced by a pair of **ovaries** in the woman, and the sperm are produced by a pair of **testes** in the man.
- It brings the eggs and sperm together. The combining of a sperm with an egg is called **fertilisation**. It is made possible by the **penis** which transfers sperms from the man to the woman during **mating** (**sexual intercourse**).
- It protects and nourishes the embryo. The organ which does this is the **uterus** or 'womb'. Here the **embryo** develops into the baby.

Keep these functions in mind as we look in detail at the reproductive system (pictures 2 and 3).

The female system

The two ovaries are on either side of the abdomen. Once every 28 days or so, one of the ovaries sheds an egg into the **oviduct**. The oviduct is also known as the **Fallopian tube** after the Italian anatomist, Gabriello Fallopio, who discovered it. The egg passes slowly down the oviduct towards the uterus. If it is not fertilised within a day or so, it will die.

The uterus is like a bag with a thick muscular wall. Its inner lining is very special, because it is here that the embryo develops. We shall have more to say about it later. The lower end of the uterus is called the neck or **cervix**, and it leads to the **vagina**.

In picture 2 you will see that the vagina opens to the outside close to the urinary opening. Just above the urinary opening is a small bump called the **clitoris**.

The external parts of the female genital organs together comprise the **vulva**. At first the vaginal opening is partly covered by a fold of tissue called the **hymen**. This becomes stretched by wearing a tampon or when sexual intercourse takes place.

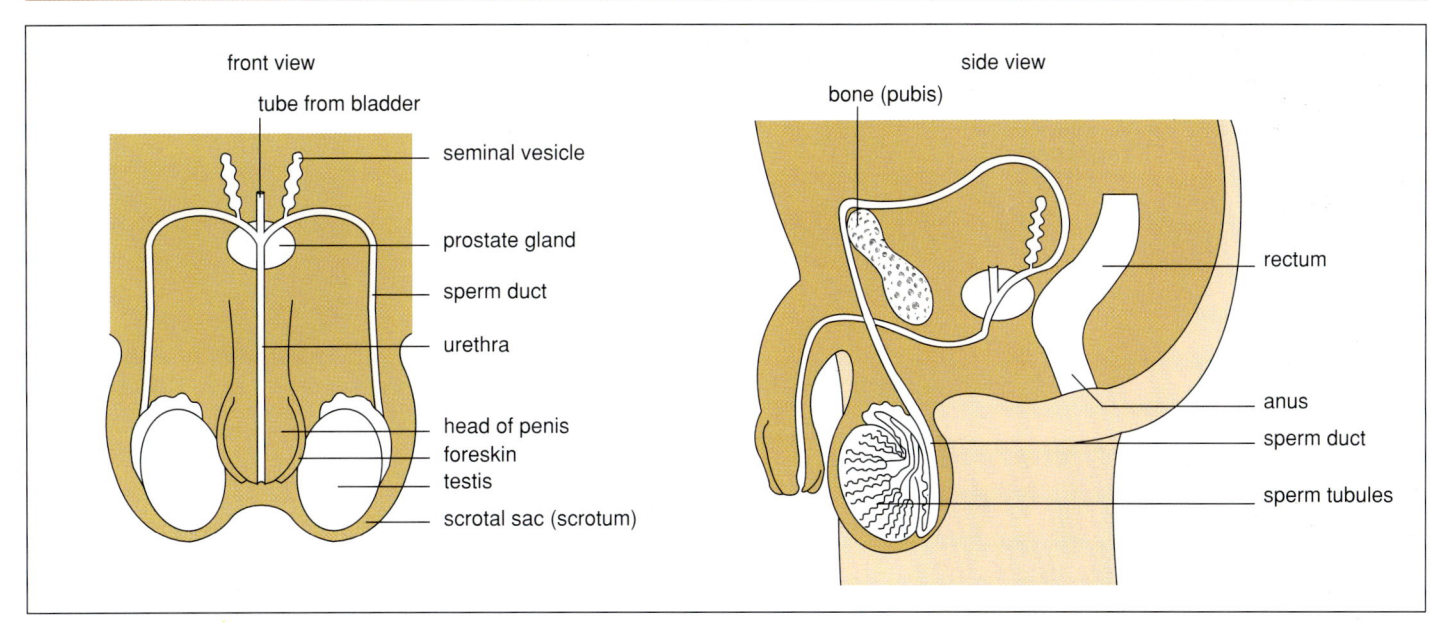

From egg and sperm to embryo 93

Picture 3 The reproductive system of the human male. The bladder is not shown.

The male system

The testes are inside the **scrotal sac** just behind the penis. They are slightly cooler than the rest of the body, because of their position outside the abdomen. This is necessary because the testes make larger numbers of sperm in cool conditions. When a baby boy is developing, the testes start off in the abdomen, but later they move down into the scrotal sac. Normally this happens before, or soon after, birth.

Each testis contains lots of narrow tubules where the sperms are made. Placed end to end, these tubules would stretch for over 500 metres – that's long enough to go right round a football pitch! This gives the testis a high production rate – it is truly a sperm factory.

Sperm are produced all the time, not just once a month like eggs are. As the sperm are produced, they move into a coiled tube alongside the testis where they are stored. This tube leads to the **sperm duct** which in turn leads to the **urethra**. The urethra runs down the centre of the penis. Notice the **seminal vesicles** and **prostate gland** at the top end of the urethra – we shall see what they do in a moment.

The head of the penis is very sensitive and is protected by the **foreskin**. The foreskin is sometimes removed in the simple operation **circumcision**. This may be done for religious reasons (for example, Jews and Muslims usually have it done), or because the foreskin is too tight. The operation is carried out at an early age, and is in no way harmful.

For sperm to leave the body, the penis has to become stiff. This is called an **erection**, and it is brought about by blood being pumped into a special spongy tissue in the penis. Rubbing of the erect penis results in **ejaculation**. Ejaculation is a reflex in which two things happen. Firstly, the seminal vesicles and prostate gland pour fluid into the sperm ducts and urethra. This fluid, together with the sperm, makes up **semen**. At the same time, repeated contractions of the muscles surrounding the sperm ducts and urethra sweep the semen out of the penis.

Ejaculation is accompanied by a pleasurable feeling called an **orgasm**. Women have orgasms too. They are brought about mainly by repeated rubbing of the clitoris which can become erect, rather like the penis.

If you look at picture 3 you will see that the bladder and sperm ducts both open into the urethra. However, urine and semen never pass down the urethra together. This is because it is impossible for urination and ejaculation to occur at the same time.

External fertilisation

In land-living animals, fertilisation is **internal**. The sperm swim in the fluid that lines the internal surfaces of the female's reproductive system.

External fertilisation occurs when the sperm and the egg meet outside the female's body. This method is used by fish and amphibians. The sperm are able to swim to the egg in the water of the pond or river.

Amphibians, which live on land for part of their lives, must return to the water to breed.

In trout, the female uses her tail to make a small hollow in the river bed. The male prods the female and as she releases her eggs, he releases his sperm onto them. The eggs lie in the hollow and, as the sperm are released very soon after the eggs, there is a good chance of fertilisation taking place.

Sticklebacks increase the chances of fertilisation by using a nest of water weeds. A special courtship dance ensures that the male and female coordinate the release of their sex cells. The nest is entered first by the female, who deposits her eggs, then by the male who releases his sperm.

In frogs, the male climbs onto the female's back. As she releases her eggs into the water, he releases a stream of sperm to fertilise them. As soon as the eggs come into contact with the water, the jelly which surrounds them swells into the familiar frog spawn.

1 What are the disadvantages of external fertilisation?

2 Why does a cod produce eight million eggs in a single spawning?

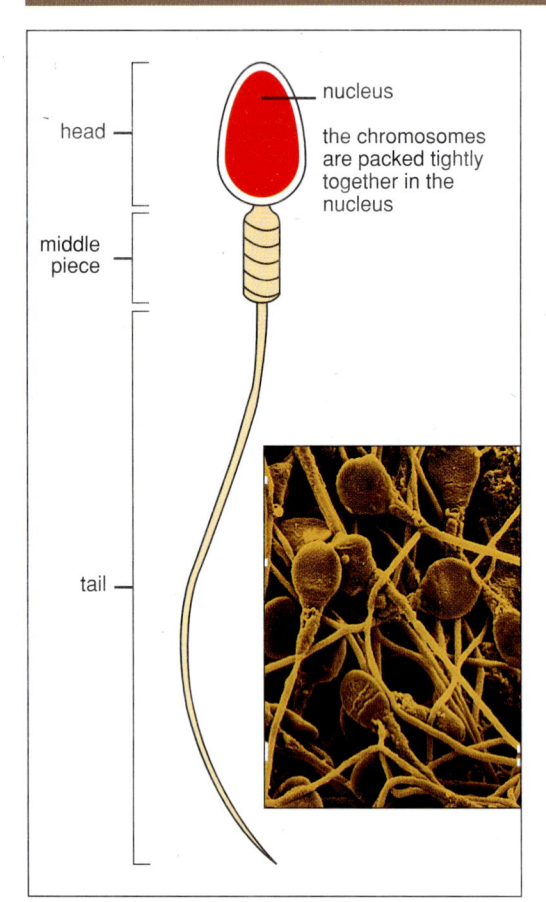

94 Animal survival

Picture 4 Human sperm. The head is about 3 μm wide. The tail lashes from side to side and the energy for this comes from the middle piece. On the right are sperms as seen in an electron microscope.

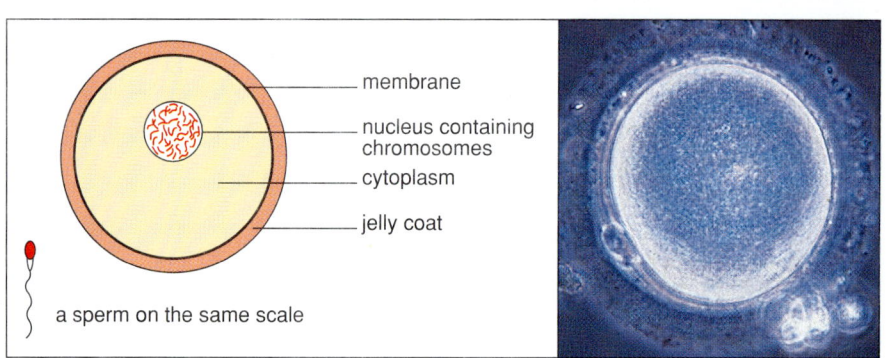

Picture 5 A human egg with a sperm alongside to show their relative sizes. The egg has a diameter of about a tenth of a millimetre. On the right is a human egg as seen under the light microscope.

Eggs and sperm

Normally the male produces about 4 cm³ of semen when he ejaculates – that's a small spoonful. This may not seem much, but it may contain as many as 500 million sperm. They are kept alive and active by substances in the semen.

The sperm are very small, and you need a microscope to see them. One is shown on a large scale in picture 4. It is shaped like a tadpole, with a head and tail. It is a single cell, with the nucleus packed tightly into the head. The sperm swims by waving its tail from side to side.

An egg is shown in picture 5. It too is a single cell, but it is much larger than the sperm. It is round like a ball, and is surrounded by a thin membrane and a layer of jelly. The nucleus is towards the centre.

The nuclei of the sperm and egg contain chromosomes, which carry the genes (see page 118). In the sperm nucleus, the chromosomes are so tightly packed that you can't see them individually. In the egg nucleus they are more spread out.

Sexual intercourse

The erect penis is placed in the vagina, and moved in and out repeatedly. Drops of fluid, secreted by glands lining the urethra, come out of the penis and serve as a lubricant. Mucus in the vagina secreted by the cervix performs the same function.

After ejaculation, the sperm swim through the mucus into the uterus. They then swim the full length of the uterus, and up the oviducts (picture 6).

Picture 6 During sexual intercourse sperm pass from the male to the female, as shown by the arrows in the diagram below. The pictures on the right show fertilisation taking place.

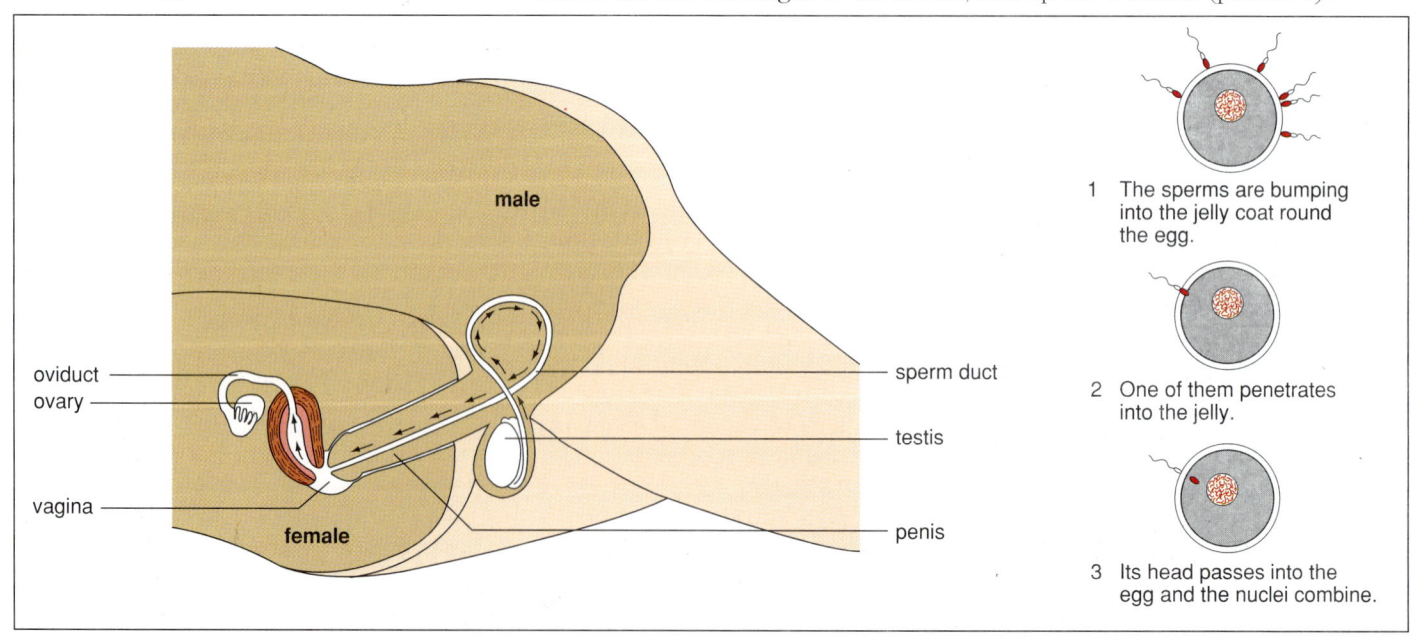

1 The sperms are bumping into the jelly coat round the egg.

2 One of them penetrates into the jelly.

3 Its head passes into the egg and the nuclei combine.

From egg and sperm to embryo **95**

Picture 7 After the egg has been fertilised it divides repeatedly to form a little ball of cells which becomes implanted in the lining of the uterus.

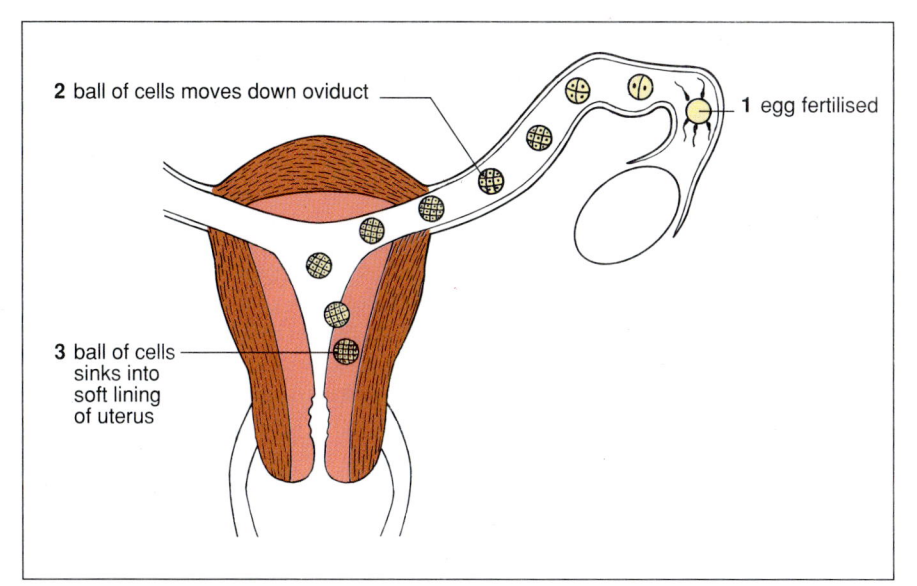

The sperm are very small and the journey is not easy. Most never make it. That is why so many are produced – it raises the chance of one of them getting through. A few days before an egg is shed from the ovary, the cervical mucus becomes more runny and plentiful and this helps the sperm to swim through it.

Fertilisation

If there is an egg in the oviduct, one of the sperm may bump into it and fertilise it. The head of the sperm penetrates the egg, and its nucleus combines with the egg's nucleus. The fertilised egg is called a **zygote**.

What happens if there is no egg in the oviduct? The sperm remain capable of fertilising an egg for two or three days. If an egg is released by the ovary within this time, it may get fertilised.

What happens if an egg is produced and there are no sperm to fertilise it? The egg is capable of being fertilised for about a day after it has been released into the oviduct. If intercourse takes place within this time, fertilisation may occur.

What happens to the fertilised egg?

After the egg has been fertilised, the zygote divides into a little ball of cells. This moves down the oviduct to the uterus (picture 7). It then sinks into the soft lining of the uterus. This is called **implantation**.

Once fertilisation has happened, **conception** has been achieved and **pregnancy** begins. The ball of cells is the **embryo**. We shall see what happens to the embryo in the next topic.

Questions

1 Why is it important that a very large number of sperm should be present in the semen?

2 Why is it an advantage for the testes to be situated in the scrotal sac outside the main body cavity? Can you think of any disadvantages?

3 Why do you think human eggs and sperm are so different in size?

4 Which structures in the female are equivalent to these structures in the male:

a penis,
b testes,
c sperm ducts,
d urethra?

In each case say in what respect the structures are equivalent.

Reproduction and behaviour

In this topic the reproductive organs of the human are described. But these splendid organs would be useless if we did not know what to do with them. This is where **behaviour** comes in. We have to respond and behave so that mating occurs in the right way and the offspring are produced successfully.

To begin with it is important that males and females should be attracted to each other and that they should want to mate. All sorts of stimuli bring the sexes together. In humans the stimuli are very varied, but in other animals they are easier to identify. The sight of the opposite sex is often important – for example, in many species of birds the female is attracted to the male by his bright colours. Smell also plays a part, as anyone who has kept a dog will know. In such cases the female produces a chemical substance which attracts the male. In animals as a whole, chemical stimuli are very important in starting up particular types of behaviour.

In some animals, especially birds, the male and female display to each other in various ways before they mate. This is called **courtship**. This kind of behaviour ensures that both partners are ready to mate at the same moment, when their reproductive organs are working fully.

Behaviour may continue to be important after the young are born. For example, many animals look after their offspring. The parents feed and protect them, and may teach them to fend for themselves. This **care of the young** is particularly well developed in mammals and birds and reaches a peak in the human, as we shall see in the next topic.

1 In what ways is behaviour important in *human* reproduction? Make a list of as many ways as you can think of.

2 Some male birds, robins for example, find a piece of territory before they mate, and defend it against intruders. Why do you think it is a good idea for a pair of breeding birds to have their own territory?

D5 Internal and external development

In this topic we will look at how embryos develop.

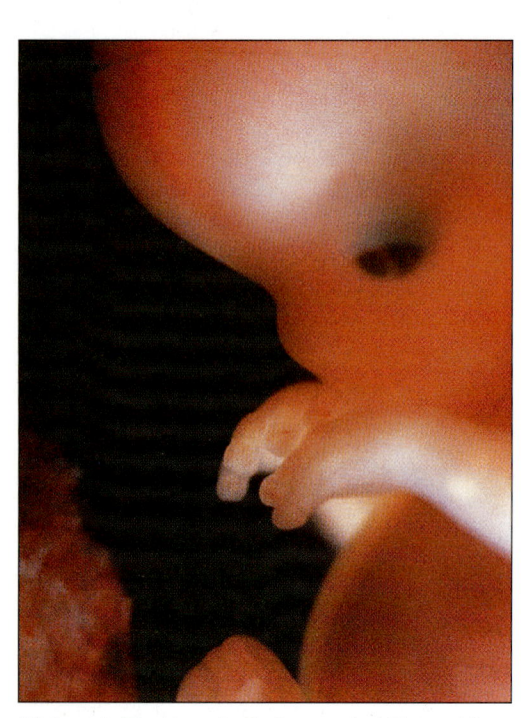

Picture 1 Photograph of a ten week old fetus. All the organs have been formed by this stage.

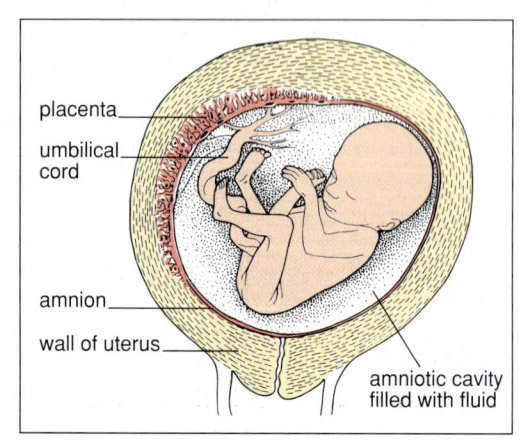

Picture 2 This diagram shows how the fetus is attached to the wall of the uterus by the umbilical cord and placenta.

Internal development

In the next few weeks, the cells of the embryo multiply and start developing into different kinds of tissue. Gradually the embryo grows into something that looks vaguely like a miniature human being. It is called a **fetus** or foetus.

The private pond of the fetus

As the embryo develops in the mother's uterus, it becomes surrounded by a thin membrane called the **amnion**. The amnion forms a kind of bag round the embryo, and it is filled with watery fluid called **amniotic fluid**.

As development goes on, the amniotic cavity expands like a balloon until it fills the entire uterus. The fetus floats in the middle of it, in a kind of 'private pond' (picture 1). The amniotic fluid cushions the fetus, protecting it from being bumped and damaged, for example when the mother runs for a bus.

How is the fetus kept alive?

Attached to the belly of the fetus is a flexible strand called the **umbilical cord**. This is its lifeline, like the tube which connects a diver with the surface. The umbilical cord brings the fetus everything it needs, such as oxygen and food substances. It also takes away unwanted substances such as carbon dioxide and excretory waste.

The umbilical cord runs from the fetus to a structure called the **placenta** which is attached to the lining of the uterus (picture 2). The placenta is shaped like a plate, and it has lots of finger-like **villi** which stick into blood spaces in the wall of the uterus. The villi contain blood capillaries which are connected to the fetus by an artery and vein in the umbilical cord: the **umbilical artery** and **vein**. A detailed picture of the placenta is shown in picture 3.

The barrier separating the fetus's blood from the mother's blood is very thin, and substances can diffuse across it easily. As the fetus's blood flows through the placental villi, it picks up oxygen and soluble food substances from the mother's blood. At the same time, waste substances like carbon dioxide and urea pass into the mother's blood.

It is not just food and oxygen that pass from the mother to the fetus. Antibodies do so too. These help to protect the newborn baby from diseases until it has had a chance to make its own antibodies.

Although the bloodstreams of the fetus and mother come very close to each other, they never mix. If the two bloodstreams were joined, the mother's blood pressure might burst the fetus's blood vessels. What's more, if the two lots of blood belonged to different blood groups, clumping of the red blood cells could occur with disastrous results.

Growth of the fetus

By the end of the third month, the fetus is fully formed right down to the fingers and toes. It now grows until it fills the uterus. Meanwhile, the uterus expands greatly as the fetus grows, and its wall becomes thicker and more muscular in readiness for birth. As the baby grows, it gets more active. It moves its arms and legs, and by the end of the fourth month the mother may feel it moving inside her.

Care during pregnancy

A pregnant woman should eat the right kinds of food, and do nothing that might injure her baby. From time to time she is examined by a doctor or midwife to make sure that everything is all right. At the same time she is given advice on how to keep fit and prepare for the birth of her baby.

Being pregnant has its problems. As well as the extra load to be carried, changes occur in the hormones and occasionally the mother may feel unwell.

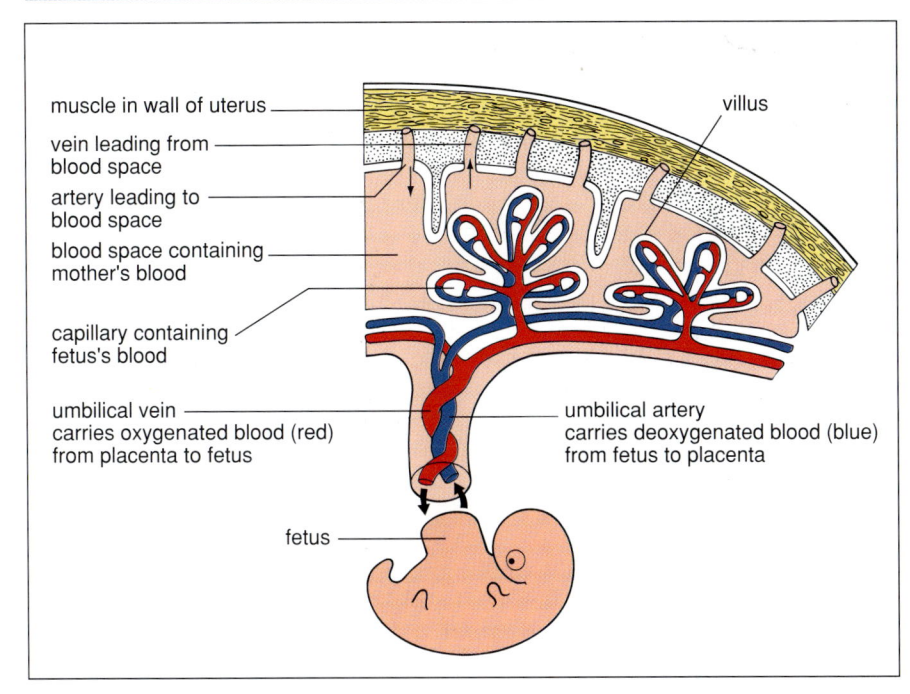

Internal and external development **97**

Picture 3 This diagram shows the placenta. Notice the close relationship between the blood of the fetus and the blood of the mother.

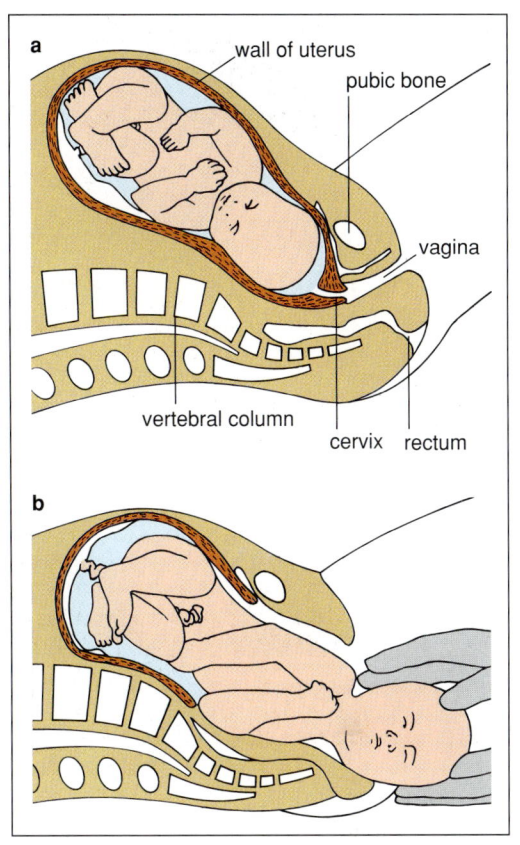

Picture 4 These diagrams show how birth takes place.

If necessary the doctor may give her some medicine to help. However, doctors do not prescribe drugs unless they have been very thoroughly tested beforehand. In the 1960s a number of pregnant women in Britain were given a tranquilliser called thalidomide. No-one realised the harm the drug was doing. Some of the mothers gave birth to babies with severe deformities such as no arms or legs.

Smoking and alcohol can also affect the health of the fetus. The placenta is very good at supplying the fetus with the things it needs, but unfortunately it does not always hold back things which the fetus does *not* need.

Certain germs may get across the placenta and harm the baby. Such is the case with the virus that causes German measles (rubella). This is a mild disease in adults, but if a pregnant woman is infected it can harm the baby. For this reason, girls who haven't had this disease are always immunised against it. Germs that cause sexually transmitted diseases can also get across the placenta.

Birth

Approximately nine months after conception the baby is ready to be born. The first sign of birth is that the uterus gives occasional contractions which become more and more frequent and strong. This is called '**going into labour**'. At about this time, the amnion bursts and the fluid escapes through the vagina, the so-called '**breaking of the water**'. Soon afterwards, the uterus contracts very powerfully and the cervix opens up (dilates). As a result, the baby is pushed through the vagina, usually head first (picture 4).

Once the baby has come out, it starts to breathe. If it does not start breathing of its own accord, the doctor or nurse may give it a tap on the bottom which makes it take a breath in. The umbilical cord is no longer needed, so it is tied and cut. The scar becomes the **navel** ('belly button'). Meanwhile the placenta comes away from the wall of the uterus, and passes out through the vagina. It is called the **afterbirth**. On average a newborn baby weighs just over 3 kg. The birth, or delivery as it's called by doctors and nurses, is now over.

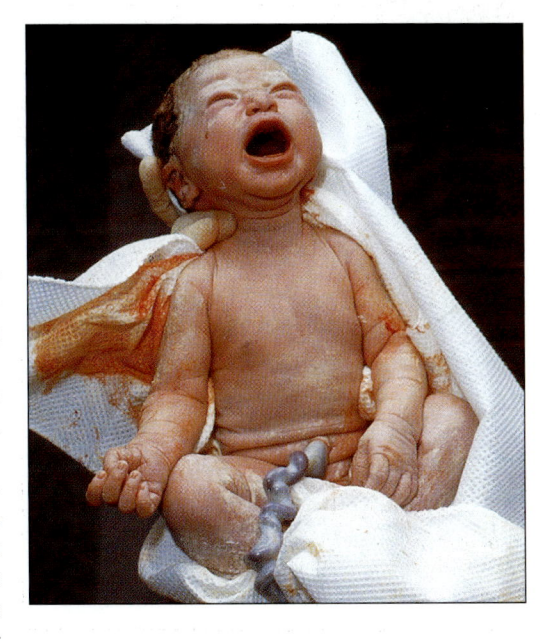

Picture 5 This baby has just been born. The umbilical cord is about to be tied and cut.

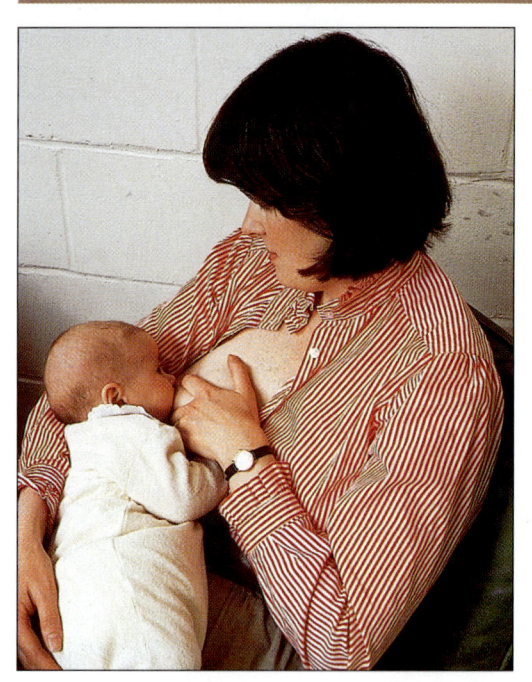

98 Animal survival

Picture 6 A mother breast-feeding her son of a few months old. Human milk contains the ideal balance of nutrients for the baby.

Caring for the newborn baby

A woman's breasts contain **mammary glands** which secrete milk. During pregnancy the breasts enlarge and the mammary glands get ready to produce milk. Soon after birth the baby sucks its mother's nipples. This stimulates the breasts to release the milk, and make more (picture 6).

Milk is the baby's only food for the first few months of life. The baby cannot cope with solid food at this stage. It has no teeth to chew it with, and its gut would be unable to digest it. The baby doesn't *have* to get milk from its mother – it can be fed on cow's milk from a bottle with a teat. However, there's a lot to be said for breast-feeding. The mother's milk is a perfect food, containing all the substances the baby needs at just the right temperature. It also contains antibodies which help to protect the baby from certain diseases and allergies. The milk produced for the first few days after birth (called **colostrum**) is particularly rich in antibodies.

Breast-feeding also allows close contact between the mother and her baby, which is good for both of them, physically and emotionally. And it's cheaper than bottle-feeding!

After several months the baby can be given semi-solid food, and gradually it moves on to a normal diet. When the baby's milk diet has been replaced by solid food, the baby is said to be **weaned**.

External development

External development takes place outside the female's body. It happens in fish, amphibians, reptiles and birds.

The eggs of fish are protected by a flexible covering and the embryo is fed from a food store (yolk) in a yolk sac (picture 7).

Once the young fish has emerged from the egg it has to look after itself. At first it feeds from the remains of the yolk in the yolk sac which is still attached to the young fish. As the food store in the yolk sac begins to run out, it starts to feed on insects or on small plants. The fish grows and develops but its chances of surviving are low, mainly because of predation. However, some of the thousands of eggs that were produced will survive to become adult fish and so the species is maintained.

In amphibians such as frogs, the eggs are protected by being clumped together in the jelly of the frog spawn. After hatching from the egg, the young tadpole must fend for itself. Three days after hatching, the tadpole feeds by scraping plant food from stones in the pond. After ten weeks it can manage to eat small plants like duckweed and after 16 weeks it will be catching insects. Like the young fish, its chance of survival is small, but so many are produced that at least some survive.

Reptiles and birds also protect their developing offspring in eggs. Reptile eggs are soft-shelled and often laid in holes in the ground dug by the female. Bird eggs are hard-shelled, laid in a nest and usually incubated by one or both parents. In both types of egg, the embryo is fed by an internal food store.

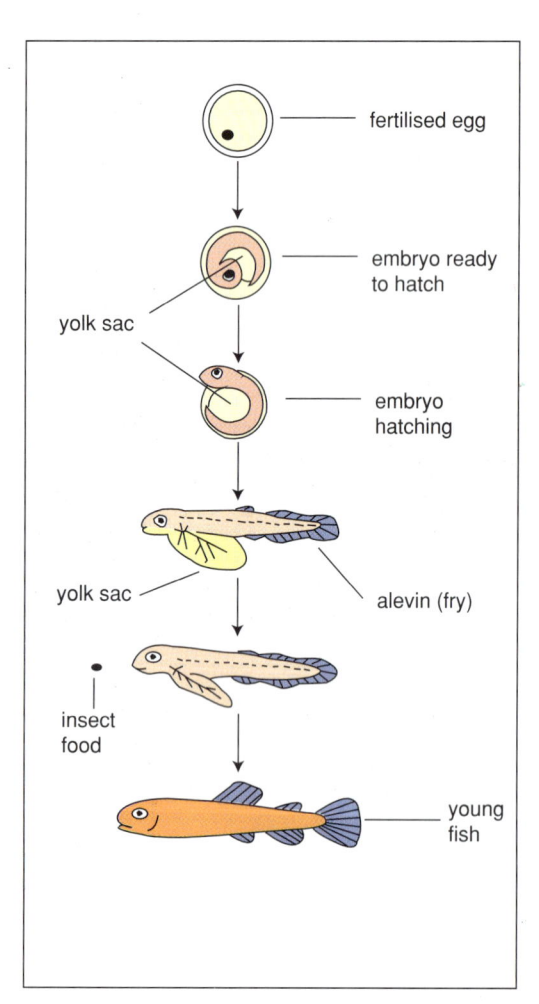

Comparing the number of eggs produced by different animals

Table 1 shows the number of eggs produced by five different animals. Why should the fish produce so many and the mammal so few? The answer lies in the way fertilisation and development are carried out by these animals.

External fertilisation followed by external development is a very risky strategy. For animals like the trout, the chances of the egg developing into an adult are small. For example, the water currents may mean that the sperm and egg fail to meet. The unprotected eggs, in a hollow in the river bed, are easily

Picture 7 The development of a trout.

swept away by the water and the lack of parental care after birth leaves the young at risk from predators.

Internal fertilisation followed by internal development is far less risky. The protection of the embryo in the mother's body, and of the young animal after birth, increases its chances of survival.

Other animals increase the survival chances of their eggs in various ways. As we have read, frogs surround the eggs in jelly. A predator would have to eat all of them or none at all. Birds protect their young with a hard-shelled egg, and the parents care for the young until they are old enough to leave the nest and feed themselves.

The number of eggs produced by these animals reflects the survival chances of the eggs and the young. Generally, the greater number of eggs produced, the smaller are the chances of survival. Animals produce enough eggs to ensure the survival of the species.

Animal	Average number of eggs produced at each mating
Trout	3000
Frog	1000
Turtle	250
Blackbird	4
Human	1

Table 1 The average number of eggs produced by different types of animal at each mating.

Factors affecting birth weight

Some babies are born under-weight, even though they are born at the right time. Why? Here are the main reasons:

The mother
- had a poor diet during pregnancy,
- was ill during pregnancy, for example she may have had anaemia,
- has parasites in her body,
- smoked during pregnancy,
- drank alcohol during pregnancy,
- took drugs during pregnancy (even medical drugs have to be carefully controlled),
- was under 16, or over 35, years old (the babies of such mothers tend to be small).

The placenta
- was diseased and had a reduced blood supply,
- was unusually small.

The baby
- was a twin (multiple birth babies are usually smaller than single-birth babies),
- possesses genes that cause it to be naturally small,
- has a chromosome abnormality, e.g. Down's syndrome.

1 Explain, as far as you can, why each of the above results in an under-weight baby.

2 Which of the factors in the list have a genetic cause, and which ones are caused by the environment?

Questions

1 What functions are performed by:
   a the muscle in the wall of the uterus,
   b the amniotic fluid,
   c the umbilical cord,
   d the mammary glands?

2 Name five jobs which are carried out by the placenta. What is it about the structure of the placenta which makes it ideally suited to do these jobs?

3 Babies are usually born head first. What advantages are there in being born this way? What changes take place in the baby's body soon after it is born?

4 Some of the daily food requirements of an adult woman with a body mass of 55 kg, and of the same woman in an advanced state of pregnancy are given in the table:

	non-pregnant	pregnant
Energy	9200 kJ	10700 kJ
Protein	29 g	38 g
Vitamin A	750 µg	750 µg
Vitamin D	2.5 µg	10 µg
Vitamin C	30 mg	30 mg
Calcium	0.5 g	1.2 g
Iron	20 mg	28 mg

a Suggest one reason why the woman requires more energy when she is pregnant.
b Name two kinds of food from which she is likely to obtain most of this energy.
c Suggest one reason why she requires extra protein when she is pregnant.
d Why do you think she needs extra vitamin D and calcium when she is pregnant?
e What are the percentage increases in the amounts of energy, protein, vitamin D and calcium which she needs when she is pregnant?
f Which substances in the table do not need to be increased during pregnancy?
g Why does she need extra iron?

D6 Controlling human reproduction

Reproduction creates new life and carries responsibilities which everyone should consider.

Picture 1 A family planning clinic where people can obtain advice about birth control.

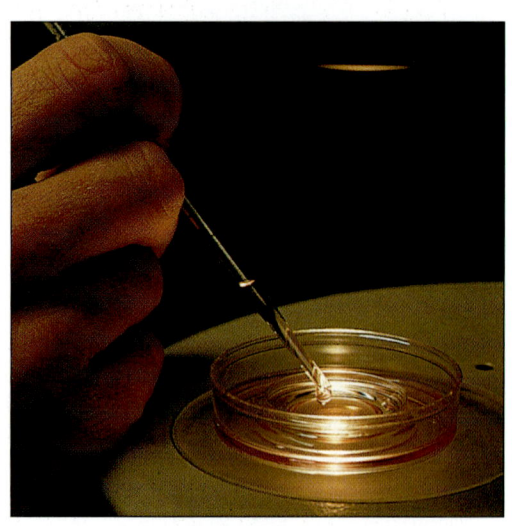

Picture 2 A technician examines a petri dish containing human eggs and sperm to see if fertilisation has taken place. The sperm were introduced with the pipette. The whole procedure is carried out under carefully controlled conditions in a dust-proof cabinet to prevent contamination.

Coping with our sex drive

Sex is one of the most powerful forces in animals, and humans are no exception. Most animals mate, or may try to mate, whenever a partner is available and they feel the urge. With humans it's different – or should be. In human society the **sex drive** has to be controlled.

The sex drive can be a particular problem during adolescence when it is developing. Adults are usually not short of advice on the subject, but they often disagree. However, most people would agree about one thing: sex should be part of a loving and caring relationship. This means not doing anything which may harm the other person, either physically or emotionally. Such a relationship stands the greatest chance of being stable and long-lasting.

How many children?

One of the most important decisions that faces every married couple is how many children to have. A sensible couple will want to give each child the support and love it needs, and this means not having too many. There may therefore be times when the couple wish to prevent pregnancy. This is called **family planning** or **birth control**.

In Britain and many other countries there are **family planning clinics** (picture 1) where people can get advice about birth control methods. These methods aim to prevent conception, so they are called **contraception**. One of the methods is natural and does not depend on the use of artificial devices. Other methods involve using a device called a **contraceptive**.

The **natural method** is simply not to have intercourse at times when the woman is likely to become pregnant. There is more about this on page 102.

One of the most widely used contraceptive devices is the **condom**, a rubber sheath which is put over the penis during intercourse (picture 2 on page 103). The condom prevents sperms getting into the vagina, and is a **barrier method** of contraception. A quite different method – a chemical one – is for the woman to take the **contraceptive pill** which prevents ovulation.

Some people who are quite sure they do not want any children (or any *more* children) may choose to become **sterilised**. In the man the sperm ducts are cut, so there are no longer any sperm in the semen. If a woman wants to be sterilised, the oviducts are cut.

Family planning is extremely important, particularly in over-populated countries which are short of food. Every couple should decide how many children they can raise. They should then consider which birth control methods, if any, are right for them and in keeping with their conscience. There is a summary of the different methods on pages 102–103.

Abortion

Despite the various birth control methods available, women may become pregnant when they do not want to. The only way to avoid having a baby then, is to destroy the embryo or fetus and terminate the pregnancy. This is known in everyday language as **abortion**.

There are various ways of carrying out an abortion, and it should always be done in hospital by a doctor. It is extremely dangerous, and indeed illegal, for it to be done in any other way.

In Britain, abortion is normally only allowed if two doctors consider that by continuing the pregnancy the woman's physical or mental health is at risk. Some people feel that abortion should be made more easily available. Others feel that it should not be allowed at all. The present law is that normally an abortion may only be carried out up to the 24th week of pregnancy. Some people have been pressing hard to get the time limit reduced to 18 weeks.

Abortion is a controversial matter which should be thought about very carefully. Many moral issues are involved.

Helping childless couples

Some couples are unable to have children, however hard they try. A common cause is that either the man cannot produce sperm, or the woman cannot produce eggs. The person is **sterile**. Sometimes the man does have sperm in his semen but there are not enough of them to ensure fertilisation, or he may not be able to get an erection and ejaculate. In the case of the woman, the oviducts may be blocked, making it impossible for the sperm to reach the egg.

A lot can be done to help childless couples these days. For example, blocked oviducts can be opened, and a man's 'sperm count' can be increased. If this fails, the woman can have semen placed in her vagina with a syringe. This is called **artificial insemination**. The semen may be taken from the husband, or it may come from a **sperm bank**, having been supplied by an anonymous donor. In a sperm bank the semen is stored in a frozen state until it is needed.

A woman who is not producing eggs can be given a **fertility drug**. This is a hormone preparation which stimulates her ovaries to start working. On occasions this treatment has proved more successful than either the doctor or the patient bargained for, and the woman has produced quadruplets, quintuplets or sextuplets.

Nowadays scientists can fertilise human eggs outside the body. An egg is taken from the ovary in a small operation, and fertilised by sperm in a dish (picture 2). This is called *in vitro* **fertilisation**. The fertilised egg divides to form a tiny embryo, and this is put into the uterus where it develops in the usual way (picture 3). Babies conceived this way are sometimes called **test tube babies**.

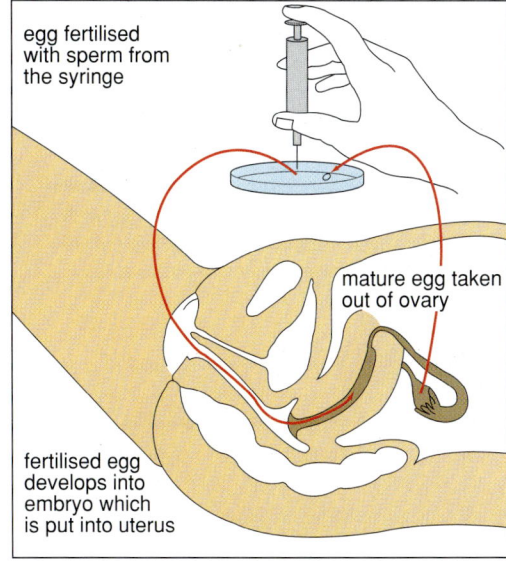

Picture 3 In *in vitro* fertilisation an egg is taken out of the ovary, fertilised in a dish and then placed in the uterus. The embryo can be placed in the uterus of the same woman or, if necessary, a different woman. In the latter case the woman is known as a surrogate mother. Under what circumstances do you think a surrogate mother would need to be used?

Research on human embryos – right or wrong?

Many people have strong views about this. Some approve, and others disapprove. You probably have opinions on this yourself, especially now that you are studying biology. But it's no use having opinions if you don't know the facts. So here, very simply, are the facts.

It all starts with a woman who can't get pregnant and chooses to have a 'test tube baby'. Now fertilising human eggs outside the body isn't easy, and sometimes it doesn't work. So the doctors don't just take one egg from the ovary, they take several. The woman is given hormone treatment beforehand to make her ovaries produce several eggs at the same time.

All the eggs are mixed with sperms, and if fertilisation is successful they may all develop into embryos. But only one embryo is needed. So what happens to the rest? The answer is that they are frozen and stored for future use. The woman herself might need them, if the first pregnancy isn't successful. Alternatively they may be used for research.

Research on what? Well, three things in particular. Firstly, doctors want to learn how to help the sperm to fertilise the egg. Secondly, doctors want to improve ways of rearing the embryos and transferring them to the mother's uterus. Thirdly, doctors want to devise methods of telling if an embryo has an inherited disease such as cystic fibrosis. A healthy embryo can then be selected for transferring to the mother.

But a basic question arises. Suppose you have an embryo, and you wish to do research on it. When should the research stop, and the embryo be destroyed? In the early 1980s a committee, headed by Baroness Warnock, was set up to look into this question and make recommendations to the government. After a great deal of deliberation, the Warnock committee recommended that the limit should be fourteen days after fertilisation.

Why fourteen days? At this stage the embryo is still very simple. The cells are all similar, and have not yet developed into particular kinds of cells. So at this stage the embryo is a bunch of undifferentiated cells. Each cell, if separated from the rest, is potentially able to develop into a new human being. So, argued the committee, the embryo at this stage can't be regarded as a single individual. Another important thing is that the nervous system has not yet started to form, and indeed won't do so for at least another week. This means that there is no possibility of the embryo feeling pain.

The fourteen day embryo is clear and easy to recognise, and a scientist would never have any difficulty knowing how old it is. At this stage a groove starts forming along the top. It's called the **primitive streak**. When the Warnock Report was first published in 1983, the expression 'primitive streak' hit the headlines. The anatomist who originally named this part of the embryo could not have guessed the publicity it would later receive!

In April 1990 the Warnock Report was debated in the House of Commons. It was decided by a majority of 362 votes to 189 that embryo research should be permitted up to the fourteenth day after fertilisation.

1 Some people (including some scientists) feel that research on human embryos should not be allowed at all. What do *you* think?

2 Some scientists would like to do research on embryos up to the stage at which the nervous system is formed. What do *you* feel about this?

3 Views about embryo research (and abortion) depend on when you feel a human life begins. Does it begin at conception, or at fourteen days after conception – or perhaps at a later stage? What do *you* think?

Methods of contraception

Life is full of choices. One choice which many people have to make is what sort of contraception to use. Doctors and family planning clinics help people to make the right choice. In making a decision, these questions have to be asked:

Is the method

- reliable at preventing pregnancy?
- likely to make sex less enjoyable or fulfilling for either partner?
- uncomfortable or difficult to use, and are there any health hazards?
- in keeping with one's religious and ethical beliefs?

The main methods of contraception are summed up in the table on the opposite page.

Other contraceptive methods

Research is always going on into new methods of contraception. For example, since 1992 a **female condom** that can be worn by women has become available. This is a soft polyurethane sheath which lines the vagina and the area just outside. Like the male condom, it also helps to prevent the transmission of AIDS and other sexually transmitted diseases.

New kinds of pill are available too. The pill described in the table is called the **combined pill** because it contains oestrogen as well as progesterone. Occasionally the combined pill may cause thrombosis in older women, particularly if they smoke. For such women a **progesterone-only pill** is available. If taken regularly according to instructions, this stops sperm entering the uterus, or prevents the fertilised egg implanting in the uterus. In some women it prevents ovulation. Its success rate is almost as good as that of the combined pill.

The trouble with pills that have to be taken regularly is that it is easy to forget to take them. This can be overcome by using an **injectable contraceptive**: a single injection given once every few months releases progesterone very slowly into the bloodstream. Or you can have an **implant**: small soft tubes placed under the skin on the inner side of the upper arm slowly release progesterone into the bloodstream for up to five years. The success rate for injectables and implants is slightly better than for the combined pill.

Research is going on into a **male contraceptive pill**. This works by preventing the testes producing sperm though semen is still produced as normal.

The natural method

Despite all the types of contraception available, some people prefer the natural method. Its advantages are that it does not involve using any artificial devices or substances, and there are no objections to it on religious grounds.

For the natural method to work, the woman needs to know when she is fertile, and this means knowing when she is going to ovulate. There are two main ways of telling when this is:

- **The calendar method**. Ovulation normally occurs about half way between one menstrual period and the next – usually between days 12 and 16 in the menstrual cycle. If you know the dates of your menstrual periods, you should be able to work out when ovulation is likely to occur.

- **The temperature method**. Just after ovulation the body temperature rises slightly (see picture 1). By recording the body temperature every day over several months, you can work out when ovulation has occurred in the past and when it is likely to occur in the future.

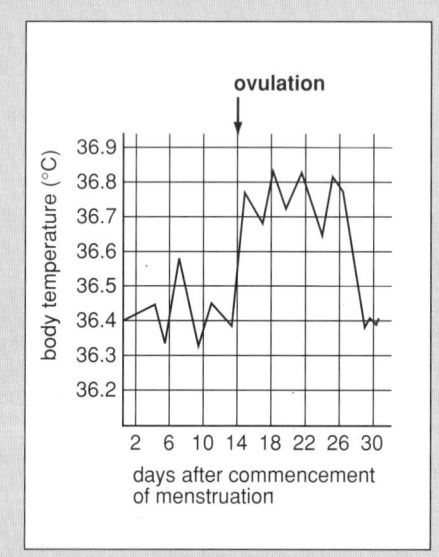

Picture 1 The basal body temperature of a woman during one menstrual cycle. The basal body temperature is the temperature at rest. It is taken at the same time each day, just after waking in the morning. Notice the slight rise in temperature following ovulation.

The time of ovulation and the time between menstrual periods may vary, particularly in teenagers, so this makes the calendar method difficult to use. The temperature method is more accurate, particularly if it is combined with other signs of ovulation. For example, the changes in the cervical mucus mentioned on page 95 are a sign that ovulation will soon take place.

In practice a combination of methods is used. Armed with all the necessary data, it is then possible to work out when it is safe to have intercourse without the risk of becoming pregnant. This is called the **safe period**.

To be successful, natural contraception requires expert guidance from a specially trained teacher. It is also important that *both* partners, i.e. the woman *and* the man, should want it to succeed.

1. What is the *scientific* basis of the natural method of contraception? Relate your answer to the menstrual cycle.

2. List as many things as you can think of which might affect the time and duration of the safe period.

3. There are cases of women becoming pregnant having had intercourse just before, or just after, menstruation. Suggest reasons.

4. In the list of birth control methods in the table on the opposite page, which ones:
   a. stop sperm reaching the egg,
   b. stop eggs being produced,
   c. stop the fertilised egg implanting in the uterus,
   d. are barrier methods,
   e. are chemical methods?

5. What does the combined pill consist of and how does it work?

6. Look at the right-hand column of the table on the opposite page. It tells you how many women in one hundred are likely to become pregnant if they use each method of contraception.
   a. Convert the information into *percentage reliability* for careful and less careful use of each method.
   b. Suppose you were put in charge of a research project to assess the reliability of a particular method of contraception. How would you go about it?
   c. Suggest possible sources of inaccuracy in assessing the reliability of contraceptive methods.

Controlling human reproduction 103

Table 1 The main methods of contraception. The reliability figures in the right-hand column are taken from *Your Guide to Contraception*, published by the Family Planning Association. The figures are based on an evaluation by a panel of experts of the results of different investigations carried out in recent years. Individual investigations into the reliability of contraceptive methods often give widely different results. For example, some suggest that the condom is more reliable, and the natural method less reliable, than the figures in this table would suggest. Why do you think different investigations give different results?

Method	How it works	Reliability
Natural method	The woman avoids having intercourse when she is fertile, i.e. during the part of the menstrual cycle when ovulation is likely to occur.	With careful use under expert guidance, 2 women in 100 get pregnant in a year. With less careful use up to 20 women in 100 get pregnant in a year.
Condom	Thin rubber sheath placed over the erect penis. Stops sperm entering the vagina. Also helps to prevent transmission of sexually transmitted diseases, including AIDS.	With careful use 2 women in 100 get pregnant in a year. With less careful use up to 15 women in 100 get pregnant in a year.
Diaphragm (cap) with spermicide	A flexible rubber cap is inserted into the vagina to cover the cervix, then a spermicide is squirted into the vagina. Stops sperm entering the uterus.	With careful use, 4 to 8 women in 100 get pregnant in a year. With less careful use up to 18 women in 100 get pregnant in a year.
Intra-uterine device (IUD)	A small plastic and copper object is placed in the uterus by a doctor. Stops sperm reaching the egg and/or the fertilised egg implanting in the uterus.	Fewer than 2 women in 100 get pregnant in a year.
The combined pill	Hormone preparation, consisting of synthetic equivalents of oestrogen and progesterone, taken regularly according to doctor's instructions. Prevents ovulation.	With careful use fewer than 1 woman in 100 gets pregnant in a year. With less careful use 3 or more women in 100
Female sterilisation	The oviducts are tied and cut so that sperm can never reach an egg.	The failure rate is 1 to 3 in 1000.
Male sterilisation (vasectomy)	The sperm ducts are tied and cut so that sperm are not present in the semen when ejaculation occurs.	The failure rate is about 1 in 1000.

Other methods of contraception are discussed on the opposite page.

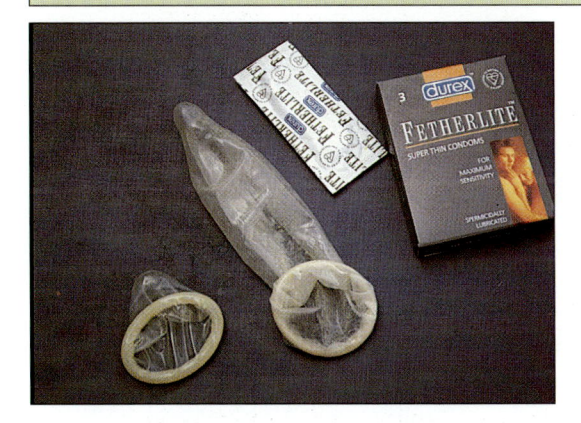

Picture 2 The condom, a widely used contraceptive. It is unrolled over the erect penis, and the semen is caught in the teat at the end. The condom may be coated with a lubricant which also acts as a spermicide (kills sperm). Oil-based lubricants should not be used as they can damage the rubber.

D7
How do we get rid of unwanted substances?

When you go to the toilet you are getting rid of unwanted substances.

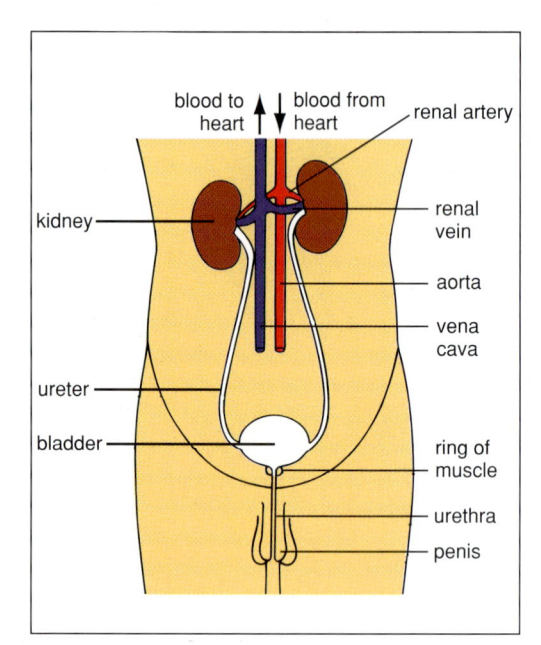

Losses and gains

The body of a mammal gains water in three ways:
- from food eaten,
- from liquid drunk,
- from chemical reactions in the body that release water as a waste product.

Mammals lose water in four ways:
- in sweat (evaporation of water keeps the body cool),
- in faeces (moist faeces are expelled more easily),
- in breath,
- in urine.

Generally we take in more water than we need, and we have to get rid of the surplus. The kidneys are the main organs which regulate the water content of the blood, keeping it at a constant level. This is called **osmoregulation**.

In addition urea, a poisonous waste product, is dissolved in the surplus water and is also expelled. This process is called **excretion**.

The urinary system

The main organs of our urinary system are the **kidneys**. We have two of them, one on each side the body. If you put your hands on your hips, your kidneys are just under your thumbs.

The urinary system is shown in picture 1. A narrow tube called the **ureter** runs from each kidney to the **bladder**. The bladder is a bag situated towards the bottom of the abdomen. Its wall is elastic and has muscle tissue in it. Leading from the bladder is a tube called the **urethra**. The urethra opens just above the vaginal opening in the female. In the male it runs down the penis and opens at its tip.

The kidneys produce a watery fluid called **urine** which contains substances that the body does not want. The urine trickles continuously down the ureters to the bladder which gradually expands like a balloon as more and more urine collects inside it. Every now and again the bladder is emptied. This is called **urination**.

How is the bladder emptied?

The top of the urethra is surrounded by a ring of muscle. When the bladder needs to be emptied, the ring of muscle opens and at the same time the muscle tissue in the bladder wall contracts. The result is that urine is forced out.

Picture 1 The urinary system of the human male. The arrows indicate the direction of the flow of blood. The ring of muscle where the bladder joins the urethra is shown here in sectional view. It encircles the urethra like a sheath. When contracted tightly it prevents the urine escaping from the bladder.

How is urea formed and why is it poisonous?

Much of the surplus food that we eat is stored by the liver. However, the liver can't store proteins or the amino acids of which they are composed. Instead the liver destroys them. Amino acids contain nitrogen, and the first thing that happens is that the nitrogen part of the amino acid molecule is broken off and turned into ammonia. This is called **deamination**. Ammonia is very poisonous so the liver quickly converts it into urea which is less poisonous. The urea is then carried by the blood to the kidneys which get rid of it in the urine.

Ammonia is not the only poisonous substance that the liver deals with. Many other poisons (including drugs) are either destroyed or made harmless by the liver. We call this process **detoxification**. It is a very important function of the liver.

How is urine formed by the kidneys?

Look at table 1. You will see that some substances are more concentrated in the urine than in the blood. These are the substances which the body does not want. The main one is urea. The figures in the table show that there is about sixty times more urea in the urine than in the blood. The reason is that as blood passes through the kidneys, urea is taken out of it and passed into the urine.

But the kidneys do more than cleanse the blood of urea. They also regulate the amounts of various substances in the blood. One of these is water.

Suppose you drink a lot of water in a short space of time. The water is absorbed from your gut into your bloodstream, and it has the effect of diluting the blood. As the blood flows through the kidneys, the unwanted water passes out of it into the urine. This is why you produce a lot of very watery urine after you have been drinking a lot.

By regulating the amount of water that goes out with the urine, the kidneys keep the concentration of the blood more or less the same all the time.

Inside the kidneys

If you slice a kidney open and look inside, you can see that it is divided into two areas, a light outer area and a darker inner area. The inner area is connected to the ureter as shown in picture 2.

To see any detail of the kidney itself you need a microscope. The microscope shows that inside each kidney there are about a million little structures called **nephrons**. One is shown in picture 3. It consists of a narrow tube, called a **renal tubule**. Its inner end is connected to a cup-like **renal capsule**. The other end is connected to a **collecting duct** which leads to the ureter.

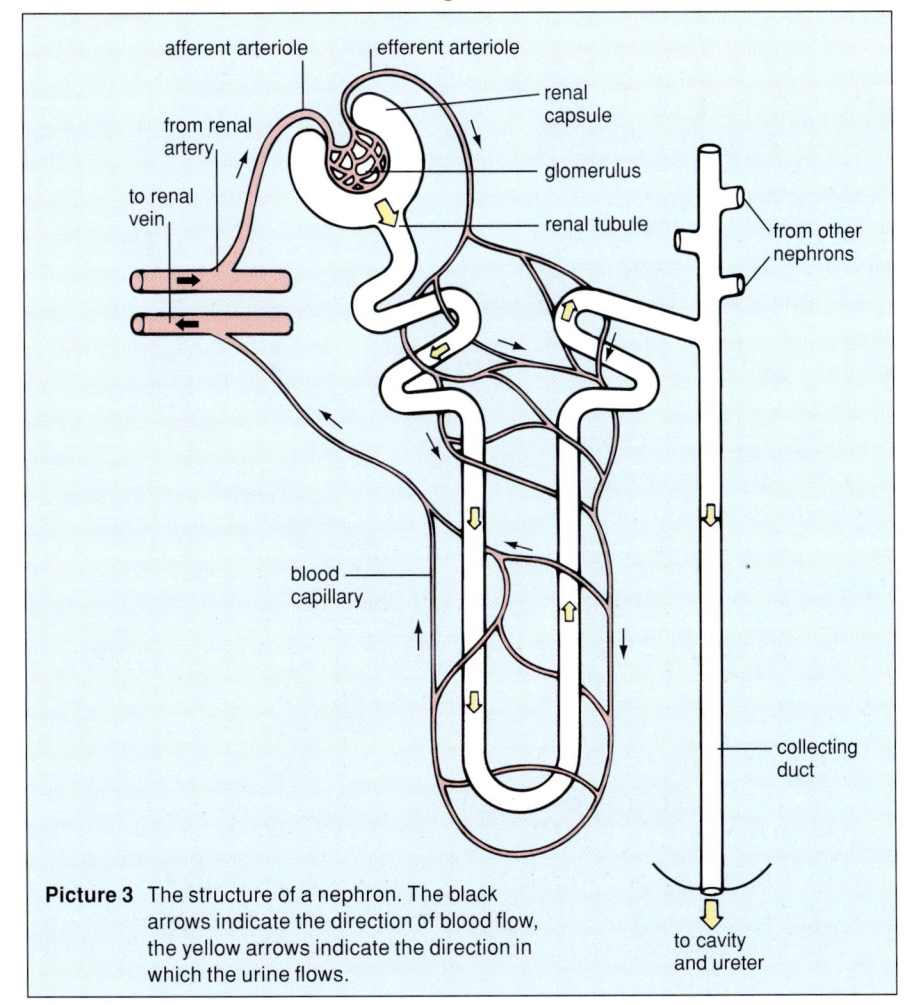

Table 1 This table compares the relative amounts of five different substances in the blood and urine of the human. The amount of water and salt in the urine varies according to the needs of the body.

Substances	Quantity (parts per hundred)	
	Blood	Urine
Water	92	95
Proteins	7	0
Glucose	0.1	0
Salt (chloride)	0.37	0.6
Urea	0.03	2

Detecting substances in blood and urine

How can we measure the concentration of substances in samples of blood and urine? Nowadays, a **biosensor** can be used.

A biosensor is a sensitive device that can detect the presence of certain substances even at very low concentrations. It consists of a probe containing immobilised enzymes or microbes. When the substance touches the probe, it reacts with the enzymes, and the reaction is turned into an electronic signal. The concentration of the substance can be measured from the number of reactions that occur.

Biosensors have many other uses in biology. Can you suggest some of them?

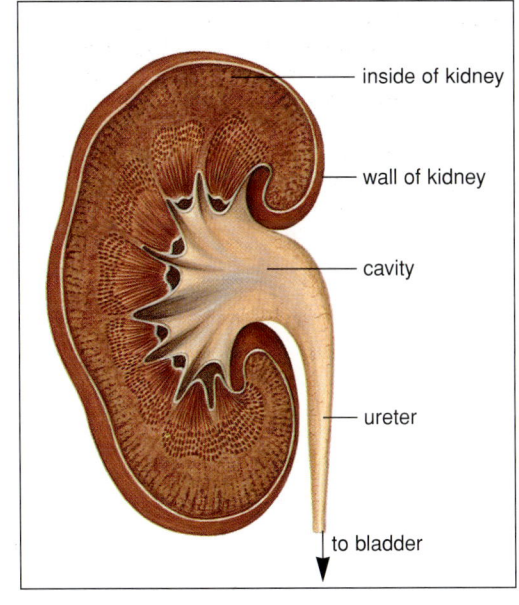

Picture 3 The structure of a nephron. The black arrows indicate the direction of blood flow, the yellow arrows indicate the direction in which the urine flows.

Picture 2 A kidney sliced horizontally to show the inside.

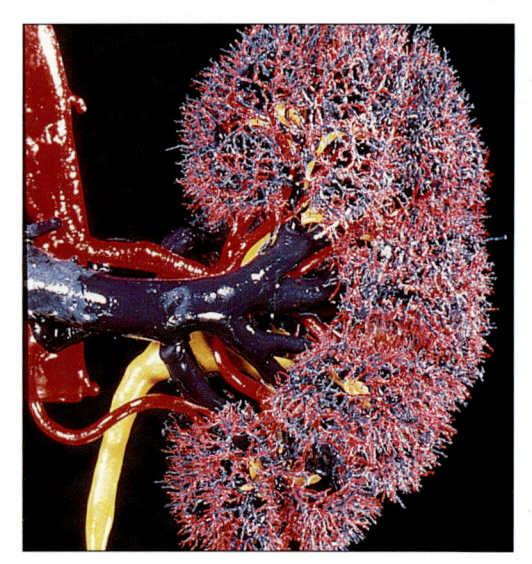

Picture 4 In this kidney all the tissues except the main blood vessels have been dissolved away. The yellow tube is the ureter which carries urine to the bladder. Arteries are red, veins blue.

The nephron's blood supply comes from a branch of the renal artery called the **afferent arteriole**. This enters the renal capsule where it splits up into a little bunch of capillaries called the **glomerulus**. The capillaries then join up again to form an **efferent arteriole** which comes out of the capsule and splits up into another set of capillaries. These capillaries are wrapped round the renal tubule – they then join up again to form a vessel which leads to the renal vein.

The two kidneys together contain about 16 km of tubules and 160 km of blood vessels (picture 4).

How do the kidneys work?

The kidneys work by each nephron 'cleaning' the blood that flows to it. Picture 5 shows what happens.

The blood which reaches the glomerulus is under high pressure. This is because the vessel which carries blood away from the glomerulus is narrower than the vessel which carries blood to it. The pressure forces the fluid part of the blood through the walls of the capillaries into the space inside the renal capsule. The fluid which goes through contains urea, glucose, water and salts. But the blood cells and proteins are too large to go through, so they stay in the capillaries. In this way the blood is filtered as it flows through the glomerulus. Because the things that are held back by the filter are very small, this process is called **ultra-filtration**.

The filtered fluid, or filtrate, then trickles along the renal tubule. As it does so, all the glucose, and most of the water and salts, are taken back into the capillaries wrapped round the renal tubule. The right amounts of water and salt are reabsorbed to give the blood its correct composition. In the meantime, urea passes on along the renal tubule and eventually reaches the bladder, together with other unwanted substances.

We can sum up by saying that the kidneys first filter the blood, and then put back into it those substances which the body needs. Reabsorbing the right amount of water is an extremely important part of the process: if the kidneys stopped reabsorbing water altogether, the body would be severely dehydrated in about three minutes.

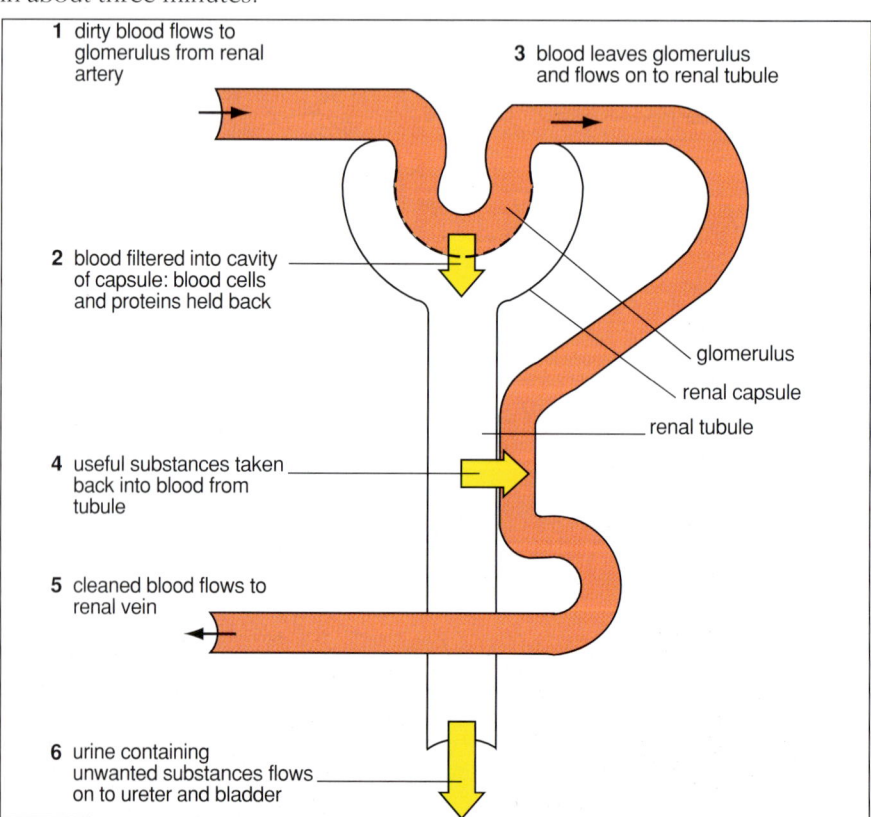

Controlling water

How do a person's kidneys know how much water to reabsorb? Well, suppose your body is short of water. Under these circumstances the concentration of salts and other solutes in the blood will be too high.

This high concentration of solutes is detected by special cells in the brain which tell the pituitary gland to secrete a certain hormone into the blood. The hormone is carried to the kidneys and tells them to reabsorb extra water into the bloodstream instead of letting it out in the urine. You will also feel thirsty and drink some water. As a result, the solute concentration of the blood is brought down to its correct value.

The hormone is called **anti-diuretic hormone**. This is because it counteracts **diuresis**, which is the excessive flow of urine from the body.

1 When is your body likely to be short of water?
2 What happens when your body contains too *much* water? Include these words in your answer: *blood, brain, pituitary gland, anti-diuretic hormone, kidneys, urine.*

Picture 5 This diagram shows very simply how the nephron cleans the blood and makes urine.

1 dirty blood flows to glomerulus from renal artery
2 blood filtered into cavity of capsule: blood cells and proteins held back
3 blood leaves glomerulus and flows on to renal tubule
4 useful substances taken back into blood from tubule
5 cleaned blood flows to renal vein
6 urine containing unwanted substances flows on to ureter and bladder

glomerulus
renal capsule
renal tubule

How do we get rid of unwanted substances? **107**

What happens if the kidneys fail?

If one kidney fails it doesn't matter very much, because we can manage with the other one. But if both kidneys fail, the concentration of substances in the blood changes and the amount of urea goes up and up. The person becomes poisoned by the body's own waste products, and death occurs in about a week.

Once again technology comes to the rescue. A person with kidney failure can be attached to an **artificial kidney** (**kidney machine**). Blood from the patient flows through the machine where it is cleansed before returning to the patient.

Another way of dealing with kidney failure is to be given a **kidney transplant** (picture 6). This involves an operation in which the person's kidney is replaced by someone else's. Usually the new kidney comes from a close relative who is willing to donate a kidney, or from the victim of a fatal accident. There's more about the kidney machine and kidney transplants on pages 108 and 109.

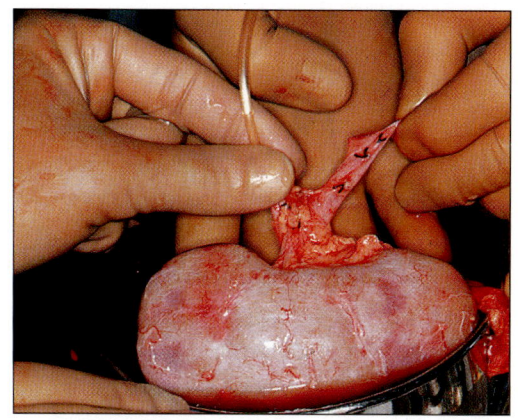

Picture 6 A kidney being prepared for a transplant operation.

Questions

1 Explain the meaning of the terms excretion and osmoregulation.

What job does the kidney do:

a as an excretory organ, and
b as an organ of osmoregulation?

2 Which of the substances listed in column A are found in each of the fluids listed in column B?

Column A	Column B
protein	blood entering kidney
glucose	blood leaving kidney
urea	fluid filtered into
water	renal capsules
	urine leaving kidney

3 What effect, if any, would you expect each of the following to have on the quantity and composition of the urine?

a Eating a large quantity of salty food.
b Having a bath.
c Drinking a lot of beer.
d Playing a hard game of squash.
e Eating two bars of chocolate.

4 It has been suggested that in hot weather a person passes less urine than in cold weather.

a Describe an experiment which could be done to find out if this is true.
b If it is true, how would you explain it?

5 Decide if these statements are true or false. If false, what word or phrase should replace those underlined?

a <u>Glucose</u> is a waste product removed in the urine.
b The <u>renal artery</u> takes blood to the kidney.

c The kidneys regulate the <u>water content</u> of the blood.
d The ureter takes urine from the kidney to <u>outside the body</u>.

6 The diagram below shows a model of an artificial kidney machine. As the blood passes along the tubing, materials pass into the surrounding fluid from the blood.

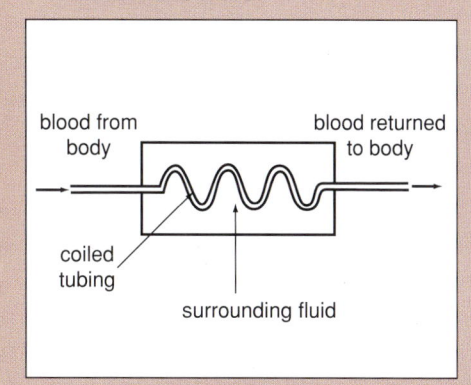

a Why is the tube coiled rather then straight?
b Name the poisonous waste product removed from the blood by the kidney machine.
c Describe how this substance moves from the blood into the fluid of the machine.
d Find out what would happen if this poisonous waste product was not removed from the body.

7 Four test tubes were set up as shown. The test tubes were left in a water bath at 37°C for 30 minutes. Urease is an enzyme which breaks down urea into ammonia. Any ammonia released is detected by the test papers. The results are shown in the table below.

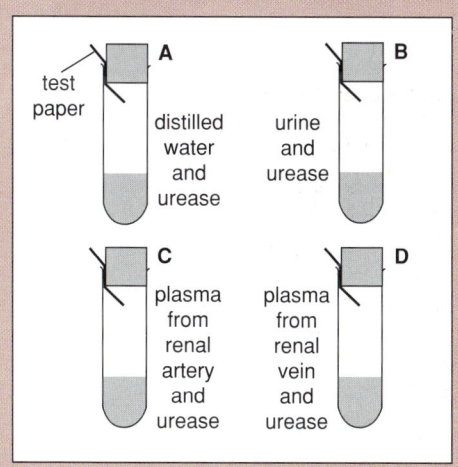

A: test paper, distilled water and urease
B: urine and urease
C: plasma from renal artery and urease
D: plasma from renal vein and urease

Test tube	Test for ammonia
A	negative
B	positive
C	positive
D	negative

Use the results to answer the following questions.

a Why were the tubes incubated at 37°C?
b Which tubes contained urea?
c Account for the difference in the results obtained from tubes C and D.

The artificial kidney

The artificial kidney, or kidney machine, can take over the job of the kidneys if they stop working.

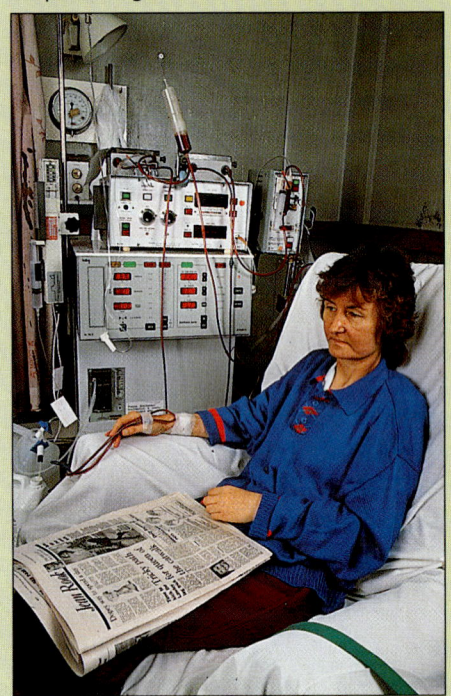

Picture 1 A person connected to an artificial kidney (kidney machine).

First a small operation is carried out in which an artery in the arm is joined directly to a vein. A tube is then connected to the vein. The blood flows along the tube to the machine.

The reason why the vein has to be joined to the artery is that the blood pressure in the vein would be too low to drive the blood to the machine. 'So why not connect the tube to the *artery*?' you ask. The answer is that the artery is narrower and more difficult to get at than the vein. The vein is just beneath the skin on the underside of the arm, and is easy to get at. Look at the underside of your own arm and you will see the veins through the skin.

Once inside the machine, the blood is pumped over the surface of a thin membrane made from a special polymer rather like cellophane. On the other side of the membrane is a watery solution containing the various substances that the body needs in the right concentrations. These substances include glucose and salts, but not urea.

The membrane will let through certain things, but not others. We call it a **dialysing membrane**, and the solution in contact with it is called the **dialysis solution**. As the blood flows over the membrane, urea and other unwanted substances pass through to the dialysis solution on the other side. Larger things in the blood, such as the cells and proteins, are held back. The dialysis solution is kept flowing all the time and is constantly replaced by fresh solution.

By the time the blood leaves the machine, the urea has gone and useful substances such as glucose have the same concentration as in the dialysis solution. The 'clean' blood is then returned to the patient by another tube inserted in the arm vein.

A person with total kidney failure needs to spend about five hours three times a week on a kidney machine, either in hospital or at home. Portable machines are now available, and people can learn how to attach themselves to them. Kidney machines are a wonderful example of how modern technology can save lives.

1. Draw a picture of what the dialysing membrane in a kidney machine might look like very highly magnified.

   Use your picture to explain how blood loses its urea as it flows through the kidney machine, and why blood cells don't pass through the membrane.

2. The dialysis solution contains glucose and salts at the same concentrations as they should be in the blood. Why is this important? Why does the solution have to be constantly replaced?

3. Kidney machines are extremely expensive and are used by relatively few people. Do you think money should be spent on expensive technology of this sort rather than on more basic things?

4. Unfortunately there are not enough kidney machines for everyone who needs them. What sort of things should be taken into account in deciding who should have them? Remember, without a kidney machine a person may die.

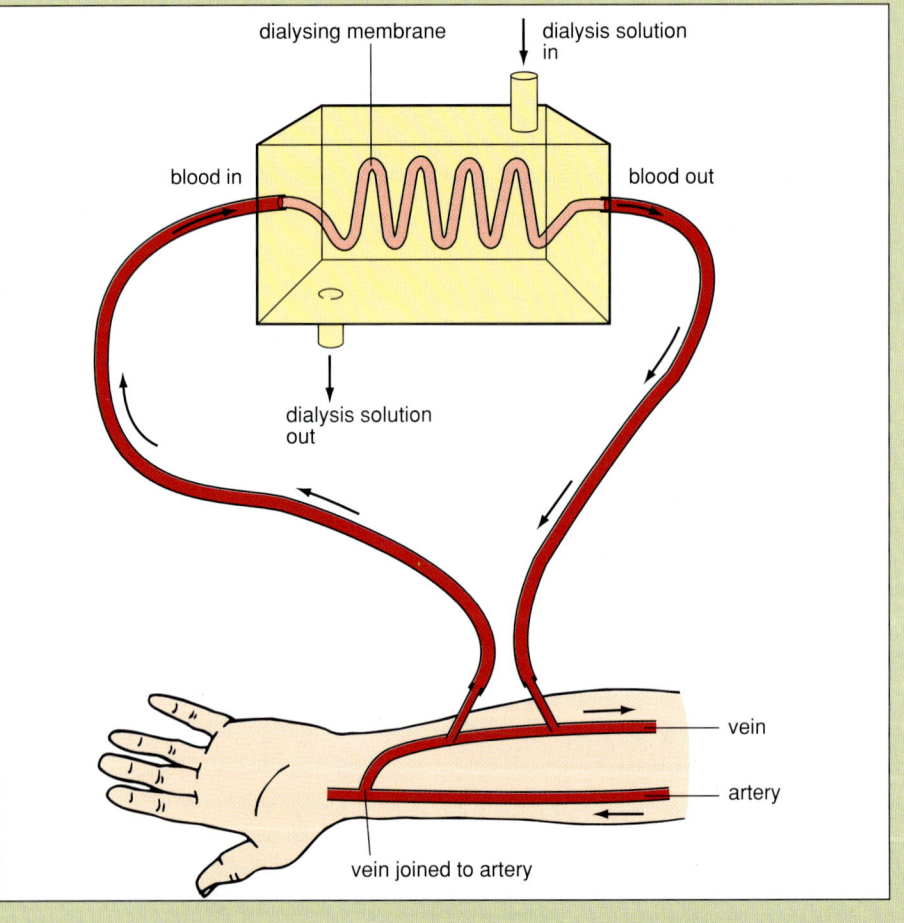

Picture 2 A greatly simplified diagram of an artificial kidney. The dialysing membrane may be in the form of flat sheets lying parallel with each other, or it may be rolled up like a swiss roll, or it may consist of lots of narrow tubes. The idea is to create a large surface area in the smallest possible space.

Having a kidney transplant

Giving someone a new kidney from a donor may sound a difficult thing to do, but a surgeon will tell you that the operation itself is relatively easy. The trouble is that the patient's immune system may treat the new kidney as an intruder and destroy it (see page 147). This is most likely to happen soon after the operation. To prevent this rejection, the patient is given drugs which suppress the immune system. Obviously this makes the body less efficient at fighting disease, so germs must be kept away from the patient until, hopefully, the kidney is accepted and the drugs can be reduced.

The more alike the donor and the patient are genetically, the less likely it is that the kidney will be rejected. So the doctors always find out how genetically similar the tissues are before the operation is carried out. This is done by a procedure called **tissue typing**. This applies not only to kidneys but to other transplanted organs too, such as hearts, lungs and livers.

There is more about organ transplants and spare part surgery on page 167.

1 What are the advantages of having a kidney transplant rather than a kidney machine. Are there any possible disadvantages?
2 Why is it important to keep germs away from a patient who has just had a transplant operation, and how do you think this is achieved?
3 A kidney transplant is most likely to be successful if the kidney comes from an identical twin. Why? If the person doesn't have an identical twin, who would be the next best donor?
4 A kidney donor can give a kidney at any time and stay alive. But a heart donor is always a person who has just died. Why the difference?

Diabetes

Some people have too much sugar in their blood. They are suffering from **diabetes** and are known as diabetics. The extra sugar in their blood makes them tired and thirsty. If nothing is done about it, the person loses weight and may eventually die.

The kidneys try to get rid of the extra sugar, so one of the signs of diabetes is that sugar is present in the urine. In the old days, doctors used to tell whether or not a patient had diabetes by tasting the urine to see if it was sweet. Nowadays, a simple test is used.

Diabetes is caused by the pancreas not producing enough insulin. The result is that the liver does not turn as much sugar into glycogen as it normally would. Diabetes may start early in life or it may develop in middle age. It cannot be cured, but it can be controlled by:

- eating carefully selected foods which do not cause a harmful increase in the concentration of sugar in the blood.
- taking tablets which lower the amount of sugar in the blood.
- taking a certain amount of insulin every day. This makes the tissues turn blood sugar into glycogen.

Unfortunately insulin cannot be taken by mouth. It's a protein and is broken down by digestive enzymes in the gut. So it must be injected through the skin with a hypodermic needle. Diabetics are taught to do this for themselves as shown in the picture.

The trouble is that it's difficult to get the dose exactly right. What sometimes happens is that diabetics give themselves too much insulin with the result that their blood sugar falls too low. This can produce all sorts of effects such as trembling, sweating and weakness. The diabetic learns to recognise these signs and, if they come on, eats a few lumps of sugar or glucose tablets to bring the blood sugar up to the right level.

With proper medical help, diabetics can learn to control their problem and to work, play games and lead a full and active life. Some leading sports figures are diabetics.

Exciting new developments in the treatment of diabetes include the use of a portable pump which is programmed to deliver exactly the right amount of insulin into the bloodstream continuously. Pancreas transplants are also possible, and research is being carried out on an artificial pancreas.

1 A person who is suspected of having diabetes produces a sample of urine which is tested for sugar.
   a Describe a suitable test which could be carried out.
   b What would be the cause of sugar being present in the urine?
2 Insulin is a protein. It cannot be taken by mouth because it would be broken down by digestive enzymes in the gut.
   a Give the names of two enzymes which would attack the insulin.
   b What would these enzymes break the insulin down into?
   c How is insulin taken by a diabetic? Mention one danger of taking insulin this way.

Picture 1 This girl has diabetes. Here you see her injecting herself with insulin.

D8 Responding to the environment

A change in the behaviour of an animal is often required in order to survive.

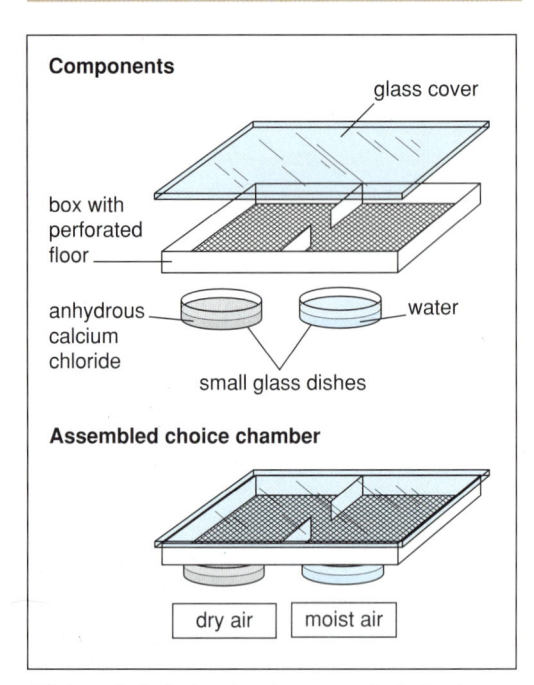

The effect of the environment on animal behaviour

The environment around us changes all the time. Changes to the immediate environment of an animal will often happen during its lifetime and in order to survive the animal must:

- sense the change in the environment,
- respond to the change.

A change in the environment is called the **stimulus**. The stimulus may be a change in the light intensity, a sound or perhaps chemicals in the air. Humans will sense the stimulus with the aid of light receptors in the eyes, sound receptors in the ears, and chemical receptors in the lining of the nose. Other animals may use different sense receptors, but they all do the same job, which is to tell the animal that something in the environment has changed.

The animal responds to the change by modifying its behaviour. For example, when the weather turns cold it may move to an area where it will stand a better chance of survival.

Choice chambers

A **choice chamber** is a piece of apparatus that can be set up to find out how small invertebrate animals respond to one altered environmental factor. Picture 1 shows how such a choice chamber can be set up.

Several woodlice are placed in the choice chamber. They begin to move about randomly. Careful observation shows that the woodlice in the dry side of the chamber move about more quickly than those in the damp side. These animals are able to sense that the air is dry. Their movement is a response to this stimulus.

This behaviour will eventually get them into the damp side. Those in the damp side move about more slowly, and so will probably stay in the damp side. This ensures that their skin remains moist and that they do not die from dehydration.

Further investigations using choice chambers show that woodlice also move into areas that are dark. One advantage of this behavioural response is that in the dark the woodlice will be less likely to be seen and therefore eaten by predators.

Rhythmical behaviour

This kind of behaviour occurs at regular intervals in response to environmental stimuli. If the interval between each response is twenty-four hours, this is referred to as a **circadian rhythm**. If it is a year, the response is said to be **annual**.

The environmental stimulus that brings on the change in behaviour is called a **trigger stimulus**.

The cockroach behaves in a circadian manner. The trigger stimulus is the onset of darkness. The animal responds by becoming active and starting to feed (it is nocturnal). The advantage of this response is that it allows the insect to feed while remaining relatively unseen by potential predators during the day.

Migration

Migratory animals have an annual behaviour pattern. The response often involves complicated trigger stimuli, which in many cases are not fully understood. The best known migrators are birds but certain fish, insects and mammals also migrate. These animals respond to unfavourable conditions in one area by travelling to another area with favourable conditions.

Birds in particular face many hazards on the way (bad weather, predators, starvation, human interference) and accurate navigation can be a problem. The casualty rate during migrations can be high, and only the best prepared,

Picture 1 A choice chamber set up to find out how woodlice react to a choice of dry or moist air.

Picture 2 Woodlice keep alive by finding moist shady places.

fittest animals will complete the journey. The benefits of migration to the flock must therefore outweigh the possible risk to individual birds.

House martins, swifts and swallows arrive in Britain during the spring from various parts of Africa. They spend the summer mating and raising their offspring. Large numbers of insects provide plenty of food for these birds. The extended hours of daylight result in longer feeding times. However, as winter approaches food becomes scarce and the birds return to Africa. The trigger stimulus for migration is the onset of shorter day lengths.

Caerlaverock, on the Solway Firth in south-west Scotland, is the winter home of barnacle geese from Spitsbergen in the Arctic Circle. Once again shorter day lengths in autumn trigger migratory behaviour. The birds avoid Spitsbergen during the winter when no food is available as the ground will be covered in snow. As the day length increases in spring, the birds migrate from Scotland to Spitsbergen. They breed successfully in Spitsbergen because there are fewer predators. Therefore, despite the yearly 1500 mile journey and the loss of some birds, the species as a whole is more successful if migrations are part of its annual behaviour pattern.

Other annual behaviour patterns

Other animals respond to the shorter day lengths of autumn and winter by **hibernating**. This avoids extreme winter conditions during which food is not easily found. Hedgehogs, bats and dormice are examples of hibernating mammals (picture 5).

Longer day lengths in spring, in some species, bring on mating behaviour. This ensures that the young are born in late spring and summer when it is warm and plenty of food is available.

Trigger stimuli must be reliable indicators of seasonal change. Day length is better than temperature. Temperature may play a part in some behavioural changes but it cannot be relied on to indicate the end of winter.

Picture 3 The Arctic tern may migrate from Arctic to Antarctic (and back again) each year, a distance of 18 000 km.

Picture 4 Barnacle geese from Spitsbergen spend the winter in south-west Scotland.

Picture 5 The dormouse – it keeps out of the winter cold by hibernating.

Questions

1 Why is day length a much more reliable indicator of seasonal change than temperature?

2 There are many more examples of species of animals that migrate. Find out the names of some others. For each, state where the animal migrates to, where it migrates from, and how many miles are covered in each migration.
What are the trigger stimuli for each migration?

3 Look at the following information.
Woodlice move slowly or settle in damp conditions.
Blowfly maggots move away from bright light.
Swallows migrate from Britain to Africa in the autumn.
Dormice hibernate during the winter months.
Hares carry out courtship displays for mating in spring.
Explain, in each case, how the survival of the animal is increased by the behaviour described.

4 Do humans show any rhythmical behaviour patterns? Are there any human activities which have a diurnal rhythm, that is, more active during the day than at night?

E1
Cells, the bricks of the body

An organism is made of cells in the same kind of way that a house is made of bricks.

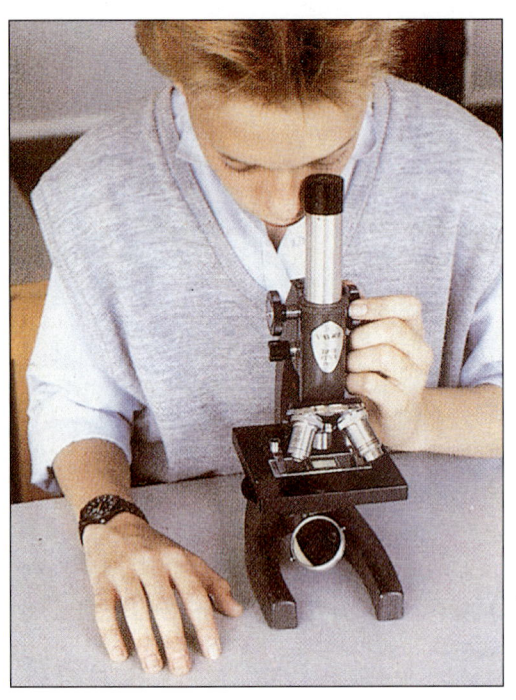

Looking at small things

In biology we often have to look at small organisms or parts of organisms. Sometimes a hand lens can help us. A typical hand lens has a magnifying power of ×10. This means that we see the object ten times larger than it really is.

If the object is too small to be seen with a hand lens then we have to use a light microscope (pictures 1 and 2).

A simple **light microscope**, similar to ones you will use, usually has three objective lenses. Each one magnifies to a different power. The total magnification of the microscope is found by multiplying the power of the eyepiece lens by the power of the objective lens being used. For example, if the eyepiece lens has a power of ×10, and the objective lens has a power of ×4, then the total magnifying power of the microscope is ×40. This means that we see the object forty times larger than it really is.

If you were to measure the width of a coin, you would probably express it in millimetres. However, for very small objects seen down the microscope we use a smaller unit called the micrometre. Its symbol is μm. It is one thousandth of a millimetre.

Usually when scientists want to look at objects using a microscope, they will **stain** them first. Staining helps to show up the different parts.

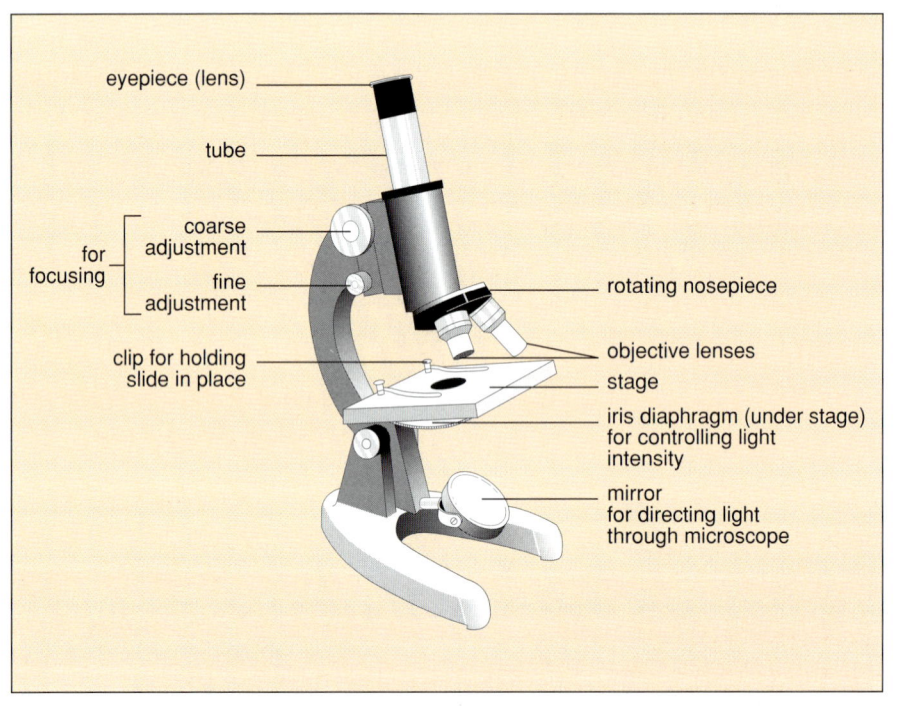

Picture 1 This kind of light microscope is used in many schools and colleges.

Picture 2 The main parts of a typical light microscope. It is known as a compound microscope because it consists of two lenses in series, the eyepiece lens at the top and the objective lens lower down.

How were cells discovered?

Cells were discovered in 1665 by the English inventor and scientist, Robert Hooke. Hooke examined a piece of bark from a tree. He looked particularly at the cork using a microscope that he had built himself. He found that the cork is made up of hundreds of little boxes, which he later called **cells** (picture 3).

As more and more organisms were examined under the microscope, it became clear to scientists that virtually all living things are made of cells. Cells became regarded as the basic unit of which organisms are made.

Cells, the bricks of the body **113**

Inside a typical animal cell

Picture 4 shows a photograph of some animal cells taken from a thin membrane in the human body, and picture 5 shows the structure of a typical animal cell. The cell is bounded by a thin **cell surface membrane**, also known simply as the **cell membrane**. In the centre is the nucleus, which is surrounded by a material called **cytoplasm**.

The cell surface membrane

The cell surface membrane (cell membrane) is thin, flexible and very delicate. It holds the cell together and plays an important part in controlling what passes into and out of the cell.

The nucleus

It is possible to remove the nucleus from certain cells by sucking it out with a very thin pipette. If this is done, the cell dies. We can conclude that the nucleus is essential for the life of the cell. It controls all the activities of the cell.

The nucleus contains a number of thread-like bodies called **chromosomes**. The chromosomes contain **genes**. These are small pieces of chemical coding which control the organism's development (see page 13). You will read more about these later.

The cytoplasm

The cytoplasm transfers energy, makes things, and stores food. Hundreds of chemical reactions take place inside it. Together, these reactions make up the cell's **metabolism**. Small dots in the cytoplasm are tiny particles of stored food. Many of them consist of a substance called **glycogen**.

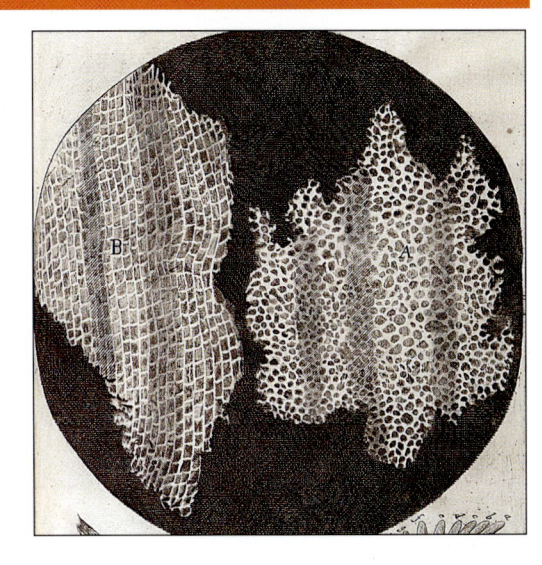

Picture 3 The first drawing of cells ever made. These cells were observed in a piece of cork by Robert Hooke. This drawing was published in 1665.

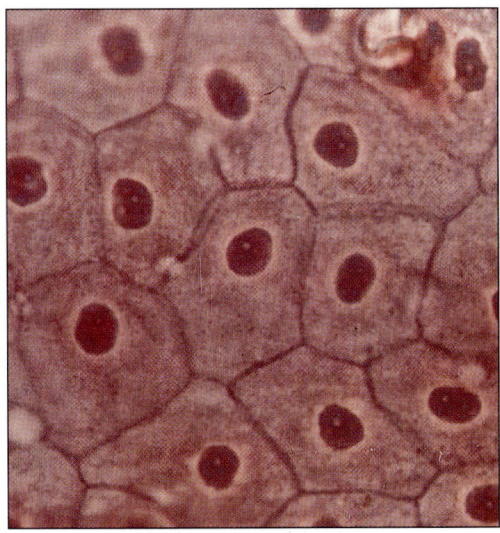

Picture 4 A simple type of epithelium seen under the microscope. It comes from one of the thin membranes inside the body.

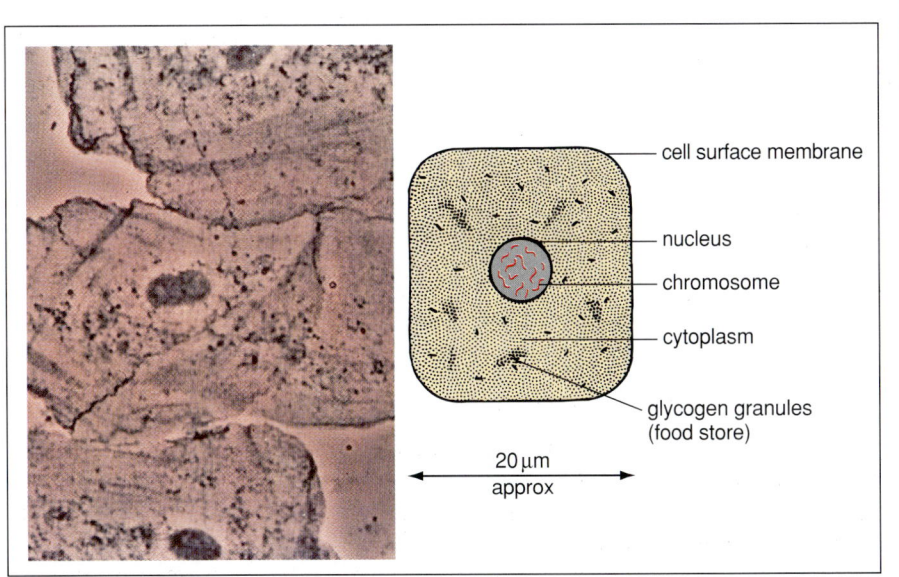

Picture 5 This diagram shows a typical animal cell. On the left are some cheek cells as they actually appear under the light microscope.

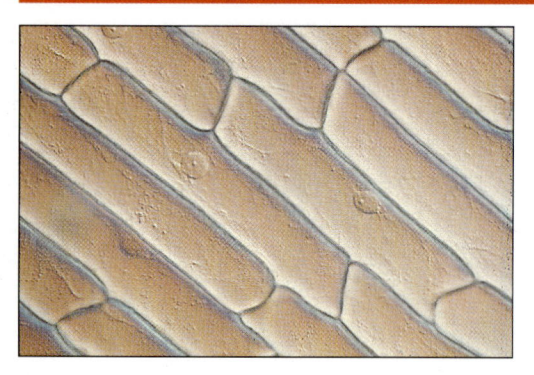

Picture 6 Plant epidermis from an onion bulb seen under the microscope.

Inside a typical plant cell

Are plant cells the same as animal cells? Not entirely, but they do have some features in common. Animal and plant cells both have a nucleus, a cell membrane and cytoplasm. Picture 6 shows a photograph of some plant cells whilst picture 7 shows a diagram of a typical plant cell. Plant cells differ from animal cells in the following ways:

- In addition to the cell surface membrane, the plant cell has a **cell wall**. It is made of **cellulose**, a tough rubbery material.
- In the centre of the cell there is a large cavity called the **vacuole**, which is filled with a watery fluid called **cell sap**. This means that the cytoplasm is pushed towards the edge of the cell. The nucleus is usually found in this layer of cytoplasm. However, in some plant cells the nucleus is suspended in the middle of the vacuole by fine strands of cytoplasm.
- The cytoplasm contains **starch grains**. This is how plants store food. The starch grains are equivalent to the glycogen granules in animal cells.
- Many plant cells possess **chloroplasts**. These are located in the cytoplasm, and they contain the green pigment **chlorophyll** which is used in **photosynthesis**. Chloroplasts only occur in the green parts of the plant which are exposed to the light. Roots and other underground structures lack them.

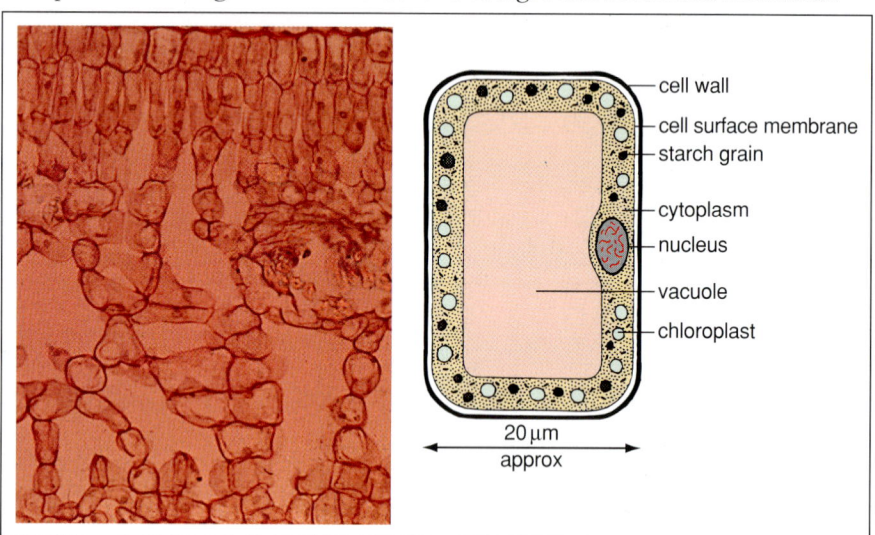

Picture 7 This diagram shows a typical plant cell. On the left are some leaf cells as they appear under the light microscope.

Different cells for different jobs

Practically all cells contain a nucleus and cytoplasm. However, they vary tremendously in their shape and form. In the human body there are at least twenty different types of cell, each specialised to do a particular job. Three are shown in picture 8.

There is thus a **division of labour** between cells. It's rather like a factory or an office in which each person has his or her own job to do. This is more efficient than if each individual tried to do everything.

Cells do not normally exist on their own. Usually large numbers of them are massed together into a **tissue**. Muscle tissue or epithelium tissue (cells which line the tubes inside the body) are examples.

Tissues are combined into **organs**. These are complex structures which have a particular job to do. Muscle tissue and epithelium tissue combine to form the wall of the small intestine. Finally, organs are grouped into **systems**, for example the digestive system. It consists of the intestine, stomach, liver and a number of other organs. Some organs belong to more than one system. If we are in good health our organ systems work in harmony with each other.

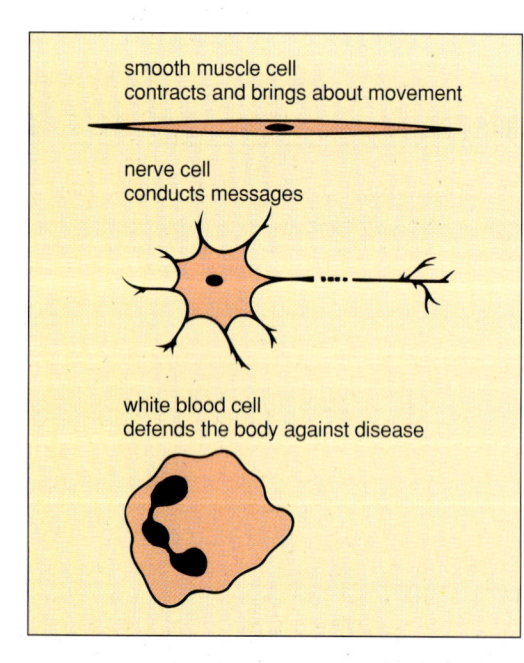

Picture 8 Three types of cell found in the human body.

Cells, the bricks of the body 115

Activities

A Learning to use the microscope
(Practical technique 5)

1 Study your microscope carefully and compare it with picture 2. Yours may be slightly different. Make sure you understand it before you use it.
2 Objects to be viewed under the microscope are first placed on a glass slide and covered with a thin piece of glass called a coverslip. Your teacher will give you a specimen which has been mounted in this way.
3 Place the slide on the stage of your microscope: arrange it so the specimen is in the centre of the hole in the stage.
4 Fix the slide in place with the two clips.
5 Rotate the nosepiece so the small objective lens is immediately above the specimen: the nosepiece should click into position.
6 Set the angle of the mirror so the light is directed up through the microscope.
7 Look down the microscope through the eyepiece. You will see a white or grey circular area. This is called the field of view. Adjust the iris diaphragm so the field of view is bright.
8 Look at the microscope from the side. Turn the coarse adjustment knob in the direction of the arrow in picture 2. This will make the tube move downwards.
9 Continue turning the knob until the tip of the objective lens is close to the slide.
10 Now look down the microscope again. Slowly turn the coarse adjustment knob in the other direction, so the tube gradually moves upwards. The specimen on the slide should eventually come into view.
11 Use the coarse and fine adjustment knobs to focus the object as sharply as possible.
12 If necessary readjust the iris diaphragm so the specimen is correctly illuminated. You will get a much better picture if you don't have too much light coming through the microscope.

> You are now looking at the specimen under low power, i.e. at low magnification. To look at it under high power, i.e. at a greater magnification, proceed as follows:

13 Rotate the nosepiece so the large objective lens is immediately above the specimen. The nosepiece should click into position, as before.
14 If the specimen is not in focus, focus it with the fine adjustment knob. Be careful that the tip of the objective lens does not touch the slide.
15 Readjust the illumination if necessary.

B Looking at plant cells
(Practical technique 6)

1 Slice an onion in two lengthways.
2 Take out one of the thick 'leaves' from inside it.
3 With forceps pull away the thin lining from the inner surface of the 'leaf'.
4 With scissors cut out a small piece of the lining, about 5 mm square.
5 Place the piece of lining on a slide and add a drop of dilute iodine solution.
  Make sure the iodine solution goes under the lining as well as above it.
  The iodine will stain the cells and make their nuclei easier to see.
6 Put on a coverslip.
7 Examine the slide under the microscope, first under low power, then high power. Choose an area of the lining where the cells are clear.
  Which of the structures shown in picture 7 can you see?
8 Draw one of the onion cells and label it as fully as you can.
  Although an onion is part of a plant, you won't have seen any chloroplasts in the cells. Why not?
9 Obtain a moss plant and pull off one of its smaller leaves with forceps.
10 Mount the leaf in a drop of water on a slide and put on a coverslip.
11 Examine the slide under low power.
  What structures, absent in onion cells, can you see in the moss cells? Explain their presence.
12 Select one of the clearest cells and examine it under high power.
13 Draw the cell and label it as fully as you can. You will have found it difficult or impossible to see a nucleus in the moss cells. Why?
  What could you do to make the nuclei show up?

> **Remember:** always treat the microscope with the greatest care: it is an expensive precision instrument. Always carry it with both hands, and keep it covered when you are not using it. Do not rest it on books or near the edge of the bench. Make sure the lenses never get scratched or damaged: if they need cleaning tell your teacher.

Questions

1 Suppose you use a microscope with one eyepiece lens and two objective lenses. The magnifying power of the eyepiece lens is ×10, and the magnifying powers of the two objective lenses are ×10 and ×40.
  What are the low and high power magnifications of your microscope?
2 Cells can be likened to the bricks of a house. In what ways are cells more than just bricks?
3 Which of the structures listed below are found (a) in animals cells only, (b) in plant cells only, and (c) in both animal and plant cells?

  cytoplasm   glycogen granules
  chloroplasts   cell wall
  starch grains   chromosomes
  nucleus   cell surface membrane
  vacuole

4 A typical cell is twenty micrometres wide.
  → Suppose that cells of this size were placed side by side. How many would there be in a row that was the same length as the third line of this question (arrowed)?
5 A certain specimen is 0.5 mm long. What is its length in micrometres?
  Suppose you drew the specimen and gave it a length of 2 cm. What would be the scale of your drawing?
  Why is it necessary for biologists to give their drawings a scale?

E2 Diffusion and osmosis

These processes enable small particles to move in and out of cells.

Moving substances in and out of cells

We saw in the previous section that all cells are surrounded by a cell surface membrane. This regulates the entry and exit of materials to and from the cell.

These materials include small particles which pass in and out of the cell by **diffusion**. To understand diffusion, you must first appreciate that a substance may be more concentrated in one region than another. For example, since the cell is continually making carbon dioxide from respiration, this gas has a higher concentration inside the cell than out. In other words there may be a **concentration gradient** between the two regions.

Diffusion is the net movement of particles from a region where they are at a higher concentration to a region where they are at a lower concentration, i.e. *down* a concentration gradient. Cells take up oxygen and get rid of carbon dioxide by diffusion (picture 1).

Diffusion is important to living cells since it provides a way by which useful substances enter and waste products leave.

Water passes in and out of cells by a special type of diffusion called **osmosis**. This is explained on the opposite page.

A Oxygen diffuses in

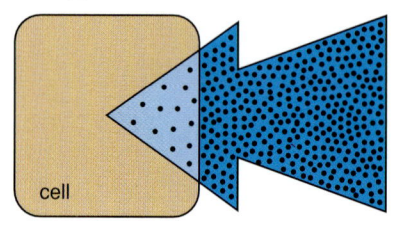

Oxygen is used up inside the cell by respiration. So the concentration of oxygen molecules is lower inside the cell than outside. As a result oxygen molecules diffuse into the cell.

B Carbon dioxide diffuses out

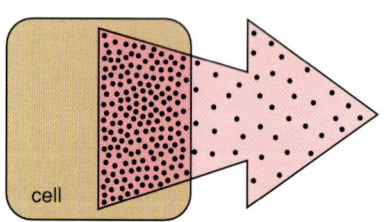

Carbon dioxide is produced inside the cell by respiration so the concentration of carbon dioxide molecules is higher inside the cell than outside. As a result carbon dioxide molecules diffuse out of the cell.

Picture 1 Cells take in oxygen and get rid of carbon dioxide by diffusion. In the diagram the closer together the dots, the higher the concentration of the gas.

Diffusion and surface area

Imagine that the box below is an organism. It is a cube whose sides are all one centimetre long:

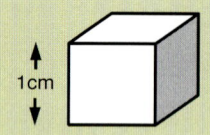

Its surface area is 6 cm², and its volume is 1 cm³.

Now suppose we double the size of the box like this:

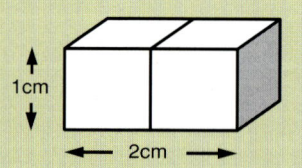

By how much have we increased its volume and its surface area? Well, its volume is now 2 cm³, twice what it was. However, its surface area is 10 cm², which is less than twice what it was.

In other words, we have doubled its volume, but its surface area has less than doubled. This is because, in the process of doubling the volume, we have lost part of the original surface (the part shaded in the first diagram).

So we can make this general statement: *as an object increases in size, the amount of surface relative to volume (the surface–volume ratio) decreases.*

This is important to organisms which take in things by diffusion. Think of it this way. A small organism, like an amoeba, has a large surface–volume ratio, so it can take in all the oxygen it needs by diffusion across the body surface. However, a large organism, like the human, has a much smaller surface–volume ratio, so it could not get all the oxygen it needs this way. Organisms of this kind need a special **gaseous exchange surface** for taking in oxygen. Examples include the **lungs** of mammals and the **gills** of fishes. These organs consist of sheets of tissue which are folded many times, thus providing a large surface area across which oxygen can be absorbed.

Larger organisms, including the human, also have a **circulatory system** which transports oxygen quickly from the gaseous exchange surface to all parts of the body. In many smaller organisms oxygen moves through the body by diffusion.

1 Having a gaseous exchange surface and circulatory system allows an organism to be more active than it would be otherwise. Why?

2 Do plants have special gaseous exchange surfaces? If so, where are they, and how are they suited for gaseous exchange?

3 Find out as much as you can about how oxygen gets from the surrounding air to the innermost parts of an amoeba, a flatworm, an earthworm, an insect, a fish and a mammal. Use books or (better still) observe the organisms themselves.

Osmosis

A bag is made out of a thin membrane and filled with a sugar solution. The open end of the bag is tied to the end of a capillary tube. The bag is then suspended in a beaker of water.

After a short time, water passes from the beaker into the bag. As a result, the sugar solution moves up the capillary tube. To understand why this happens, look at picture 1. The sugar molecules are larger than the water molecules. The membrane of which the bag is made has tiny holes in it. These holes are large enough to let the water molecules through, but too small to let the sugar molecules through. We call this kind of membrane a **partially permeable membrane.**

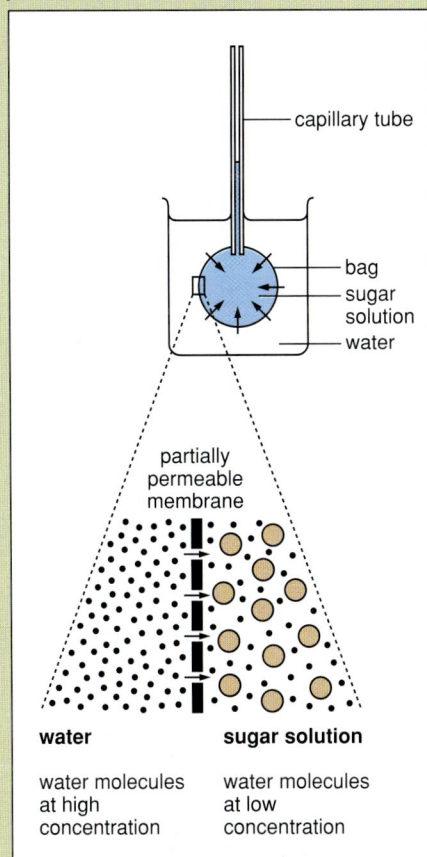

Picture 1 Osmosis is the one-way diffusion of water across a partially permeable membrane.

Now the presence of the sugar molecules in the bag means that there is less room for water molecules in the bag than in the beaker. So the water molecules in the bag are less concentrated than in the beaker. As a result, water molecules *diffuse* into the bag.

The diffusion of water across a partially permeable membrane is called **osmosis**. *Osmosis will take place wherever two solutions of different water concentrations are separated by a partially permeable membrane.*

The general term for any substance dissolved in a solution is solute. In the case we have been considering, the solute is sugar, but it could be some other substance such as salt.

What has all this got to do with biology? Well, cell surface membranes are partially permeable, so osmosis is important in organisms.

Osmosis in human cells

Human cells contain a solution of salts and other solutes. These are enclosed inside the partially permeable cell surface membrane.

Suppose you immerse a human red blood cell in water. What happens? Water enters the cell by osmosis, and the cell swells up and bursts (picture 2). The cell bursts because the cell surface membrane is too thin and delicate to withstand the pressure inside the cell.

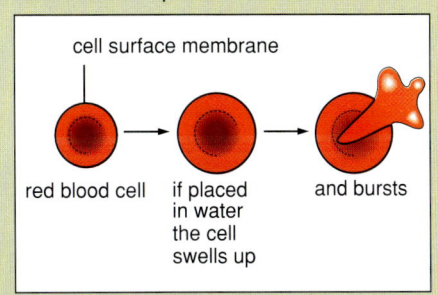

Picture 2 The result of immersing a red blood cell in water.

Obviously cells must not be allowed to burst inside our bodies. What stops this happening? The answer is that our blood and other body fluids have the same concentration as the cells, so water does not enter the cells by osmosis. In a later topic we shall see how the concentration of the blood and body fluids is maintained at just the right value.

Osmosis in plant cells

Plant cells have a cell surface membrane, just like animal cells, but outside this there is the cellulose cell wall. Inside a plant cell there is a solution of salts and other solutes, many of which are located in the vacuole. The cell surface membrane is partially permeable, just as it is in animal cells. But the cellulose cell wall is *fully* permeable to solutes as well as to water.

What happens if you immerse a plant cell in water? Water flows through the cell wall and cell surface membrane into the vacuole from the outside. As a result, the cell swells up. But it does not burst. This is because the cell wall stops the cell expanding too much. The wall stretches but it does not break. It is like trying to blow up a football into which no more air can be forced. When this point is reached, we say the cell is **fully turgid** or at **full turgor** (picture 3).

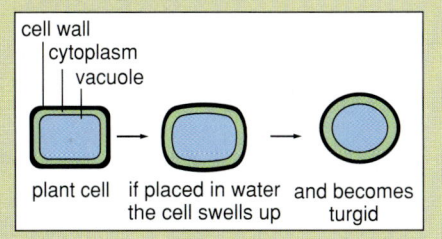

Picture 3 The result of immersing a plant cell in water.

Turgor is very important in land plants. It helps to make them firm. For example, when all the cells in a leaf are fully turgid, the cells press against each other and the leaf is held out in a open, expanded position. If the plant runs short of water, the cells may lose their turgor and the leaves droop. This is called wilting. Herbaceous plants which do not contain much wood depend on turgor to keep their stems erect. When such a plant wilts, the stem bends.

Picture 4 A melon plant when it is turgid (left) and when it has wilted (right).

1. Suggest an explanation for each of the following:
   a. If a lettuce becomes floppy, you may be able to make it firm and crisp by putting it in water for a while.
   b. If you sprinkle sugar on a bowl of strawberries, juice oozes out of them.

2. When a person swims in fresh water, you might think that water would enter the body through the skin by osmosis. But it does not. Suggest a reason.

3. What would happen to (a) a red blood cell and (b) a plant cell if they were immersed in a solution whose solute concentration was greater than that inside the cells?

E3 Cell division

Here we look closely at cell division and the chromosomes in the nucleus.

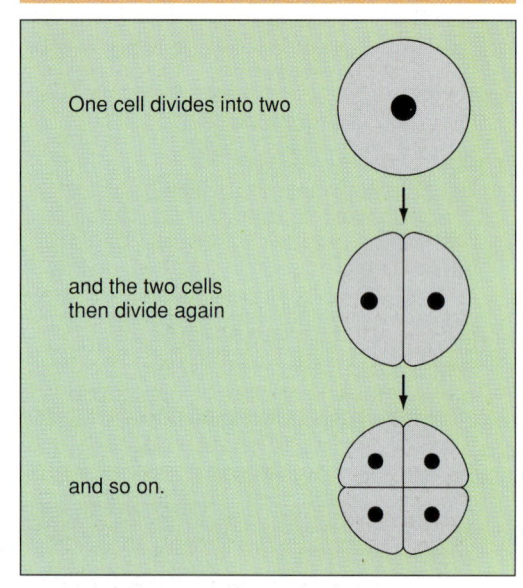

The purpose of cell division

Cell division, called **mitosis**, allows an organism to increase the number of cells in its body. In some single-celled animals and plants, mitosis is the process which takes place during **asexual reproduction**. In plants and animals mitosis permits an organism to **grow**.

What happens during mitosis?

Picture 1 shows what happens when a cell divides. First the nucleus splits into two, then the rest of the cell divides across the middle. At first the new cells are smaller that the original, but they soon grow to full size.

We have already seen that the nucleus of the cell controls most of the cell's activities. This includes mitosis. It contains chromosomes, thread-like structures containing the information to control how the cell develops and what sort of chemical reactions will take place in it. They are usually spread about in the nucleus and are not easily seen. During mitosis they shorten and coil up and become visible.

Picture 2 shows a complete set of the chromosomes from a human cell arranged in pairs.

The total number of chromosomes in a human is 46 (23 pairs). Other species have different numbers of chromosomes. For example, a chimpanzee has 48 (24 pairs), a dog 78 (39 pairs), a Siamese fighting fish 42 (21 pairs) and a cabbage 18 (9 pairs).

The fact that the chromosomes can be paired suggests that there are two complete sets of instructions in the nucleus of every cell. *The process of mitosis must be able to pass on both sets of information to each of the two new cells that will be produced.*

Look at pictures 3 and 4. They show what happens to the chromosomes at different stages of mitosis. Perhaps you will be able to see some of the stages from the diagram in the photograph. Mitosis proceeds smoothly from one stage to the next and is a continuous process.

Notice that the two **daughter cells** in picture 4 have the same number of chromosomes as the parent cell. This is called the **diploid number** as there are two of each type of chromosome. We can see that each daughter cell has obtained both sets of instructions from the parent cell, and it should therefore be able to develop normally. Mitosis has maintained the diploid number. However, before each daughter cell can divide to produce two more cells, the sets of instructions must be replicated again. This is achieved by each chromosome producing a replica of itself.

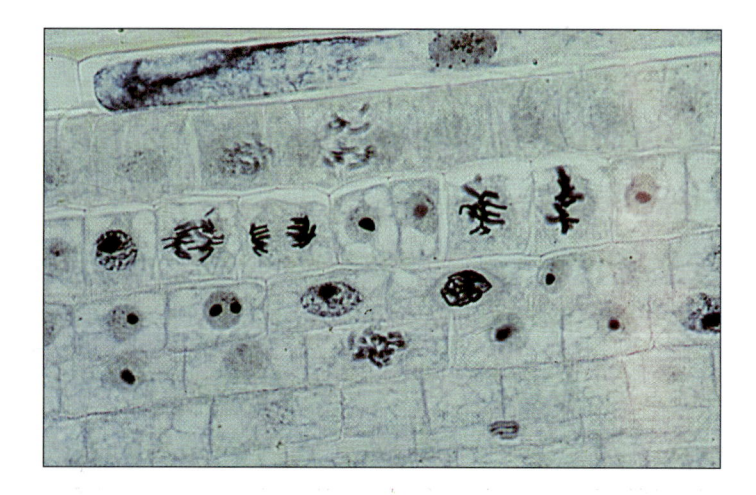

Picture 1 Cell division is the basis of growth in animals and plants.

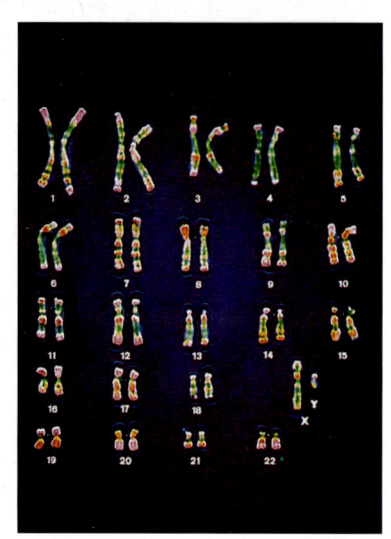

Picture 2 Human chromosomes sorted out and arranged in matching pairs. Each pair of chromosomes is given a number for identification purposes. The **X** and **Y** chromosomes are sex chromosomes which make this person a male. A female would have two **X** chromosomes.

Picture 3 Cells from an onion root tip during mitosis.

Cell division 119

MITOSIS

parent cell

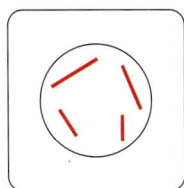

The chromosomes shorten and fatten and become visible.

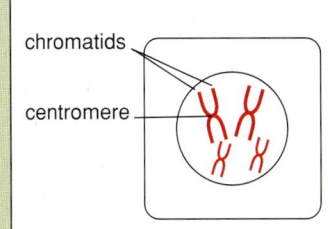

chromatids
centromere

Each chromosome produces a replica of itself. The original chromosome and its replica are called chromatids. They are held together at a point called the centromere.

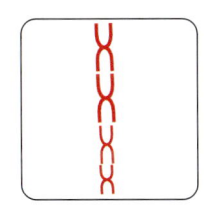

The chromosomes line up in the middle of the cell.

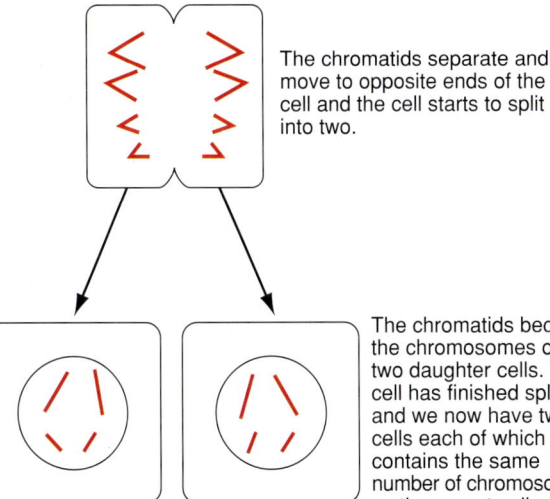

The chromatids separate and move to opposite ends of the cell and the cell starts to split into two.

The chromatids become the chromosomes of the two daughter cells. The cell has finished splitting, and we now have two cells each of which contains the same number of chromosomes as the parent cell.

daughter cells

Picture 4 The main stages of mitosis.

Questions

1 Look at the cell shown below, then answer the following questions.
   a How many chromosomes are there altogether?
   b How many *pairs* of chromosomes are there?
   c If this cell divided by mitosis, how many chromosomes would there be in each daughter cell?

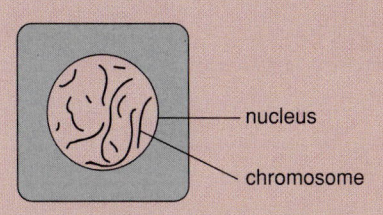

nucleus
chromosome

2 A cell can divide to produce two daughter cells. Each daughter cell grows and then divides.
   a How many cells would there be after ten divisions?
   b If each division takes 30 minutes, how many cells would there be after 24 hours?
   c If the parent cell had five pairs of chromosomes, how many chromosomes, in total, would a cell have after five divisions?

3 The following diagrams show cells at different stages of mitosis.
   Arrange the letters in the correct order.

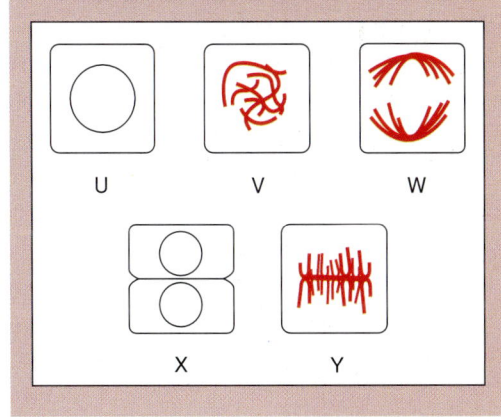

U   V   W

X   Y

E4 Enzymes

In this topic we shall see how the cell's chemical reactions are controlled.

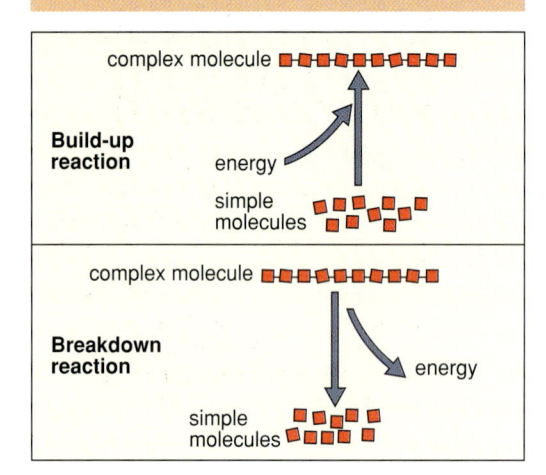

Chemical reactions in living things

Lots of chemical reactions take place inside living cells. Together, they comprise **metabolism**. Some metabolic reactions build things up (**anabolism**), others break things down (**catabolism**). Build-up reactions use up energy: they are **endothermic**. Breakdown reactions release energy: they are **exothermic** (picture 1).

An example of a build-up reaction is the linking of glucose molecules to form glycogen or starch for storage (picture 2). Another example is the linking of amino acid molecules to form proteins for body-building.

One of the most important examples of breakdown reactions is the oxidation of glucose to carbon dioxide and water in respiration (see page 124). This happens in almost all living cells.

Chemical reactions also take place in the gut. They are not part of metabolism but are concerned with **digestion** (see page 86). Starch, proteins and lipids are all broken down into simpler substances in the gut.

What enables all these reactions to occur and keeps them going? The answer is **enzymes**.

What are enzymes?

Enzymes are **biological catalysts**. They speed up the chemical reactions which go on inside living things. Without them the reactions would be so slow that life would grind to a halt!

Enzymes are extremely efficient at doing their job. Here is an example. Some of the chemical reactions which take place in our cells, for example in the liver, produce a by-product called hydrogen peroxide. Hydrogen peroxide is very poisonous so it must be got rid of quickly. Under the influence of an enzyme called **catalase**, the hydrogen peroxide is broken down into harmless water and oxygen. Catalase acts very quickly: one molecule of it can deal with six million molecules of hydrogen peroxide in one minute!

Types of enzymes

Enzymes are made inside cells. Once formed, the enzyme may leave the cell and do its job outside. Such enzymes are called **extracellular enzymes**. They include the digestive enzymes which break down food substances in our gut.

Other enzymes do their job inside the cell. They are called **intracellular enzymes**. Their job is to speed up the chemical reactions occurring in our cells. But they do more than just speed up the reactions; they also control them.

At this moment, thousands of chemical reactions are taking place in your body. Each reaction is controlled by a particular enzyme. Our enzymes make sure that the right reactions occur in the right place and at the right time.

An enzyme-controlled reaction

Here is an example of a reaction which is controlled by an enzyme:

$$\text{maltose (substrate)} \xrightarrow{\text{maltase (enzyme)}} \text{glucose (product)}$$

The substance which the enzyme acts on is called the **substrate** – in this case maltose. The new substance or substances formed as a result of the reaction are the **products**. In this case there is just one product: glucose. The enzyme catalysing this particular reaction is maltase.

This reaction will go in either direction. In other words the reaction is **reversible**: maltose can be turned into glucose, or glucose into maltose. The enzyme will work either way. If there is a lot of maltose present compared with glucose, the reaction will go from left to right; if there is a lot of glucose present compared with maltose, it will go from right to left. Most metabolic reactions are reversible.

Picture 1 This diagram illustrates two important types of chemical reaction which take place in living organisms.

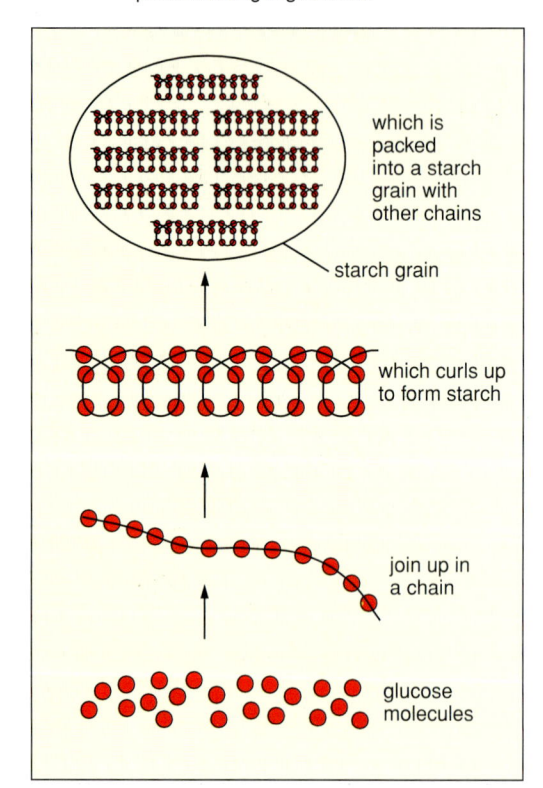

Picture 2 Starch is a convenient way of storing glucose molecules. These diagrams are not drawn to scale.

The properties of enzymes

Enzymes have five important properties:

1 They are always proteins
This is one reason why we need proteins in our food.

2 They are specific in their action
What this means is that each enzyme controls one particular reaction, or type of reaction. Thus maltase will only act on maltose, and sucrase on sucrose.

3 They can be used over again
This is because they are not altered by the reactions in which they take part. However, an enzyme molecule eventually runs down and has to be replaced.

4 They are destroyed by heating
Enzymes, in common with all proteins, are destroyed by heating. This is called **denaturation**. At first, as the temperature rises the activity of the enzyme increases (see graph 1 in picture 4). Raising the temperature by 10°C can double the rate of reaction. Heating increases the random movements of the molecules and heightens the chances of the enzyme and substrate meeting and reacting.

At a certain temperature, called the **optimum**, the enzyme will be working as fast as it can. A further rise in temperature results in the denaturation of the enzyme and the activity drops rapidly. Most enzymes stop working if the temperature rises above 45°C (picture 3).

5 They are sensitive to pH
The term pH refers to the degree of acidity or alkalinity of a solution. Most intracellular enzymes work best in neutral conditions. Graph 2 in picture 4 shows the effect of pH on two enzymes, catalase (see page 120) and pepsin (see page 88). There is an optimum pH at which the enzyme activity is greatest. It is not the same for both enzymes.

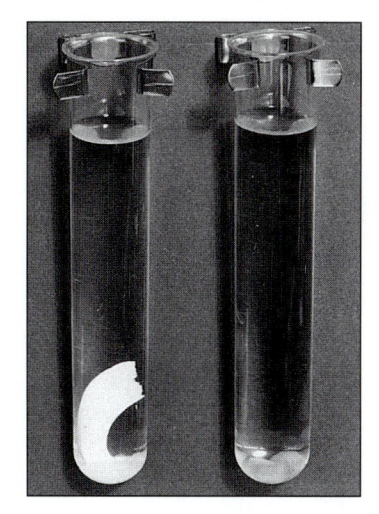

Picture 3 The effect of heating trypsin, a protein-digesting enzyme in the small intestine. In the left tube a piece of hard egg-white was covered with trypsin which had been heated to 50°C beforehand and then allowed to cool. In the right tube a piece of egg-white was covered with trypsin that had not been heated beforehand. Note that the pre-heated trypsin has failed to digest the egg-white.

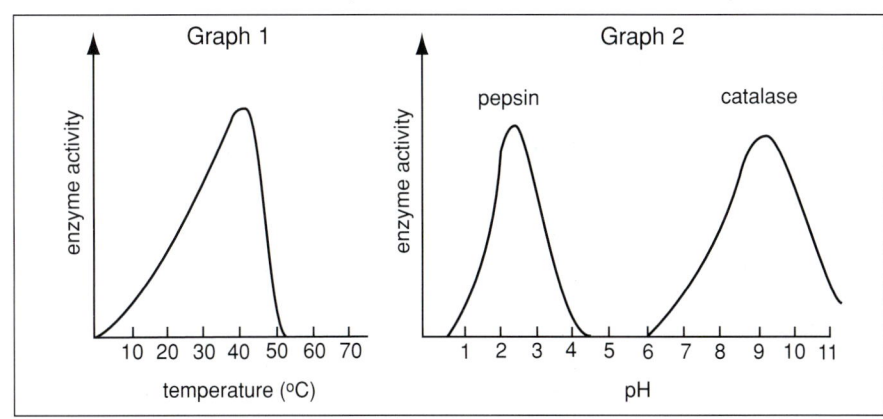

Picture 4 Graphs to show the effects of temperature and pH on enzyme activity.

How do enzymes work?

Look at picture 5. This shows in a very simple way how enzymes are believed to work. As you know, molecules are constantly moving about and bumping into each other. Now when a substrate molecule bumps into a molecule of the right enzyme, it fits into a depression on the surface of the enzyme molecule. This depression is called the **active site**. The reaction then takes place and the molecules of product leave the active site, freeing it for another substrate molecule.

The active site of a particular enzyme has a specific shape into which only one kind of substrate will fit. The substrate fits into the active site rather like a key fits into a lock. This is why enzymes are specific in their action.

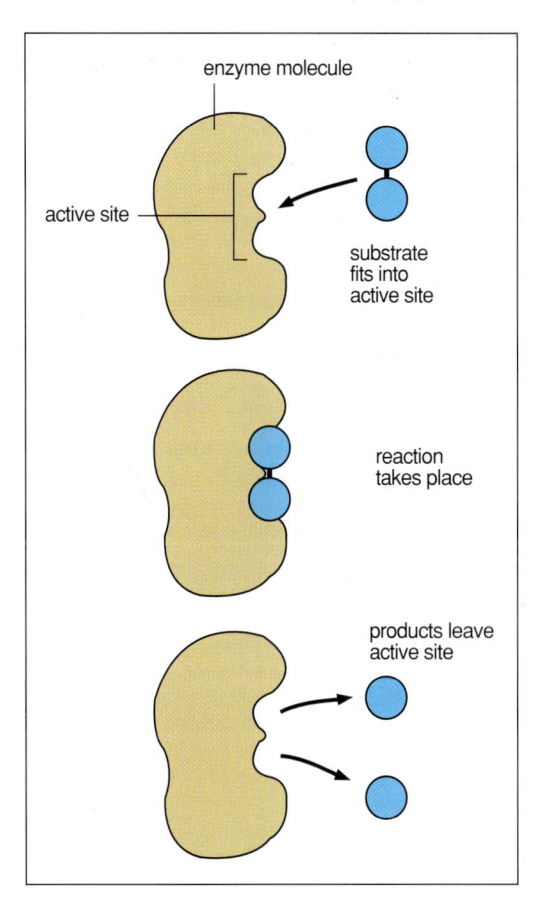

Picture 5 How an enzyme works. The substrate fits into the active site where the reaction takes place.

When an enzyme is denatured by heating, the shape of the active site is changed so that the substrate no longer fits. A change in the pH has a similar effect.

The uses of enzymes

Enzymes can be extracted from organisms in a purified form and then used in all sorts of scientific and industrial processes. An everyday use in the home is in **biological washing powders**. Various protein-digesting enzymes (proteases) are added to the washing powder, and these are supposed to dissolve protein stains (see page 201).

The advantage of biological washing powders is that they work at relatively low temperatures. This makes them particularly useful for delicate fabrics, and it saves electricity too. However, some people are allergic to them and they can cause skin trouble.

Biological washing powders are an example of how enzymes can be useful in the home. Enzymes are useful in industry too. Here are some examples:

- **Proteases** are used for tenderising meat, skinning fish, removing hair from hides, and breaking down proteins in baby foods.
- **Amylases** convert starch to sugar in making syrups, fruit juices, chocolates and other food products.
- **Cellulase** breaks down cellulose and is used for softening vegetables, removing the seed coat from cereal grain, and extracting agar jelly from seaweed.
- **Isomerase** converts glucose into fructose. Fructose is much sweeter than glucose; this makes it useful in slimming foods as only small amounts are needed.
- **Catalase** releases oxygen from hydrogen peroxide and is used in making foam rubber from latex.

Nowadays enzymes for human use are obtained mainly from microbes. The microbes are grown on a large scale in **industrial fermenters** (see page 191) so large amounts of the enzymes can be obtained.

Picture 6 Enzymes are used in manufacturing sweets, in biological washing powders and for tenderising meat.

How enzymes were discovered

Enzymes were discovered in 1897 by a German scientist called Eduard Buchner. He discovered them by accident.

Buchner was interested in yeast. This little organism had long been known to convert sugar into alcohol. We call this process fermentation (see page 188). However it wasn't fermentation that Buchner was interested in; he had the idea that yeast might contain proteins which could be useful medically. So he gave up a holiday in order to investigate this idea.

He decided to extract the juice from yeast and test it on people to see if it might help to cure certain diseases. He obtained a large amount of yeast and squeezed it. Out of it oozed a brown liquid, rather like treacle. But before he had a chance to try it out on anyone, it went bad.

What could he do to preserve it? His laboratory assistant remembered that sugar was used to preserve fruit, so he suggested that they might add some sugar to the yeast extract. They did this, and to their surprise the brown liquid converted the sugar into alcohol!

Until now people had thought that sugar could only be fermented by *living* yeast cells. Buchner showed that fermentation does not depend on living cells, but is achieved by a chemical substance in the cells. We now know that this substance is a mixture of enzymes.

(Adapted from '*The Science of Life*' by Gordon Rattray Taylor, Thames and Hudson)

1 What do you think caused Buchner's yeast extract to go bad?

Suggest two things that could be done with it today to prevent it going bad.

2 What is the advantage to yeast of being able to convert sugar into alcohol?

3 How could you show that the substance in Buchner's yeast extract was an enzyme and not some other kind of substance?

Picture 1 Eduard Buchner who discovered enzymes.

Questions

1. Look at picture 3 on page 121 and read the caption carefully. Describe an experiment which you would do to find out, as closely as possible, the exact temperature at which trypsin is destroyed.

2. A technician carried out an experiment to investigate the effect of temperature on a certain metabolic reaction. Her results are shown in the graph.

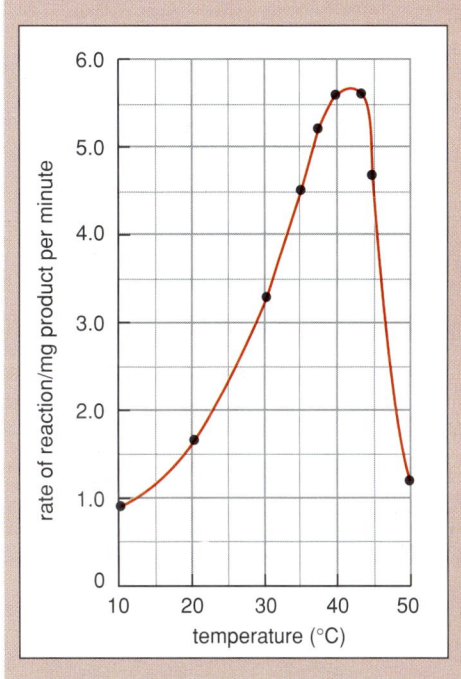

    a Between which temperatures does the rate of the reaction (i) increase, (ii) decrease?
    b At what temperature is the rate of the reaction fastest? (This is called the optimum temperature.)
    c Explain the effect of temperature on the rate of the reaction.

3. Small samples of starch were added to a solution of the enzyme amylase made up at different pH values. The table below shows the time taken for the complete digestion of starch at the different pH values.

    a Where, in the human body, would the enzyme amylase be found? Suggest two places.
    b Plot a line graph of these results.
    c Describe the effect of pH on the action of amylase.
    d What is the optimum pH for the action of this enzyme?
    e Is this investigation a fair test? What factors or variables must be kept constant during this investigation?
    f What can be done to increase the accuracy and validity of these results?

4. The graph below shows the effect of pH on the activity of the enzyme pectinase.

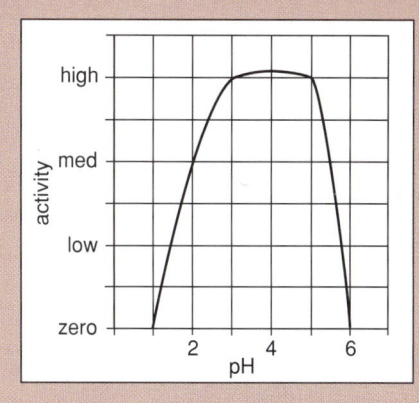

    a Between which two pH values is pectinase active? This is the working range of the enzyme.
    b What term is used to describe the pH at which an enzyme is most active?
    c Pectinase only breaks down pectin. It has no effect on any other substrate. How would you explain this?

pH	5.0	5.5	6.0	6.5	7.0	7.5	8.0
Time taken for digestion of starch (minutes)	6.00	5.60	4.20	1.30	1.30	2.40	3.50

Naming enzymes

Enzymes are usually named by putting 'ase' on the end of the name of the substance, or type of substance, on which the enzyme acts. So

- enzymes which act on carbohydrates are called **carbohydrases**,
- enzymes which act on lipids are called **lipases**, and
- enzymes which act on proteins are called **proteases**.

Each of these major groups of enzymes includes specific enzymes which act on particular substances. For example, carbohydrases include **amylase** which catalyses the breakdown of starch to maltose, and **maltase** which catalyses the breakdown of maltose to glucose.

Using enzymes to manufacture syrups

Enzymes, obtained mainly from bacteria, are used for making sweet syrups from starch. The syrups formed contain two sugars, maltose and glucose.

The starch is obtained from plants from which it is extracted by milling. The milled starch consists of masses of starch grains (see page 120). The grains are broken open by heat treatment so as to release the starch itself.

After cooling, the starch is rather like unsweet jelly. It is now mixed with certain enzymes which liquefy it and turn it into maltose. Treatment with other enzymes turns some of the maltose into glucose. Both these sugars are sweet.

By varying the amounts of the different enzymes, it's possible to produce syrups consisting of mainly maltose with relatively little glucose, or mainly glucose with relatively little maltose.

High maltose syrups are used in the brewing industry, whereas high glucose syrups are used for making jam and confectionery. By further enzyme treatment, glucose syrups can be turned into fructose syrups. Fructose is sweeter than glucose and is used as a sweetener in foods and drinks.

1. Before enzymes were used, starch was converted into sugars by heating it with an acid. Why is the enzyme method better? Think of as many reasons as you can.

2. Draw a flow chart to summarise the process outlined in the passage.

E5 Obtaining energy

We need energy for almost everything we do. We get it from our food which serves as a fuel.

Food as a fuel

We can show that food is a fuel by burning it. When the food is burned, energy is transferred to the surroundings, warming them.

Now for practical details. We weigh a sample of food. Then we put the sample of food under a measured quantity of water. We set fire to the food and let it heat up the water. The rise in temperature of the water tells us how much energy has been transferred from the food. To do this accurately we use an apparatus called a **food calorimeter** (picture 2). Picture 1 shows a simple but less accurate method based on the same principle.

The energy is measured in a unit called the **kilojoule** (**kJ**). The unit of energy used to be the Calorie. This is still used sometimes, and you hear people talking about losing calories or eating low-calorie foods. However, this unit has now been officially replaced by the kilojoule.

The three main substances found in food are carbohydrate, fat and protein. We can estimate the amount of energy obtainable from each of these substances. We can then compare their energy values. Here they are:

- Carbohydrate: 1 gram gives 17 kJ
- Fat: 1 gram gives 39 kJ
- Protein: 1 gram gives 18 kJ

Notice that fat gives about twice as much energy as either carbohydrate or protein.

How much energy is given by different foods?

Table 1 tells you how much energy is given by some everyday foods. The amount of energy given by a particular food depends on the substances it contains. For example, margarine and butter consist almost entirely of fat, so they give a lot of energy. On the other hand, a cabbage is ninety per cent water, so it gives very little energy.

Another thing that determines how much energy a particular food gives is how it is cooked. For example, potatoes fried in fat give three times as much energy as potatoes boiled in water.

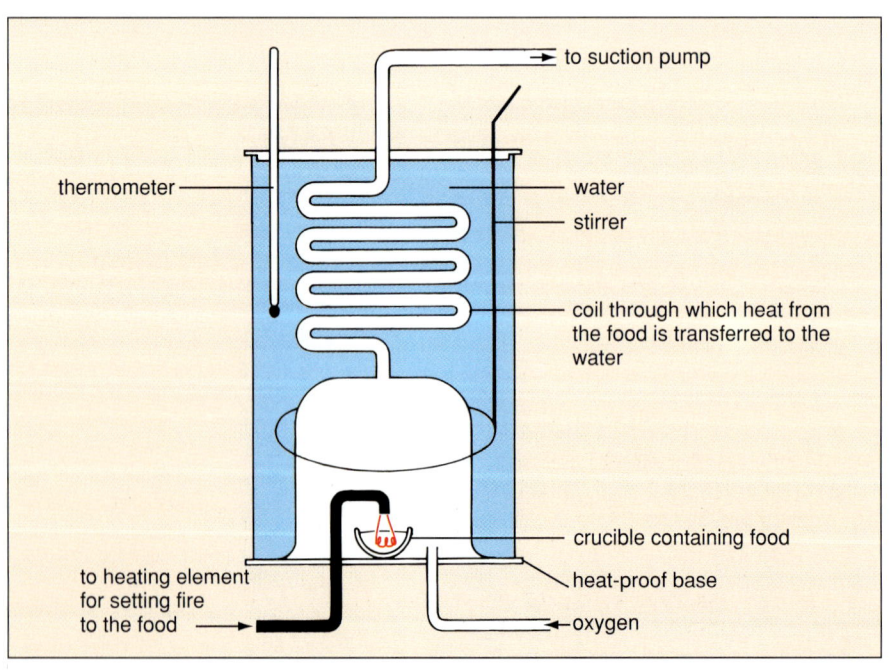

Table 1 How much energy is there in various everyday foods? You can find out by looking at this list.

	kJ per gram
margarine	32.2
butter	31.2
peanuts/groundnuts	24.5
chocolate (milk)	24.2
cake (plain)	18.0
sugar (white)	16.5
sausages (pork)	15.5
cornflakes	15.3
rice	15.0
bread (white)	10.6
chips	9.9
chicken (roast)	7.7
eggs (fresh)	6.6
potatoes (boiled)	3.3
milk	2.7
beer (bottled)	1.2
cabbage (boiled)	0.34

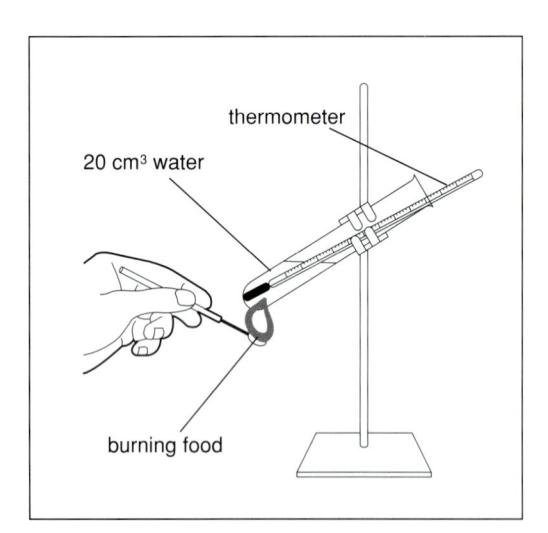

Picture 1 To calculate the energy content of the food, multiply the mass of water by the rise in temperature and then by 4.2. The answer is in joules (J). Convert to kilojoules (kJ) by dividing by 1000.

Picture 2 A food calorimeter. It is used to find how much energy there is in a sample of food.

What is energy needed for?

Here are the main things that organisms need energy for.
- All organisms need energy for growth, cell division, transporting chemicals, and just staying alive.
- Animals need energy for making muscles contract, sending messages along nerves and keeping warm.
- Plants need energy for taking up mineral salts from the soil and opening and closing their air pores (stomata).

What happens to the food?

First, think what happens when a fuel like petrol is burned. Oxygen is used up and carbon dioxide and water are produced. At the same time, energy is transferred to the surroundings, warming them.

The same kind of thing happens in our bodies. Substances, derived from our food, are oxidised to give carbon dioxide and water, and energy is transferred.

The main substance oxidised is glucose. We can summarise what happens as an equation:

glucose + oxygen → carbon dioxide + water + energy

$C_6H_{12}O_6$ $\quad\quad$ $6O_2$ $\quad\quad$ $6CO_2$ $\quad\quad$ $6H_2O$

This process takes place in our cells. We call it **respiration**. The glucose serves as a fuel. The oxidation of glucose in respiration drives our bodies, just as the burning of petrol drives a car.

When respiration takes place with oxygen present it is called **aerobic respiration**. We will read more about this later.

Picture 3 A sprinter in action. How do his muscles get the energy they need?

Confirming the respiration equation

Various experiments can be carried out to show that organisms take in oxygen and release carbon dioxide, and also that they transfer energy to the surroundings by warming them.

The apparatus in picture 4 has been set up to find out if germinating peas give out carbon dioxide. If lime water turns cloudy white in flask C, then this indicates the presence of carbon dioxide. The carbon dioxide has come from the peas. They have used up their internal food store (see page 52) to produce energy for growth. Respiration has taken place in the peas.

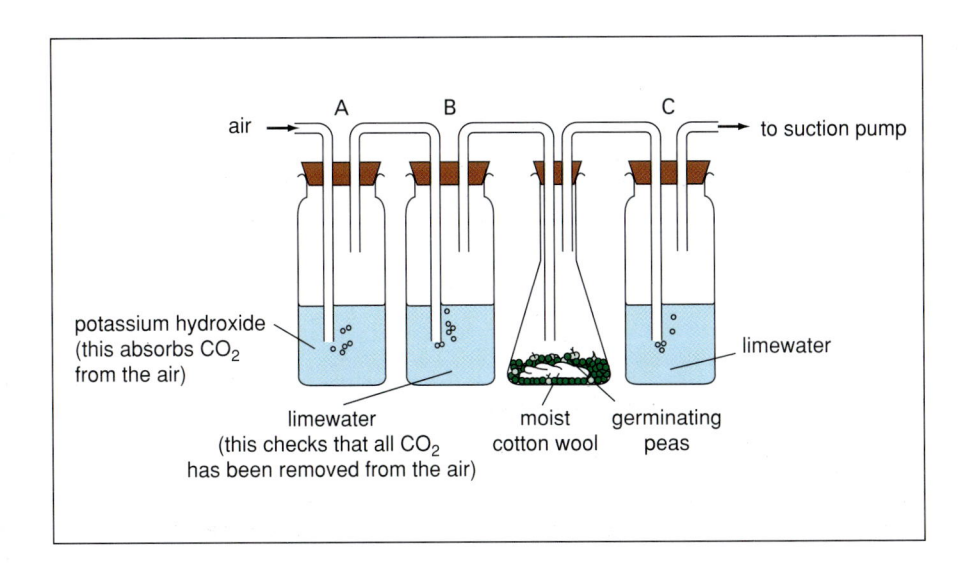

Picture 4 Apparatus required to find out if germinating peas release carbon dioxide.

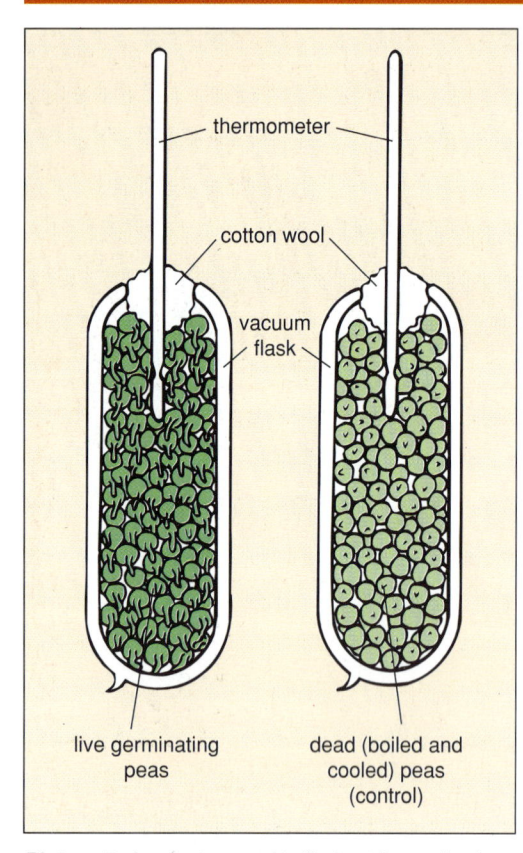

Picture 5 Apparatus used to find out if germinating peas release energy to their surroundings.

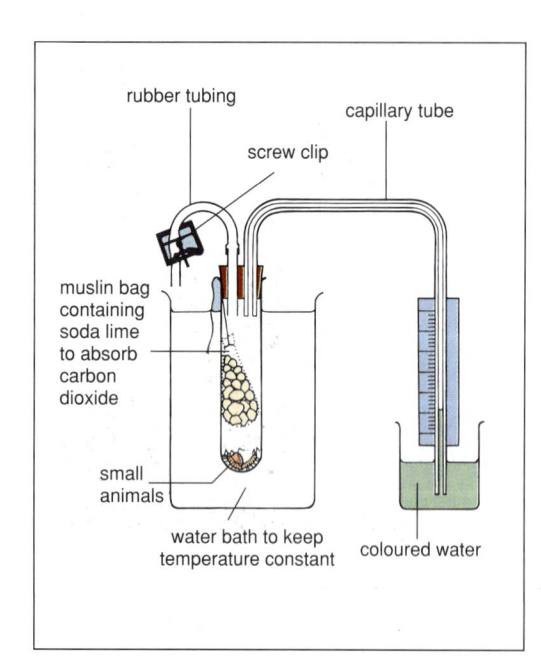

Picture 6 A simple respirometer.

A second set of the apparatus would have to be set up to act as a **control**. It would contain dead peas that would *not* be respiring.

To be a fair test, there should be only one difference between the experimental apparatus and the control. In this case, it is that the peas are living or dead. All other conditions must be the same for both sets of apparatus. The difference in the results obtained must be due to the one difference between the two sets of apparatus.

In this case the living peas would respire and release carbon dioxide; the lime water would turn cloudy. In contrast, the dead peas would not respire and would not release carbon dioxide; the lime water would remain clear.

An alternative indicator to lime water can be used. For example hydrogencarbonate (bicarbonate) indicator changes from red to:

- **yellow**, if the air contains more than the normal atmospheric level of carbon dioxide.
- **purple**, if the air contains less than the normal atmospheric level of carbon dioxide.

The apparatus in picture 5 can be used to show that germinating peas release energy (in the form of heat) to their surroundings. Once again you will notice this experiment has a control: a control flask is used to compare the results with the experimental flask.

Measuring the rate of respiration

The uptake of oxygen can be used to measure the **rate of respiration**. The apparatus, shown in picture 6, is called a **respirometer**.

Small animals, such as woodlice, are put in a large test tube. A muslin bag filled with soda lime, a chemical which can absorb carbon dioxide, is suspended in the tube. Care must be taken to avoid contact between the animals and the soda lime. The tube is made air-tight with a screw clip on the rubber tubing and the open end of the capillary tube is dipped into some coloured water.

The animals take in oxygen and the coloured water gradually rises up the tube. Any carbon dioxide given out by the animals is absorbed by the soda lime. The volume of oxygen taken in over a period of say 30 minutes can be measured, and the rate or respiration calculated.

Once again a control apparatus is needed. It will differ from the experimental apparatus in that there will be no living organisms in it.

One of the investigations that can be carried out using a respirometer is to find the effect of increasing temperature on the **rate of respiration** of an organism. The respiration rate rises as the temperature increases up to about 40°C. Above that temperature, respiration slows down and soon stops altogether. At this temperature enzymes are destroyed (see page 121). This suggests that respiration is a chemical process catalysed by enzymes.

ATP, the essential link

The energy released when glucose is oxidised is not used directly. It is linked to activities such as muscle contraction by another substance called **ATP**. ATP stands for **adenosine triphosphate**. When glucose is oxidised, the energy is transferred to ATP. When a muscle contracts, energy is transferred from the ATP to the muscle. ATP is a kind of 'energy carrier', taking the energy from the glucose to the muscle.

If you put a drop of glucose solution on a muscle fibre, nothing happens. But if you put a drop of ATP solution on the muscle fibre, it contracts. This shows that glucose, by itself, cannot provide the energy needed for muscle contraction. It is the ATP, made as a result of oxidising glucose, that provides the energy. ATP supplies energy in all living organisms.

Questions

1. Look at the following statements and say if each one is true for respiration.
   a. occurs only in plant cells
   b. produces oxygen
   c. occurs only in animal cells
   d. releases energy
   e. only takes place during the day
   f. produces carbon dioxide

2. Look at the graph which shows the temperature at the centre of a mound of decomposing grass, measured at noon each day for a month.
   a. What was the highest temperature recorded?
   b. Why was the temperature recorded at noon each day?
   c. Name the process, occurring in the cells of the decomposers, which causes the release of heat energy.
   d. Why does the temperature in the centre of the mound fall from 9 September onwards? 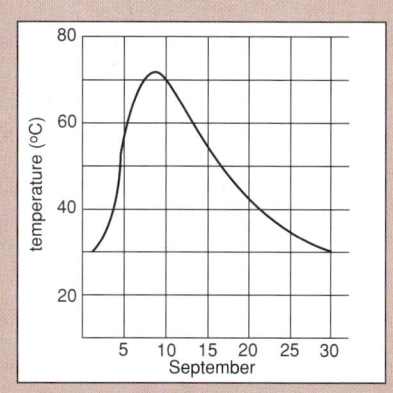
   e. Describe the effect of the increasing numbers of decomposers on the amount of oxygen present at the centre of the mound of cut grass.

3. Under what circumstances, if any, would you expect a plant to:
   a. respire but not photosynthesise,
   b. photosynthesise but not respire,
   c. respire and photosynthesise,
   d. neither respire nor photosynthesis?

4. The apparatus shown was set up to demonstrate respiration. After a few days, it was found that the level of water had risen in the tube on side B.
   a. What name is given to this kind of apparatus?
   b. Name two factors which must be kept constant in the experiment.
   c. Explain why small changes in room temperature during the experiment can be ignored.
   d. Suggest a reason to explain why, on repeating the investigation, a small rise in the water level on side A occurred in addition to a large rise on side B.

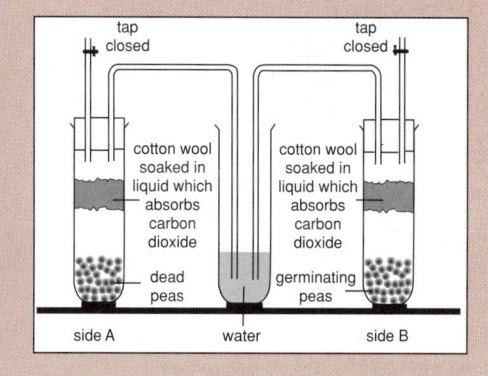

On being a good scientist

When respiration takes place, glucose is not oxidised in a single chemical reaction but in a series of small steps.
Many of the individual steps were discovered by the late Sir Hans Krebs who was a pupil of a great German scientist called Otto Warburg. Sir Hans Krebs was awarded a Nobel Prize in 1953 for his research on respiration.
Here he suggests some of the qualities which a successful scientist should have:

'Technical skills are, of course, prerequisites for successful research. What is critical in the use of skills is how to assess their potentialities and their limitations; how to improve, to rejuvenate, to supplement them. But perhaps the most important quality is humility, because from it flows a self-critical mind and the continuous effort to learn and to improve. If I try to summarise what I learned from Warburg, I would say it was asking the right kind of question, forging new tools for tackling the chosen problems, being ruthless in self-criticism, taking pains in verifying facts, and expressing results and ideas clearly and concisely.'
Asking the right kind of question in research means avoiding those which may give a quick result and concentrating on those which are really worthwhile tackling. Paul Weiss remarked: 'The primary aim of research must not be more facts and more facts, but more facts of strategic value'. Goethe expressed the same idea much earlier. 'Progress in research is much hindered because people concern themselves with that which is not worth knowing, and that which cannot be known'.

Medawar has stated very succinctly: 'If politics is the art of the possible, science is the art of the soluble'. How to select worthwhile soluble problems and how to create the tools required to achieve a solution is something that scientists learn from the great figures in science rather than from science books.

(Adapted from Hans Krebs. *Reminiscences and Reflections*, Oxford University Press, 1981)

1. Why is it important for scientists to show humility?
2. What are 'facts of strategic value'? Can you think of examples?
3. Suggest examples of things which, in your opinion, are not worth knowing or cannot be known.

Picture 1 Hans Krebs in his laboratory at Oxford.

F1
How we move

Can you imagine what life would be like if you couldn't move?

Picture 1 A ballet dancer caught in mid-action.

The skeleton

Look at the ballet dancer in picture 1. Without her skeleton the dancer would not be able dance; in fact she would be little more than a mass of pink material on the floor.

The skeleton has three important functions:
- to support the body, giving it shape and form,
- to provide points of attachment for muscles so the body can move,
- to protect the soft internal organs of the body.

What do we need in order to move?

To move we need three things: nerves, muscles and a skeleton. The nerves carry messages to the muscles, which respond by shortening. The shortening of a muscle is called **contraction**. The muscles are attached to the skeleton at both ends by a **tendon**. The tendons are tough and non-elastic, so they do not stretch when they are pulled. The individual bones that make up the skeleton are held together by **ligaments**. These are tough but elastic and will stretch when pulled.

So, when a muscle contracts, it pulls on one part of the skeleton and, since the tendons do not stretch, the contracting muscle is able to move the bones.

The arm, an example of how we move

Two main muscles move the arm: the **biceps** and the **triceps**. The biceps bends the arm at the elbow: it is a **flexor muscle**. The triceps straightens the arm: it is an **extensor muscle** (picture 2). These two muscles produce opposite effects and are known as **antagonistic muscles**.

For our muscles to do their job properly, the bones must move easily against each other. This happens at the **joints**.

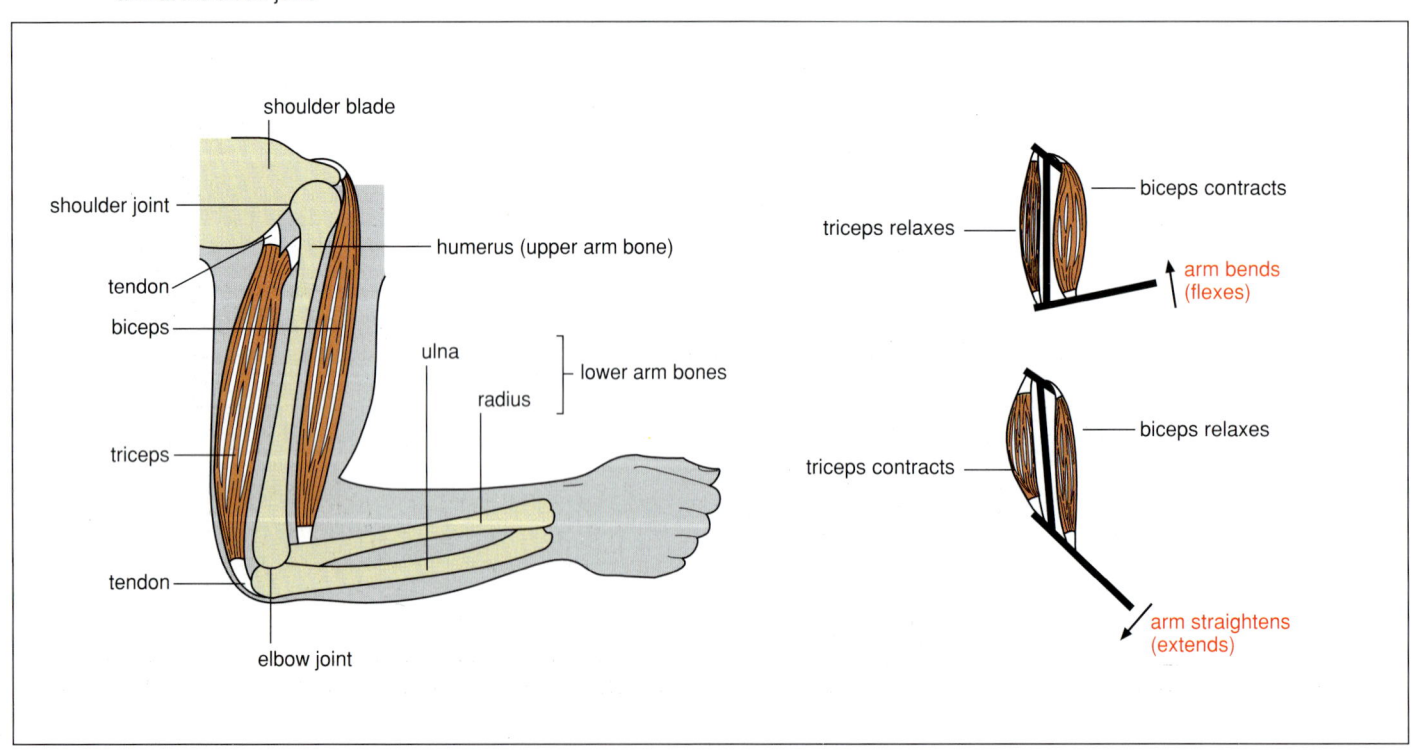

Picture 2 The biceps and triceps muscles move the arm at the elbow joint.

Joints, movement with minimum friction

A joint is shown in picture 3. Notice how the two bones fit together. The two bones are separated by a special fluid called **synovial fluid**. This serves as a lubricant, enabling the knob to move smoothly inside the socket with very little friction. It's like the oil between the moving parts of a machine. Synovial fluid is the best lubricant in the world: manufacturers of artificial lubricants have never been able to better it.

The ends of the two bones are made of **cartilage**. This is softer than bone and slightly springy. It helps to prevent jarring when the two bones move against each other.

Joints are weak points in the skeleton, and they must be protected. The joint is surrounded by a tough **fibrous capsule**. Knees are particularly vulnerable because of their exposed position. The knee is protected in front by a small bone called the **knee cap**. Behind and in front of the knee cap there are cavities filled with synovial fluid which cushion the knee.

Different kinds of joints

The hip joint is called a **ball and socket joint** (picture 4A). This kind of joint allows movement in any direction. Test this for yourself by standing up and moving your leg around at the hip. You can move it forwards and backwards and from side to side, and you can rotate it.

Now try bending your leg at the knee. You will find that you can bend it in only one direction: backwards and forwards. This is because of the way the knee joint is constructed. It consists of two knobs which fit into two cups (picture 4B). This is called a **hinge joint** because it operates rather like the hinge on a door.

What sort of joint is the shoulder joint? And the elbow? How can you tell what sorts of joints these are?

Holding the bones together

If the bones were not held together in some way, they would fall apart at the joints. They are held together by the fibrous capsules which cover the joints, and by the muscles and ligaments which run from one bone to another. Some of the ligaments are inside the joints, others outside. You can see ligaments inside the joints in picture 4.

The ligaments limit the amount of movement which is possible at a joint. Collectively, though, the joints enable the human skeleton to be amazingly flexible. Flexibility of the body is an aspect of fitness (see page 164).

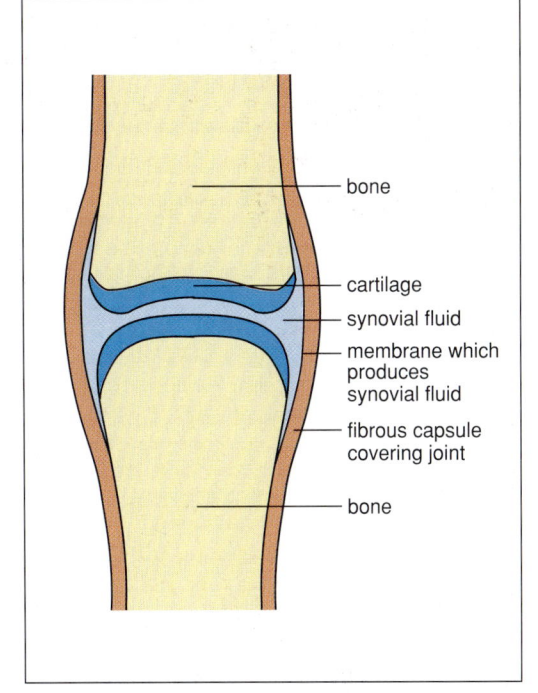

Picture 3 The structure of a typical joint.

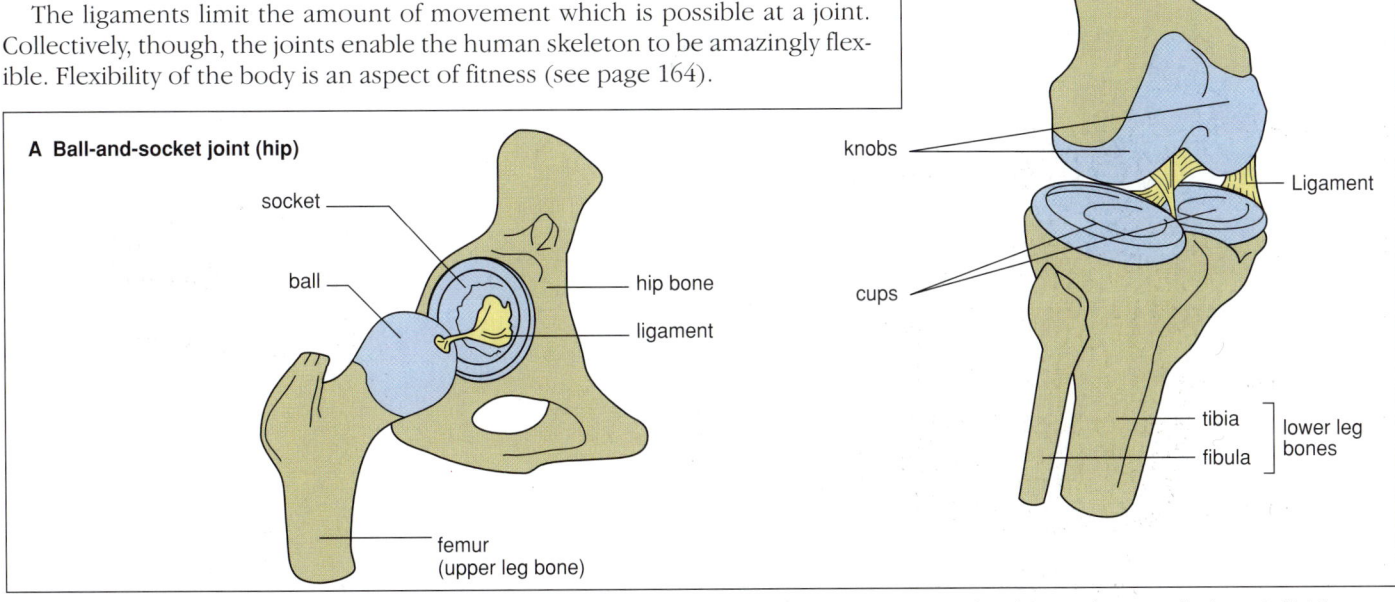

Picture 4 A ball and socket joint and a hinge joint. In each case the fibrous capsule has been removed and the two bones pulled apart slightly.

The structure of a bone

A bone consists of two main parts, the **shaft** and the **head**.

The shaft has an outer layer composed of dense compact bone. In the centre of the shaft there is a cavity filled with **bone marrow**. This consists mainly of fat, but at the two ends of the bone the bone marrow is able to make red blood cells (see page 146).

The head contains a lattice arrangement of bony fibres. These, and the hollow shaft, make the bone light but very strong.

Bone is a living tissue. It is composed of flexible fibres which contain blood vessels and nerves. Special bone cells make new bone and repair it when damaged.

Bone is very hard. This is because the living tissue contains minerals. The main mineral is calcium phosphate, obtained from our food. Growing children need plenty of calcium and phosphorus if their bones are to grow properly (see rickets on page 84).

Two simple experiments can be done to show the chemical make-up of bone.

Burning a piece of fresh bone (in a fume cupboard) destroys the living material, leaving only the minerals. The bone becomes blackened and is very brittle.

However, placing a fresh piece of bone in acid for a few days results in it becoming very flexible and soft. In this case, the acid has removed the mineral content of bone, leaving only the flexible tissue.

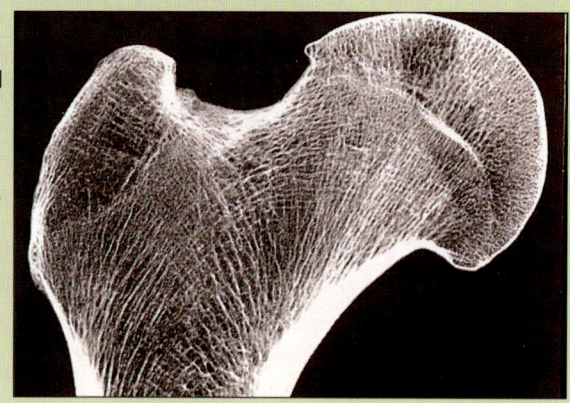

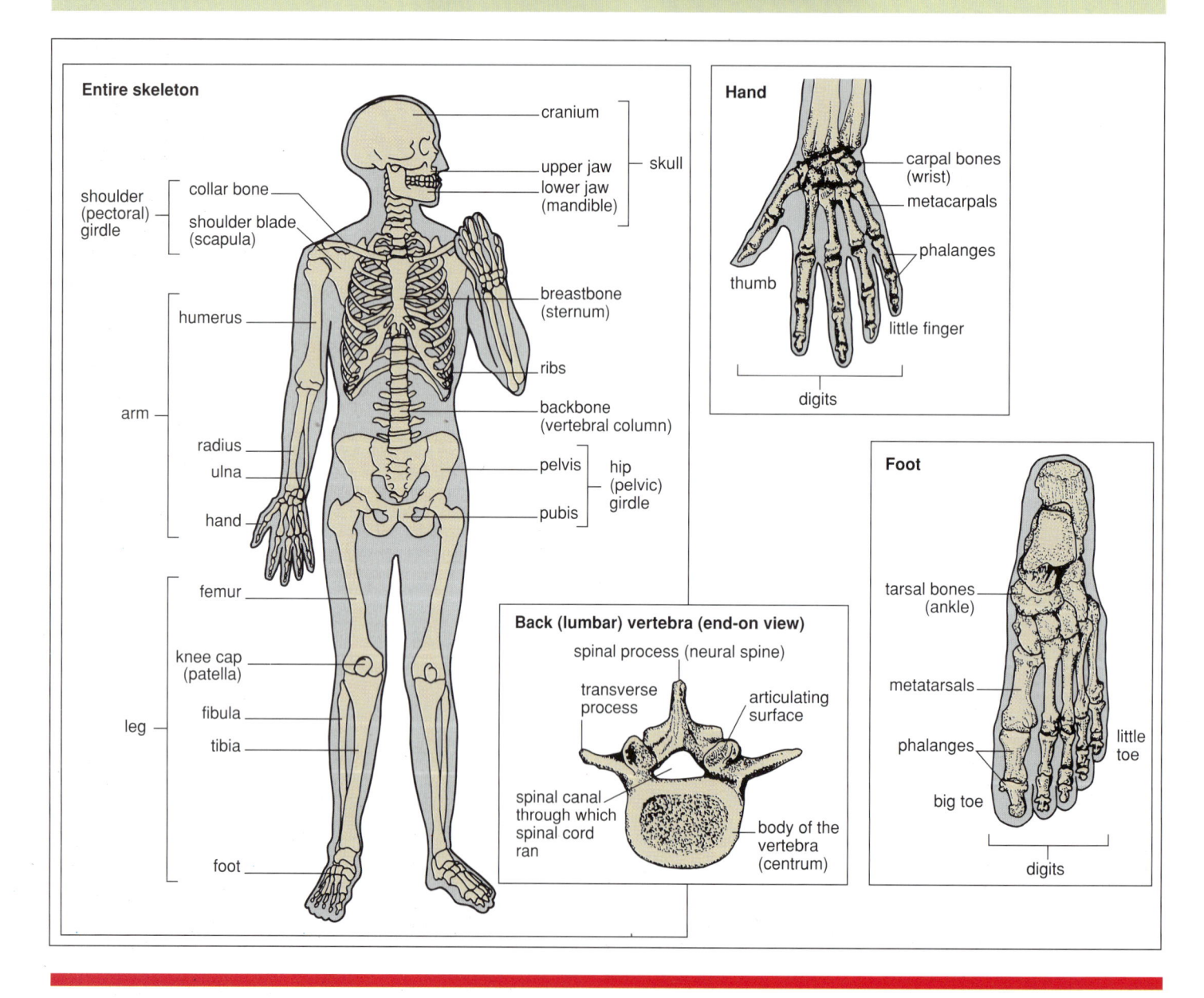

Picture 1 Radiograph of the top part of a femur showing its internal structure.

Questions

1 The diagram below represents some structures of the human leg. Match the letters on the diagram with the following structures and functions.
   a bone
   b joins bone to bone
   c ligament
   d produces force to move bones at a joint
   e muscle
   f framework for attachment of muscle
   g tendon
   h joins muscle to bone

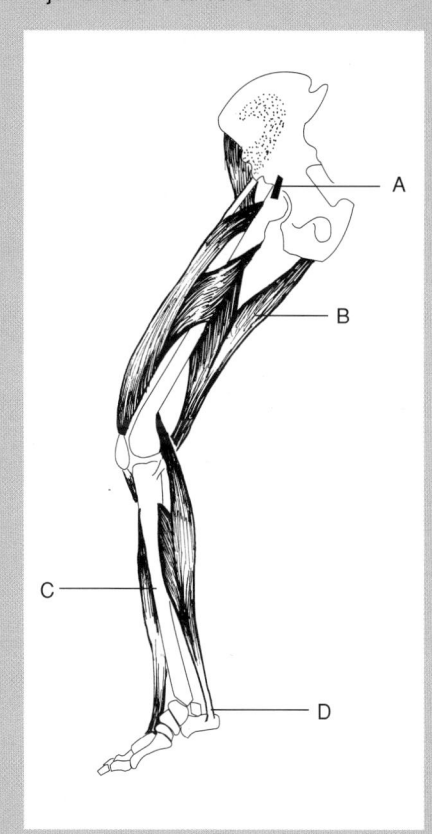

2 The information below refers to parts of the skeleton and to organs in the body.
   Skeleton: vertebrae, skull, rib cage
   Organs: brain, heart and lungs, spinal cord
   a Match each part of the skeleton with the organ that it protects.
   b State two other functions of the skeleton.

3 The list below contains words relating to joints. Use the words from the list to answer the questions below.
   ligament
   ball and socket
   cartilage
   hinge
   tendon
   bone cells
   a Which tissue holds bones together at a joint?
   b Which tissue cushions and protects the ends of bones?
   c Which type of joint allows the fingers to bend?
   d Which tissue attaches muscles to bones?
   e Which type of joint allows movement in all directions?

4 The following diagrams show a model of the human leg in a resting position and in one other position.

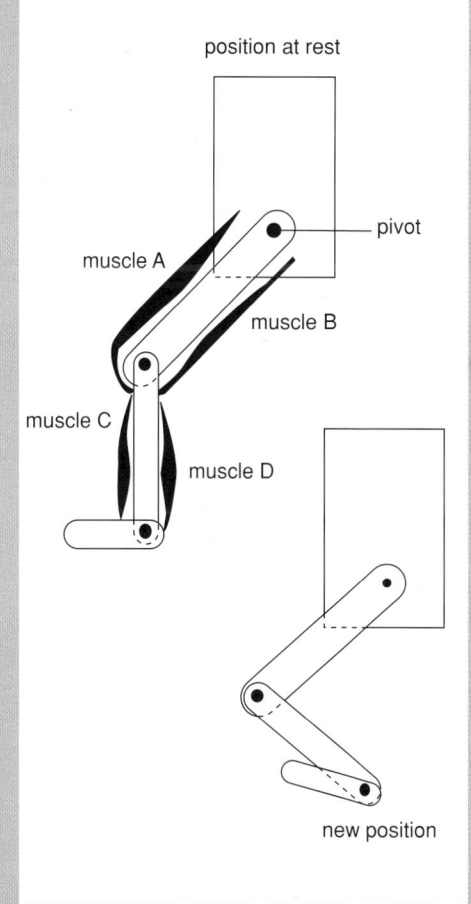

   a Which two muscles contracted to bring about the change from rest to the new position?
   b Which muscles are antagonistic to each other? Explain your answer.

5 Decide if the following statements are true or false. If false, suggest a correction for the part underlined.
   a A hinge joint allows movement in every direction.
   b Ligaments attach muscles to bones.
   c Cartilage reduces friction at a joint.

6 Explain why two muscles are needed to control the movements of the bones on either side of a hinge joint.

7 Answer these questions, which are about the skeleton on page 130.
   a Name two bones which protect vital organs of the body.
   b Name two bones which help to move parts of the body.
   c Name two bones which help to support the body.
   d Which three bones meet at the shoulder joint?
   e Which three bones meet at the knee joint?
   f What bones form the pelvic and the pectoral girdles?
   g Which bones form the palm of the hand?
   h What similarity is there in the bone arrangement of the arm and the leg?
   i Find out what sort of differences there are between the skeleton of a male and a female.
   j The cranium is really several bones joined together. Find out how they are joined together. Find out how the cranial bones of a newborn baby are different from those of an adult.

Aches, pains and broken bones

A break in a bone is called a **fracture**. There are many kinds of fracture. Some are shown in picture 1.

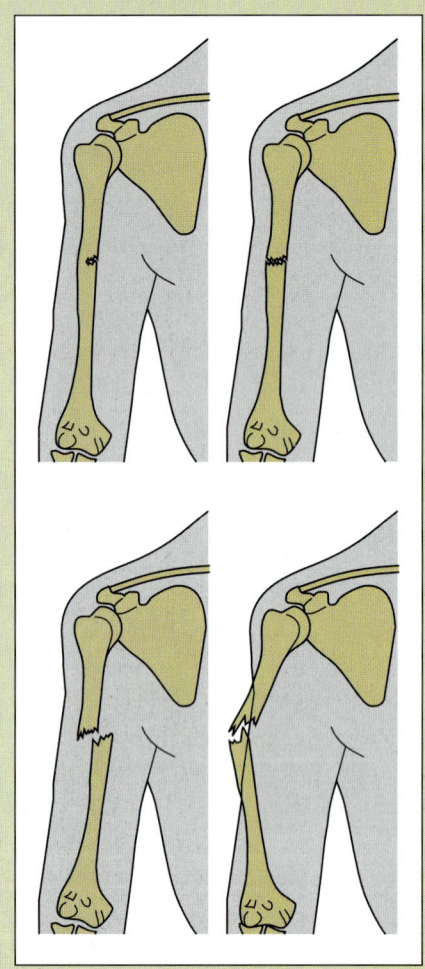

Picture 1 Four ways in which the upper arm bone (humerus) can be fractured.

Let's take the type of fracture where a limb bone breaks right across. Picture 2 shows how such a fracture mends. For the bone to heal neatly the two ends must be in contact but not allowed to move against each other. This is achieved by putting the limb in plaster or holding it in position with a splint.

Fractures heal much more slowly than cuts in the skin. This is because it takes a long time for bone tissue to grow and harden. However, if all goes well the final mend is almost undetectable in an X-ray (picture 3).

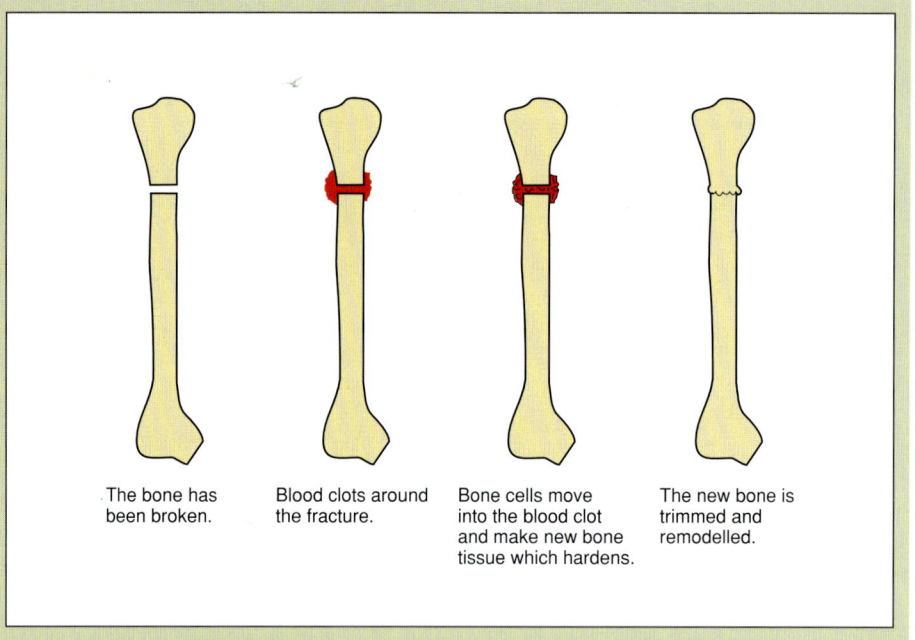

- The bone has been broken.
- Blood clots around the fracture.
- Bone cells move into the blood clot and make new bone tissue which hardens.
- The new bone is trimmed and remodelled.

Picture 2 How a fracture mends.

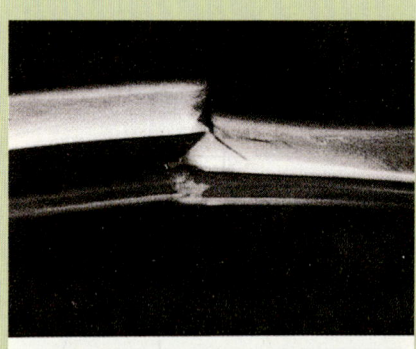

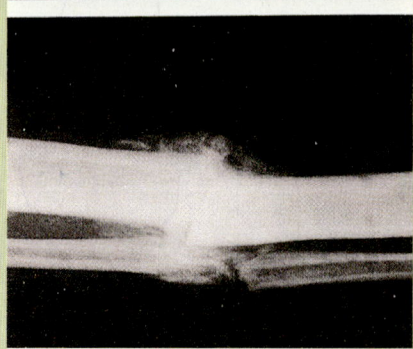

Picture 3 The top X-ray shows a fractured tibia and fibula (the lower leg bones) just after a car accident. The bottom X-ray shows the same bones six months later, after the leg had been in plaster.

A common mishap is to wrench a joint, thereby tearing a ligament or tendon. This is called a **sprain**. A sprained ankle may be caused by suddenly twisting the foot inwards, which tears the ligament on the outer side. The same kind of thing can happen in the wrist.

Sometimes two bones may come apart at the joint. This is called a **dislocation**. For example, the upper arm bone (humerus) may come out of the shoulder socket. With some people this can happen remarkably easily. Usually a doctor can put the humerus back by moving it about in a particular way.

Occasionally a baby is born with the head of the femur outside the hip socket (picture 4). In this case the doctor moves the legs about in such a way that the head of the femur is forced into its socket. The child is then put in plaster with the legs pushed wide apart. After many months the plaster is removed and the head of the femur stays in its socket.

Dislocated hips run in families. Nowadays a simple test is carried out on babies immediately after birth to see if their hip joints are working properly.

Many people suffer from **arthritis**. In one type of arthritis the cartilage wears away and the joint surfaces become roughened. In another type of arthritis fibrous tissue grows over the joint surfaces and destroys them. Either way, movement becomes painful and difficult.

Most of us get **cramp** from time to time. This is caused by a muscle suddenly contracting so powerfully that it hurts. Cramp is brought on by cold, or by using a muscle a great deal. **Stitch** is a type of

(Continued on next page)

cramp which occurs in the abdominal muscles, usually after a hard bout of exercise.

1 Look at picture 4. Make a drawing of a normal hip joint.
2 What sort of injuries are likely to arise from different sports, and why?

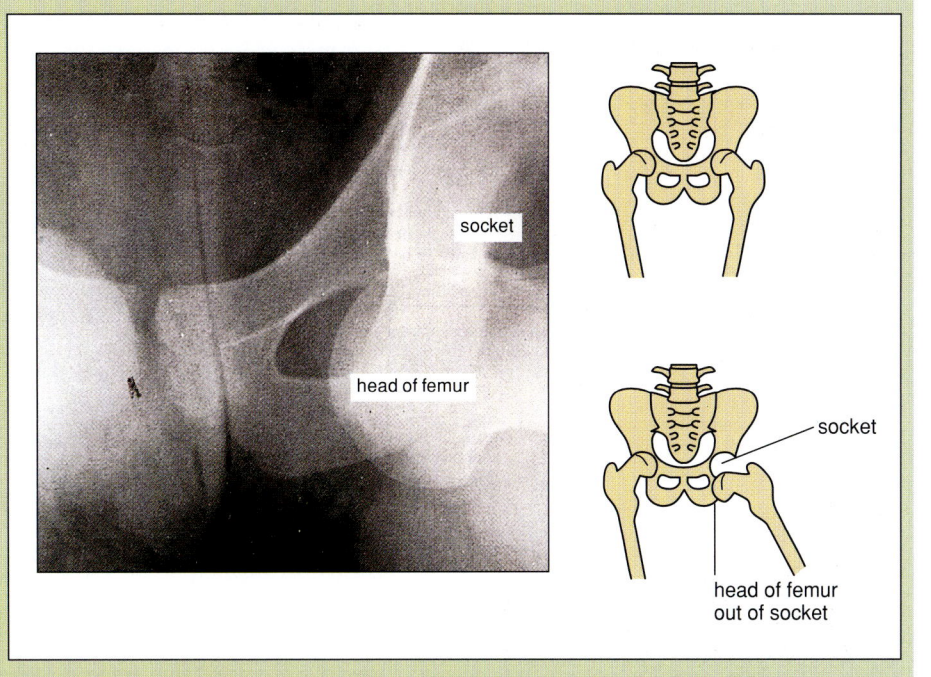

Picture 4 X-ray of a dislocated hip joint. The diagram on the right will help you to interpret the X-ray.

Replacement surgery

You probably know someone who has had a hip or knee replacement operation because they were suffering from severe arthritis.

Hip replacement is one of the commonest types of **replacement surgery**. In the operation the surgeon cuts off the head of the femur and replaces it with a stainless steel ball. The ball is held in place by a metal rod which is pushed into the marrow cavity of the bone and fixed securely with an acrylic cement.

The socket in the hip bone is usually lined with a plastic cup, and this too is fixed securely with an acrylic cement. The stainless steel ball is then inserted into the plastic cup in which it should fit snugly.

A person's life can be transformed by a hip replacement. People who could barely get around with two sticks find they can walk, and even run, again – and without pain.

1 What sort of things might go wrong during, or after, a hip replacement operation? Think of as many possibilities as you can.
2 A knee replacement is more difficult to do than a hip replacement. Why do you think this is?

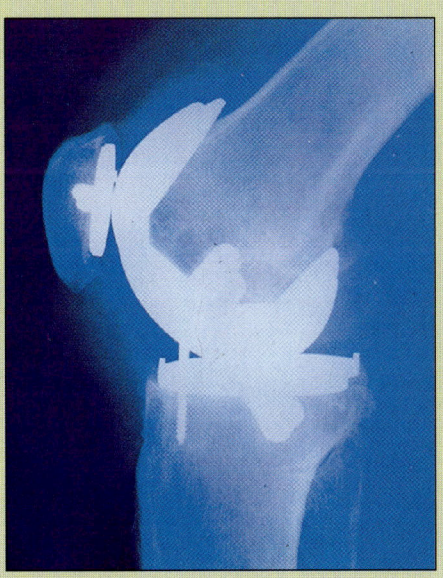

Picture 1 X-rays of an artificial hip joint (far left) and an artificial knee.

F2 Energy balance

Exactly how much energy do we need? In this topic we shall find out.

How much energy do we need?

Imagine you are lying in bed doing nothing. Even in this inactive state you need energy to breathe, make your heart beat, and drive all those countless chemical reactions which keep you alive. The rate at which these 'ticking over' processes take place is called your **basal metabolic rate**.

How much energy do you need to maintain your basal metabolic rate? It is difficult to say, because it varies from one individual to another. Very roughly, the amount needed is 7000 kJ per day. This is about the same amount of energy needed to boil water for 100 cups of tea.

Few of us spend our days lying in bed – most of us do something. Table 1 tells you roughly how much energy is needed by different people in the course of a normal day. You will see that it depends on the person's age, sex and occupation. A person who spends most of the time sitting in an office needs far less energy than a very active person.

What happens if we eat too much?

Suppose you eat more food than is needed for supplying you with energy. What happens to the food left over? Most of it is turned into fat and stored. The result is that your body weight increases. (Strictly speaking we should call this the body *mass*. However, the word 'weight' is normally used in this context so we shall use it here.) If your body weight increases, you run the risk of becoming fat – or **obese**, to use the proper word.

We can think of a person as taking in energy (**energy intake**) and giving out energy (**energy output**). Obesity is caused by a person's energy intake being greater than the energy output. The most fattening foods are therefore those that provide most energy, such as cakes, sweets and butter.

In our bodies, fat is stored in **fat cells** under the skin. An overweight person has too much fat in these cells, and the total number of fat cells is too high.

For everyone there is a 'correct' weight. This will depend on the person's sex, age and height.

How can we lose weight?

The only way to lose weight is to make our energy intake less than the output. This can be done in two ways:

- By taking more exercise; this will increase the energy output.
- By eating less energy food; this will decrease the energy intake.

The first method is certainly helpful, but it is no use taking exercise if you don't keep a check on your diet as well. For example, yesterday I played tennis for half an hour. During the game, I lost about 700 kJ of energy. Afterwards, I felt thirsty and had a glass of beer. The result was that I put back all the energy I'd just lost!

The second method is very good if carried out properly. A person on a well planned weight-reducing diet can lose about 1 kg of body mass per week. Such diets contain relatively little high-energy food and a lot of low-energy food. The result of going on a diet of this sort is shown in picture 1.

The best results can be obtained by combining both methods, i.e. by going on a diet *and* taking more exercise. Regular sessions of steady exercise are better than occasional bouts of very strenuous exercise. The ultimate aim should be to achieve a balance between energy intake and energy output. Then your weight should stay more or less constant.

Why lose weight?

Look at the bar chart in picture 2. It shows the relationship between people's body weight and the death rate. We may draw this simple conclusion from the

	kJ per day
Newborn baby	2 000
Child 1 year	3 000
Child 2–3	6 000
Child 5–7	7 500
Girl 12–15	9 500
Boy 12–15	12 000
Office worker	11 000
Factory worker	12 500
Heavy manual worker	15 000
Pregnant woman	10 000
Woman breast-feeding	11 000

Table 1 Approximate amounts of energy required daily by different types of people.

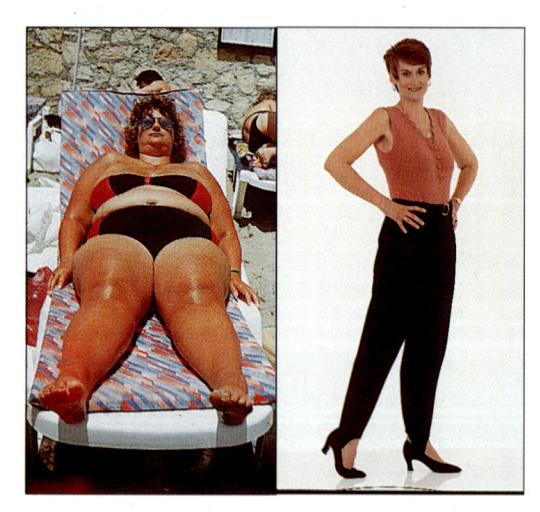

Picture 1 Going on a diet can be a good way of losing weight. This lady reduced her weight dramatically in a few months.

chart: there are more deaths amongst people who are overweight than amongst people of normal weight. In other words, overweight people don't live as long, on average, as people who are the normal weight.

An overweight person has a greater chance of having a stroke or heart attack (see page 144). Other illnesses, too, are connected with being overweight. The risk of death is greater for men than for women, and it increases with the amount of excess weight.

What happens if we eat too little?

Suppose you eat no energy foods at all. What happens? At first you obtain energy from your fat stores. As a result you lose weight.

Eventually all your fat gets used up. In order to stay alive, the body starts getting energy from your tissue proteins, particularly your muscles. As a result, you waste away, becoming thin and weak. Death will occur after about two months. This has happened in concentration camps, and in famine areas.

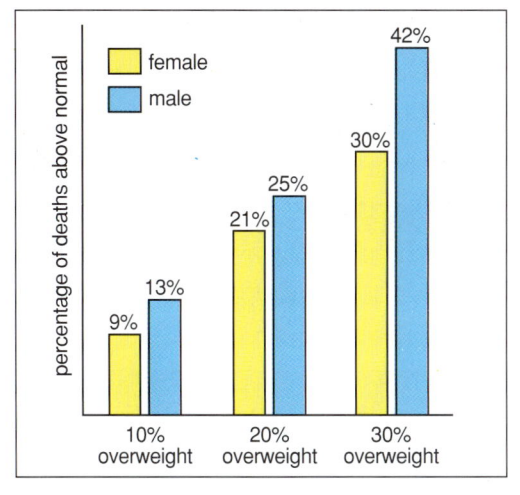

Picture 2 This bar chart shows the relationship between people's body weight and the death rate in the United States.

Questions

1. What mass of roasted peanuts (groundnuts) would the heavy manual worker referred to in table 1 have to eat in a day to just satisfy his energy needs? (See table 1 on page 124.)

2. The data summarised in picture 2 were compiled by an American life insurance company.
   a Explain in full how you think the data were obtained.
   b Why should a life insurance company want to compile such data?

3. Give examples of the sort of food you would recommend to:
   a someone who is going on a hiking holiday and
   b someone who wishes to lose weight.

4. The following table shows the approximate amounts of energy used up in different activities by a normal person.

Activity	Energy used
sleeping	4.5 kJ per min
sitting	5.9 kJ per min
standing	7.1 kJ per min
washing/dressing	14.7 kJ per min
walking slowly	12.6 kJ per min
walking fairly fast	21.0 kJ per min
walking up stairs	37.8 kJ per min
carpentry	15.5 kJ per min
playing tennis	26.0 kJ per min
playing football	36.5 kJ per min
running	42.0 kJ per min

a From these figures work out the approximate total amount of energy which you yourself use up in 24 hours. Show your working in full.
b Using table 1 on page 124 draw up a menu for breakfast, lunch and supper which would give you just enough energy to satisfy your need. Give the amount of each food item which you would need.
c A person who ate the food listed in your menu might still be getting an inadequate diet. Why?

5. The table below shows the daily energy requirements of people of different ages.

Age (years)	Energy requirements (kJ per day)
1	3 000
2	6 000
6	7 500
12	10 000
15	12 000
18	13 000

a Plot these figures as a graph.
b How would you explain the shape of the graph?
c What assumptions are made in drawing up figures of this sort?
d What can you predict about a person's energy requirements after the age of 18?

6. If all the food produced in the world was evenly distributed, no one would starve. Discuss why this has never happened. Is there any sign that it might happen in the future?

Anorexia and bulimia

Some people suffer from a psychological condition in which they eat very little. This is called **anorexia nervosa**. It sometimes happens to young people, particularly women, and it may stem from an obsessive fear of becoming fat. Such people often become thin and frail, and if nothing is done to remedy the condition, they may die.

The opposite also occurs. A person may go on eating and eating and eating. This is called **bulimia nervosa**. Such people may deliberately make themselves sick.

Anorexia and bulimia are both distressing conditions which may require the expert help of a doctor or psychiatrist.

F3 How we breathe

Breathing is the process which moves air in and out of the body.

Why is breathing important?

Breathing enables us to obtain oxygen and get rid of carbon dioxide. You can show this by comparing the air we breathe in (**inhaled air**) with the air we breathe out (**exhaled air**). Picture 1 shows such a comparison. You will see that the person's exhaled air contains less oxygen and more carbon dioxide than inhaled air.

When we breathe in, oxygen is taken out of the air and used for respiration (see page 124). Meanwhile carbon dioxide, produced by respiration, is added to the air which we breathe out. This exchange of oxygen and carbon dioxide is called **gaseous exchange**. It is a life-giving process in nearly all living things.

Our breathing system

When we breathe in, air is drawn into our **lungs**. These are the main organs of our **breathing system**.

The breathing system is shown in picture 2. There are two lungs, situated in the chest (**thorax**). The sides of the chest are bounded by the **ribs**. Between the ribs are **intercostal muscles**. Below the lungs is a sheet of muscle tissue, shaped like a dome, which separates the thorax from the abdomen. This is called the **diaphragm**.

The lungs are surrounded by two thin sheets of tissue with fluid in between. The fluid serves as a lubricant, allowing the membranes to slide over each other smoothly as we breathe in and out.

The rest of the breathing system consists of a series of cavities and tubes through which air flows to and from the lungs. Here are a few notes about the structures through which the air passes.

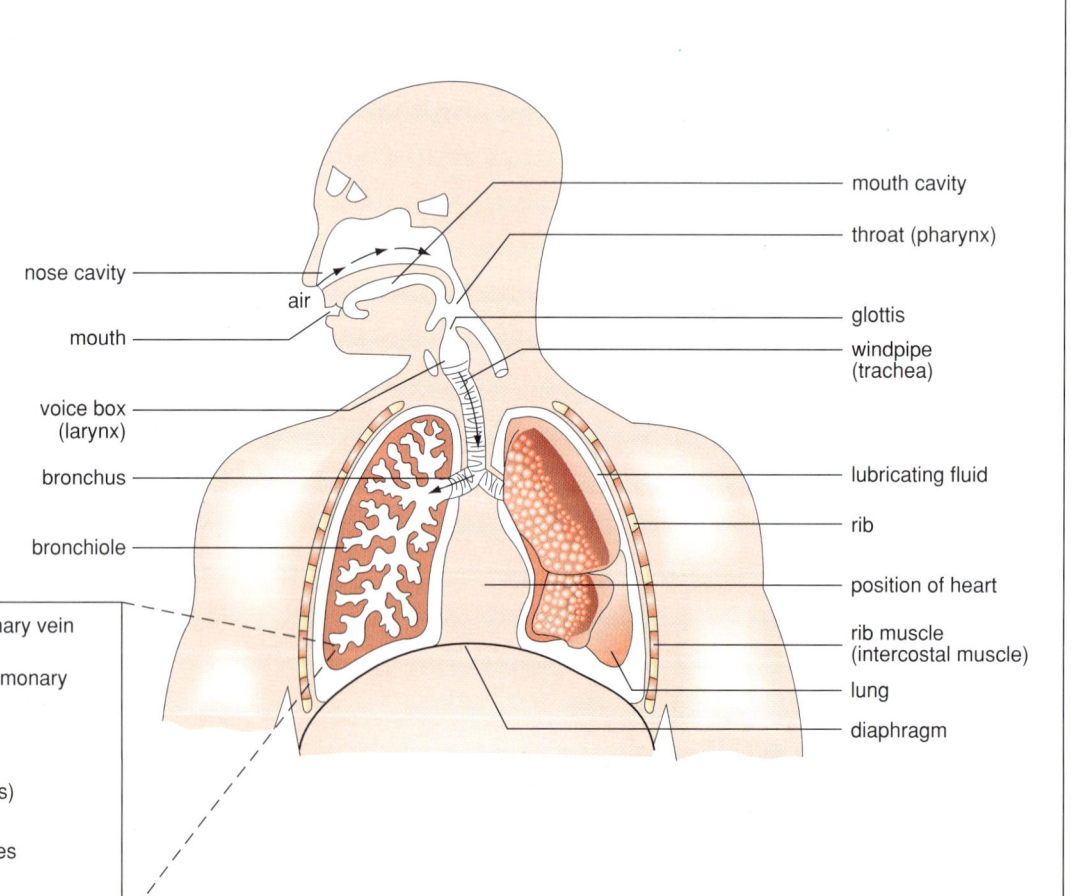

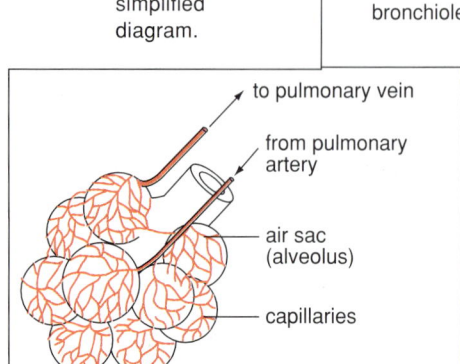

	Inhaled air	Exhaled air
Oxygen	20.93	16.4
Carbon dioxide	0.03	4.1
Nitrogen (and argon)	79.04	79.5

Picture 1 The air we breathe out contains less oxygen and more carbon dioxide than the air we breathe in.

Picture 2 The human breathing system. There are really far more bronchioles and air sacs than are shown in this simplified diagram.

The nose

The cavity inside the nose is divided up by shelf-like partitions rather like the radiator of a car. As air passes through, it is warmed, moistened and cleaned. Dust and germs get caught up in mucus on the lining and are wafted towards the throat by thousands of tiny, beating 'hairs' called **cilia**. The cilia project from a special kind of epithelial tissue called **ciliated epithelium**. Dust and germs, thus trapped, are expelled from the nose and throat by **sneezing** and **coughing**. These are both reflexes which help to protect us from infection.

The throat (pharynx)

Here the airway crosses the throat. Air passes from the nose cavity across the throat and into a little hole called the **glottis** which leads to the **windpipe** (**trachea**). You cannot breathe and swallow at the same time. When you swallow, the breathing pathway is closed off so food does not go the wrong way (page 87). If a bit of food does get stuck in the airway, you can choke.

The windpipe (trachea)

Before air reaches the windpipe it has to go through the **voice box** (**larynx**). The windpipe itself runs from the voice box into the chest. For the air to flow freely, the windpipe must be open at all times. It is kept open by rings of cartilage in its wall (picture 3).

Dust and germs which escaped being caught in the nose and throat get trapped in mucus lining the windpipe. They are then wafted towards the throat by cilia. Every now and again you need to clear your throat to get rid of the mucus.

The bronchi and bronchioles

Inside the chest the windpipe splits into two short tubes called **bronchi** (singular: **bronchus**). These then divide like a tree into lots of small branches called **bronchioles** which get narrower and narrower towards their ends (picture 4).

The air sacs

Each bronchiole leads to a bunch of tiny air sacs called **alveoli** (singular: **alveolus**). The air sacs are surrounded by a network of blood capillaries, rather like a string bag (see inset in picture 2). Here, in the depth of the lungs, gaseous exchange takes place.

How does gaseous exchange take place?

The air sacs inside our lungs are in close contact with the blood capillaries, and the two are separated by a very thin membrane. Across this membrane gaseous exchange takes place. Oxygen diffuses from the air sacs into the blood, and carbon dioxide diffuses from the blood into the air sacs. The inner surface of the air sacs is covered by a thin layer of fluid in which the gases dissolve before they diffuse through (picture 5).

There are about 150 million air sacs in each lung, and together they cover a

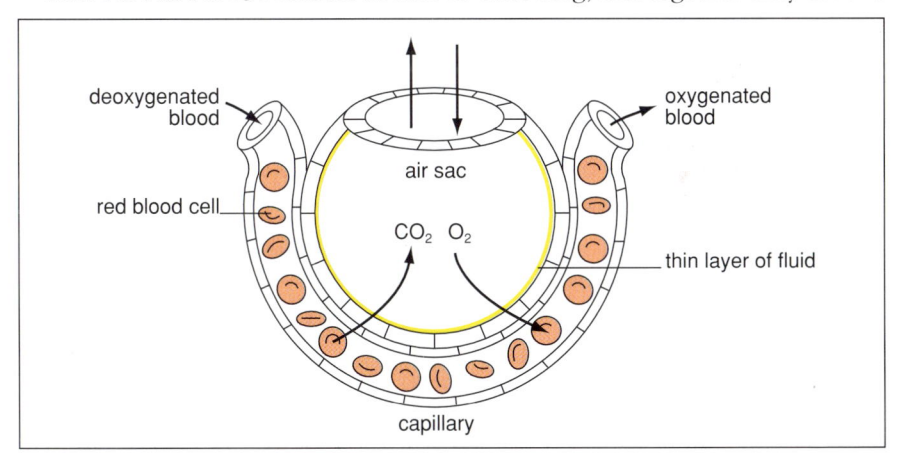

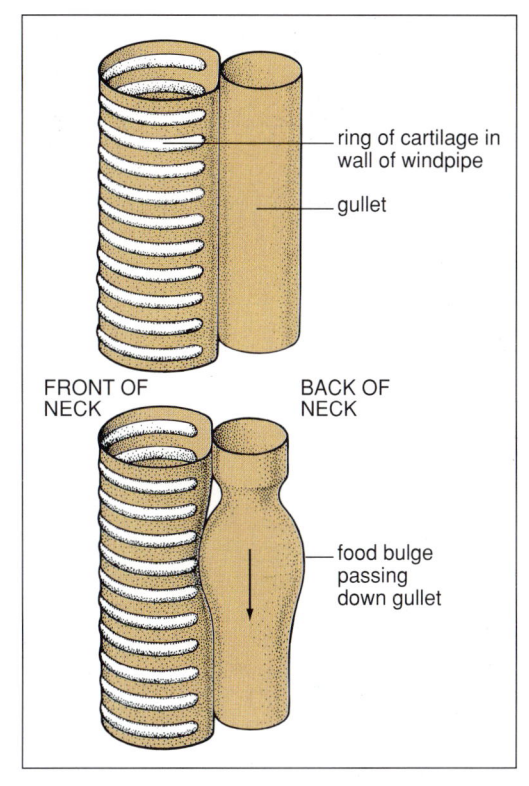

Picture 3 Rings of cartilage keep the windpipe permanently open and prevent its wall caving in. The rings are incomplete, like a pile of Cs. The open side of the C is next to the gullet; this allows the gullet to expand when food is passing down.

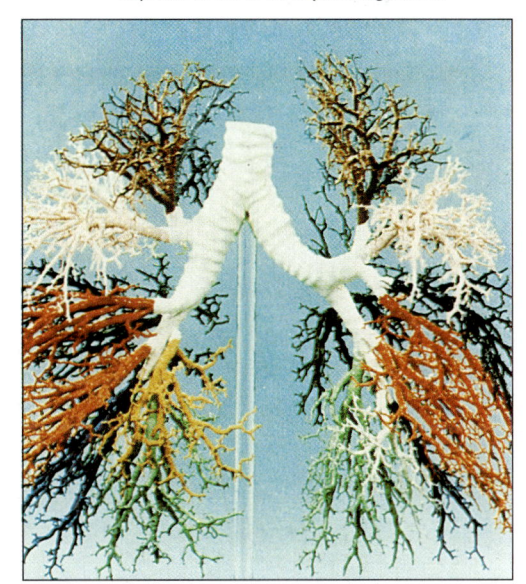

Picture 4 A museum exhibit of human lungs. The bronchial tree was filled with a solution which hardened. The rest of the lung tissue was then dissolved.

Picture 5 As blood flows past an air sac, it gives up carbon dioxide and picks up oxygen. These gases move in and out of the air sac by diffusion.

138 *The body in action*

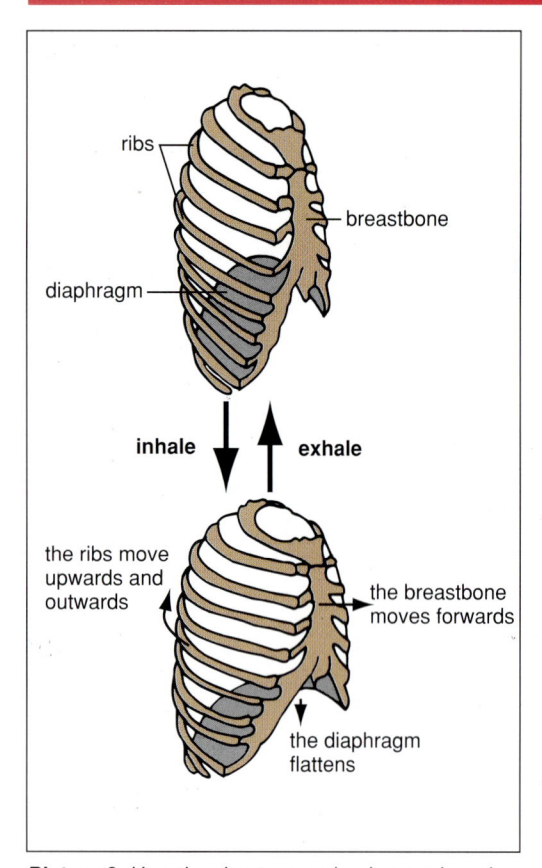

Picture 6 How the chest expands when we breathe in. Notice that its volume increases in all directions.

very large surface area. Someone has worked out that if you were to flatten them out like a sheet, they would cover an area the size of a tennis court! It is important that the lungs should have a large surface area, because it means that plenty of oxygen can be taken up by the blood when we breathe in.

The air sacs always contain some air, even when we breathe out as hard as we can. If there was no air inside the air sacs, their walls would cave in and stick together. The gaseous exchange surface would then be so reduced that we would suffocate.

How does air get in and out of the lungs?

Our breathing system works rather like a pair of bellows, sucking air in and then forcing it out. The details are shown in picture 6.

Inhaling is brought about by the chest expanding. The ribs, moved by their muscles, swing upwards and outwards and the breast bone moves forward. At the same time the diaphragm flattens. The result is that the volume of the chest increases. This lowers the pressure in the chest, so air passes into the lungs.

Exhaling is brought about by the reverse process. The ribs and breastbone return to their original positions, and the diaphragm bulges upwards again. The result is that the volume of the chest decreases. This raises the pressure in the chest, so air is forced out of the lungs.

Questions

1 Suggest why it is a good idea to:
   a breathe through your nose rather than through your mouth,
   b take deep breaths rather than shallow ones,
   c stop talking when you swallow,
   d blow your nose when necessary.

2 Explain each of the following in terms of breathing in and out: a yawn, a gasp, a cough, a sigh, a laugh.

3 Picture 1 on page 136 gives the percentage volumes of oxygen and carbon dioxide in the air inhaled and exhaled by a human.
   a What is the other main gas in inhaled air? Would you expect it to be in exhaled air as well?
   b Explain how the change in the composition of the air is brought about.

4 An experiment was carried out on a young man in which the volume of air taken in at each breath, and the number of breaths per minute, were measured at rest and after running. The table shows the results.

	Volume of air per breath	Breaths per minute
at rest	450 cm^3	20
after running	1000 cm^3	38

   a What is the total volume of air breathed in per minute at rest and after running?
   b Twenty per cent of the air breathed in consisted of oxygen, but only sixteen per cent of the air breathed out consisted of oxygen. Assuming that these figures remain constant, work out the volume of oxygen entering the blood per minute at rest and after exercise.
   c Why does the amount of oxygen taken up into the blood increase after exercise?

5 The diagram represents an air sac (alveolus) and a blood capillary alongside it.

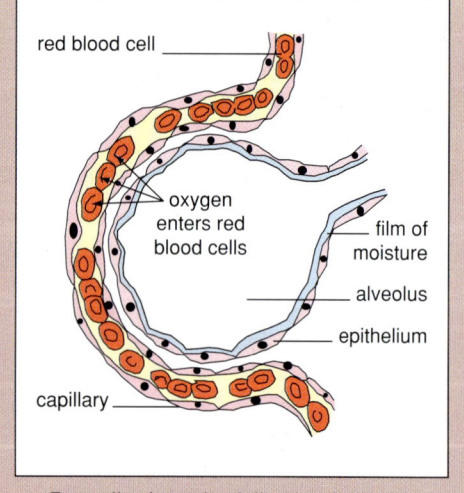

Describe how the following features, shown on the diagram, help to make gaseous exchange efficient.

   a the film of moisture
   b a thin epithelium

6 The diagram below shows part of the human breathing system.

   a Identify and name two muscular structures which bring about changes in the volume of the lungs.
   b Identify parts A and B. Why is A important during breathing? 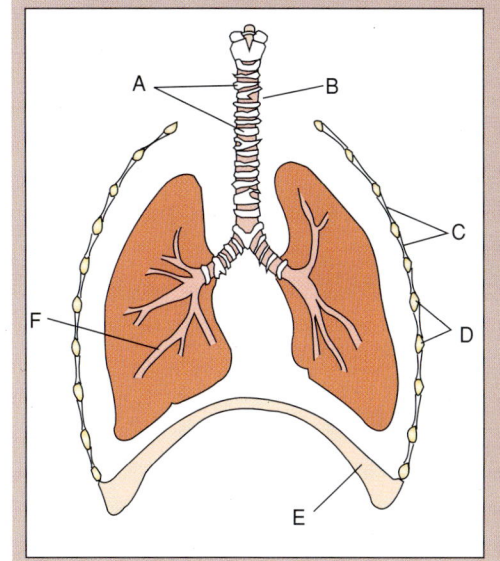
   c Which of the following statements correctly describes inhalation? Pick three.
      i   intercostal muscles contract
      ii intercostal muscles relax
      iii diaphragm contracts
      iv diaphragm relaxes
      v rib cage moves up and out
      vi rib cage moves down and in
   d Choose one option in each group to make this sentence correct: 'During inhalation, the lung volume *increases/decreases/stays the same*, and as a result, the lung pressure *increases/decreases/stays the same*.

7 The graphs show changes in lung pressure and volume during one complete breathing cycle.

   a Calculate the volume of air exhaled.
   b State the relationship between the pressure and the volume of air in the lungs during stage B of the breathing cycle.
   c What evidence supports the statement that the lungs are never completely empty of air?

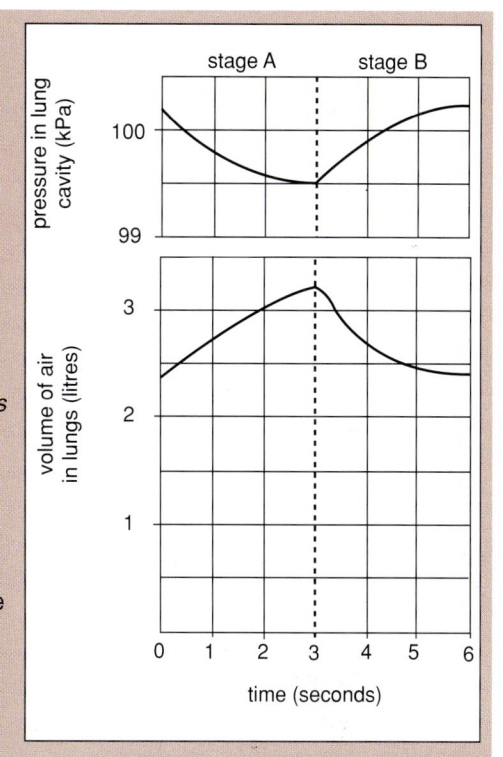

Artificial respiration

If a person has an accident, the brain may stop working for a time and breathing stops. However, the person's life may be saved by **artificial respiration**. This must be carried out as soon as possible, otherwise the brain cells may run so short of oxygen that they die.

1 Pinch the nostrils shut with the fingers of one hand, then tilt the head back and push the lower jaw forward so the chin juts out. This will force the tongue forward and open the air passages.

The best method of artificial respiration is **mouth-to-mouth resuscitation** or 'kiss of life'. With the person lying down, you keep breathing out into his or her mouth as shown in the pictures. There's enough oxygen in your exhaled air to keep life going, and hopefully the victim will soon start breathing again. Mouth-to-mouth resuscitation is something everyone should be prepared to do if necessary.

In a severe accident, such as a car crash, the brain may be so badly damaged that the person cannot start breathing again.

2 Take a deep breath, then open your mouth and seal your lips against the person's mouth. Breathe out firmly but gently into the person's mouth and so into the lungs.

It may then be necessary to attach the person to a **resuscitator**, a machine which forces air in and out of the lungs. An unconscious person can be kept alive for weeks or even months on a machine like this. Sometimes the brain recovers sufficiently for the person to start breathing again. If recovery does not take place, the family and doctors have to decide whether to keep the person alive on the machine or switch it off. Obviously this is an agonising decision to have to make.

3 Lift your mouth off, then turn your head so as to look at the person's chest. If you have been successful you will see that it has risen and is now falling as air comes out of the lungs.

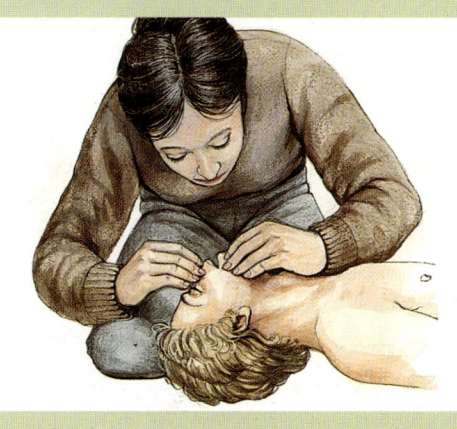

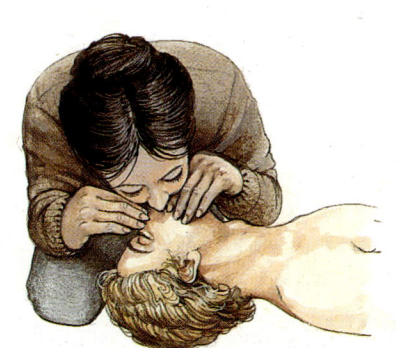

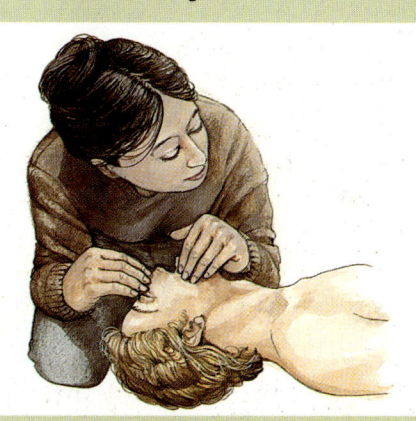

4 Repeat steps 2 and 3 at a steady rate. The person's colour should improve, and eventually breathing should start up again.

F4
The heart and circulation

Blood constantly flows round and round the body. This is called the circulation.

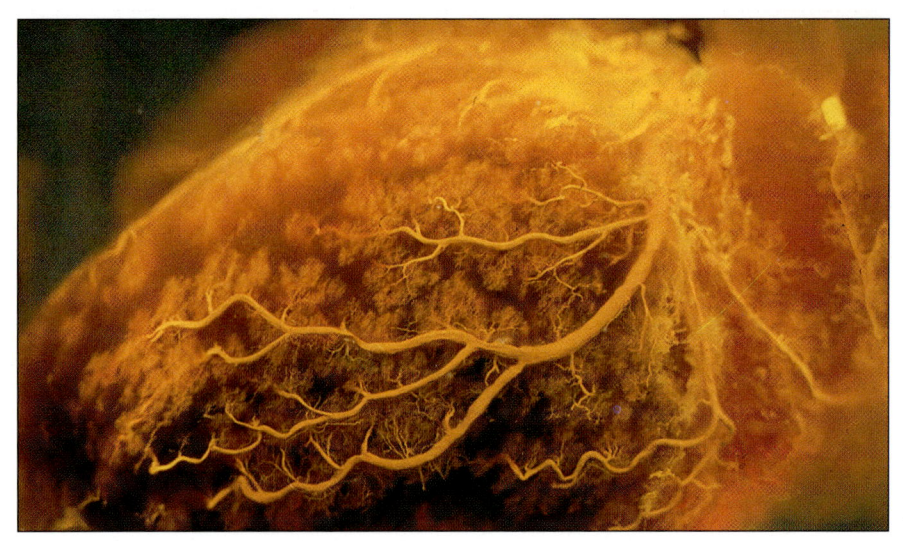

Picture 1 The heart, the body's life-giving pump. The branched tubes on the surface are the coronary arteries which carry oxygen to the heart muscle.

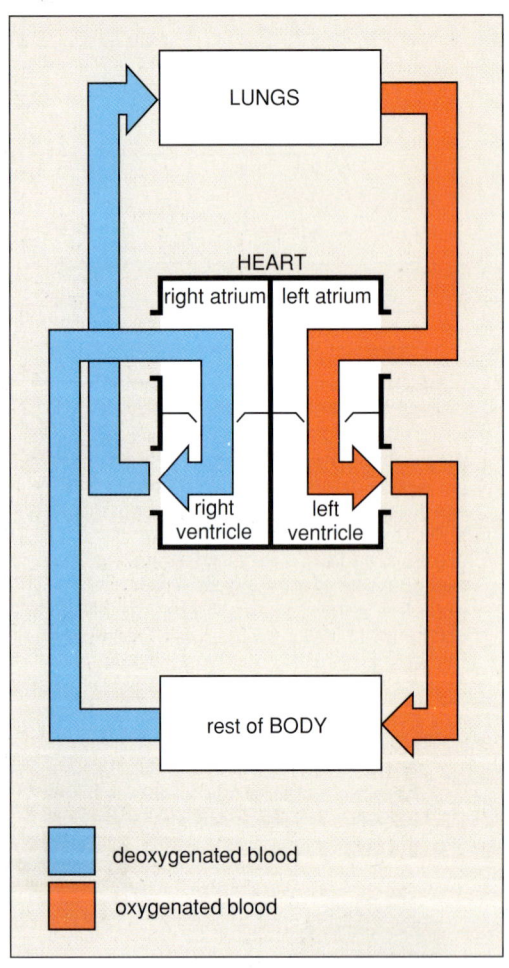

The general plan of the circulation

The structures which blood flows through as it goes round the body make up the **circulatory system**. The main organ in the circulatory system is the **heart**, which is situated between the lungs in the chest (picture 1). The heart's job is to pump the blood round the body. More about that presently.

The rest of the circulatory system consists of tubes called **blood vessels**. These are of two types: **arteries** carry blood away from the heart to the various organs, and **veins** carry blood back from the organs to the heart. Within each organ the arteries and veins are connected by numerous very narrow blood vessels called **capillaries**.

As blood flows along the capillaries, oxygen and other useful substances diffuse out to the surrounding cells, and unwanted substances diffuse in the other direction. In this way the capillaries keep our tissues in a healthy state.

The capillaries are extremely numerous and every organ contains thousands of them. No cell is more than a twentieth of a millimetre from the nearest one. If a person's capillaries were laid end to end, they would stretch round the world two and a half times!

We really have two circulations

Look at picture 2. The heart is divided by a partition into two halves, left and right. Blood is pumped from the right side of the heart to the lungs where it takes up oxygen. The **oxygenated blood** then passes back to the left side of the heart, which pumps it to the rest of the body. The oxygen is then taken up by the various organs, and the **deoxygenated blood** returns to the right side of the heart.

So there are really two circulations, one serving the lungs and the other serving the rest of the body. Putting it a different way: blood passes through the heart twice for every complete circuit of the body.

When blood arrives at the heart from the veins, it goes first into a chamber called the **atrium** (plural: **atria**). This is the Latin word for an entrance hall. From here the blood flows through an opening into another chamber called the **ventricle**. This has a very thick, muscular wall for pumping the blood into the arteries. So the heart has four chambers altogether: left and right atria, and left and right ventricles.

The human heart and circulation are shown in detail in pictures 3–6. Follow the route by which blood flows through the heart and round the body.

Picture 2 A simple view of the human circulation. It is usual to show pictures of human anatomy from the belly (ventral) side, so in this diagram the right side of the heart is on your left, and the left side is on your right.

The heart and circulation **141**

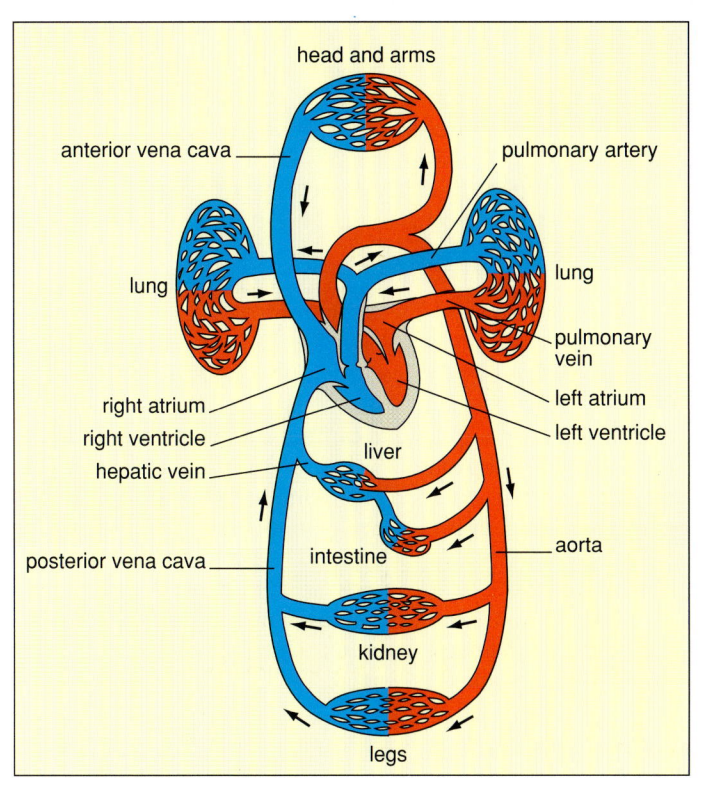

Picture 3 General plan of the human circulatory system. Oxygenated blood, red; deoxygenated blood, blue.

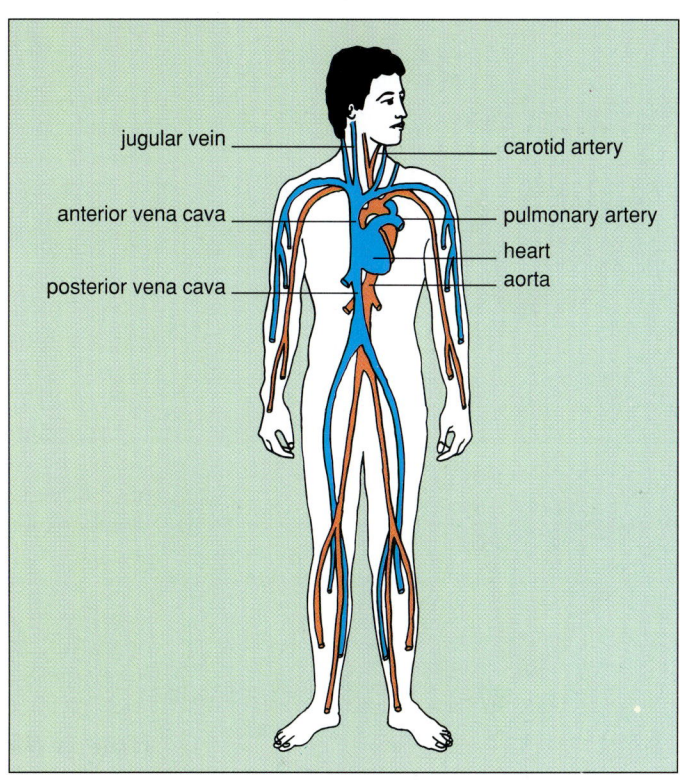

Picture 4 The main blood vessels of the human. Oxygenated blood, red; deoxygenated blood, blue.

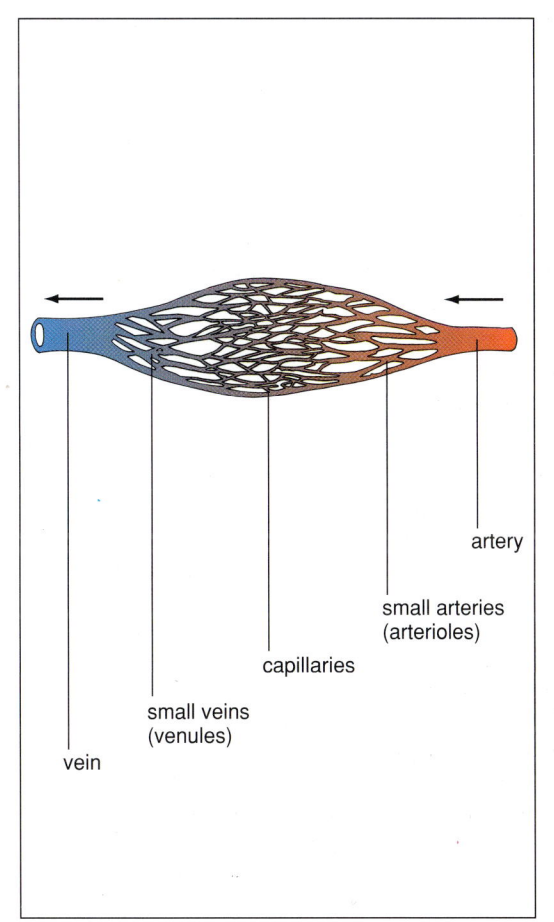

Picture 5 A capillary system. The arrows show the direction of blood flow.

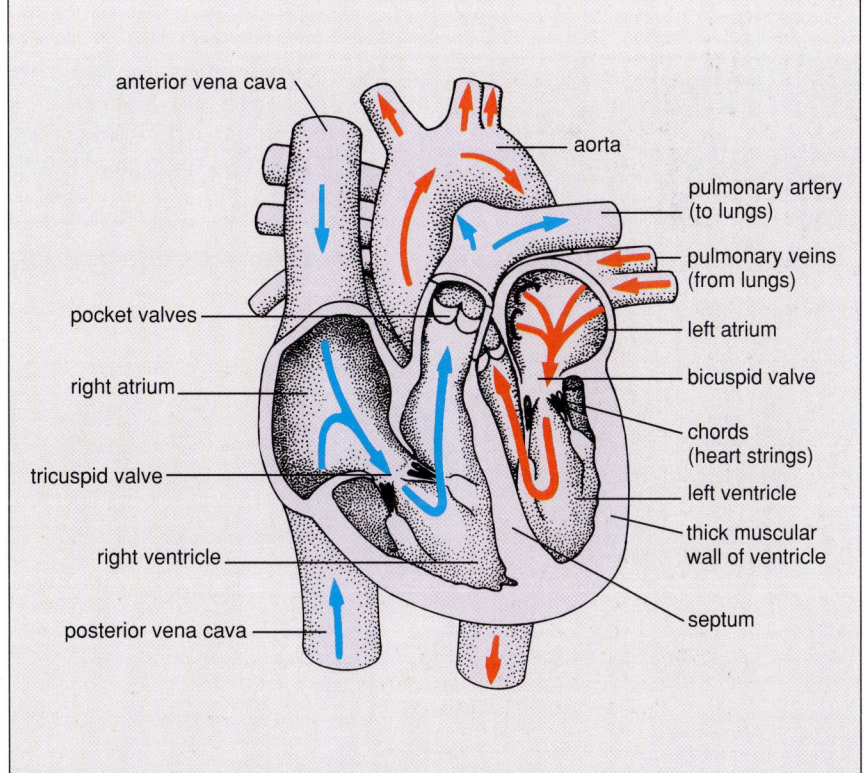

Picture 6 The heart, cut open to show the inside. Notice how the aorta and pulmonary artery twist round each other. The bicuspid and tricuspid valves consist of flaps whose free ends are attached to the sides of the ventricle by tough chords, the 'heart strings'. The bicuspid valve has two flaps, the tricuspid valve has three. The pocket valves at the entrance to the aorta and pulmonary arteries are similar to the valves in the veins (see picture 10).

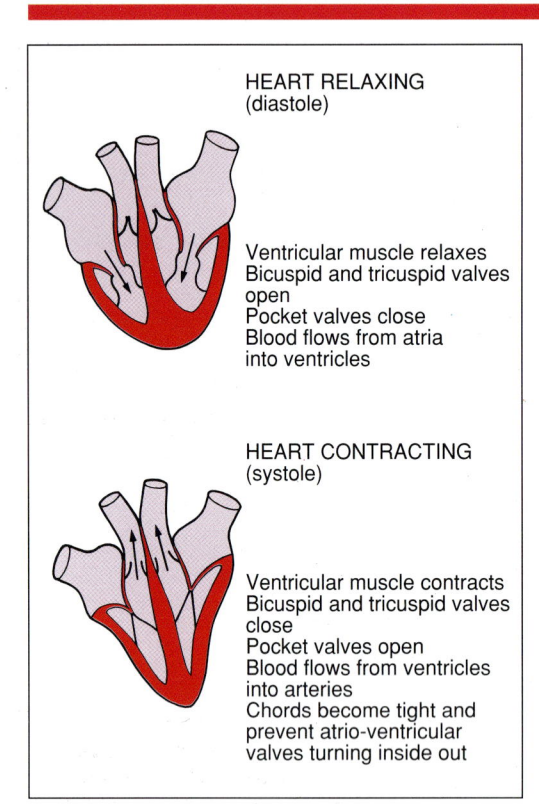

HEART RELAXING (diastole)

Ventricular muscle relaxes
Bicuspid and tricuspid valves open
Pocket valves close
Blood flows from atria into ventricles

HEART CONTRACTING (systole)

Ventricular muscle contracts
Bicuspid and tricuspid valves close
Pocket valves open
Blood flows from ventricles into arteries
Chords become tight and prevent atrio-ventricular valves turning inside out

Picture 7 These diagrams show how blood flows through the heart. The valves stop the blood flowing backwards.

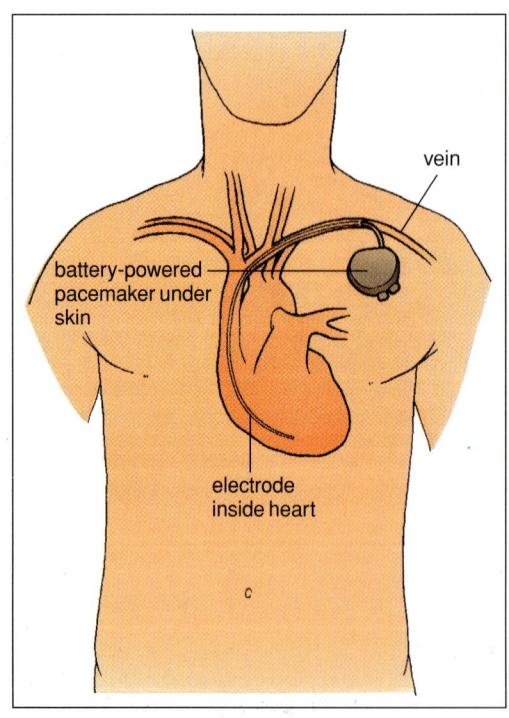

Picture 8 An electronic pacemaker. In this particular type an electrode is inserted into the heart through a vein, so there is no need for the surgeon to cut the chest open. Electrical pulses pass from the pacemaker into the heart muscle via the electrode.

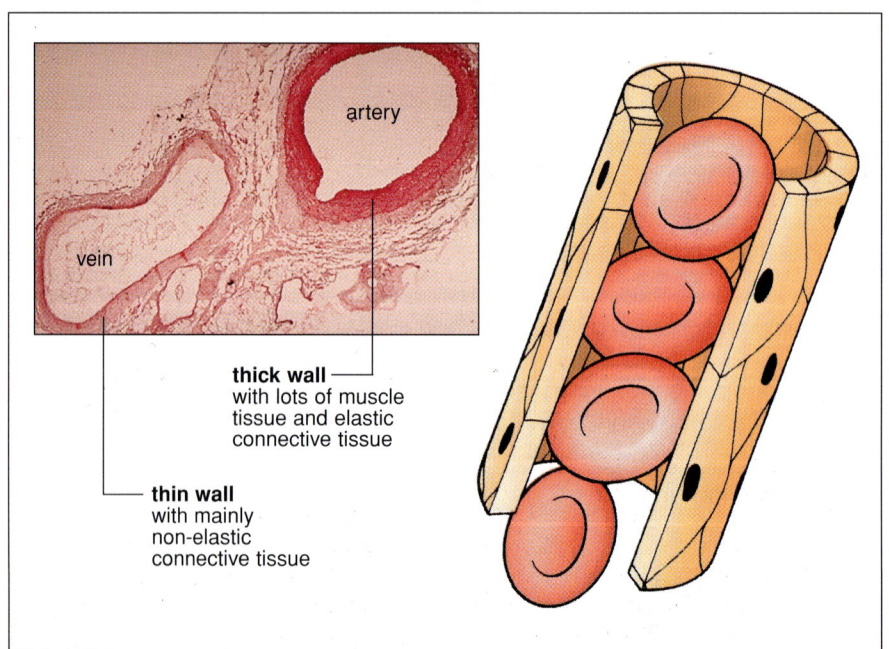

The heart as a pump

The heart beats about 70 times a minute, that's over 100 000 times a day. This is made possible by the muscle tissue in the wall of the ventricles. **Heart muscle** (**cardiac muscle**) differs from other kinds of muscle in being able to contract repeatedly without getting tired. Try clenching your fist 70 times per minute and your hand muscles will soon give up. Heart muscle, however, has no difficulty working at this rate.

After the heart has contracted, it relaxes back to its original position. When it relaxes, blood flows into it from the veins. When it contracts, blood is pumped out of it into the arteries. So blood flows through the heart in only one direction. This is made possible by flap-like **valves** which prevent the blood flowing backwards (picture 7).

Every time the heart beats it sets up a wave of pressure which travels along the main arteries. This is called the **pulse**. If you put your finger on your skin just above the artery in your wrist, you can feel your pulse as a slight throb. Doctors and nurses feel a patient's pulse to check whether the heart is beating at its normal rate.

In order to keep contracting, the heart muscle needs a good supply of oxygen. It gets this from a system of **coronary arteries** which branch out over the heart wall. You can see them in picture 1. A **heart attack** is caused by one of the coronary arteries becoming blocked (see page 144).

How is the heart controlled?

Here is a remarkable fact: if the heart was removed from the body, it would go on beating on its own. In other words the mechanism which makes the heart beat is in the heart itself. The heart is made to beat by tiny electrical pulses which are sent out from a patch of special tissue in the wall of the right atrium. This is called the **pacemaker**.

Sometimes the pacemaker fails to work properly, or a block develops between it and the heart muscle. If this happens, the person may need to be fitted with an **artificial pacemaker**. This is an electronic device, placed under the skin on the wall of the chest (picture 8). It sends electrical stimuli through an electrode into the heart muscle, making it contract.

Picture 9 The left picture is a cross-section of an artery and a vein. The artery has a thicker wall than the vein. The right picture shows a capillary with four red blood cells inside it.

The blood vessels

Picture 9 shows an artery and a vein as they appear in a thin section under the microscope. The **arteries** have tough elastic walls containing muscle tissue. The high pressure from the beating of the heart forces the blood along quickly, much as water is forced along a narrow hosepipe.

By the time the blood reaches the **veins** the pressure pushing it along is much less. Also a lot of the blood is now moving against gravity as it flows upwards from the legs. This makes it difficult for the blood to get back to the heart. However, the veins are relatively wide and let the blood flow along easily. Also they contain **valves** which prevent the blood slipping back (picture 10).

Nevertheless the bloodflow through the veins may become sluggish. The pressure of blood may stretch the walls of the veins, making them flabby like thin bags. These are called **varicose veins** and they often develop in the legs, particularly in older people. Movement and exercise help to prevent varicose veins: contraction of the leg muscles squeezes the blood along and helps to keep it moving.

The **capillaries** are just wide enough to let the red blood cells pass along in single file. Their walls are very thin, consisting of just one layer of flattened cells. This enables oxygen and other substances to diffuse through easily.

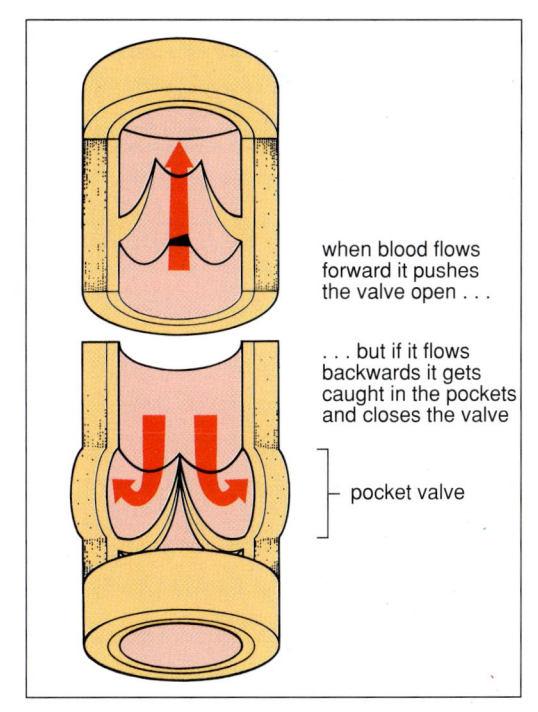

Blood pressure

The pumping of the heart, combined with the narrowness of the smaller blood vessels, produces a considerable pressure in the arteries. This is what we mean by **blood pressure**. It is important that our blood pressure should be reasonably high because it keeps the blood on the move.

Our blood pressure varies according to what we are doing. In general anything which makes the heart beat faster, or the arteries get narrower, will increase the blood pressure. For example, anger, excitement and exercise all have this effect.

Some people's blood pressure is too high all the time. This puts an extra strain on the heart. The pressure may even burst a blood vessel, particularly in old people whose vessels have become weak with age. If this happens in the brain, the cells in the region of the burst are killed, resulting in a **stroke**. A stroke may leave a person partly paralysed and unable to speak properly. A severe stroke can be fatal. A stroke can also be caused by a blood vessel in the brain becoming blocked by a blood-clot.

What causes high blood pressure? We don't know for certain, but it seems to be connected with stress and tension, over-eating, smoking and drinking too much alcohol. If a person feels tired and run down, one of the first things the doctor does is to measure the blood pressure (picture 11).

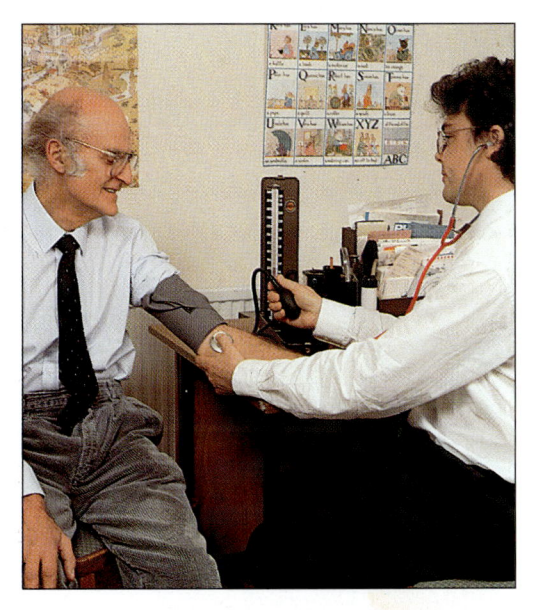

when blood flows forward it pushes the valve open . . .

. . . but if it flows backwards it gets caught in the pockets and closes the valve

pocket valve

Picture 10 Pocket valves inside the veins stop blood flowing backwards. The valves at the entrance of the aorta and pulmonary artery work in the same way.

Picture 11 A doctor taking a patient's blood pressure. The pressure is registered by a U-tube containing mercury. The pressure is highest when the heart contracts, and lowest when the heart relaxes. Both pressures are measured and expressed as a fraction with the highest figure on top. A healthy person's blood pressure should be around 120/70 millimetres of mercury.

Activity

How fast is your heart beating?

1. Sit down comfortably in a chair with the palm of one hand facing upwards.
2. Gently place the middle finger of your other hand on the thumb side of your wrist. Move it around until you can feel a repeated throb. This is your **pulse**.
3. Count the number of heart beats in one minute. Repeat this three times. Calculate an average value. This is your **resting heart rate**.
4. Stand up for one minute. Still standing, make three measurements of your pulse rate. Calculate an average value. This is your **standing heart rate**.

How do the resting and standing heart rates differ?

Why do you think they differ?

There is more on this subject on page 164.

Questions

1. Suggest a reason for each of the following:
   a the right atrium is larger than the left atrium,
   b the left ventricle has a thicker, more muscular wall than the right ventricle,
   c arteries have more muscle in their walls than veins,
   d capillaries have very thin walls,
   e veins contain valves.

2. The chart below shows the pulse rate of a patient measured at four hourly intervals every day.
   a Can you detect a regular pattern in the way the pulse rate changes? If so, describe the pattern.
   b Do you have any criticism of the way the pulse rate is graphed in the chart?
   c What were the highest and lowest pulse rates and when were they recorded?
   d Give possible reasons why the pulse rate reached these particular values.

3. The average speed of the blood in the arteries is 45 cm per second, but the average speed in the capillaries is only 0.5 mm per second.
   a Give the speed in the capillaries as a percentage of the speed in the arteries.
   b What do you think causes the difference?
   c Why is it desirable for blood to flow through the capillaries slowly?

4. The diagram below shows some of the structures in the mammalian heart viewed from the ventral (belly) side.

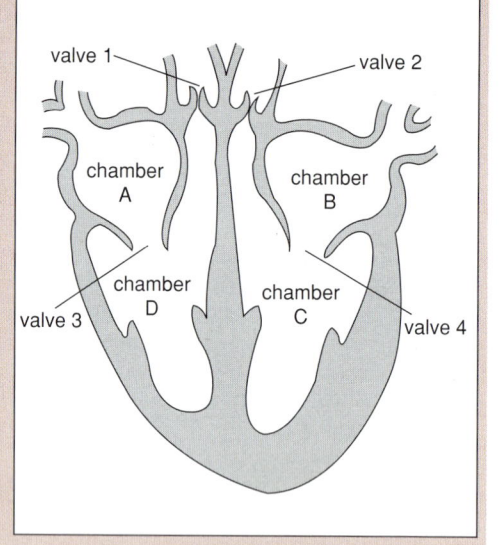

   a What is the name of chamber A?
   b What is the name of chamber C?
   c What is the name of valve 4?
   d What type of valve is valve 2?
   e Describe the function of valves 1 and 2.
   f From which organ of the body does blood return to chamber B?
   g What sequence of letters gives the order of the chambers through which the blood passes?
   h Why does chamber C have a thicker wall than chamber D?
   i Name the blood vessel that supplies the heart with oxygen.

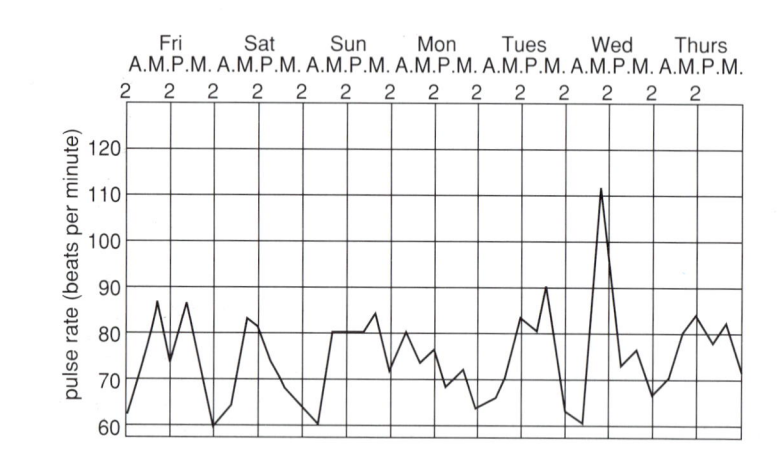

What caused Jim's heart attack?

It all started many years before, when Jim's arteries began to harden. The culprit was the fat-like substance **cholesterol** (page 79). Cholesterol was laid down in the walls of some of Jim's arteries, making them narrower and slowing the flow of blood through them.

Jim didn't realise this was happening. Why should he? He had been goalkeeper for the local football team for many years, and although he had a desk job now, he felt fit. He had no idea that blood was likely to clot inside one of his hardened arteries.

One day it happened. Jim was watching his team play a match. He suddenly felt stabbing pains in his chest, then he passed out. A **clot** had formed in one of his coronary arteries. The artery was blocked, and the heart muscle served by it was starved of oxygen and stopped beating. He had had a heart attack. Fortunately an ambulance was at hand: the driver massaged his chest to keep the blood flowing. It turned out that only a small part of Jim's heart was damaged, so he recovered. If a larger part had been affected, he would have died.

How could Jim have avoided having a heart attack? Well, he should never have got hardening of the arteries. This would have meant keeping down the amount of cholesterol in his blood. He might have done this by eating unsaturated rather than saturated fat, and by not smoking. He knew these were linked with heart disease. But he loved his food and smoked twenty cigarettes a day.

1. What is saturated fat, and what sort of foods contain it? (Use the index if necessary.)
2. What advice would you give Jim on how to avoid having another heart attack?
3. In some cases hardening of the arteries causes pain. In what way can the pain be helpful?
4. Some people eat a lot of saturated fat and live to an old age without ever having a heart attack. What conclusions do you draw from this?

How the circulation was discovered

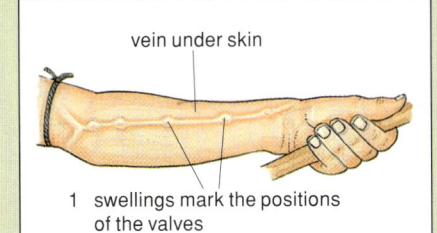

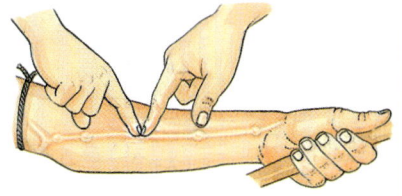

Some of the best experiments are very simple. A simple, but clever, experiment led William Harvey to discover the circulation of the blood in the early 1600s.

Harvey was Charles I's doctor. At that time scientists thought that blood seeped out of the heart to the various parts of the body, and then back again in the same vessels – rather like the tide flowing in and out of an estuary. This 'ebb and flow' theory was put forward by a Greek physician called Galen in the second century AD and it was still believed at the time of Harvey.

But Harvey had a different idea. He thought that the blood circulated round the body, flowing away from the heart in the arteries, and back to the heart in the veins.

Harvey's experiment is illustrated in picture 1. Study it carefully. The experiment shows that blood flows in only one direction in the arm vein – towards the heart. The valves stop the blood flowing in the other direction.

Picture 2 shows Harvey demonstrating this experiment to some young doctors in London. Try the experiment yourself, on a friend. But be careful: tying a band round the arm can be dangerous, so do the experiment only when your teacher is present.

This is only one of many experiments which Harvey did. He also dissected animals, studied the heart and blood vessels, and made calculations on the flow of blood. All his observations supported the idea that blood is pumped by the heart into the arteries and returns in the veins.

However, he never discovered the connection between the arteries and veins, namely the capillaries. He predicted that such a connection must exist, but he never found it.

Harvey has been called the father of modern medicine. He saw the human body as a machine, obeying the laws of physics and chemistry in the same way that non-living things do. At that time most people believed that the human body was created by God and obeyed special laws. The heart was the seat of the soul, not just a pump. Some of Harvey's patients were so upset by his ideas that they went to other doctors. Even his fellow scientists were critical, particularly as the final piece of evidence – the capillaries – was missing.

The capillaries were discovered seven years after Harvey's death by an Italian scientist, Marcello Malpighi. Malpighi used a microscope to examine the webbed foot of a frog. There before his eyes were the capillaries, with the blood flowing through them. Although the microscope was invented during Harvey's lifetime, he never used it in his work.

1. How did Malpighi's approach differ from Harvey's? Which approach provided the best evidence that the blood circulates, or is it impossible to say?
2. Harvey made a prediction which was tested by Malpighi. What was the prediction, and what piece of technology enabled Malpighi to test it?
3. How do you think people's lives were changed by Harvey's discoveries?

Picture 1 Harvey's famous experiment showing that blood flows towards the heart in the veins.

1. swellings mark the positions of the valves
2. Block vein with fingers as shown
3. Keep right finger where it is, then push blood to next swelling with left finger
4. Take left finger away. Note that blood does not flow back …
5. … even if you try pushing it with your finger

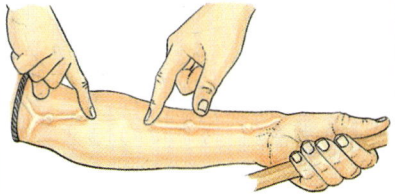

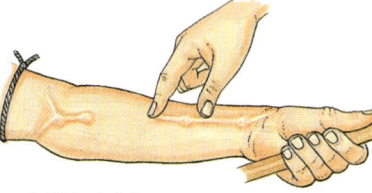

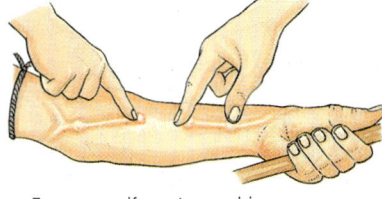

Picture 2 William Harvey showing his experiment to a group of young doctors at the Royal College of Physicians.

F5 Blood, the living fluid

Blood is much more complicated than you might think.

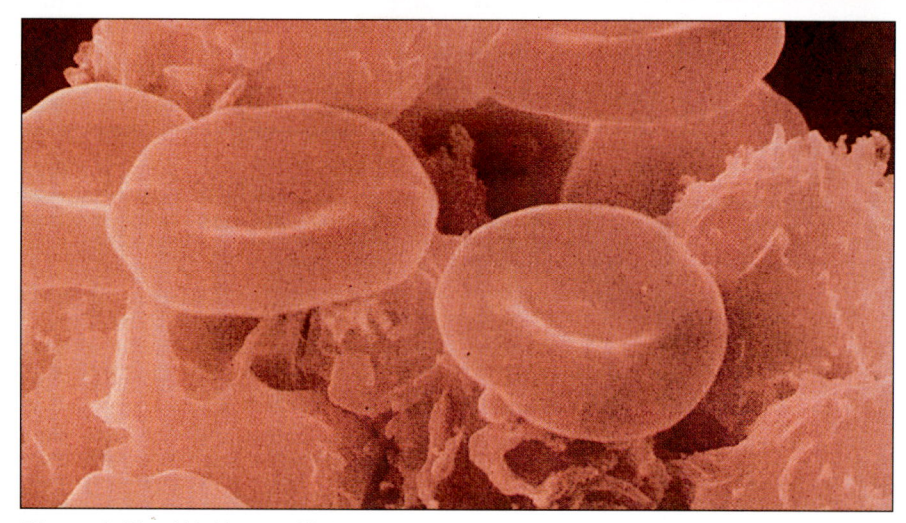

Picture 1 Blood highly magnified.

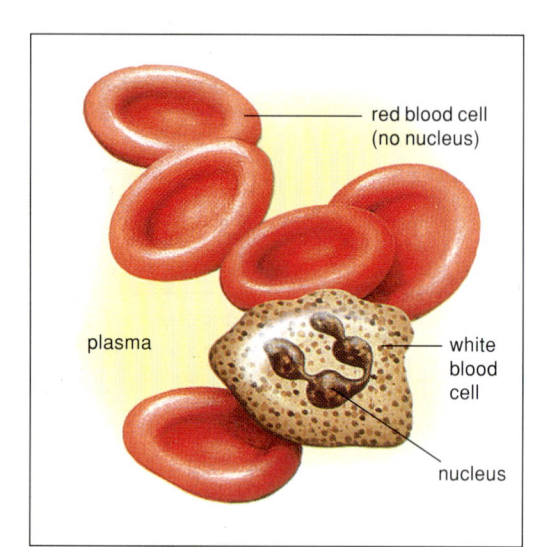

What does blood consist of?

An average sized person has about five litres of blood, that's nearly a bucket full. To the unaided eye blood looks like a simple fluid. But if you look at a sample of it under the microscope, you can see that there is more to it than that. It is a special type of tissue consisting of millions of cells in a fluid.

The cells are of two kinds: **red blood cells**, and **white blood cells**. The fluid part of the blood is called **plasma** (picture 2).

What does our blood do?

Our blood does three main things for us:
- It transports substances, including oxygen, within the body.
- It helps to defend us against disease.
- It keeps conditions right for the working of our cells.

Most of the substances that the blood transports are carried in solution in the plasma. They include soluble food substances (e.g. glucose), excretory products (e.g. urea) and hormones (e.g. insulin).

Its other jobs, carrying oxygen and fighting disease, we shall now look at in detail.

How does blood carry oxygen?

Oxygen is carried by our red blood cells. A single drop of blood contains millions of these cells. The red blood cell has a distinctive shape: it's like a disc which has been pressed in on each side, like the wheel of a car (picture 3). This gives it a large surface area for taking up oxygen.

The red blood cell does not have a nucleus. The inside is filled with a red pigment called **haemoglobin** – this is what makes blood look red. Haemoglobin is a special protein and contains iron. The iron enables the haemoglobin to carry oxygen. That is why we need iron in our food.

How does haemoglobin work? It combines with oxygen to form a substance called **oxyhaemoglobin**. In this form the oxygen is carried by the blood from the lungs to the tissues. When it gets to the tissues, the oxyhaemoglobin lets go of the oxygen and is turned back into haemoglobin.

The blood also carries carbon dioxide from the tissues to the lungs. The carbon dioxide is picked up by the red blood cells, but is then carried mainly in the plasma until it gets to the lungs. The carriage of oxygen and carbon dioxide is summarised in picture 4.

The remarkable thing about haemoglobin is how readily it takes up oxygen in the lungs. It's as if it has a special liking for oxygen.

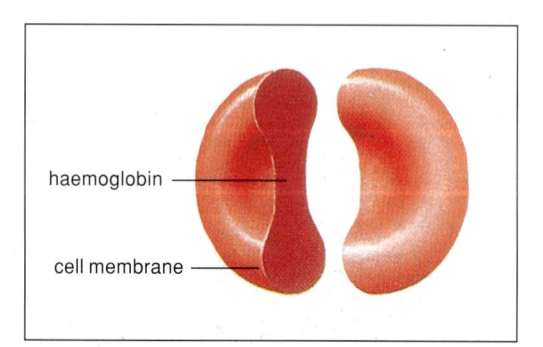

Picture 2 The main components of blood. There are several types of white blood cell of which only one is shown here. A cubic millimetre of blood (that's one small drop) contains about five million red cells and seven thousand white cells.

Picture 3 A human red blood cell cut in half to show its inside.

Haemoglobin has an even greater liking for another substance: carbon monoxide. This is present in motor vehicle exhaust. It combines with haemoglobin about 300 times more readily than oxygen does. If we breathe it in, less oxygen can combine with the blood, so the tissues are starved of oxygen.

Breathing carbon monoxide gas can kill you in a few minutes – that's why car exhaust is poisonous, even though less than five per cent of it is carbon monoxide. Small amounts of carbon monoxide are also present in cigarette smoke – not enough to kill you, but enough to make you feel faint if you're not used to smoking.

Non-stop production

Red blood cells live for only about four months. They are then destroyed in the liver, rather like used cars are destroyed when they're finished with. To keep up the right number in our bloodstream, new ones must constantly be produced. They are made in the **bone marrow**, a soft tissue inside certain bones (see page 130). About two million are manufactured every second!

A person who doesn't have enough red blood cells or haemoglobin suffers from **anaemia**. It can make you feel very tired. We can become anaemic by not having enough iron in our food, or by losing a lot of blood.

What happens if we lose a lot of blood?

People sometimes lose a lot of blood, haemophiliacs for example and people injured in car accidents. If more than a couple of litres are lost, the person's life is in danger for two reasons:
- The blood pressure falls, and this slows down the flow of blood round the body.
- The number of red blood cells falls, so the oxygen-carrying ability of the blood is reduced.

All sorts of consequences follow, but the main one is that not enough oxygen gets to the brain. The result is that the person goes unconscious and may die. However, life may be saved by a **blood transfusion**.

Blood transfusions

In a blood transfusion the person is given blood which has been donated by a **blood donor** (picture 5). If the person is very short of blood cells, a blood cell transfusion is given. Otherwise plasma alone will do. This restores the blood pressure, so the blood flows round the body at its normal speed. Over the next few weeks the patient makes new red blood cells to replace the ones which have been lost.

Before carrying out a transfusion with red blood cells the doctors make sure that the donor's blood and the patient's blood belong to the same **blood group**. Otherwise the donor's red blood cells may clump together, blocking the patient's blood vessels and causing death. Blood groups are explained on page 149.

How does blood fight disease?

Fighting disease is the job of the white blood cells. They are fewer in number than the red blood cells. They do not contain haemoglobin, and they have a nucleus. Their job is to attack and destroy germs which get into the body. This is part of our **immune system**. Like the red blood cells, the white blood cells are manufactured in the bone marrow.

There are two main kinds of white blood cell: **phagocytes** and **lymphocytes**. They attack germs in different ways. Phagocytes surround and digest invading germs. Lymphocytes destroy germs by producing **antibodies**. These are proteins which match protein **antigens** on the surface of the germ. Antibodies combine with the antigens and kill the germ.

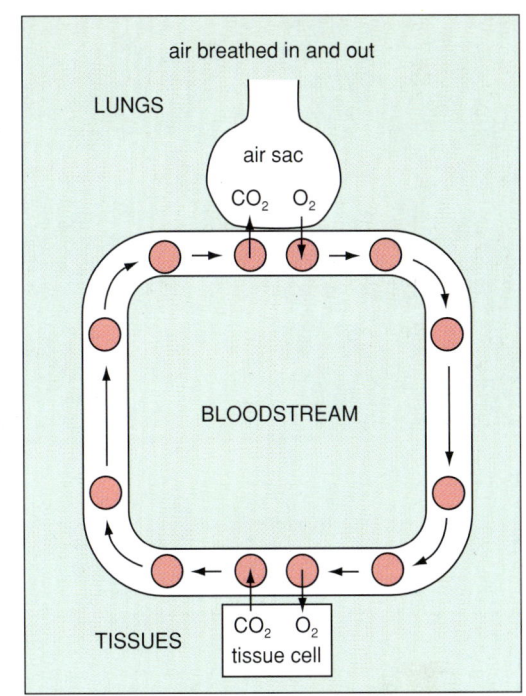

Picture 4 Blood carries oxygen from the lungs to the tissues, and carbon dioxide from the tissues to the lungs. Oxygen is carried from the lungs to the tissues by haemoglobin inside the red blood cells. In the tissues carbon dioxide enters the blood via the red blood cells, but most of it is then carried in the plasma as hydrogencarbonate ions. In the lungs carbon dioxide leaves the blood via the red blood cells.

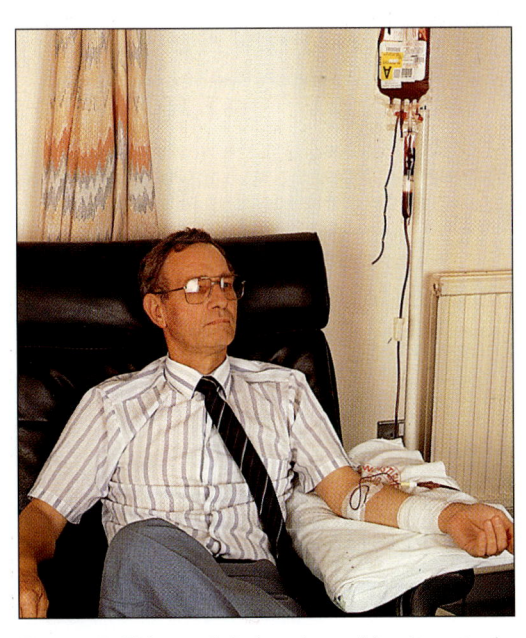

Picture 5 This man is being given a blood transfusion.

Blood clotting

If you cut yourself, you usually bleed for a short time, but soon the blood thickens and the bleeding stops. The thickening of the blood is called **clotting**. Clotting is important because it plugs up wounds, preventing blood being lost and stopping germs getting in. It is also the first step in the healing process in which the damaged tissues join up again.

How does clotting take place? Damage to a blood vessel causes tiny cell fragments in the blood, called **platelets**, to start a chain reaction. The final part of the chain is shown in picture 6. A soluble protein called **prothrombin** turns into an enzyme called **thrombin**. The thrombin then causes another soluble protein called **fibrinogen** to turn into solid threads of **fibrin**. This is the clot.

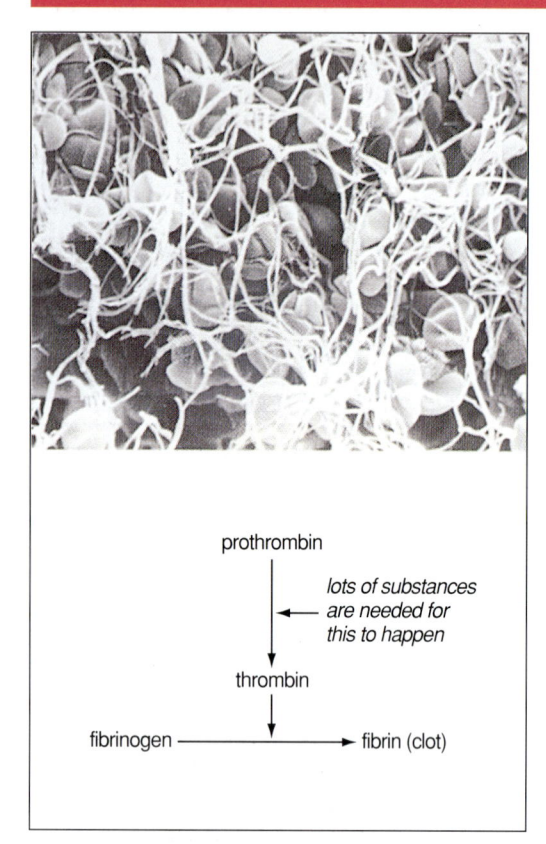

Picture 6 When blood clots a meshwork of fibres (called fibrin) is formed. The picture was obtained with an electron microscope. The things that look like deflated footballs are red blood cells. The main chemical reactions involved in the clotting process are shown below the picture.

prothrombin
↓ ← lots of substances are needed for this to happen
thrombin
fibrinogen ⟶ fibrin (clot)

First aid for bleeding

1. Get the person to lie down and relax.
2. Press the edges of the wound together with thumb and finger, or press down on the wound with the palm of your hand.
3. Raise the site of the wound above the level of the heart.
4. Place a thick pad (e.g. a folded handkerchief) on the wound, continuing to press all the time.
5. Bandage the pad very firmly with, say, a tie or stocking. If blood oozes through the bandage, add a further pad and bandage.
6. If a lot of blood has been lost, raise the legs above the level of the head and trunk.

Give a reason for each of the steps in this procedure.

Questions

1. Write down *three* ways in which red and white blood cells differ in their appearance.
   What job does each do?

2. Why is it dangerous to breathe in motor car exhaust? Explain your answer.

3. There are approximately five million red blood cells in a cubic millimetre of human blood, and the total volume of blood in the whole body is about five litres. Each red blood cell has a surface area of about 120 square micrometres.
   a How many red blood cells are there in the entire bloodstream?
   b What will be the total surface area of all the red blood cells? Give your answer in square metres.
   c What is the significance of these measurements?

4. A scientist investigated the number of red blood cells possessed by people living at sea level and in a mountainous region at a height of 5860 metres. Here are her results:

sea level	5.0 million per mm^3
5860 metres	7.4 million per mm^3

   Why do you think they differ?

5. Explain the reasons for each of the following:
   a Not more than half a litre of blood is normally taken from a blood donor.
   b After giving blood, the donor is advised to sit down quietly for about half an hour.
   c A little sodium citrate is usually added to blood which has been given by a donor.
   d Complete blood is only kept for about a month after it has been obtained from a blood donor, but plasma may be kept much longer.

6. Use the following words or phrases to complete the sentences below. You may use the word or phrase once, more than once or not at all.

   red blood cells
   white blood cells
   plasma
   oxygen
   carbon dioxide

   Blood arriving at muscle cells has a high concentration of .... and a low concentration of ....
   Most of the oxygen is carried by the .... and most of the carbon dioxide is carried by the ....

7. Mice, living at low altitude, were transported to a high altitude for 100 days.
   During the first 50 days their average number of red blood cells increased from 7.5 to 10.5 million per mm^3. After 100 days, however, this figure had stabilised at 9.5 million per mm^3.
   a Calculate the percentage increase in the average number of red blood cells per mm^3 after 50 days at high altitude.
   b Name the substance, in the red blood cells, which combines with oxygen.
   c Explain why an increase in the number of red blood cells helps the mice to live at higher altitudes.
   d Suggest a reason why the number of red blood cells stabilised at a level below the maximum value attained.
   e Suggest a suitable control for this investigation.
   f What variables would have to be kept constant in order for a fair comparison to be made?

What are blood groups?

The ABO system

Everyone's blood belongs to one of four groups called **A**, **B**, **AB** and **O**. The letters refer to particular protein antigens which may be present on the surface of the red blood cells:

Group A blood has type A antigens on the red blood cells.

Group B blood has type B antigens on the red blood cells.

Group AB blood has both types of antigen on the red blood cells.

Group O blood has neither type of antigen on the red blood cells.

In the plasma there are antibodies. If these antibodies were to combine with the antigens on the red blood cells, they would cause havoc.

However, a person never possesses blood in which the antigens and corresponding antibodies occur together. Nature simply doesn't allow it. For example, group A blood has type A antigens on the red blood cells but anti-B antibodies in the plasma; and group B blood has type B antigens on the red blood cells but anti-A antibodies in the plasma.

If the corresponding antibodies were present in the plasma, they would combine with the antigens and cause the red blood cells to clump together. It's as if the red blood cells were treated as germs.

In a blood transfusion the patient must be given blood from a donor with the right blood group. The donor's red blood cells will clump together if the patient's plasma contains the corresponding antibodies (see picture 1). This is what doctors have to avoid. The best way is to use blood which belongs to the same group as the patient's.

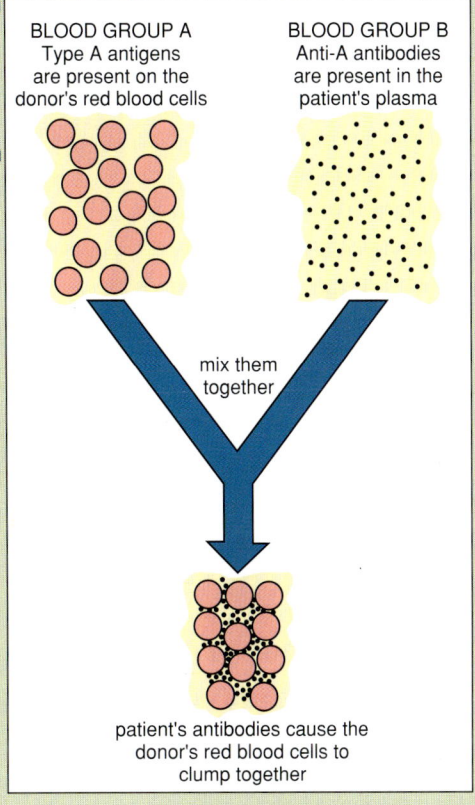

BLOOD GROUP A Type A antigens are present on the donor's red blood cells

BLOOD GROUP B Anti-A antibodies are present in the patient's plasma

mix them together

patient's antibodies cause the donor's red blood cells to clump together

Picture 1 This diagram shows what may happen if blood of different blood groups is mixed.

The rhesus system

There are other blood groups besides the ABO system. For example, some people are described as **Rhesus positive**. They have a certain type of antigen on their red blood cells. People who don't have these antigens are called **Rhesus negative**.

Now suppose a Rhesus negative person is given Rhesus positive blood in a transfusion. In this case the Rhesus negative person makes antibodies which combine with the antigens on the donor's red blood cells. This can cause the donor's red blood cells to clump together and burst. Here again, the red blood cells are treated as germs.

Blood groups and transfusions

Before blood transfusions are carried out, doctors always make sure that the patient's blood is compatible with the donor's blood. Their blood groups are found by carrying out a simple test on small drops of blood.

We inherit our blood groups from our parents. The percentages of people belonging to the different blood groups in Britain are as follows:

ABO system		Rhesus system	
O	47%	Rh+	85%
A	41%	Rh–	15%
B	9%		
AB	3%		

These figures tell us which blood groups are most likely to be needed for transfusions.

Blood which has been given by donors is stored in blood banks. The blood is kept in bottles which are labelled with the blood groups.

1 People belonging to blood group O have anti-A and anti-B substances in their plasma.
  a What sort of antigens, if any, do they have on their red blood cells?
  b What sort of antibodies and antigens are present in the blood of a person belonging to blood group AB?

2 Four young people donate blood in a blood donation centre. A medical technician finds their blood groups by mixing drops of their blood with different kinds of serum.

John's blood goes lumpy with anti-A serum but not with anti-B.

David's blood goes lumpy with anti-B serum but not with anti-A.

Anna's blood goes lumpy with both kinds of serum.

Susan's blood does not go lumpy with either kind of serum.

Which blood group does each person belong to?

Allergies

Sometime we produce antibodies against harmless substances such as certain foods, pollen or even clothing. This can cause unpleasant effects, as anyone who has suffered from hay fever knows. Hay fever is caused by pollen, and it particularly affects the nose and eyes. People differ in the way they react to food substances. Some people are sensitive to lettuces – something in the lettuce leaf makes you feel really ill.

These sort of reactions are called **allergies**. Sometimes it is difficult to know exactly what is causing a particular allergic reaction, and various tests have to be carried out. Once the cause has been discovered, steps can be taken to prevent it or at least make it less severe.

A well known symptom of allergic reactions is the release from certain cells in the body of a substance called **histamine**. One way of treating allergies therefore is to give the person an **anti-histamine drug**.

F6
The eye

Close your eyes and imagine what it must be like to live in darkness. Our eyes are amongst our most important sense organs.

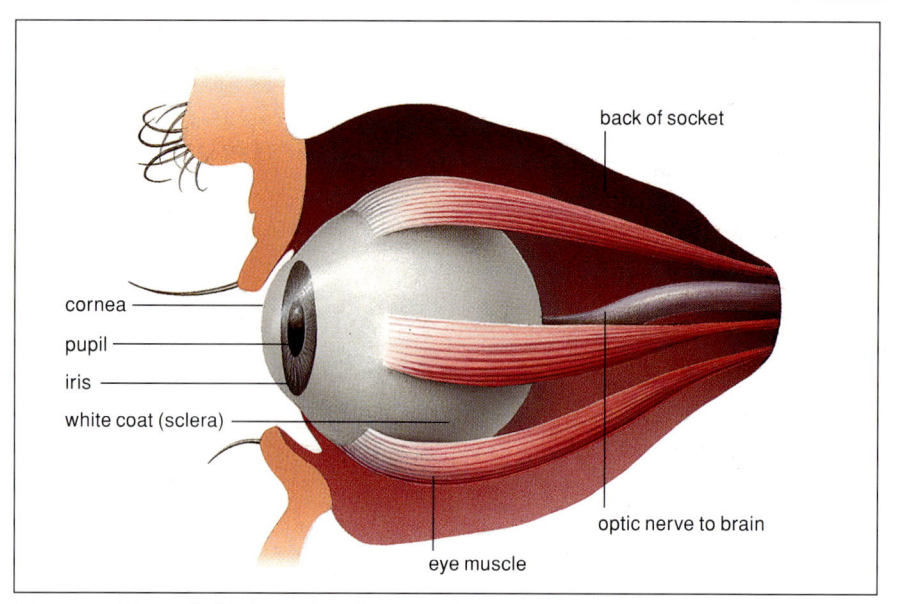

Picture 1 The eyeball in its socket. There are six eye muscles altogether, of which only three are shown here.

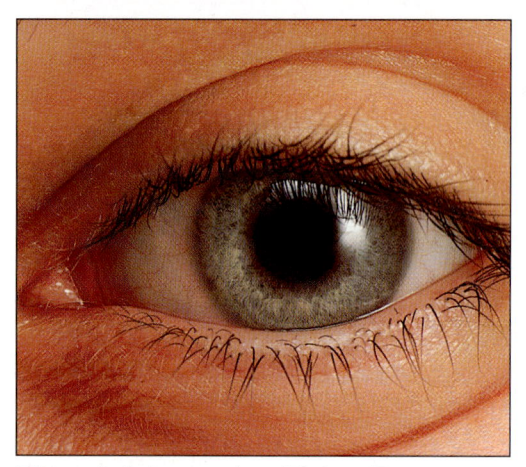

Picture 2 A close-up view of the eye. Tears are produced by a gland just under the upper eyelid on the right, and they drain away into a duct in the corner of the eye on the left.

The outside of the eye

Each eye consists of an eyeball which rests in a socket in the skull (picture 1). The sides and back of the eyeball are thick and tough – this is the 'white of the eye'. The front is transparent and is called the **cornea**. The cornea is covered by a thin and delicate membrane called the **conjunctiva**.

The conjunctiva is kept moist by **tears**, a lubricating fluid produced by a gland under the eyelid (picture 2). Tears also contain the enzyme **lysozyme** which kills bacteria.

In the centre of the eye is the **pupil**. This is surrounded by the **iris**, the coloured part of the eye.

The eyeball is held in place by muscles which can move it up and down and from side to side. A large **optic nerve** runs from the back of the eye to the brain. When you look at an apple, millions of impulses are sent off in this nerve and when they reach the correct part of the brain you see the apple.

Picture 3 The internal structure of the human eye. You must imagine that the eye has been sliced across the middle and that you are looking inside.

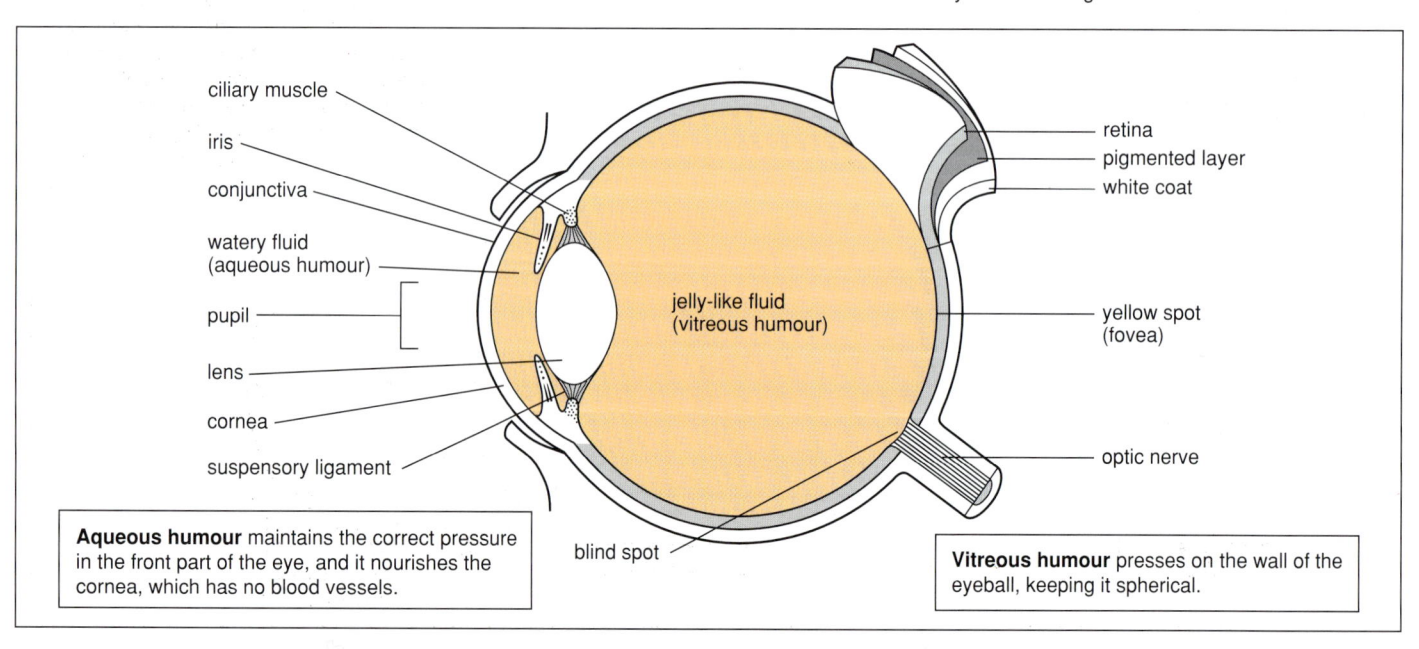

Aqueous humour maintains the correct pressure in the front part of the eye, and it nourishes the cornea, which has no blood vessels.

Vitreous humour presses on the wall of the eyeball, keeping it spherical.

The inside of the eye

Picture 3 shows the inside of the eye. For seeing things, the two main parts are the **lens** and the **retina**.

The lens is soft and transparent – rather like a polythene bag full of water – and its shape can change. It is encircled by a ring of muscle called the **ciliary muscle**. The lens is held in position by fine threads which run from it to the surrounding ciliary muscle. The threads are called the **suspensory ligament**.

The retina lines the inside of the eyeball. It contains millions of receptor cells. These cells are sensitive to light which has entered the eye through the pupil – this is how the eye sees things. The part of the retina responsible for seeing things most clearly is right in the middle – the **yellow spot** (**fovea**).

Behind the retina is a layer of tissue containing a dark pigment. The pigment absorbs light and prevents it being reflected within the eye. Why would it be a bad thing if this happened?

The pigmented layer also contains lots of blood vessels. They supply the retina with oxygen and food substances.

The point where the optic nerve is attached to the eye is called the **blind spot**. The blind spot has no receptor cells, so it is unable to see things.

Controlling the amount of light that enters the eye

If you look at a bright light, a reflex action occurs: the pupil gets smaller and this stops too much light getting into the eye. The opposite happens in the dark: the pupil gets larger, so more light can enter the eye.

The widening and narrowing of the pupil is brought about by the iris. Picture 4 shows how it works.

How does the eye see things?

When you take pictures with a television camera, light enters the camera and is focused by a lens onto a light-sensitive film at the back. The eye works in the same kind of way.

Suppose you are looking at a dot on the wall. Light rays, reflected from the dot, enter your eye as shown in picture 5. As the light rays pass through the cornea and lens, they are bent inwards so that they meet on the retina. Here they produce an image of the dot.

For the image to be clear and sharp, i.e. in focus, the light rays must meet exactly on the retina. This is achieved by the lens which makes sure that the light rays are always bent to just the right extent. We'll come back to this in a moment.

The bending of the light rays is called **refraction**, and it plays an essential part in giving us good eyesight.

Picture 5 How the eye focuses on a dot.

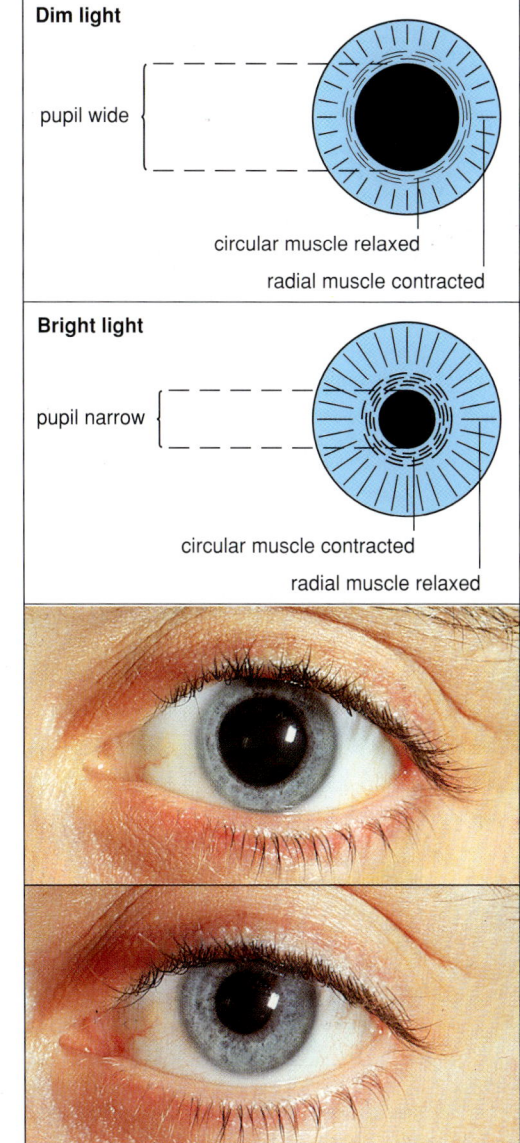

Picture 4 What happens to the pupil when the light intensity changes. These changes are brought about by the iris. Inside the iris there are muscles which can make it either constrict or open up. The photographs show a real eye with the pupil wide open and narrow.

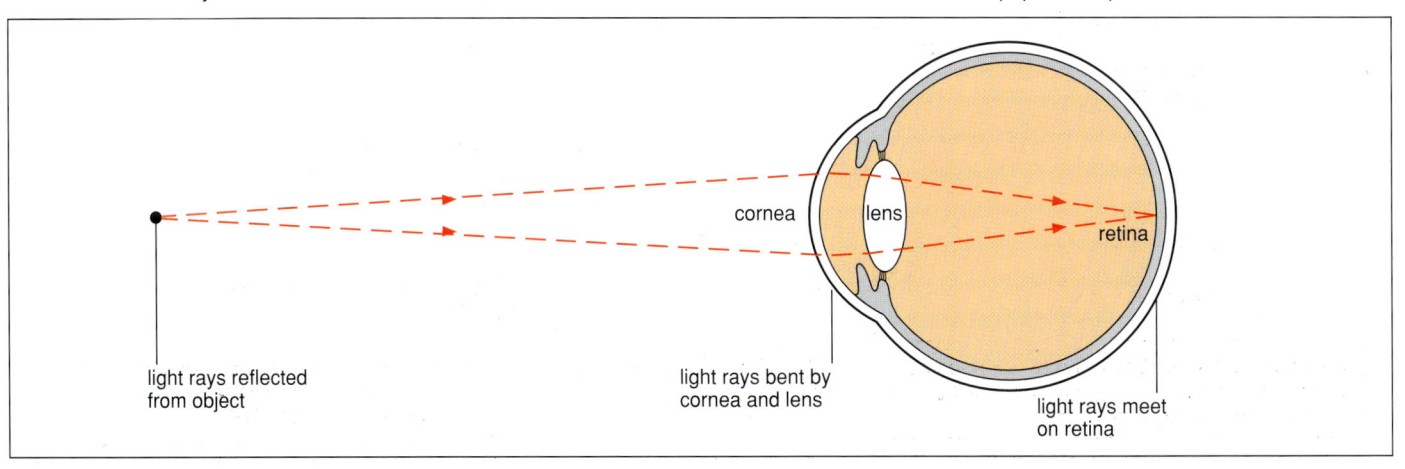

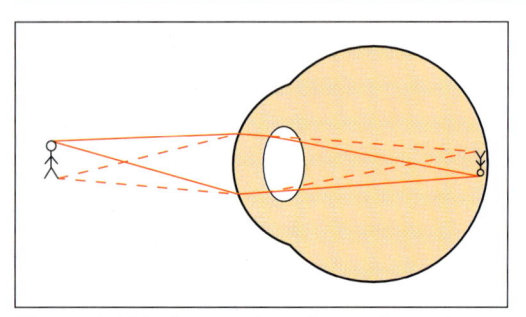

Picture 6 This diagram shows how an image is turned upside down by the lens in the eye. The same thing is done by the lens in a camera.

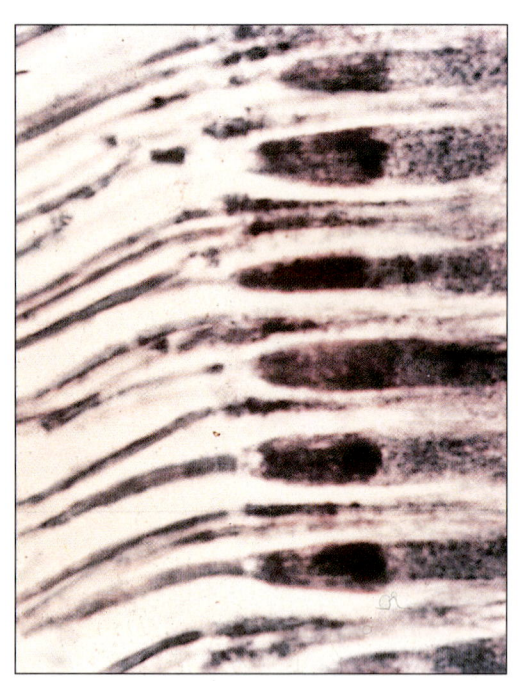

Picture 7 A small part of the retina seen under the microscope. It shows the cone cells and rod cells.

Picture 8 How the eye keeps a ball in focus as it gets closer.

Seeing things the right way up

Suppose you are looking at a person. Picture 6 shows how the light rays, reflected from the person, pass into your eye. The result is that the image is upside down on the retina.

Why then don't we see everything upside down? The answer is that the brain comes to the rescue and turns the picture the right way up for us.

Some years ago an experiment was done in which a man was given special glasses that made him see everything upside down. After a while his brain made the necessary correction and he began to see things the right way up again, even though he went on wearing the glasses. What do you think happened when he took the glasses off?

How does the retina work?

If you look straight at an object, and then look at it out of the corner of your eye, its appearance changes. From being clear and sharp, it becomes fuzzy and indistinct. Also it's hard to tell what colour it is.

How can we explain this? Well, there are two types of receptor cells in the retina. They are called **cone cells** and **rod cells** (picture 7). When you look straight at something, you are using the central part of the retina – the yellow spot. This part of the retina contains mainly cone cells, which detect things clearly and in colour.

However, when you look at something out of the corner of your eye, you are using the part of the retina further out. This contains mainly rod cells. They detect things less clearly, and in black and white.

Seeing in dim light

From what we have just said, you might have got the idea that the outer part of the retina is not much use. However, it is good at seeing things in dim light. You can prove this for yourself by looking at a faint star on a dark night. It is much easier to see it out of the corner of your eye than by looking straight at it.

The reason for this is that the rod cells are stimulated by even very small amounts of light, so they work in gloomy conditions. The cone cells, on the other hand, are less sensitive and will only work in reasonably bright conditions.

Have you noticed that when you go into a gloomy room from bright sunlight, you can't see anything at first but gradually things become visible? The reason is that the bright light causes your rod cells to lose their sensitivity. So when you go into the gloomy room, the rod cells don't work. They need time to become sensitive again. As their sensitivity returns, you begin to see things.

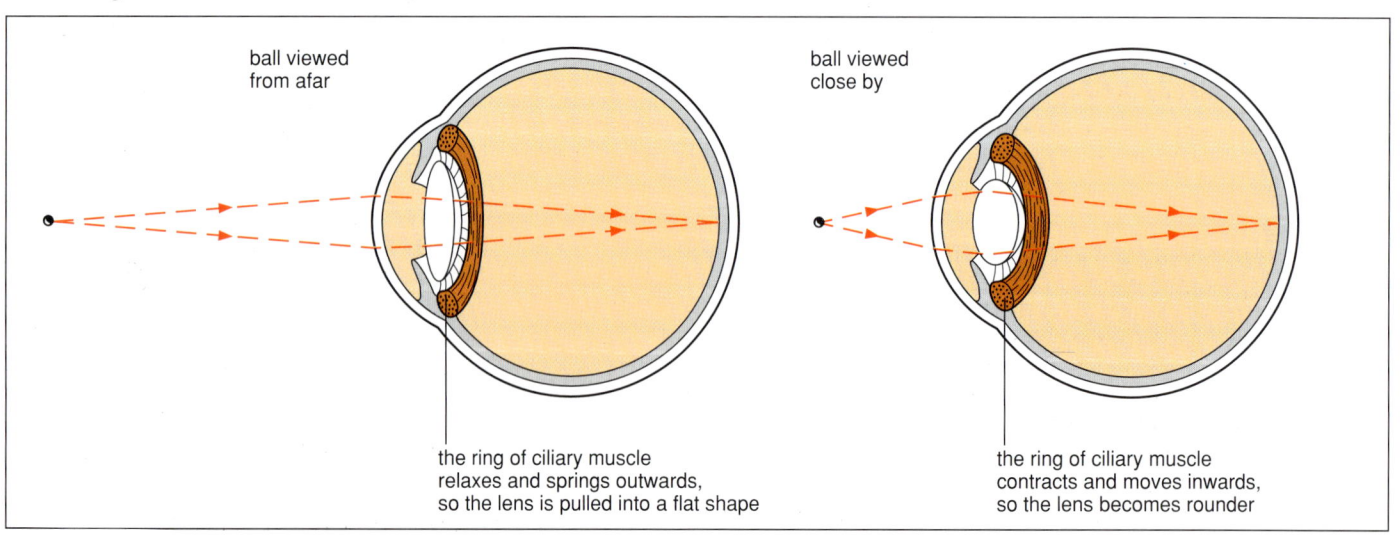

ball viewed from afar

the ring of ciliary muscle relaxes and springs outwards, so the lens is pulled into a flat shape

ball viewed close by

the ring of ciliary muscle contracts and moves inwards, so the lens becomes rounder

Colour vision

If you have ever been involved with stage-lighting, you will know that almost any colour can be obtained by mixing red, green and blue lights in the right proportions. These are the **primary colours**.

The same principle applies to the way we see colours. Scientists have shown that we have three different kinds of cone cells, each sensitive to one of the primary colours. The colour which we actually see depends on how many cones of each kind are stimulated.

Some people cannot see certain colours – they are **colour blind**. In rare cases colours cannot be seen at all, so everything looks black, white or grey. A more common condition is where people cannot tell the difference between red and green.

Keeping things in focus

Suppose you are watching a ball hurtling towards you. If the eye did not adjust, the light rays would stop meeting on the retina as the ball got close to you – so the ball would become out of focus. However, the eye does adjust. The lens becomes rounder and bends the light rays more. So the light rays continue to meet on the retina, and the ball stays in focus.

The eye is able to keep things in focus because the lens is soft and can change its shape. The shape of the lens is changed by the ciliary muscle. This makes the lens flat or more rounded, depending on whether you are looking at something in the distance or close to (picture 8).

Despite this wonderful adjustment mechanism, many people cannot focus properly. Such people may be either **short-sighted** or **long-sighted**.

Short-sighted people

A short-sighted person can focus on things close by, but not a long way off. This is due to the lens bending the light rays too much, or to the eyeball being too long. The result is that the light rays meet in front of the retina.

Short-sightedness is corrected by wearing glasses which bend the light rays outwards before they reach the eye (picture 9).

Long-sighted people

A long-sighted person can focus on things a long way off, but not close by. This is due to the lens not bending the light rays enough, or to the eyeball being too short. The result is that the light rays are directed to a point behind the retina.

Long-sightedness is corrected by wearing glasses which bend the light rays inwards before they reach the eye (picture 10).

Long-sightedness is also caused by the lens becoming hard, so it no longer changes its shape in the usual way. This tends to happen in old people, and is one of the main reasons why they often need glasses.

A more serious problem is that the lens may become cloudy and stop letting light through. This is called a **cataract**. The only remedy is to take the lens out in an operation and give the person very strong glasses or contact lenses. In the latest operations, the person's own lens is replaced with an artificial acrylic lens.

Three-dimensional vision

If you look at a chair, it appears to have depth. In other words you see it in three dimensions. You need two eyes for this. What happens is that each eye sees a slightly different aspect of the chair. In the brain the two images are combined to give a single three-dimensional view of the chair. Seeing with two eyes is called **binocular vision**.

Binocular vision gives us a more complete view of our environment, and it helps us to judge distances. For example, if you're cycling along the road and there's a car in front of you, you know roughly how far away it is.

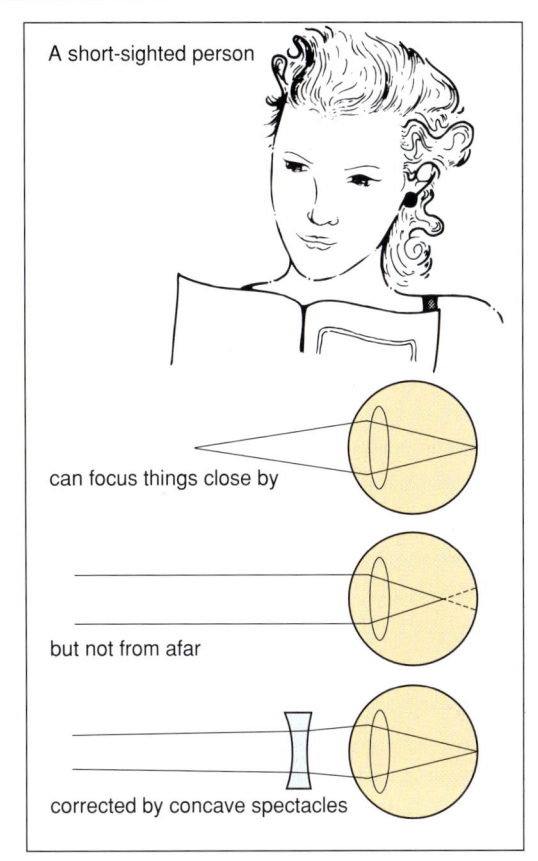

Picture 9 Short-sightedness and how it can be corrected by wearing glasses.

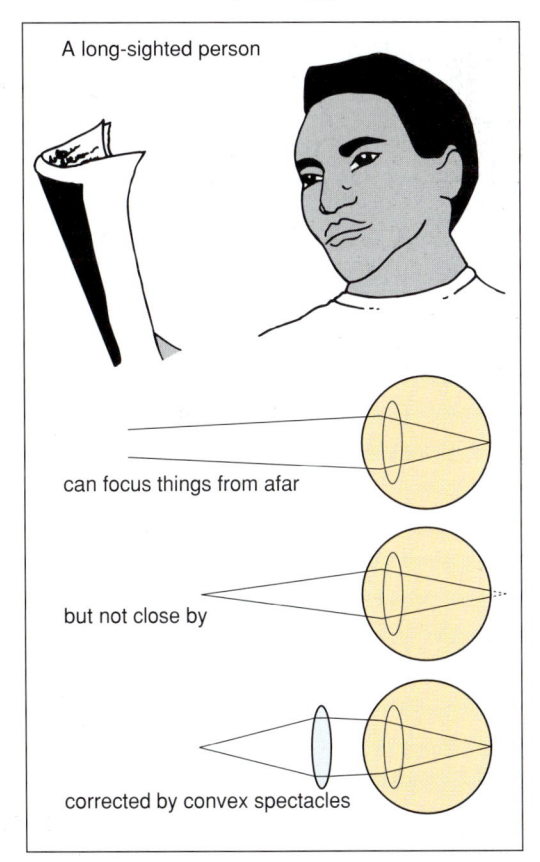

Picture 10 Long-sightedness and how it can be corrected by wearing glasses.

154 *The body in action*

Activities

A The pupil reflex

Work in pairs, with one person acting as observer and the other as subject. This is what the observer should do:

1 Get the subject to close his/her eyes for ten seconds, then open them. What happens to the pupils when the eye opens?
2 Shine a torch in the subject's eye and watch the pupil. What happens to the pupil? Explain your observations.
3 Get the subject to look at an object in the distance and then nearby. What happens to the pupil when the subject does this, and why?

B Demonstrating the blind spot

1 Look at the picture below: hold it about 10 cm from your eyes.

2 Close your left eye, and look at the house with your right eye.
3 Slowly move the picture away from your eyes, keeping your right eye focused on the house all the time.
   What happens to the ghost as you move the picture away from you?
   How would you explain this?
4 Repeat the experiment with both eyes open.
   What happens this time?
   How would you explain the difference?

C How good is your eyesight?

1 On a white card draw two parallel lines one millimetre apart. Hang the card on the wall.
2 Gradually back away from the card until the two parallel lines appear as one, then stop.
   How far are you from the card?
   Compare your distance with that of other people in the class.

D Seeing colours

1 Obtain two cards, one red and the other green.
2 Look at the two cards out of the corner of your eye.
   Can you tell which colour is which?
   How would you explain your observation?
3 Obtain a set of colour blindness test cards.
   Test your eyes with the cards, following the instructions carefully.
   Can you see colours normally, or are you colour blind?
   If you are colour blind, are you totally colour blind or are you colour blind only to red and green?

E How the brain can help

With a piece of straight-edged paper cover the top half of the following phrase:

HAPPY BIRTHDAY

Can you read it?

Now cover the bottom half of the phrase. Can you read it now?

This experiment tells us something about the part played by our brain when we look at things.

Try to explain your result.

Questions

1 What are the advantages of having two eyes rather than only one?
2 Explain the reason for each of the following:
   a When you go into a cinema from bright sunlight, you cannot see the seats at first, but gradually they become visible.
   b If you are trying to see a faint star in the night sky, it is better to look slightly to one side of it rather than straight at it.
   c When it is getting dark at night, it is impossible to make out the colours of cars on the road.
   d If you look at a cinema screen out of the corner of your eye, you can see it flickering.
   e If both your eyes are open and you press the side of one of your eyeballs, you see double.
3 The diagram shows some of the structures in a human eye.

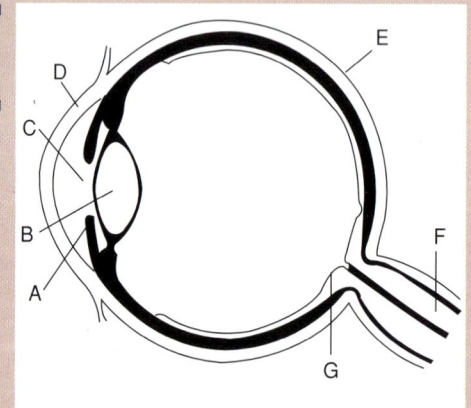

   Use the letters from the diagram to identify the following structures and functions.
   a lens
   b produces a nerve signal in response to light energy
   c cornea
   d controls the amount of light entering the eye
   e focuses the image by changing shape
   f optic nerve

4 Nocturnal animals, i.e. animals which sleep during the day and come out at night, tend to have wide pupils and lots of rods in their retinas. Suggest a reason for this.
5 Select from the list the correct words to complete the sentences.

   optic nerve
   focusing
   lens
   pupil
   contracting
   retina

   The iris is a muscular layer behind the cornea. By ...., the iris can alter the size of the.......... This controls the amount of light reaching the light-sensitive ....

6 Why is it important for a person to know if he or she is colour blind?

   People who are red-green colour blind say that they have no difficulty telling whether the traffic lights are red or green. How would you explain this?

Living in darkness

Close your eyes for at least one minute, and imagine what it must be like to be blind. Suddenly the sense organs which make you most aware of your environment stop working.

Although blind people have serious problems, most of them manage very well. One reason for this is that they make much more use of their other senses, particularly hearing and touch. In blind people these senses become very well developed.

Take touch, for example. Blind people identify things by feeling them. Their fingertips become very sensitive, and this enables them to read Braille. This system was invented in France by Louis Braille. Each letter of the alphabet is represented by a character consisting of one to six dots embossed on thick paper (see picture 1).

Picture 1 A blind person reading Braille.

Another system was developed by an Englishman called Dr Moon. In this case the letters are represented not by dots but by shapes. They are easier to feel and to learn, but they take up more room.

1 Close your eyes. Your teacher will give you a flat shape made of wire. Feel it. Your teacher will then take it away. Open your eyes and try drawing the shape.

2 With your eyes closed, feel the characters on a Braille card with your fingertips. Do you find it difficult to tell the difference between the various characters?

Repeat the process with a sheet of Moon. Are the characters easier to tell apart than the Braille characters? If so, why? How could you prove that they are?

3 People who go blind when they are young usually learn Braille, but elderly people who go blind usually learn Moon. Why the difference?

Lasers and the eye

A laser is an instrument which produces very intense beams of light. There are many types of laser, and they produce light at different frequencies. Laser beams can be used for all sorts of purposes. For example, they may be used to destroy or cut tissues, or to get tissues to stick together.

The eye was the first organ in the human body to be treated with lasers (see pictures 1 and 2). Let's look at an example. Sometimes a hole develops in a person's retina. Fluid in the eyeball gets through the hole and lifts the retina away from the tissue underneath. This is called a **detached retina**. If nothing is done about it, the person may go partially blind.

Detachment of the retina can be prevented by laser treatment. Short pulses from the laser are sent into the eye, one after the other, and focused on the retina. The pulses are not all directed at the same spot, but form a ring round the hole in the retina. It's like firing a gun at a target, but instead of aiming at the bull each time, you aim slightly to one side and make a circle round the bull. The laser beam makes the retina stick to the tissue behind it, and stops it coming off – it 'welds' it into position.

The beam is so fine that very few sensory cells in the retina are damaged – certainly not enough to affect the person's eyesight. The pulses are extremely quick – each one lasts only a tenth of a second, and you hardly feel anything at all.

But there's a snag. The treatment *must* be carried out before fluid has a chance to get behind the retina. Once the retina gets lifted off the underlying tissue, the laser can't stick it back again. The only remedy then is to perform an operation on the eye.

Lasers are a modern invention, but way back in 1949 a German professor made a sort of home-made laser to treat people with holes in the retina. He set up a tube with a system of mirrors to gather sunlight and focus it on the retina. One day he was looking down the tube and suddenly the sun caught one of the mirrors and burned the central part of his own retina. The result was that he became blind in one eye. This story illustrates the point that very intense light destroys living tissue.

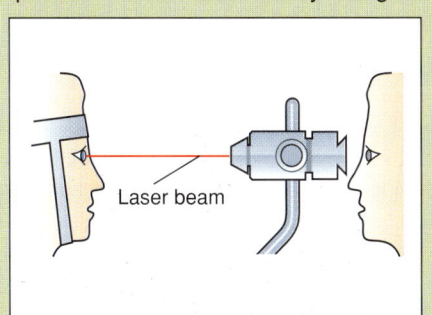

Picture 1 This diagram shows a laser beam being shone into a patient's eye. The patient wears a special kind of contact lens which allows the doctor to see into the eye and focus the laser beam on exactly the right part.

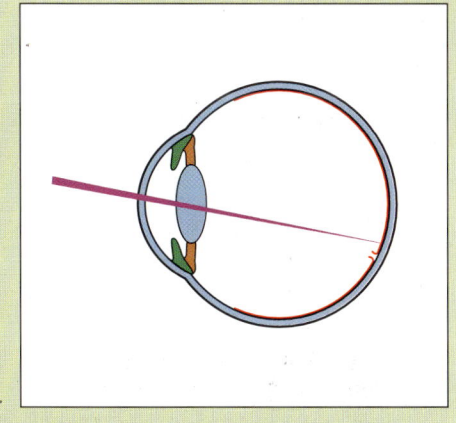

Picture 2 A laser beam being used to stick back a detached retina.

1 What advantages does a laser have over an operation for treating the eye? Think of as many advantages as you can.

2 Why do you think a laser beam makes the retina stick to the tissue underneath?

3 A person who develops a hole in the retina may not know that it has happened. How would you explain this?

F7 The ear and hearing

Block your ears with your fingers and imagine what it's like to live in silence.

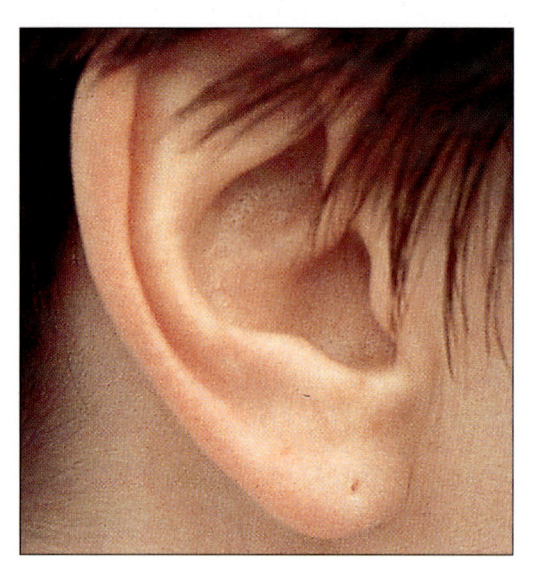

Picture 1 Our ears tell us a lot about what's going on around us.

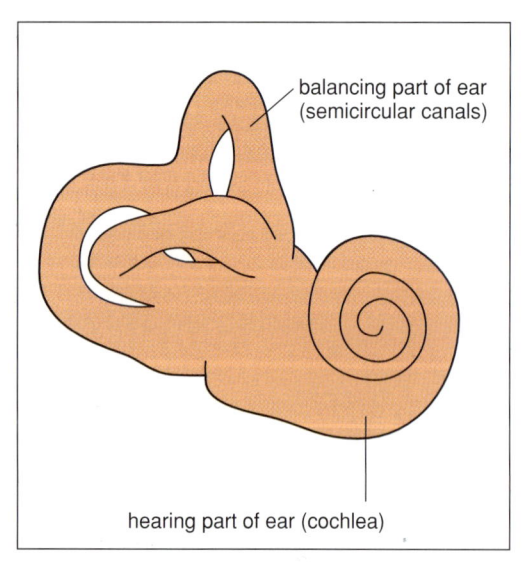

Picture 2 Imagine that the inner ear was taken out of your head. This is what it would look like.

- balancing part of ear (semicircular canals)
- hearing part of ear (cochlea)

The outside of the ear

Most people think of the ear as just a flap on the side of the head. But there is much more to it than that. The flap is simply a device for catching sounds and directing them into the **ear hole** in front. The flap is called the **pinna** and it contains gristle to keep it stiff.

Inside the ear

The 'business' part of the ear is embedded in the side of the head. Picture 2 shows it on its own outside the head. It is made up of two parts which do quite different jobs. One part helps us to keep our balance – we shall return to that later. The other part enables us to hear. The hearing part consists of a coiled tube rather like a snail's shell. It is called the **cochlea**. The ear hole is connected to the cochlea by a series of channels and chambers which are shown in picture 3.

Let's go on a guided tour of the ear, using picture 3 to help us. The hole leads into a short tube called the **outer ear channel**. The skin lining the first part of the channel secretes wax which catches germs and dust, preventing them from getting into the ear.

Stretched across the inner end of the channel is a tough membrane, the **ear drum**. On the other side of the ear drum is a chamber filled with air. It is called the **middle ear chamber**, and it contains three tiny bones called the **ear ossicles**. They are the smallest bones in the body. Because of their shape, they are called the **hammer**, **anvil** and **stirrup**. They run from the ear drum to a small hole on the other side of the middle ear chamber. This is called the **oval window**, and it leads to the cochlea which is part of the **inner ear**.

The cochlea is full of fluid and it contains receptor cells which are connected to the brain by the **auditory nerve**.

How does the ear hear?

It's Guy Fawkes night and there's a loud bang. The noise sets off **sound waves** which travel through the air. Within a fraction of a second the sound waves reach your ear, and the pinna directs them into the outer ear channel.

The sound waves pass along the channel to the ear drum. When they hit the ear drum, the drum vibrates. This moves the ear ossicles backwards and forwards, causing the foot of the stirrup in the oval window to vibrate. The vibrations of the stirrup then move the fluid in the cochlea.

The function of the ear ossicles is to transmit the vibrations of the ear drum to the cochlea. But they do more than this. They also amplify the vibrations. Why do you think this is necessary?

What happens in the cochlea?

Inside the cochlea there are two membranes stretched across from one side to the other. These membranes run the full length of the cochlea. You can see them in picture 3. The lower one has receptor cells attached to it.

Vibrations of the cochlea fluid make the cochlea membranes vibrate. When the lower membrane vibrates, it stimulates the receptor cells. The receptor cells then send off impulses in the auditory nerve. When the impulses reach the brain, we hear the sound.

That's not quite the end of the story. Look once more at picture 3. You'll see that between the middle ear chamber and the cochlea there is a hole called the **round window**. You may have wondered what it's for. Obviously the pressure which develops in the cochlea fluid has got to be taken up by something. It's taken up by the membrane covering this hole.

We can sum up by saying that the sound waves make the ear membranes vibrate, and the movements are then changed, i.e. transduced, into electrical signals which are sent to the brain.

Picture 3 Inside the human ear. The arrows show how sound waves are transmitted to the receptor cells in the cochlea.

Telling the difference between loud and soft sounds

If you play a note on a guitar, its loudness depends on how hard you pluck the wire. The harder you pluck, the greater is the distance through which the wire vibrates and the louder is the sound.

The loudness of a sound is registered by the ear in the same way. Soft sounds cause small vibrations of the cochlea membranes. Louder sounds cause larger vibrations.

Telling the difference between high and low notes

With a guitar, the note depends on how rapidly the wire vibrates – in other words, the frequency. High frequency vibrations give high notes, whereas low frequency vibrations give low notes.

Although the details are different, the ear works in the same kind of way. The membrane to which the receptor cells are attached vibrates at different frequencies in different parts of the cochlea. In other words, the membrane **resonates**, and this enables different notes to be heard.

How can you tell where a sound comes from?

Normally when you hear a sound, you know where it comes from. This is because you have two ears, one on each side of the head.

Suppose you hear a sound from the right. Sound waves reach the right ear a fraction of a second before they reach the left ear (picture 4). The result is that nerve impulses are sent to the brain from the right ear slightly before they are sent from the left ear. From this the brain knows that the sound must have come from the right. Although other effects play a part, this is the basis of how we tell where sounds come from, and how we appreciate stereo music.

Picture 4 Where did that bang come from?

158 *The body in action*

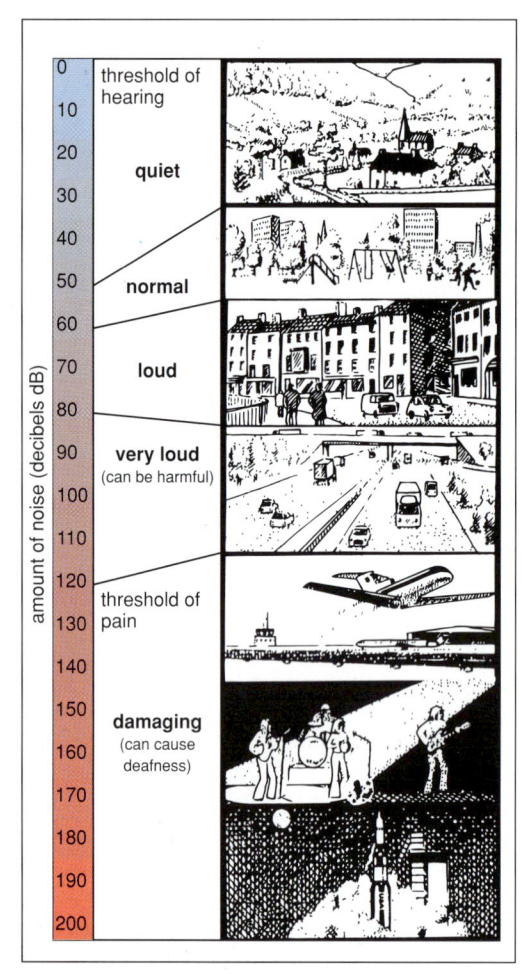

Picture 5 This illustration shows the noise scale as expressed in decibels, the standard unit of noise as measured with a sound meter.

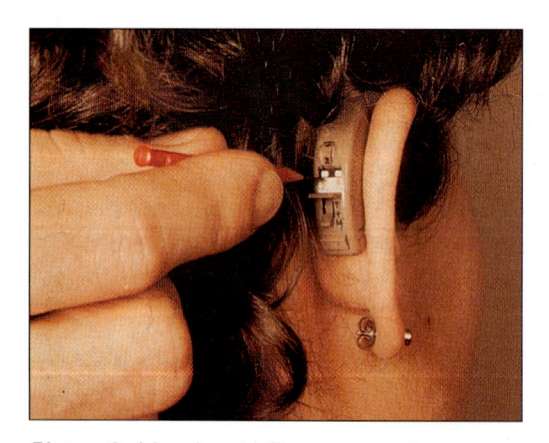

Picture 6 A hearing aid. The case contains a microphone, battery and earphone. The case fits neatly behind the ear. Sound waves are transmitted through a plastic tube to a mould which is placed over the opening of the ear.

The audible range

The frequency (pitch) of a sound is measured in cycles per second or Hertz (Hz). The human ear can detect frequencies from about 20 Hz (very low notes) to about 20 000 Hz (very high notes). This is called the **audible range**. Animals such as dogs and cats can hear higher notes than we can, and bats can hear ultrasonic sounds at a frequency of 100 000 Hz! You can hear high notes best when you are young. Elderly people lose this ability.

Within the audible range an average person can distinguish between about 2000 different notes, though a trained musician can do better than this. We are best at distinguishing between notes in the 1000 to 4000 Hz range.

How about intensity?

The intensity (loudness) of a sound is measured in decibels (dB). The quietest sound that the human ear can detect is called the **threshold of hearing** and is given a value of zero decibels. Picture 5 shows the range of intensities from the threshold to the loudest sounds that the human ear can bear. Notice that a sound of 120 dB is on the **threshold of pain**. Sounds louder than this can actually hurt your ears and give you a headache. Prolonged noise above 150 dB can cause permanent deafness. The reason is explained below.

Because of its harmful effects, it is important for noise in the environment to be controlled. Sound levels above 90 dB are not normally allowed in factories, but many of the noises which we hear in our everyday lives are much louder than this. Can you think of examples? People who work close to noisy machinery wear ear plugs. Perhaps we should all wear ear plugs!

What causes deafness?

There are several types of deafness, depending on which part of the ear is affected.

■ **Outer ear deafness**

Lots of people become slightly deaf from time to time because the outer ear channel gets blocked with hard wax. This is easily removed by the doctor syringing out the ears with warm water. It helps if the wax is first softened by putting a few drops of olive oil into the ear several days beforehand.

An explosion, or a blow on the side of the head, may rupture the ear drum, causing partial or complete deafness. However, the ear drum usually heals quite quickly and then hearing returns.

■ **Middle ear deafness**

More serious deafness is caused by bone tissue growing round the stirrup in the middle ear chamber. This can prevent the stirrup moving, in much the same way as a piston may seize up with rust. If nothing is done about it, this can lead to permanent deafness. However, the person's hearing may be improved by wearing a hearing aid which amplifies the sound waves (picture 6). In severe cases the stirrup may be replaced by an artificial one made of plastic. This type of deafness runs in families, and it can begin when you are quite young.

■ **Inner ear deafness**

Sometimes deafness is caused by the cochlea not working properly. For example, suppose you listen to a very loud sound of a particular pitch for a long time. The cochlea membrane vibrates so much that eventually the receptor cells which detect that particular frequency get damaged. The result is that you become deaf to that particular note. Some pop singers have become deaf to certain notes because of this; so have young people who listen to very loud music through headphones. There is no cure for this kind of deafness.

People often get deaf as they grow old. This is usually caused by the auditory nerve failing to carry impulses to the brain in the usual way.

Activities

A Experiments on hearing

These experiments involve using a signal generator.

1 Your teacher will use a signal generator to compare the audible ranges of people in your class. How do people differ in their ranges, and why? (Hint: read page 168.) Do you think it matters?

2 Plan an experiment to find out if a person's threshold of hearing (i.e. the quietest sound which he or she can hear) depends on the frequency of the sound.

If facilities permit, your teacher will help you to carry out the experiment.

3 It is said that females can hear higher notes than males. With the help of your teacher, test this idea on your class.

B Comparing the noise levels in different places

Using a sound meter, find the maximum amount of noise above the hearing threshold in different places such as a street corner, railway station, airport, children's playground, school dining hall, reference library, motorway, factory, park, disco.

Compare your results with picture 5, and decide whether each place is quiet, normal, loud, very loud or damaging. Do you have any difficulty in deciding? If so, why?

Questions

1 What jobs are done by each of these: the ear drum, the oval window, the receptor cells in the cochlea, the auditory nerve?

2 What is the pinna, and what job does it do? The pinna of an Alsation dog is more efficient than the pinna of a human. What makes it more efficient?

3 People who drill holes in the road or work in very noisy factories should wear ear muffs. Why?

4 Suppose someone became deaf to low notes but not to high notes.
  a This is unlikely to have been caused by a ruptured ear drum. Why?
  b What would be the most likely cause? Explain your answer.

5 To enjoy listening to music with stereophonic sound, we need two ears.
  a How could you show that this is true?
  b What is the explanation?

6 The middle ear chamber contains three ear bones. Why three rather than one? (To answer this question you'll need to find out exactly what the ear bones do. This will mean reading about them in more advanced books.)

Balance

As well as enabling us to hear, the ear helps us to keep our balance. This function is mainly carried out by three **semicircular canals** located close to the cochlea. You can see them in picture 2 on page 156.

The canals are filled with fluid, and they contain receptors which are stimulated when moved. If you move your head the fluid pulls on the receptors. As a result messages are sent to the brain. The brain then causes certain reflexes to take place so that you keep your balance and don't fall over.

The picture on the right shows the positions of the three canals. Notice that they are at right angles to each other. This means that movement of the head in any plane can be detected by the receptors.

1 What sort of reflexes take place when the receptors are pulled, and how do they help you to keep your balance?

2 Why do you think you feel dizzy after going on a roundabout?

3 What part do our eyes play in helping us to keep our balance?

4 We have receptors in the soles of our feet which are sensitive to pressure. How might these pressure receptors help us to keep our balance?

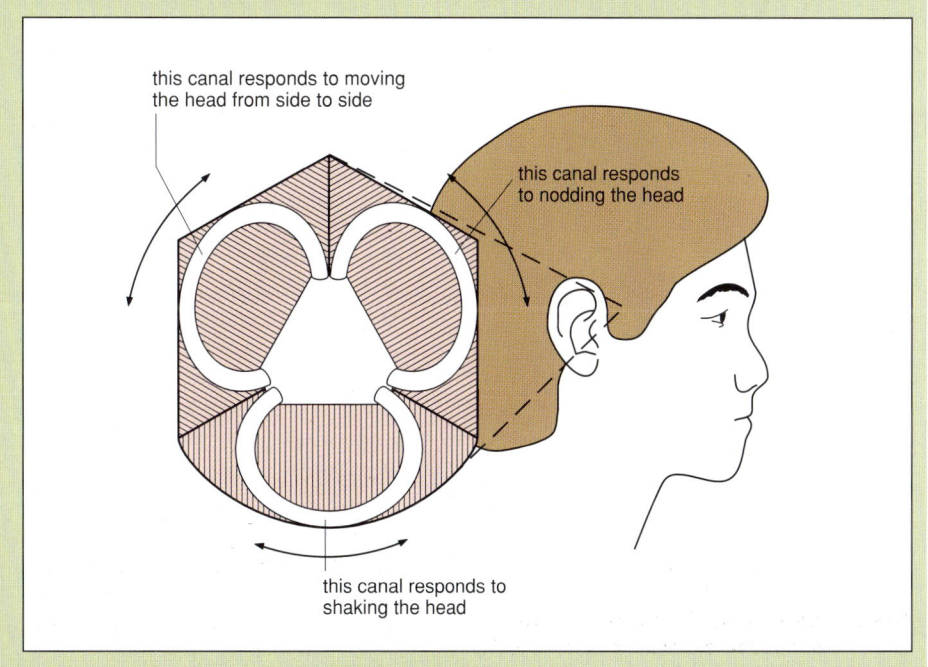

Picture 1 The three semicircular canals are at right angles to each other, so movement of the head in any plane can be detected by the sense organs.

F8 The nervous system

At this moment you are reading this sentence. You can't do this without your nervous system.

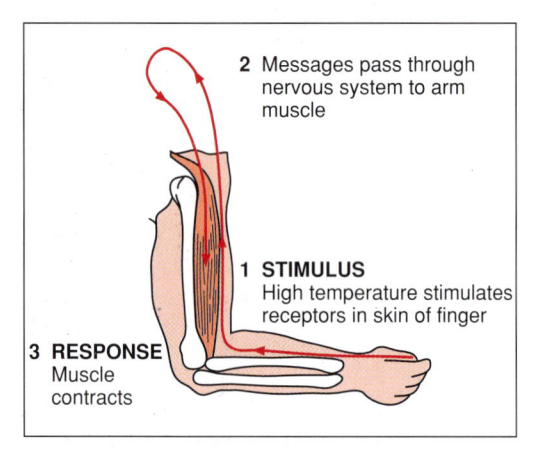

Picture 1 What happens when you pull your hand away from a hot object.

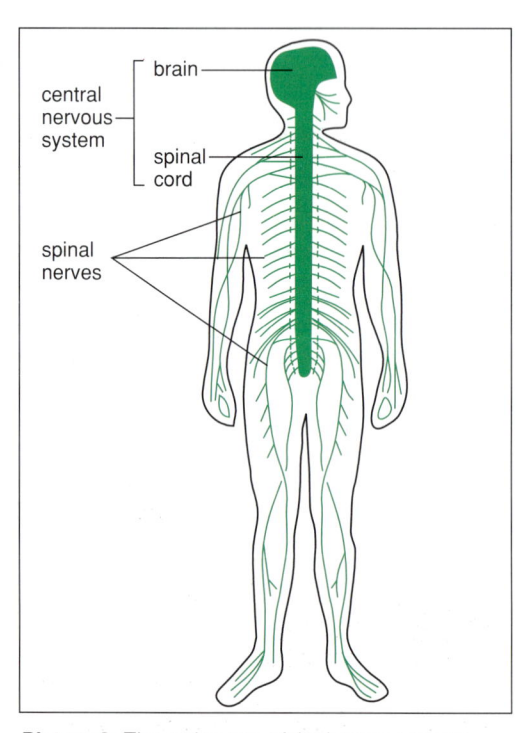

Picture 2 The main parts of the human nervous system.

Reflex action

Reading, writing and thinking thoughts are all very complicated functions of our nervous system. Let's start with something much simpler. If you accidentally touch a hot plate, you pull your hand away. This is an example of a **reflex action**.

A reflex action involves making a **response** of some kind. In the case of the hot plate, the response is pulling your hand away. But you will respond only if something makes you: this is called the **stimulus**. In the case of the hot plate, the stimulus is the high temperature of the plate.

The high temperature stimulates certain **receptors** in the skin. Messages then pass through the nervous system to the muscle in your arm. The muscle then shortens (**contracts**), and pulls your hand away from the plate (picture 1). The whole reflex takes only a fraction of a second, and this shows how quickly the messages travel through the nervous system.

When you pull your hand away from a hot plate, the structure that responds is a muscle. However, this is not the case with all reflexes. Sometimes it is a gland that responds. The general term for something which responds when it receives a message from the nervous system is **effector**.

The receptors which are stimulated when you touch a hot plate are sensitive to temperature and pain. But we have other receptors too. They are sensitive to **smell** (nose), **taste** (tongue), **touch** (skin), **light** (eyes) and **sound** (ears).

How the nervous system is organised

The human nervous system is shown in picture 2. The main parts are the **brain** and **spinal cord.** The brain is inside the skull, and the spinal cord runs down the centre of the vertebral column (backbone). The brain and spinal cord together make up the **central nervous system**.

The central nervous system is connected to the various parts of the body by **nerves**. Some of the nerves come out of the brain, others out of the spinal cord. The nerves that come out of the brain go mainly to structures in the head, such as the eyes and jaws. Those that come out of the spinal cord go to the rest of the body. These are called **spinal nerves**.

The reflex arc

The messages which bring about a reflex action travel through the nervous system by a particular route. The route is called a **reflex arc**.

A reflex arc of the kind found in humans is shown in picture 3. Work your way round the arc, starting with the receptor and finishing with the effector. It is like a chain with three links. The links are **nerve cells** or **neurones**:

- A **sensory neurone** carries messages from the receptor to the spinal cord.
- A **connector neurone** carries messages through the spinal cord.
- An **effector neurone** carries messages from the spinal cord to the effector.

If the effector is a muscle, the effector neurone is called a **motor neurone**. The part of the neurone which carries the messages to the muscle is a long thread-like structure called an **axon**. The main part of the cell from which the axon projects is called the **cell body**. It contains the nucleus and other things that animal cells normally contain.

Only one reflex arc is shown in picture 3. In reality there would be lots of reflex arcs in a part of the spinal cord like this, and the spinal nerve would be full of neurones serving all sorts of receptors and effectors.

How are the messages carried?

The messages are tiny pulses of electricity. We call them **nerve impulses**. The axons are like electric cables, and nerve impulses pass along them very quick-

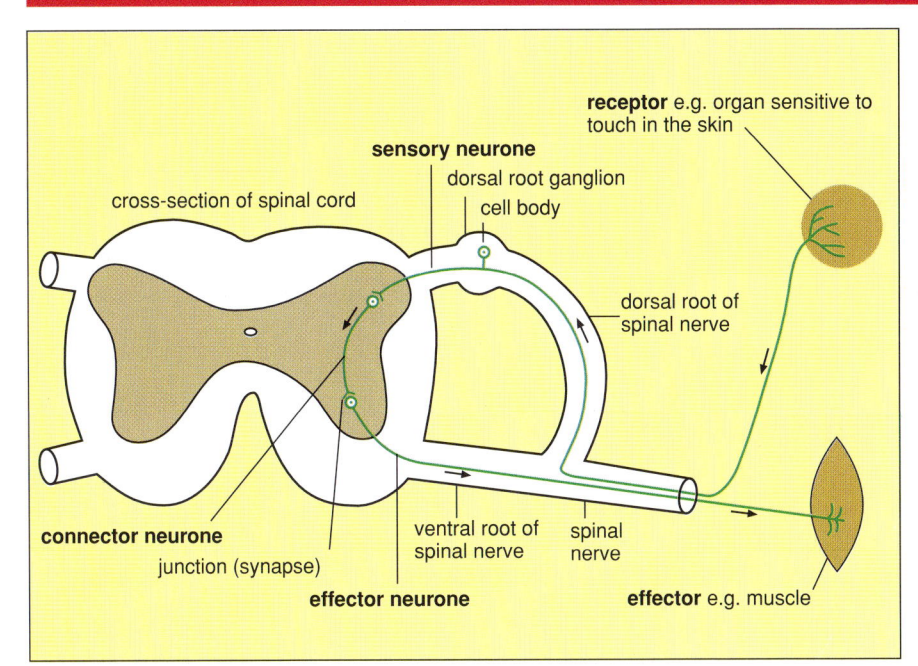

Picture 3 A generalised reflex arc. The dorsal root ganglion contains the cell bodies of many other sensory neurones besides the one shown – that is why it is swollen. The white matter contains axons which run up and down the spinal cord, connecting this reflex arc with other reflex arcs and with the brain.

Picture 4 This doctor is testing a patient's knee jerk.

ly. Nerve impulses are all separate, like cars whizzing along a road, and they travel along the axon one after the other.

In picture 3 you will see that the neurones are connected to each other by junctions in the spinal cord. These junctions are called **synapses**. At the synapse there is a tiny gap. When an impulse reaches the end of a neurone, a small amount of a chemical substance, called a **neurotransmitter**, is released into the gap. This then activates the next neurone, so that it starts carrying an impulse. The chemical can be produced only on one side of the gap, and this ensures that the impulses always travel in the right direction – *from* the receptor *to* the effector.

When nerve cells and synapses go wrong

All three neurones must be working properly if the impulses are to get right through the reflex arc. If one of them dies, the reflex cannot occur. Some people suffer from a condition called **motor neurone disease**. The neurones serving the muscles gradually degenerate and stop carrying impulses. As a result the muscles can't be made to contract, and the person becomes paralysed.

It is also important that our synapses should work properly. Synapses are readily affected by drugs and poisons. Some block them, others make them work too easily. One reason why drugs such as alcohol are harmful is that they interfere with synapses in the brain, slowing down our reactions. This is why it's so dangerous to drive after drinking alcohol.

Doctors can see if the various parts of our nervous system are working properly by testing our reflexes. One such reflex is the **knee jerk**: if your knee is tapped in a certain place, your leg gives a little kick (picture 4). This particular reflex involves only the spinal cord. It does not involve the brain. For this reason it is called a **spinal reflex**.

A closer look at neurones

Look at picture 5. This shows a motor neurone in detail. Notice the axon which carries impulses to the muscle. It leaves the spinal cord and, along with lots of other axons, enters one of the nerves. At the far end it breaks up into branches which go into the muscle.

The axon is enclosed in a **fatty sheath**. This insulates it and speeds up the impulses. If the fatty sheath wasn't there, the axon wouldn't be able to carry

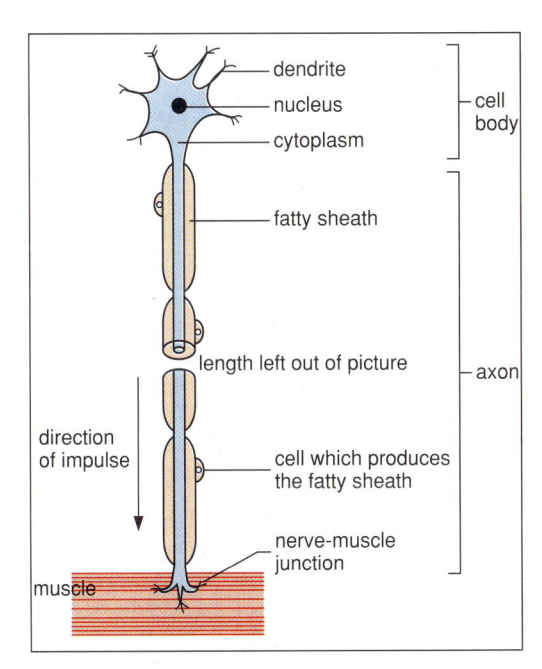

Picture 5 A motor neurone in detail. The axon runs out into a spinal nerve.

162 *The body in action*

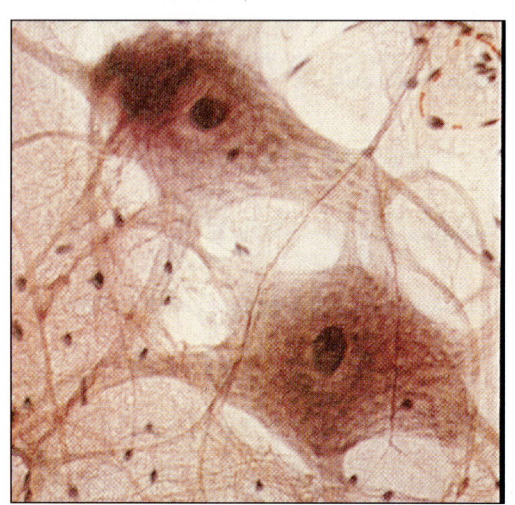

Picture 6 This is a thin section of the spinal cord seen under the microscope, greatly magnified. Two motor neurones can be seen.

First aid for unconsciousness

Unconsciousness can occur when the brain does not work properly. Causes include a reduced oxygen supply to the brain, a severe blow to the head, or an overdose of drugs (including alcohol).

If the person stops breathing, give mouth-to-mouth resuscitation. If the person is still breathing, put him or her in the **recovery position**, like this:

The head must be on its side so that any saliva or vomit flows out of the mouth. This is vital, otherwise the person may inhale these fluids into the lungs, which can be fatal.

The head should also be tilted slightly back. This helps to keep the airway open to the lungs.

Remove false teeth and anything else in the mouth, loosen clothes, cover the person with a blanket or coat and call a doctor.

1 In what circumstances might there be a reduced oxygen supply to the brain?
2 Suggest a reason for the arrangement of the arms and legs in the recovery position.

impulses properly. In the disease **multiple sclerosis** the person gradually loses the use of the muscles. This is because the fatty sheaths break down, so impulses can't get to the muscles.

When the axon reaches the muscle, it splits into branches which make connection with the muscle fibres. The point where the two join is called the **nerve–muscle junction**. There is a gap here, and the message gets across by means of a chemical substance just as it does between neurones.

In pictures 5 and 6 you can see lots of 'arms' sticking out of the cell body. These are called **dendrites**, and they link up with other nerve cells to form a dense network. It is this network which enables the spinal cord and brain to carry out their important job of coordination.

Coordination

Let's go back to the hot plate. If the plate was very hot, you would jump back and let out a cry. This shows that the reflex involves the brain as well as the spinal cord. The nerve impulses travel into the spinal cord, then up to the brain where they produce the sensation of pain. Then impulses travel out to the various muscles involved in the response.

What exactly is the brain doing here? Put simply, it makes sure that the right muscles contract at the right time. This is called **coordination**. All our responses require coordination. This function is carried out by the brain and, to a lesser extent, the spinal cord.

Pulling your hand away from a hot plate is a relatively simple response. Many of our actions are more complicated than this. Think of the coordination that's necessary, for example, in walking or running. Even more coordination is needed for skilled activities like skiing and ballet dancing.

In all these cases the brain *processes* the information it receives and ensures that the right actions take place.

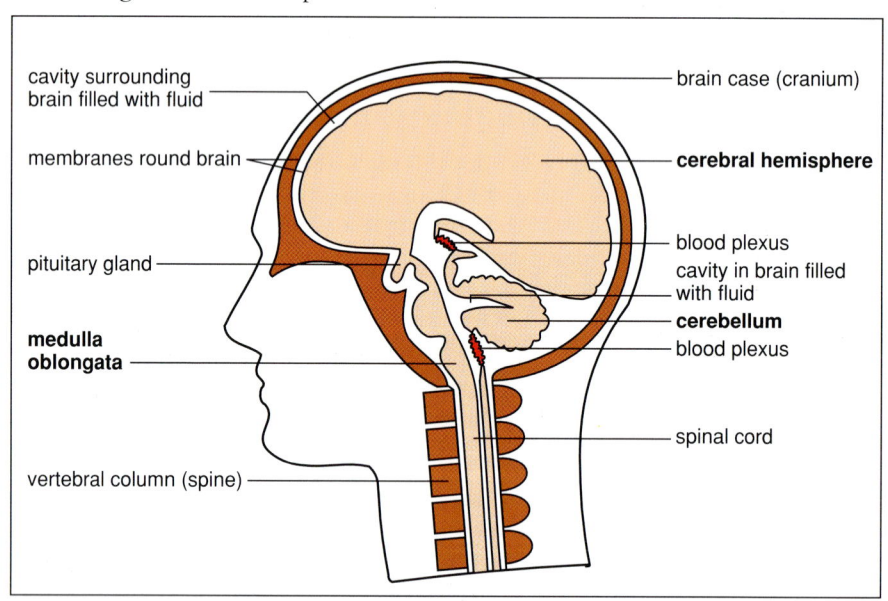

Picture 7 The human brain seen in its natural position inside the head.

The brain

There are over one thousand million neurones in the brain and each one may be connected with as many as 25 000 others. This makes the brain like an extremely complex computer and enables it to coordinate all our actions. But the brain is more than a computer for it gives us feelings and emotions – we are human beings not machines.

You can see a human brain in picture 7. Three of its most important parts are labelled in bold print:

- The **medulla oblongata** controls various automatic processes such as breathing and the circulation.
- The **cerebellum** helps us to keep our balance and enables us to make precise and accurate movements.
- The **cerebral hemispheres** control our sensations and movements, and are also responsible for memory, thought and intelligence.

Our feelings and emotions stem mainly from the front part of the cerebral hemispheres just behind the forehead. This is the part of the brain that gives us our individuality and personality. It is the least understood part of the brain, and perhaps will never be understood.

Drugs and the brain

Drugs which affect the brain fall into four main groups: **stimulants, sedatives, hallucinogens** and **painkillers**.

Stimulants speed up the brain, whilst sedatives slow down its activity. Hallucinogens make you see or hear things which do not really exist, and painkillers suppress the part of the brain which gives us our sense of pain.

Alcohol is a sedative. It sedates the higher centres in the brain, making people feel less inhibited. It slows down reaction time and impairs judgement.

Prolonged use of alcohol kills brain and liver cells. In the liver it can cause a disease called cirrhosis, in which the liver cells are gradually replaced by useless fibrous tissue. It is particularly easy to get addicted to alcohol.

The amount of alcohol that a person drinks can be expressed in 'units'. A unit of alcohol is 10 cm^3 (10 millilitres). This is the amount present in half a pint of standard beer or lager, a glass of wine, a small glass of sherry or a single measure of spirits or vermouth.

When you drink, the alcohol goes into your bloodstream, and the more you drink the greater will be the concentration of alcohol in your blood. This is shown in the bar chart. However, other factors affect the way a person's blood alcohol rises – body mass, for example.

The bar chart also shows the legal limit for driving. If you have more than the equivalent of 5 units of alcohol in your blood, you are breaking the law. This does not mean that it is safe to drive after drinking just under 5 units. the only safe level is zero.

The alcohol we drink gets into the cells and is eventually broken down. It takes about an hour for each unit to be destroyed. An average-sized man who drinks more than 21 units a week is seriously risking his health – for women the figure is 14 units.

Because of the problems connected with alcohol, most countries have licensing laws which limit the sale of alcohol to certain hours of the day.

1. Why do you think the risk figure is lower for women than for men?
2. Some people say you should drink no alcohol at all before driving. Do you agree?
3. Do you think alcohol should be classified as a dangerous drug and banned?

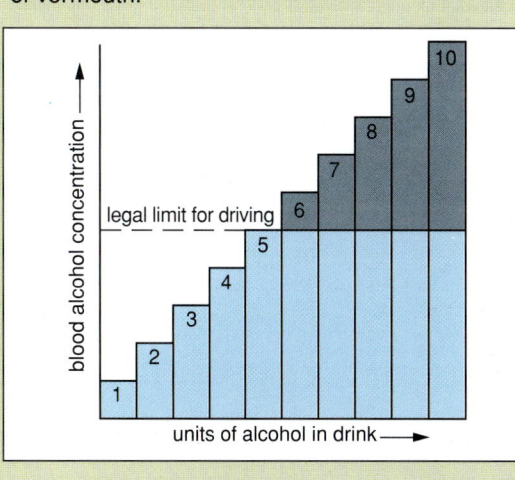

Picture 1 This bar chart shows how the concentration of alcohol in the blood rises as you drink more and more alcohol.

Questions

1. A person walks across a room in bare feet and treads on a drawing pin. He lets out a cry. Explain what happens in his nervous system in bringing about this response.

2. Which of the following responses are reflex actions?
   a. Pupil of the eye getting smaller in bright light.
   b. Eating when hungry.
   c. Running cold water over a burnt hand.
   d. Swallowing when food touches the back of the throat.

3. The picture below shows the route through which messages travel in bringing about the knee jerk. When the tendon is tapped, receptors in the muscle are stretched and this causes the messages to be sent off.

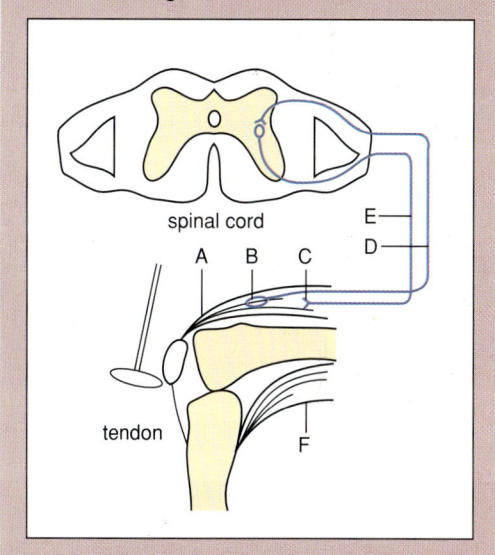

   a. Which structure is stimulated by the hammer?
   b. Which structure carries impulses away from the spinal cord?
   c. Which structure shortens as a result of the reflex?
   d. What would be the approximate length of structure E in a human?
   e. Assuming that the impulses travel at 100 metres per second, how long would it take for an impulse to travel through this reflex arc?
   f. How does the structure of this reflex arc differ from the one in picture 3 (page 161)?

F9 Exercise and fitness

During exercise various changes need to occur in the body.

Picture 1 Exercise is an important aspect of being fit.

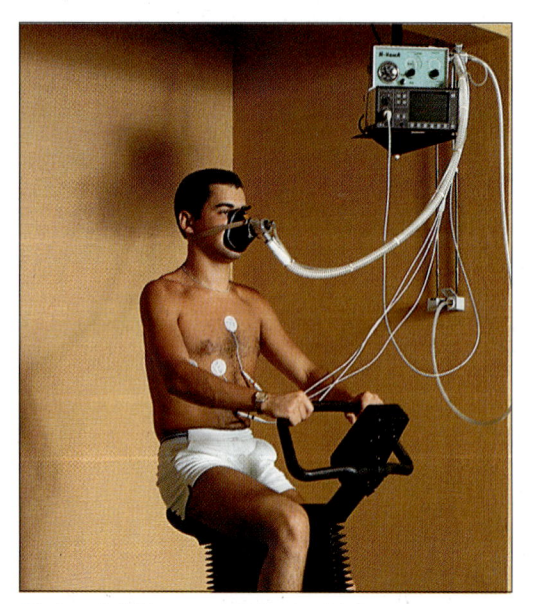

Picture 2 This person is having his oxygen consumption measured while he pedals an exercise cycle.

Why be fit?

Here are six reasons why it is a good idea to be fit:
- It keeps our body mass down.
- It increases our resistance to disease.
- It helps to prevent heart disease and varicose veins.
- It helps us cope with everyday tasks.
- It makes us feel better, physically and mentally.
- It helps us to withstand stress.

The effects of exercise

Being fit does not mean that our bodies can exercise without getting tired but it does mean that we should be able to easily endure such physical activity. Walking up a steep hill, for instance, will result in an increase in both our breathing and pulse rates. This is because our muscles require more energy, which they get by burning more glucose. This is **aerobic respiration** (see page 125). We have to increase our breathing rate to get more oxygen into our bloodstream (picture 2). At the same time our heart rate increases to get the oxygen (and glucose) to the muscle cells.

Whether we are fit or not, really strenuous exercise puts a great strain on the body's circulatory and breathing systems. In running a 100 metre sprint we cannot breathe fast enough, and our circulatory system is not efficient enough, to get oxygen to our muscles to keep them going. So the muscles obtain extra energy by respiring without oxygen. This is called **anaerobic respiration**.

Anaerobic respiration in animal cells

In the absence of oxygen, animal cells break down glucose in a series of small steps into **lactic acid**. Carbon dioxide is not given off and a much smaller amount of energy is released compared to aerobic respiration.

glucose → lactic acid + energy

Unfortunately, lactic acid is a mild poison and its build-up in our muscles makes them ache. Also, the muscles gradually contract less powerfully. This is called **muscle fatigue**.

When the race is over, lactic acid is broken down into carbon dioxide and water. Oxygen is needed for this and the volume of oxygen required to get rid of all the lactic acid is called the **oxygen debt**. In a long distance race, lactic acid builds up to begin with, but soon the body adjusts and the acid is destroyed while you are actually running.

The importance of training

Trained athletes and other fit people find that during exercise their breathing and pulse rates do not rise as much as in non-trained people (picture 3). In addition, an athlete's breathing rate, lactic acid level and pulse rate should all return to normal sooner after the exercise has stopped. This is called the **recovery time** and it is a good way of measuring fitness (picture 4).

Training improves the effiency of the heart, lungs and circulation. The volume of the heart increases and the muscle tissue gets stronger. Lung capacity gets larger and the delivery of oxygen to the muscles is better. Regular exercise also improves the coronary blood supply, so more oxygen is sent to the heart muscle.

Exercise and fitness **165**

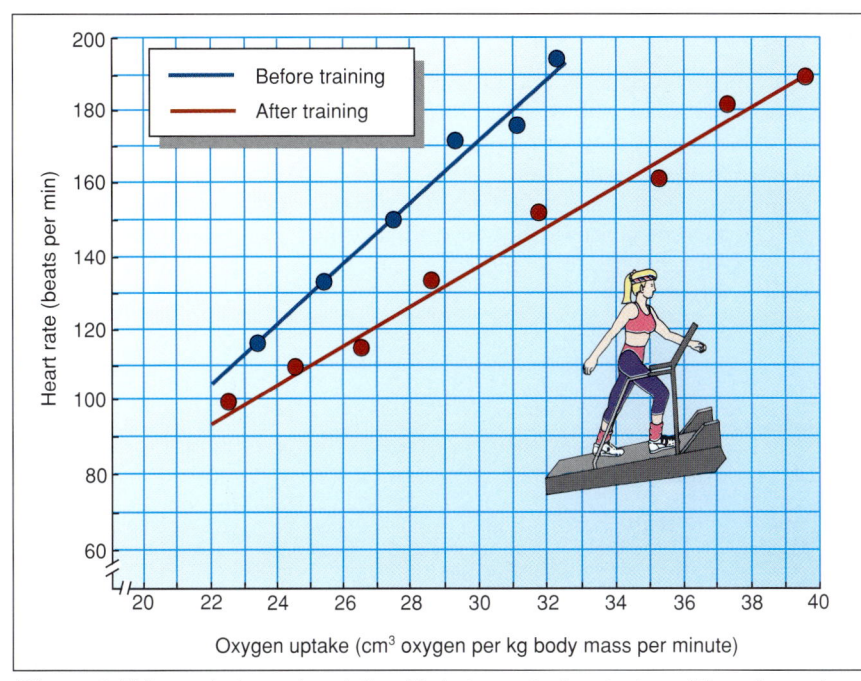

Picture 3 This graph shows the relationship between the heart rate and the volume of oxygen taken up during exercise on a treadmill.

Picture 4 The breathing and heart rates of these fit athletes will take a relatively short time to return to normal after a race.

Questions

1 A pupil was asked to raise his arm above his head. He was then asked to clench and relax his hand for five minutes.
  a What word is used to describe the effect that this activity has on the muscles?
  b Name the substance which builds up in the rapidly contracting muscles.
  c Recovery time is the time taken for certain variables to return to normal after vigorous exercise. Select two such variables from the list:
    breathing rate,
    body temperature,
    sweating,
    urine production,
    pulse rate.
  d If the exercise was carried out by a trained and a non-trained athlete, how would the variables in the list alter, during the exercise and recovery, in each athlete?

2 Mr Jones sits at a computer all day and watches television all evening. The only exercise he gets is walking to and from his car.
  What dangers are there in his lifestyle?

3 The graph below shows changes in the number of capillaries supplying blood to the heart muscle of an individual who started on a programme of daily training by running.

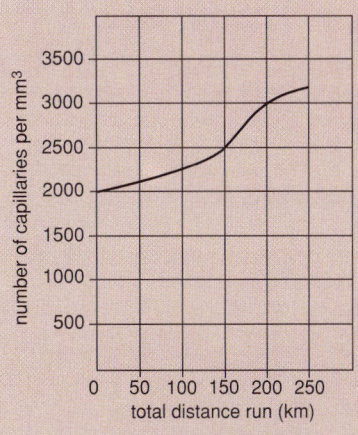

  a Calculate the percentage increase in the number of capillaries per mm^3 in the heart muscle after running a total distance of 200 km.
  b How many kilometres did this individual run in order to increase the number of capillaries per mm^3 in the heart muscle by 25%?
  c During the running what changes occurred to the following variables?
    i lactic acid in muscles
    ii pulse rate
    iii carbohydrate store
    iv breathing rate

4 The graph shows the heart rates of two students before, during and after a three-minute bout of exercise.

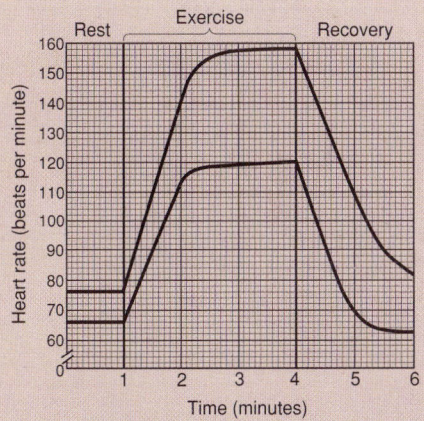

  a Comment on the possible life styles of the two students.
  b What can you say about the working of the students' hearts?
  c Suppose you wanted to carry out the same investigation on a student in your class. Describe in detail how you would do it.

5 One hundred years ago the world record for one mile was 4.5 minutes. In 1954 Dr Roger Bannister ran the mile in just under 4 minutes. The current record is 3 minutes 44.39 seconds.
  a Suggest why athletes continue to improve on world records.
  b Do you think a time will come when further improvements cannot be made? What do you think will set the limit?

F10 Staying fit for life

In this topic we find out how to stay healthy and examine ways in which our bodies are helped back into action.

Keeping healthy and avoiding illness

Much more is involved in keeping healthy than just taking exercise. Table 1 shows ways of avoiding some major illnesses. Of course, following the advice does not mean that you will never get any of these illnesses. It simply means that you are less likely to get them.

Some interesting anomalies have been discovered. For example, fish oil and olive oil help prevent heart attacks. So does alcohol – in moderation!

What sort of investigations would have to be carried out to obtain the information in the table?

	No smoking	Little or no alcohol	Low fat diet	High fibre diet	High vegetable and fruit diet	Low salt diet	Exercise and weight control
Heart attack	★★★		★★★		★★	★	★★★
Stroke	★				★★	★★★	★★
Diabetes (adult)			★★★	★	★★		★★
Cancer: lung	★★★		★		★		
liver		★★★			★★		
colon			★★★	★★★	★★★		★
breast			★★★	★	★★		★

Table 1 How to avoid some major illnesses. ★★★ very effective, ★★ fairly effective, ★ slightly effective.
The table is based on information from the American Medical Foundation.

Activities

A Measuring your fitness

WARNING! Do not attempt this activity if you have a health problem or are recovering from an illness.

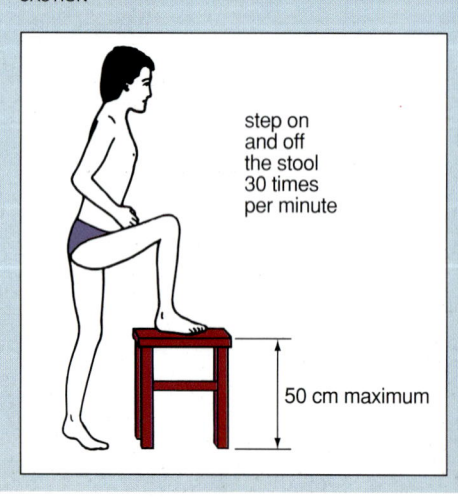

⚠ CAUTION

step on and off the stool 30 times per minute

50 cm maximum

We shall use a simple test which is used in the army. It involves stepping up onto a stool or chair, 43 cm high, 30 times per minute. Each step (up and then down) should take 2 seconds.

Work in pairs: one of you (the subject) should take the exercise, and the other one (the tester) should administer the test. The tester should count the seconds to keep the subject stepping at the right rate. Try it for a short time to get used to the rhythm. Also practise taking the subject's pulse (see page 143).

Now proceed as follows:

1 Step up and down for 5 minutes.
2 Sit down and rest for 1 minute.
3 Take the pulse for 30 seconds = **A**.
4 Rest for 30 seconds.
5 Take the pulse for 30 seconds = **B**.
6 Rest for 30 seconds.
7 Take the pulse for 30 seconds = **C**.
   Add together **A** + **B** + **C**.

Assess your fitness from the scale.

These figures, suggested by former Olympic athlete and coach, Bruce Tulloh, are suitable for teenagers.

	Male	Female
Very fit	175 or less	190 or less
Fairly fit	200 approx	220 approx
Rather unfit	215 approx	235 approx
Very unfit	230 or more	250 or more

Which attributes of your body are being measured by this test? Do you think it is a valid test of fitness? What criticisms have you of it? Could it be used to find the best athlete in your school?

B Devising your own fitness test

Devise a fitness test, with a scoring system, which assesses as many physical attributes of the human body as possible, e.g. muscular strength, efficiency of the heart, flexibility and so on.

The test can be divided into a number of parts, each assessing a particular attribute, but a person on whom the test is carried out should finish up with a single score that reflects his or her overall fitness.

Discuss your test with your teacher, then try it out on students in your class.

New parts for old

If you cut yourself, the skin eventually knits together and the wound heals. Most tissues are quite good at mending themselves like this. But if an organ gets badly damaged, or stops working properly, a new one won't grow in its place.

Fortunately some of our organs occur in pairs, the lungs and kidneys for example, and we can manage with only one. People who have had a lung removed because of cancer can live for years. In fact it's amazing what we can do without. A person can survive with less than half the intestine and only fifteen per cent of the stomach.

You may have heard of people who have been given a new organ in a **transplant operation** – a kidney perhaps, or a heart.

Transplant operations are carried out on patients who have an organ that is working so badly that their life is in danger. The bad organ is removed and replaced with a healthy one taken from another person, the **donor**.

The donor is usually a healthy person who has died suddenly, often as a result of a car or motorcycle accident. The organ is removed from the donor's body and quickly taken to the hospital where the operation is to be performed. The organ is kept alive in a sealed bag containing a special fluid.

The trouble with transplant operations is that the transplanted organ may be destroyed after it has been put into the patient's body. Why this happens, and how it is overcome, is explained on page 109.

In the last thirty years or so, great progress has been made in replacing parts of the body, not only with transplants but also with artificial structures. The picture shows some of the 'spare parts' now available.

'Spare part surgery' is important because the human body is so bad at regenerating its own lost parts. However, certain other organisms are very good at regeneration. For example, an earthworm accidentally cut in two by a gardener's spade will grow a new back end; and small pieces of certain plants can grow into complete new plants. We make use of this in propagating plants (see page 62).

1 What features would you expect the 'special fluid' mentioned in this section to have?
2 Mr X is in hospital waiting to have a heart transplant. Make a list of all the difficulties facing the team of doctors who are hoping to carry out the operation.
3 Many people carry a card saying that if they die they are willing for their organs to be used in transplant operations. Suppose a card-carrying person has a fatal car accident. Should the relatives have any say in whether or not the person's organs are used?
4 Some people object to transplants on ethical grounds. Discuss possible ethical problems connected with transplant operations.
5 The picture showing spare parts is not complete. Other parts are available, and other materials can be used. Ask a doctor (who isn't too busy!) to bring the picture up to date for you.

Key
Transplants
1 Cornea
2 Heart
3 Lung
4 Heart valve
5 Liver
6 Kidney
7 Bone
8 Bone marrow
9 Hair
10 Brain tissue
11 Small intestine
12 Pancreas

Artificial structures
13 Skull plate (metal)
14 Ear flap (plastic or silicone rubber)
15 Ear ossicles (stainless steel)
16 Eye lens (plastic)
17 Nose cartilage (plastic)
18 Jaw bone (metal)
19 Teeth (ceramic with titanium jaw attachment)
20 Hearing aid
21 Blood pressure regulator (electronic)
22 Windpipe (plastic)
23 Shoulder joint (metal or plastic)
24 Elbow joint (metal or plastic)
25 Wrist joint (metal)
26 Knuckle (plastic or silicone rubber)
27 Breast (silicone rubber)
28 Heart valve (metal or plastic)
29 Heart pacemaker (electronic)
30 Arm (metal or plastic, powered)
31 Artery (Fluoro-ethene polymer or cultured tissue)
32 Bladder stimulator (electronic)
33 Hip joint (femur head: metal; cup: high density polythene)
34 Bone plate (plastic, dissolves as bone heals)
35 Blood vessel (plastic, dissolves as vessel knits)
36 Knee joint (metal or plastic)
37 Tendon (plastic)
38 Leg (metal or plastic, powered)
39 Calf stimulator (activated by foot)
40 Voice tone generator
41 Penis (silicone rubber erector)

Picture 1 'Spare parts' available to humans.

G1 Variation

The people in the picture are all different. This topic is about variation.

Picture 1 People differ from each other in all sorts of ways.

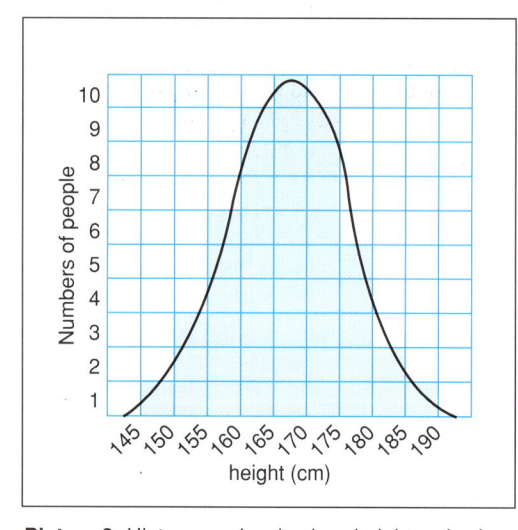

Picture 2 Histogram showing how height varies in an adult human population. Each bar represents the number of people who fall within a particular height group, e.g. 145–150 cm, etc.

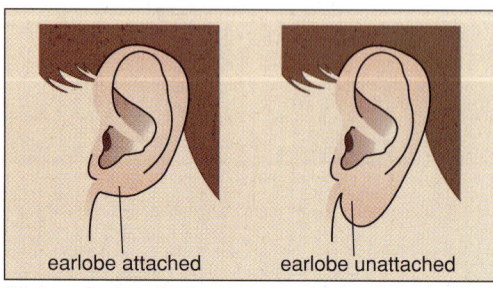

Picture 3 Attached and unattached earlobes.

What are species?

Look around you at the members of your class. There are some really obvious differences between them. For example, differences exist in hair colour, eye colour or sex. (You will read more about these differences shortly.) Yet despite these differences, we all belong to the same species. We all share certain characteristics in our body plan (two legs, two arms, etc.) and in our biochemistry. We can communicate with each other in spoken language, but, most of all, we only interbreed amongst ourselves. In addition, the offspring that are produced are fertile, and they too can interbreed to produce more fertile offspring. Our species is *Homo sapiens*, and we are just one of millions of species on this planet.

A species is a group of similar looking interbreeding organisms whose offspring are fertile.

However, we are all different. Apart from identical twins, no two people can be exactly alike. This is called **variation**, and it occurs in *all* species. Variation in humans is easy to spot but it is less easy to see in other organisms. We can see differences in a group of cats or dogs, but only experienced eyes can tell the difference between, for example, one sheep in a flock and another. Experienced naturalists have been able to name individual whales in a school by the shapes of the fins, whilst others can recognise individual zebras by the pattern of their stripes. It just takes practice.

There is also variation in plant species. The leaves of one plant are not exactly the same as the leaves of another plant of the same species. The number and colour of the petals may also vary.

Continuous and discontinuous variation

There are two types of variation in a species.

1 **Continuous variation**. In this case there are two extremes of a characteristic and a whole range of forms in between; for example the tallest and the shortest adult in the country, with the heights of all other adults fitting into the range between.

   Other examples of continuous variation in humans are the resting pulse rate, the length of the index finger, and the mass of the femur bone. Examples in other species are the number of petals on a buttercup flower, the width of snail shells and tail length in adult mice.

   Continuous variation can be measured and is shown as a histogram or line graph (picture 2).

2 **Discontinuous variation**. In this case there is a limited number of forms for a particular characteristic. Sometimes there are only two forms, for example in humans, attached or unattached earlobes (picture 3). There are no in-betweens. The ABO blood group system is another example (see page 149).

   There are many more examples in other species. These include flower colour in foxgloves, green or variegated leaves of geranium (see page 66) and black or brown coat colours in mice.

   Discontinuous variation can be displayed by means of a bar chart or a pie chart. An example is given in question 2 on the opposite page.

Differences caused by the environment

Many people grow hydrangeas in their gardens. This plant has large clumps of flowers which may be white, pink or blue. What decides the colour of the flowers? In this case it's not the genes. Instead it's the type of soil the plant is growing in. If the soil is acidic, blue flowers develop; if the soil is alkaline, white or pink flowers develop (picture 4).

This is an example of variation being caused by the environment. Many differences between people, particularly in their behaviour and attitudes, can be explained by the fact that they have been brought up in different environments. Environment here includes our diet, surroundings, home, school and the people with whom we live and work.

We still don't know how important the environment is, compared with our genes, in making us different from each other. This particularly applies to features like intelligence and artistic ability.

In trying to find an answer to this question, studies on identical twins can be useful. Identical twins have the same genes, so any differences between them must be due to the environment. Such studies suggest that our environment helps us to develop motivation and plays an important part in overall achievement.

Picture 4 The colour of hydrangea flowers depends on the environment.

Activity

Looking at an example of variation

1 Measure the height of each person in your class.
2 Divide the heights into 5 cm groups, starting with 120 cm and finishing up with 180 cm (i.e. 120–25, 125–130, 130–135, etc.) and write down the groups in a list.
3 Work out how many people in your class fall into each group. Write the numbers alongside the groups in your list.
4 Construct a histogram (like the one in picture 2) showing how height varies in your class.
   Which group contains (a) the largest number of people, and (b) the fewest people?
   What is the **height range** (that is, the difference in height between the shortest and tallest pupils)?
   What is the average height in your class?
   Does it correspond to the tallest bar?
5 Join the tops of the bars in your histogram with a smooth curve.
   What does the shape of the curve tell us about the way height varies?
   Suggest reasons why the members of your class should vary in height.
   What other variable features in humans, or in animals or plants, could you measure and present in this way?

Questions

1 What kind of offspring are produced in a cross between a male horse and a female donkey? Are the offspring fertile? Find out the names of other 'hybrids' whose parents are of different species.

2 Look at the bar chart. It shows the distribution of the four blood groups in three different human populations. 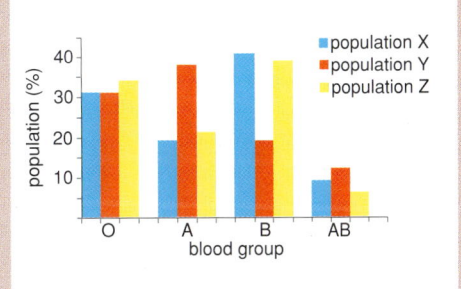
   a What is the percentage in population X of blood group A, B and AB?
   b 400 people are selected from population Y. How many of them can be expected to belong to blood group AB?
   c There are 600 people in population Z. How many have blood groups O and B?

3 You have been asked to plan investigations on identical twins to find out the extent to which intelligence is inherited from parents or acquired from the environment. Let us see your plan.

4 Make a list of your own features which you think you have inherited, and those which you think you have got from your environment. Which aspects of your environment have affected you most, and in what ways?

5 The length of the right index finger of a number of pupils was measured. The results are shown in the histogram. 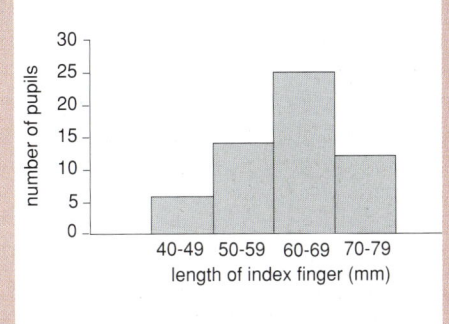
   a How many pupils have finger lengths of 50–59 mm?
   b What is the full range of index finger lengths?
   c How many pupils had an index finger shorter than 70 mm?

G2 Introducing inheritance

Why are we like our parents, and why do we differ from them? This is the science of heredity.

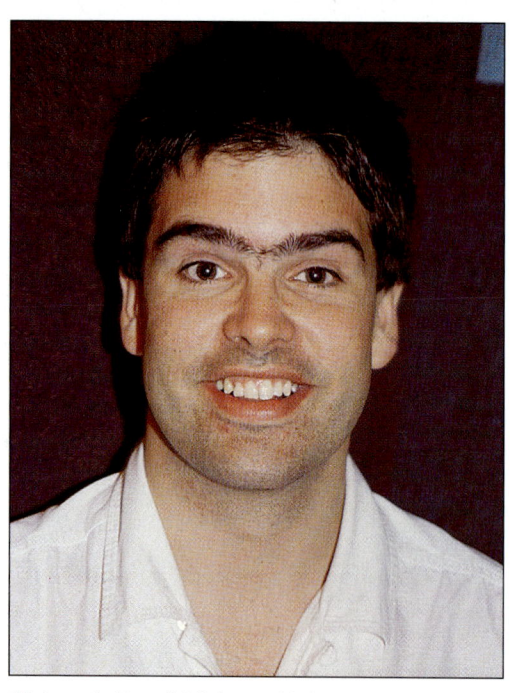

Picture 1 How did John get his brown eyes?

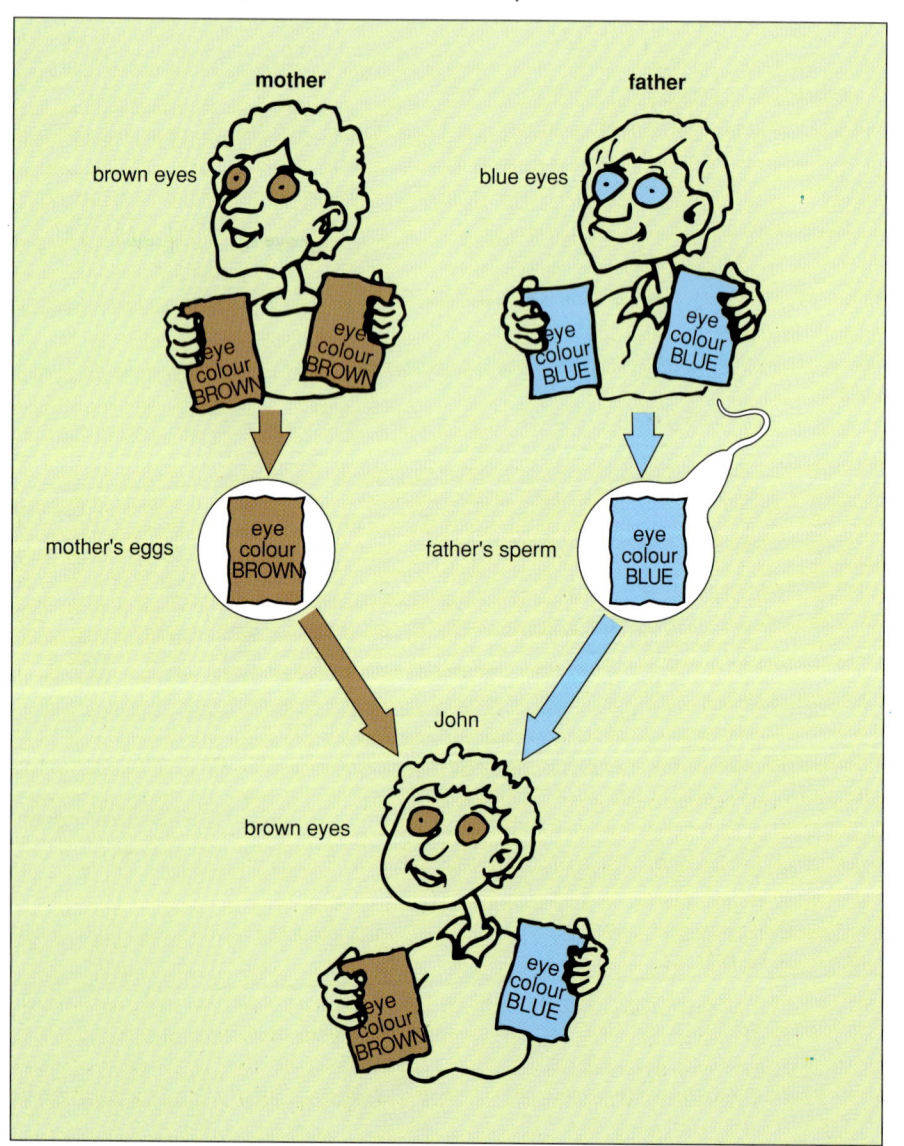

Picture 2 How John got his brown eyes.

How John got his brown eyes

John has brown eyes. His mother has brown eyes too, but his father has blue eyes. How can we explain how John got brown eyes?

Let's suppose that people are born with **instruction cards** telling them what sort of eyes to have. John's mother has two eye-colour instruction cards which make her have brown eyes. John's father has two eye-colour instruction cards which make him have blue eyes. For convenience, we will call mother's cards 'brown cards', and father's cards 'blue cards'. John's parents and their cards are shown at the top of picture 2.

First of all, notice the eggs and sperm. Mother's eggs each contain one brown card, and father's sperm each contain one blue card. This is one of the most important things about heredity: *a person has two cards for controlling a particular feature, whereas the sperm and eggs have only one*.

John was conceived when one of his father's sperm fertilised one of his mother's eggs. When this happened, one of father's blue cards was combined with one of mother's brown cards. So John has two cards, a brown one from his mother and a blue one from his father.

John has a blue card as well as a brown card. Why, then, does he have brown eyes? The reason is that the brown card *overrules* the blue card. Putting it another way, the brown card is **dominant** to the blue card. So although John carries the blue card, it has no effect on his eyes.

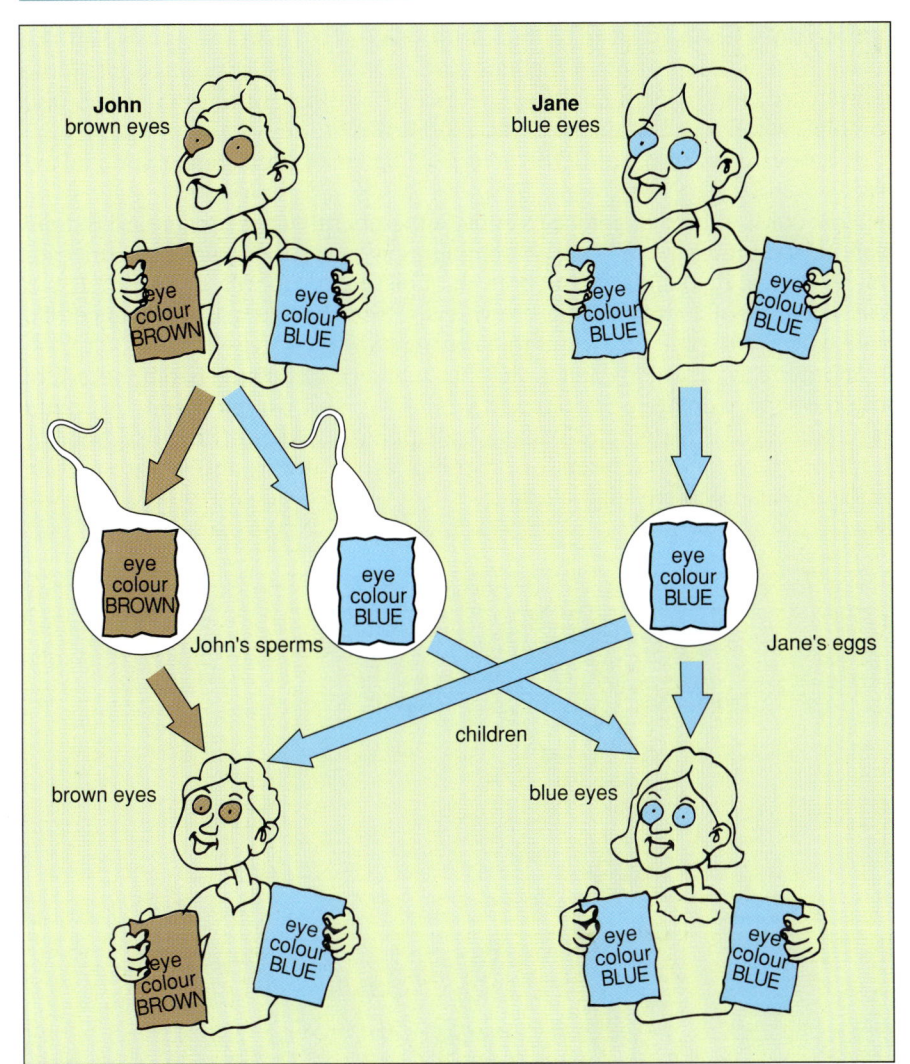

Introducing inheritance 171

Picture 3 How John and Jane pass their eye colours on to their children.

Activity

Heredity in action

To study heredity you need animals or plants that reproduce quickly and have clear-cut features which you can observe easily. Suitable animals are the fruit fly *Drosophila* and the flour beetle *Tribolium*. Suitable plants are tobacco, tomato, pea and maize.

Whatever organism you use, you must first decide which feature or features you wish to study the inheritance of. In the fruit fly it might be the colour of the eyes (some have white eyes, others red). In maize it might be the height of the plants (some are tall, others dwarf).

The next step is to choose the parent organisms, and get them to reproduce. Male and female fruit flies will reproduce if you put them together in a container with the right food. Once the offspring have developed, you can anaesthetise them and count the different types.

With plants the parents have to be cross-pollinated by hand (see page 183). You then collect the seeds and sow them. Later, when the seedlings have grown sufficiently, you count the different types.

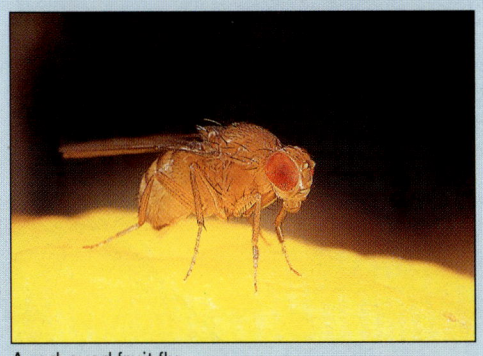

A red-eyed fruit fly.

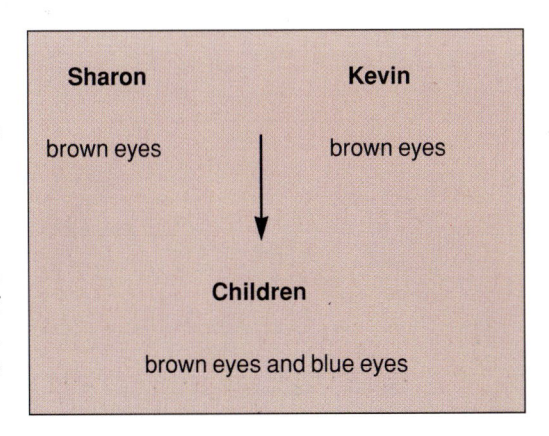

John marries Jane

John marries Jane who has blue eyes. They have two children: one has brown eyes and the other has blue eyes. How can we explain this?

The explanation is given in picture 3. John has a brown card and a blue card, as we've already seen. Now half John's sperm contain one brown card, and the other half contain one blue card. This is because the two types of card are equally distributed amongst the sperm rather like dealing cards. All Jane's eggs contain a blue card.

When fertilisation takes place, Jane's egg may receive one of John's brown cards or one of his blue cards. Fertilisation is random – it's pure chance as to which kind of sperm fertilises the egg. So there's an equal chance of a brown card or a blue card combining with the egg's blue card. This means that there's a 50:50 chance (one in two) of any of the children being brown-eyed or blue-eyed. It happens that one of the children has brown eyes, and the other blue eyes. But both *could* have had brown eyes, or both blue eyes – it's just like tossing coins.

John has a sister

John has a sister called Sharon. Sharon has brown eyes, like John's. Sharon marries Kevin who also has brown eyes. They have lots of children: most of them have brown eyes, but to their surprise one has blue eyes, as shown on the right. How can we explain this? Think about it before you turn over the page.

Sharon **Kevin**
brown eyes brown eyes
↓
Children
brown eyes and blue eyes

The explanation is given in picture 4. Half of Sharon's eggs contain the brown card, and half contain the blue card. Half of Kevin's sperms contain the brown card, and half contain the blue card. The different ways the cards may combine when fertilisation takes place is shown at the bottom of the picture. Fertilisation is random, so there's an equal chance of each combination taking place.

What colours are the children's eyes? Remember that the brown card is dominant to the blue card: as long as a child has at least one brown card, the eyes will be brown. If you look at the bottom of picture 4 you will see that there is a 3 in 4 chance of a child having brown eyes. And there is a 1 in 4 chance of a child having two blue cards, and thus having blue eyes.

Another way of looking at it is like this. If Sharon and Kevin had hundreds of children, approximately 3/4 of them would have brown eyes, and 1/4 would have blue eyes. This is hardly likely to happen in practice, because humans don't produce large numbers of offspring. But it does happen with certain other organisms, as we shall see later.

Picture 4 How Sharon and Kevin pass their eye colours to their children.

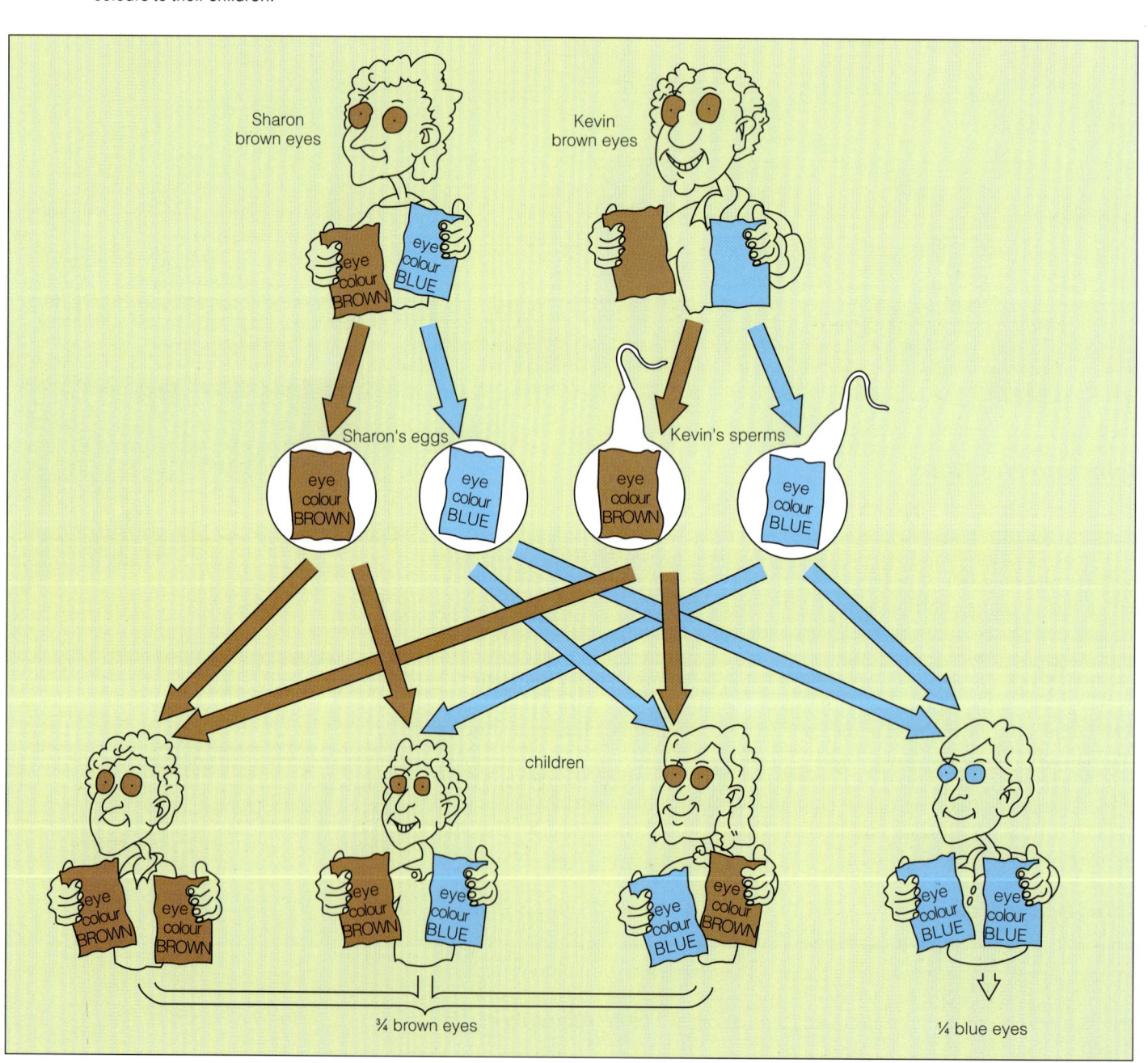

What are the instruction cards?

What we have been calling instruction cards are really our **genes**. Genes are found in all our cells and they control the way we develop, causing us to have certain features. Later we shall see what genes are made of. For the moment let's use the idea of instruction cards to illustrate some important things about genes.

There are different versions of the instruction card for eye colour. One version says 'have brown eyes', another version says 'have blue eyes'. In the same way the gene that controls eye colour may exist in different forms, each one telling the person to develop a particular eye colour. These different forms of a gene are called **alleles**.

The cards are in packs

We don't just have instruction cards for eye colour. We have cards for hundreds of other features as well. These cards are arranged in 'packs'.

In the same way, our genes are grouped together into **chromosomes**. Chromosomes occur in the nuclei of all living cells. They are like pieces of thread. The genes are strung out along the chromosomes, like strings of beads. Each gene controls a particular feature such as eye colour, hair colour, the length of the nose and so on (picture 5).

The card that says 'have brown eyes' is in a separate pack from the card that says 'have blue eyes'. But these two cards are in exactly the same position within each pack. In the same way, the alleles that call for brown or blue eyes are in the same positions within two separate chromosomes. These two chromosomes look exactly alike: they belong to a pair. And just as the chromosomes are in pairs, so too are the alleles which they carry.

Putting all the pairs of chromosomes together gives each body cell two matching sets. Sex cells or **gametes** contain only one set of chromosomes. The reduction of the number of sets from two to one occurs during **gamete-formation**. This takes place in the ovaries or testes of animals and in the ovaries and anthers of plants.

Normal development of an animal or plant can only take place if two sets of chromosomes are present. The two sets are put together again during **fertilisation** (see page 93 for fertilisation in animals and page 57 for plants).

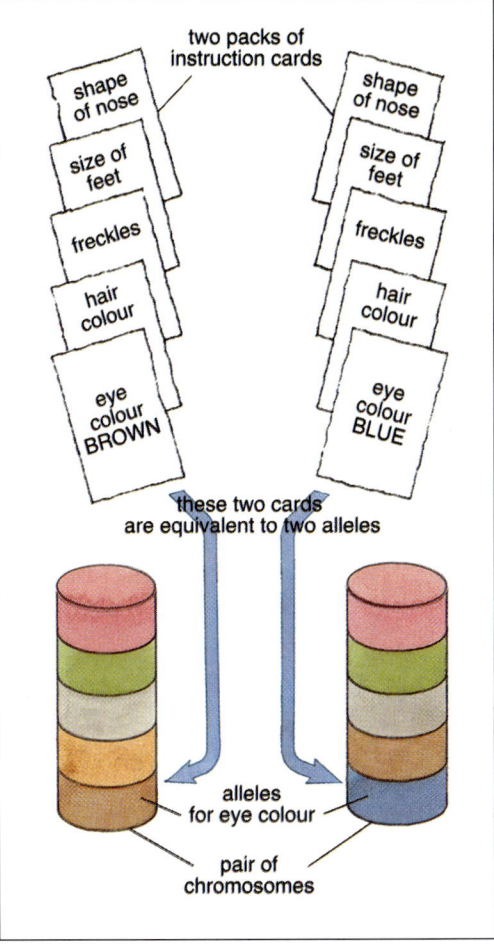

Picture 5 Genes in a chromosome can be likened to instruction cards in a pack.

Questions

1. The blue-eyed child in picture 3 thinks she got her blue eyes from her mother. Is this true? Explain your answer.
2. John, in picture 3, has a sister with brown eyes. Could she have had blue eyes? Explain your answer.
3. Suppose Kevin in picture 4 had two brown cards instead of a brown card and a blue card. What difference would this make to the colour of the children's eyes? Explain your answer.
4. Human features sometimes 'skip a generation'. What does this mean, and why does it happen? Use the pictures in this topic to illustrate your answer.
5. In picture 3 both children might have had brown eyes, or both might have had blue eyes. Explain this. (Hint: when you toss a coin, what decides whether you get heads or tails?)
6. A black mouse mates with a brown mouse, and all the offspring are black.
    a Why are no brown offspring produced? Use instruction cards to illustrate your answer.
    b If two of the black offspring mate with each other, what kind of offspring would you expect and in what proportions? Draw a diagram to show what happens.

Life is full of surprises

Do not make the mistake of thinking that blue-eyed parents can only produce blue-eyed children. The inheritance of eye-colour is complicated and not fully understood. A group of genes seems likely to be controlling eye-colour and they can produce an effect which may not be expected. And of course there are many other eye-colours besides blue and brown.

G3
More about heredity

In this topic we explain heredity properly in terms of genes and their alleles.

Picture 1 Diagram showing how John inherited his brown eyes. The alleles are indicated by letters: **B** is the allele for brown eyes, **b** is the allele for blue eyes. In diagrams of this sort it is usual to represent the alleles by the same letter, a capital letter for the dominant allele and a small letter for the recessive allele.

How are genes passed from parents to offspring?

Let's go back to John with his brown eyes (see page 170). You will remember that his mother has brown eyes, but his father has blue eyes. On page 170 we explained this, using the idea of instruction cards. Now we shall explain it in terms of genes.

John and his parents have in all their body cells a gene which controls eye colour. This gene has two alleles which we will call **B** and **b**. **B** is the allele for brown eyes, and **b** is the allele for blue eyes. The **B** allele is **dominant** to the **b** allele – that is why it is written with a capital letter. The **b** allele is described as **recessive**. So brown eyes are dominant to blue eyes.

John's mother contains in her cells two **B** alleles which give her brown eyes: we can call her **BB**. John's father contains in his cells two **b** alleles which give him blue eyes: we can call him **bb**. The way these alleles are passed to John is shown in picture 1.

The gametes (eggs and sperm) contain only one allele. This is because of the way the gametes are formed. Each of mother's eggs contains a **B** allele, and each of father's sperm contains a **b** allele.

When a sperm fertilises the egg, the **B** and **b** alleles are brought together. John develops by the fertilised egg dividing repeatedly in such a way that each of his body cells contains a **B** allele and a **b** allele. Because **B** is dominant to **b**, he has brown eyes. However, he is a carrier of the allele for blue eyes and can pass it on to his children.

Picture 1 on this page is really the same as picture 2 on page 170, but it explains how John got his brown eyes in terms of alleles rather than instruction cards. Try re-drawing pictures 3 and 4 on pages 171 and 172 in the same way.

In this way, genes which control particular characteristics are passed from parents to offspring in all living organisms. Examples of these characteristics include flower colour and stem length in pea plants, eye colour in fruit flies, leaf shape in tobacco plants, coat colour in mice and the taste of cucumbers.

Characteristic	Possible phenotypes
Eye colour in humans	Blue, brown
Earlobes in humans	Attached, free
Flower colour in peas	Red, white
Eye shape in fruit flies	Round, bar, kidney
Coat colour in mice	Black, brown, agouti, yellow, white
Coat colour in horses	Black, chestnut

Table 1 Some characteristics and their phenotypes.

Some technical terms

There are two ways of describing John and his parents. We can describe their outward appearance, e.g. brown eyes or blue eyes. Alternatively, we can describe their alleles, e.g. **BB**, **Bb** or **bb**.

The outward appearance of a person is called the **phenotype**. The person's alleles make up the **genotype**. So John's phenotype is 'brown eyes' and his gentoype is **Bb**.

Characteristics usually have at least two phenotypes. For example, eye colour can have the phenotypes of brown or blue. Table 1 shows the possible phenotypes for a range of characteristics in humans and certain other organisms.

When the genotype for a particular feature consists of two identical alleles, e.g. **BB** or **bb**, we say that the person is **homozygous**. If the two alleles are both dominant, e.g. **BB**, the person is **homozygous dominant**. If the two alleles are both recessive, e.g. **bb**, the person is **homozygous recessive**. John's mother is homozygous dominant for eye colour, whereas his father is homozygous recessive.

Organisms that are homozygous are also described as **true breeding**. This is because crossing two identical homozygous parents will result in homozygous offspring. A **pure line** is produced where all the individuals have the same genotype. This is useful because organisms can be produced which have a guaranteed phenotype. For example, a market gardener may want nothing but white-flowered plants. Using true-breeding white-flowered plants ensures that nothing but white-flowered offspring are produced.

When the genotype for a particular feature consists of two different alleles, e.g. **Bb**, we say that the person is **heterozygous**. So John is heterozygous for eye colour.

These technical terms are applied not just to humans but to other organisms as well. They may seem long-winded and difficult, but they are a useful shorthand. They help us to describe examples of heredity without using too many words.

We shall now apply the principles of heredity which we've learned about in the human, to a completely different kind of organism – plants. This is important for market gardeners and others who grow plants to sell.

Picture 2 Red and white flowered busy Lizzie plants. As in many other kinds of plants, the colour of the flowers is controlled by genes.

Crossing plants

Suppose we have a bed of plants like the ones in picture 2. Some have red flowers, others white. We take some pollen from a red flower and place it on the stigma of a white flower: in this way we cross the two plants. When the seeds develop, we sow them in the soil. In time new plants grow up from the seeds. They all have red flowers.

How can we explain this? Look at picture 3. Each of these plants has in its cells a gene which controls the colour of its flowers. The alleles of this gene include two which we shall call **R** and **r**. **R** is the allele for red flowers, and **r** is the allele for white flowers. **R** is dominant to **r**. The red-flowered parent is homozygous dominant (**RR**), whereas the white-flowered parent is homozygous recessive (**rr**).

Now the gametes (pollen grains and egg cells) contain only one of these alleles. Each gamete produced by the red-flowered plant contains an **R** allele, and each gamete produced by the white-flowered plant contains an **r** allele.

When fertilisation takes place, the **R** and **r** alleles are brought together, so the offspring are heterozygous (**Rr**). As **R** is the dominant allele, the offspring have red flowers.

From these results we can put forward a general rule. In a cross between homozygous parents with different phenotypes of the same characteristic, the offspring produced are identical to each other. In addition, the phenotype of the offspring shows which one of the two alleles is dominant.

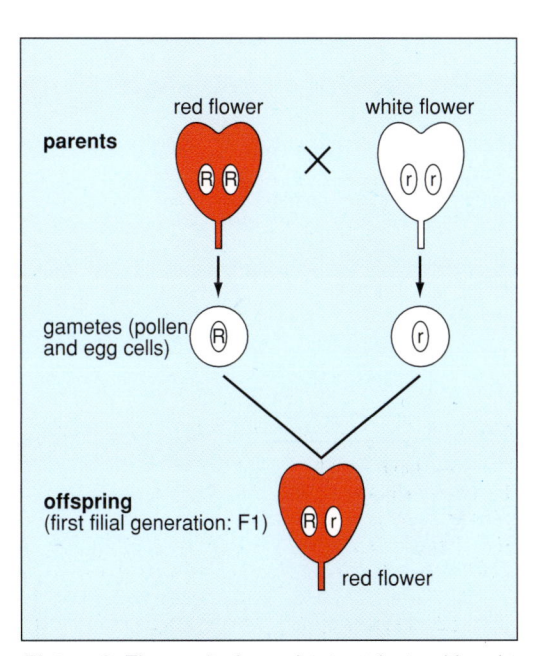

Picture 3 The result of crossing two plants with red and white flowers. The alleles are indicated by letters: **R**, red; **r**, white.

176 Inheritance

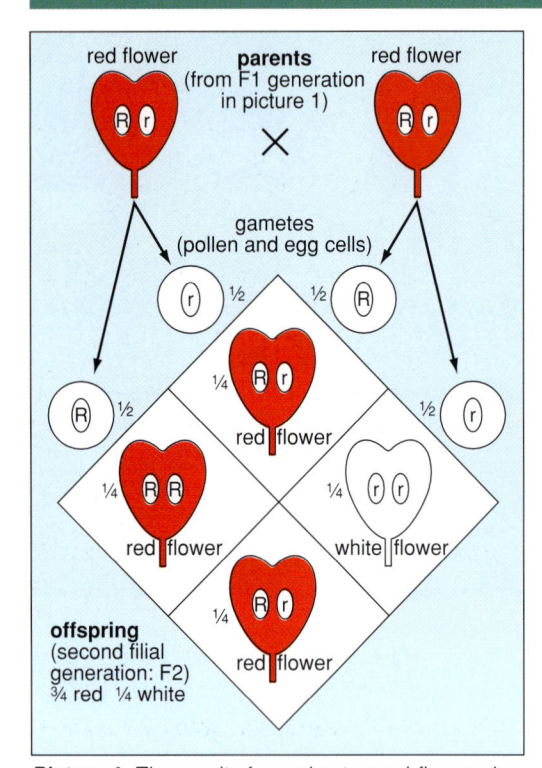

Picture 4 The result of crossing two red-flowered offspring from picture 3. The same result would be obtained by self-pollinating one of them. Symbols as in picture 3. Instead of using lines to show which gamete joins up with which, here the same thing is shown by means of a grid. A grid has the advantage of not having lots of lines crossing each other, like there are in picture 4 on page 172.

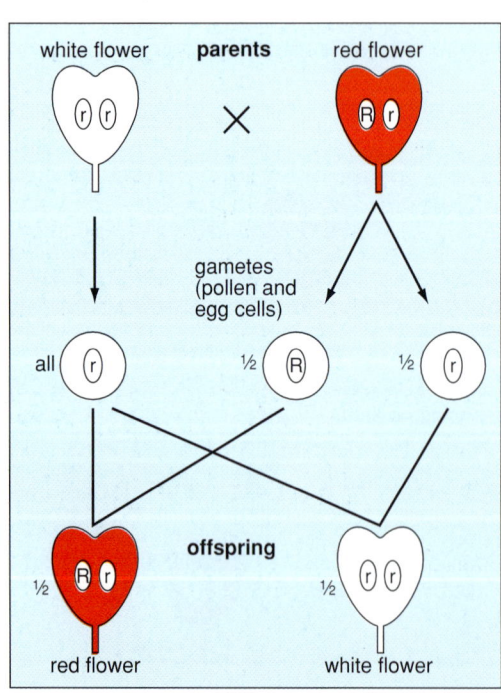

Picture 5 The result of crossing a white-flowered plant with a red-flowered plant containing the **R** and **r** alleles. Symbols as in pictures 3 and 4.

Another plant cross

The red-flowered offspring from the previous cross belong to the **first filial generation**, or **F1** for short. (The parents are sometimes abbreviated to **P**.)

Now suppose we take two of these red-flowered plants and cross them. Or alternatively we could self-pollinate one of them. The resulting seeds are planted, and the new plants grow up and bear flowers. They belong to the **second filial generation** or **F2**.

This time we get a mixture of red-flowered and white-flowered plants. On counting each type, we find that roughly three-quarters are red, and one quarter white. In other words, they are in a ratio of 3 to 1.

How can we explain this? Look at picture 4. The two parent plants are both heterozygous (**Rr**), as we have already seen. Now the gametes produced by these plants contain either an **R** allele or an **r** allele. In fact there should be equal numbers of each.

Fertilisation is random, and it is sheer chance as to which kind of pollen fertilises which kind of egg cell. Picture 4 shows the possible combinations, and the offspring resulting from each. Can you see why we get a 3 to 1 ratio between the red and white-flowered offspring?

Observed and predicted ratios

When crosses are carried out using fruit flies or pea plants, very large numbers of offspring are produced. This allows ratios to be calculated with considerable accuracy. It is found that an exact ratio of 3:1 hardly ever arises. The observed ratios, that is those actually counted by the experimenter, are very close to the expected ratio, but not exactly 3:1. The reason for this is that fertilisation is a random process. An exact 3:1 ratio would only happen if the two types of male gametes joined with the two types of female gametes in exactly equal numbers (see picture 4).

The element of chance (or luck) means that slightly more of one combination will occur and slightly less of another. This means that the ratio is never exactly 3:1.

Doing a test cross

The red-flowered offspring from the previous cross have two genotypes: some are homozygous (**RR**), and others are heterozygous (**Rr**). Both look exactly alike, so you can't tell which is which just by looking at them. How, then, could you find out if a particular red-flowered plant is homozygous or heterozygous?

One way would be to cross it with a white-flowered plant. If the red-flowered plant is homozygous (**RR**), the offspring will all be red-flowered (as in picture 3). On the other hand, if the red-flowered plant is heterozygous (**Rr**), we would expect to get a mixture of red-flowered and white-flowered plants in roughly equal proportions (picture 5).

A cross which is done to find the genotype of an organism is called a **test cross**.

More about heredity **177**

Inherited diseases of humans

Certain genes can cause diseases which may be passed from parents to their children. In some cases the dominant allele is harmful, but more often it is the recessive allele.

An example of such an inherited disease is **cystic fibrosis** (picture 6). It is caused by a recessive allele which is inherited in a straightforward way. Only people who are homozygous for the harmful allele get the disease. Heterozygous people do not get the disease. However, they are **carriers** of the allele and may pass it to their children, as you can see in picture 7.

If a couple give birth to a child with a disease such as cystic fibrosis, their doctor can arrange for them to see a **genetic counsellor**. The genetic counsellor will try to work out the chance of their next child being born with the disease. Knowing the risks, the parents can then decide whether or not to have any more children.

Sometimes couples who have not yet had any children know that there is a history of a particular disease in one or other of their families. For example, the wife may have had a grandparent or an uncle with the disease. Here too a genetic counsellor can be helpful.

In order to advise people, the genetic counsellor must know as much as possible about the parents' **pedigrees**.

What is a pedigree?

You come from your parents, and they came from *their* parents – and so on. This is your pedigree.

Building up a person's pedigree involves tracing back his or her history through the parents, grandparents, great-grandparents and so on. A pedigree can be built up for any kind of organism whose ancestors are known. You can then use it to show how certain features or **traits** are inherited. This is done in the form of a **family tree.**

A family tree is shown in picture 8. It shows the occurrence of **night-blindness** in the males and females of a family over three generations. Having built up a chart like this, we can work out the genotypes, or possible genotypes, of the various individuals. From this it may be possible to work out the chance of the problem arising in the next generation.

It is remarkable how some features persist in a family. A famous example is the drooping lower lip of the Habsburg family (picture 9). By looking at family portraits, this feature can be traced back through several centuries. It is thought to be caused by a dominant allele.

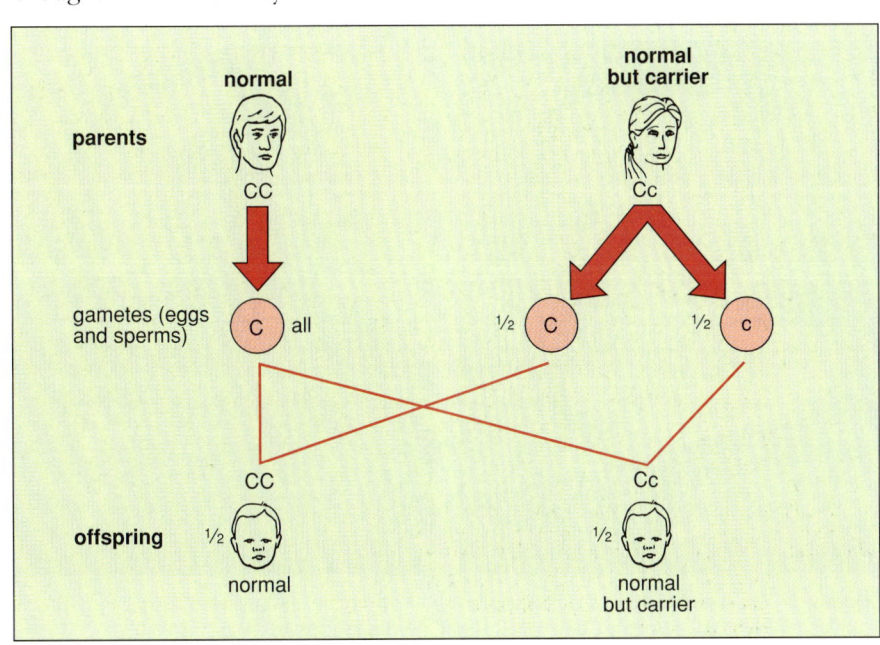

Picture 6 Cystic fibrosis is a disease of the pancreas, lungs and certain other organs. It is an inherited condition occurring about once in every 2500 births. Scientists have been working hard to find a way of preventing this disease which is known to be caused by a particular gene. Much of the research is funded by voluntary donations.

Picture 7 How cystic fibrosis is inherited. The diagram shows what happens if a normal person (genotype **CC**) mates with a carrier (genotype **Cc**). None of their children will have the disease, but there is a one in two chance that a child will be a carrier. If two carriers mate there is a one in four chance that they will produce a child with the disease. Can you see why?

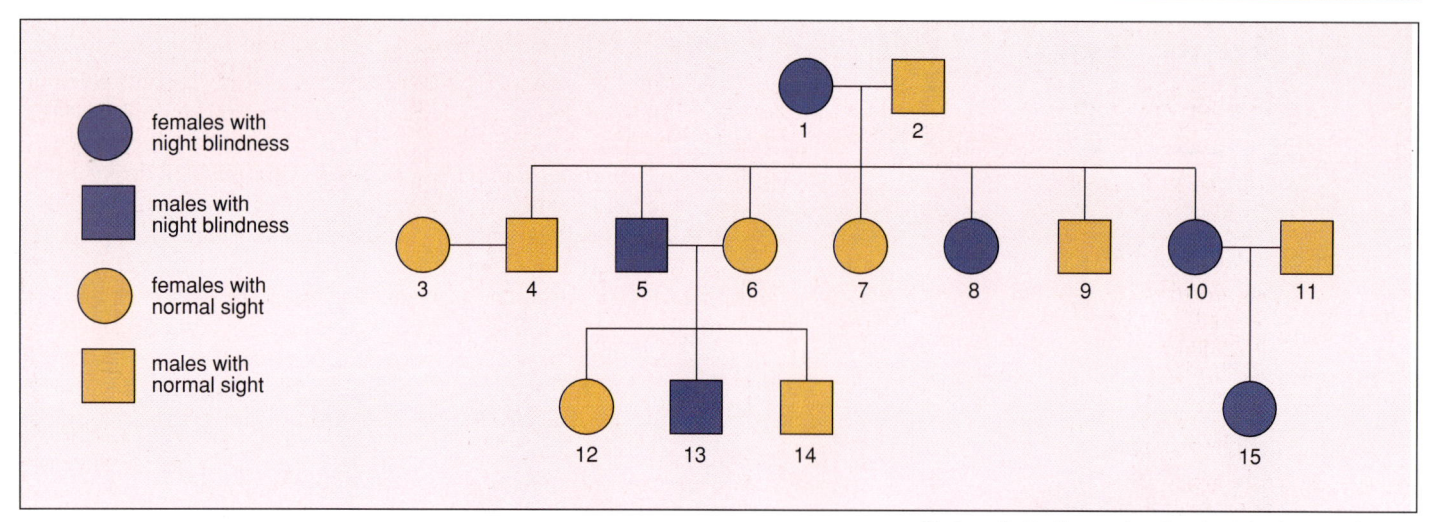

Picture 8 Pedigree showing the inheritance of night-blindness in a family. In this condition it is difficult to see in dim light. This type of night-blindness is controlled by a gene which has two alleles; the allele for night-blindness is dominant to the allele for normal vision.

A boy or a girl?

What decides whether the fertilised egg develops into a boy or a girl? Well, it depends on what kind of chromosomes the fertilised egg contains.

We have in our cells a pair of **sex chromosomes**: they decide the person's sex. One is longer than the other. The long one is called the **X chromosome**, and the short one is called the **Y chromosome**. Males possess an **X** and a **Y** chromosome in their cells, whereas females possess two **X** chromosomes.

Now the sperm which the male makes in his testes contain only one of these two chromosomes, either **X** or **Y**. In fact, half the sperm should contain an **X** chromosome and half should contain a **Y** chromosome. (For shortness we will call them **X** and **Y** sperm.) On the other hand, the eggs which the female produces in her ovaries will all contain an **X** chromosome. This is shown in the top part of picture 10.

When fertilisation occurs, the egg may be fertilised by either an **X** sperm or a **Y** sperm. In fact, fertilisation is random so there is an equal chance of either happening. If an **X** sperm fertilises the egg, the fertilised egg will contain two **X** chromosomes, and this will develop into a female. On the other hand, if a **Y** sperm fertilises the egg, the fertilised egg will contain an **X** and **Y** chromosome and will develop into a male. This is shown in the bottom part of picture 10.

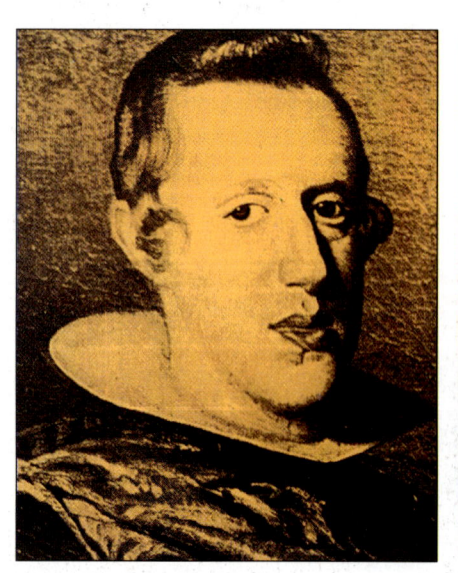

Picture 9 Two members of the Habsburg family, showing the famous 'Habsburg lip'. Left: Philip IV of Spain, 1605–1665. Right: Ferdinand I of Austria, 1793–1875.

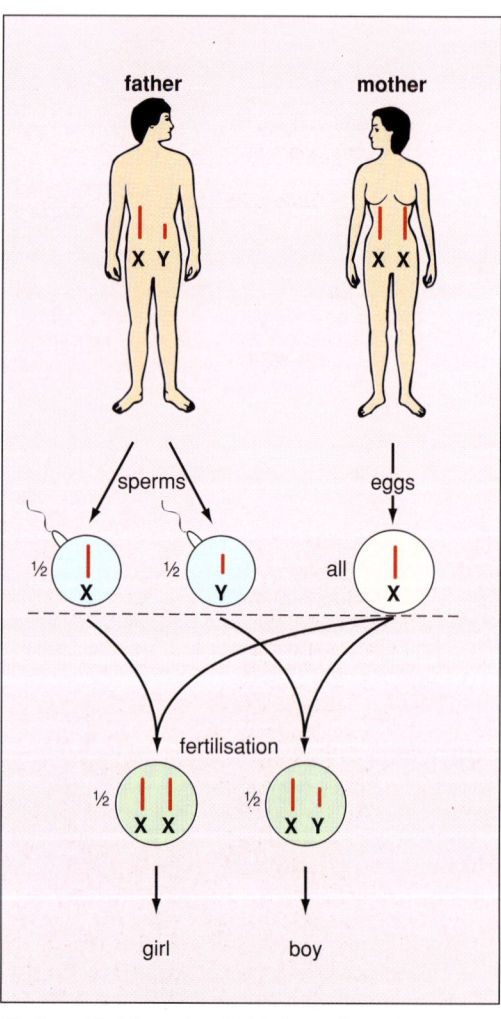

Picture 10 A boy or a girl? It depends on the sex chromosomes. The chromosomes are shown in red. There is a pair of sex chromosomes in every body cell.

Questions

1 You have to decide if the following statements are true or false. If false, you should give the correct alternative to the part that is underlined.
   a Sex cells are known as <u>gametes</u>.
   b Each sex cell contains a <u>double set of chromosomes</u>.
   c The genetic make-up of an individual is called its <u>phenotype</u>.
   d The human sex chromosomes are <u>Y and Z</u> chromosomes.

2 Seed colour in pea plants is genetically controlled. Look at the following cross.

Generation A

○ × ●

true-breeding white pea seeds   true-breeding grey-brown pea seeds

all seeds are grey-brown in colour; only these seeds were used in the cross below

Generation B

● × ●

grey-brown pea seeds   grey-brown pea seeds

Generation C

○ ●

25 white pea seeds   75 grey-brown pea seeds

   a Identify generations A, B and C using the symbols F1, F2 and P.
   b Which seed colour is dominant?
   c Which of the following seeds are true breeding?
      i   white seeds from generation A
      ii grey-brown seeds from generation A
      iii grey-brown seeds from generation B
      iv white seeds from generation C
   d Draw a pie chart to illustrate the results for generation C.

3 In cucumber plants, the presence of a chemical giving the cucumber a bitter taste is under genetic control. The bitter taste (B) is dominant to the non-bitter taste (b). A market gardener wanted to obtain a supply of plants which produced non-bitter cucumbers. She carried out the crosses shown below.

   cross 1   BB × BB
   cross 2   BB × bb
   cross 3   Bb × bb

   a What phenotypes, and in what ratios, did she obtain in the F1 offpring from crosses 1, 2 and 3?
   b In a fourth cross she obtained only non-bitter offspring in the F1. Write down the genotypes of the parent plants.

4 The alleles responsible for coat colour in leopards are spotted coat (B) and black coat (b).

A spotted-coat female was crossed with a black-coated male in a Scottish zoo. Both spotted and black-coated cubs were produced. Their phenotypic ratio agreed with the predicted ratio. The following year the same parents produced two black cubs. Account for the difference in the two results.

5 In a certain type of plant, white fruit colour is dominant to yellow. A fruit-grower crosses a white-fruited plant with a yellow-fruited one. About half the offspring have white fruit, and half have yellow fruit.

   a What are the genotypes of the parent plants? How do you know?
   b If you were to self-pollinate one of the white-fruited offspring, what phenotypes would you expect to obain, and in what proportions?

6 In pea plants, the allele for long stem is dominant to the allele for short stem. A long-stemmed pea plant was crossed with a short-stemmed pea plant. 123 offspring were produced. Of these, 68 had long stems and 55 had short stems.

Explain this result, using the following terms: phenotype, genotype, homozygous and heterozygous. You may draw a diagram if you like.

7 The picture below shows fruit flies with different types of wings. The flies of type 1 are true breeding and have normal wings. The flies of type 2 are also true breeding but have small short (vestigial) wings.

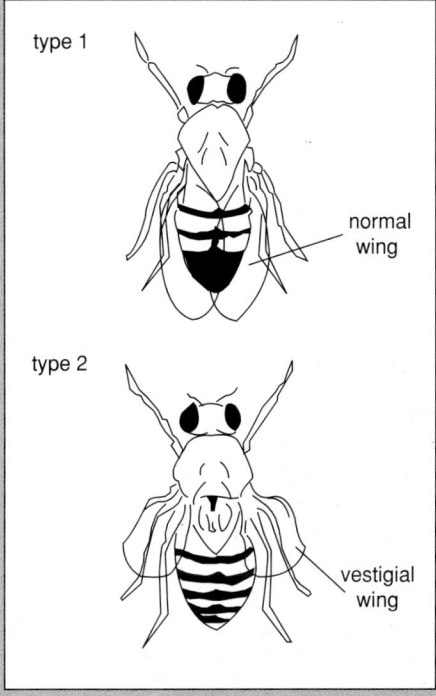

type 1 — normal wing

type 2 — vestigial wing

A cross was set up between flies of each type. The resulting F1 generation all had normal wings. Some of the F1 flies were selected and bred together. The F2 generation of flies was examined and counted. The results were:

flies with normal wings   153
flies with vestigial wings   39

   a In a cross like this, what would be the expected number of flies with vestigial wings in the F2 generation?
   b Give a reason to account for the difference between the expected number and the actual number with vestigial wings in the F2 generation.

8 A woman has ears with free (unattached) earlobes, but her husband's earlobes are attached (see page 168). Their four children (three boys and a girl) have the same ears as their mother. Ear shape is controlled by a single gene which has two forms.

   a What are different forms of the same gene called?
   b Using **E** to represent the form of the gene for free earlobes and **e** to represent the form of the gene for attached earlobes, work out which of the following statements are true or false. If false, suggest a correction for the part underlined.
      i The genotype of the woman could be **EE** or **Ee**.
      ii The form of the gene for free earlobes is <u>recessive</u> to the form of the gene for attached earlobes.
      iii The genotype of the man is <u>**EE**</u>.
      iv If the daughter marries a man with the genotype **ee**, there is a <u>1 in 2</u> chance that their child would have ears with attached earlobes.

9 Suppose that in humans the allele for short fingers is dominant to the allele for long fingers. Short-fingered Sue marries long-fingered Larry, and they have five children. Three of the children have short fingers, and two have long fingers. Using **S** as the allele for short fingers, and **s** as the allele for long fingers, give the genotypes of Sue, Larry and their five children.

10 Look at the family tree in picture 8 on page 178. In answering the following questions, use **B** as the symbol for the night-blindness allele (dominant), and **b** for the normal allele (recessive).

   a Write down the possible genotypes of all the people in the chart.
   b Explain how you know the genotype of person 1.
   c How do you know the genotypes of persons 13 and 15?
   d If persons 13 and 15 should marry, what is the chance that any of their children will be night-blind? Explain your answer.
   e If persons 14 and 15 should marry, what is the chance that any of their children will be night-blind? Explain your answer.

11 Huntington's chorea is a genetic disorder. When one of the chromosomes in a pair carries the abnormal form of the gene, that person develops the disorder. The abnormal form of the gene is represented by **H** and the normal form of the gene by **h**. The genotype of an affected individual is **Hh**. The tree below shows the inheritance of this disorder in one family.

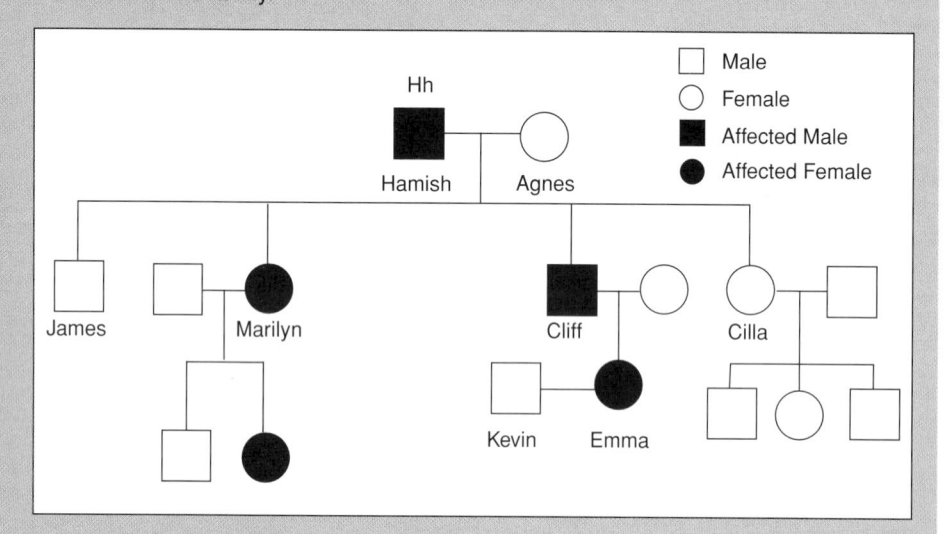

   a How many sons do Hamish and Agnes have?
   b How many grandchildren do they have?
   c State the phenotypes of Agnes and Emma.
   d State the genotypes of Marilyn and James.
   e Kevin and Emma are expecting a baby. What is the chance of the baby inheriting the disorder?
   f If the baby is unaffected, what is the chance of their next child being affected?

12 Albinos have no pigment in the skin, so they are very pale. This condition is caused by a recessive allele. Dave marries Joan. Dave and Joan are both normal, but each of them has a parent who is an albino.

   a How likely is it that Dave and Joan's first child will be an albino? Give your reasons in full.
   b Certain individuals in this family are 'carriers'. Which ones are carriers, and what does this word mean?

13 Mr and Mrs Cross have three children, all boys. They are sure that their next child will be a girl. Do you agree? Explain your answer.

14 Imagine you are a genetic counsellor. You are visited by Mr and Mrs Flap. They are worried because Mrs Flap and her father both have huge ears, and they don't want to bring a child into the world with ears like Mrs Flap's. There is no history of huge ears in her husband's family. What advice would you give them? Explain your reasoning, and state any assumptions that you need to make.

Gregor Mendel, the father of genetics

Gregor Mendel was a monk. He belonged to an Augustinian monastery in a town called Brunn in Austria (now Brno in the Czech Republic). He was a teacher in the local school and everyone liked him. One of his pupils remembered him as a cheerful clergyman, kind to everyone while contemplating the world through his gold-rimmed spectacles.

Picture 1 Gregor Mendel, the Austrian monk who discovered the principles of genetics.

Mendel had always been interested in heredity, so he decided to do some experiments on pea plants. He chose pea plants because they had a number of clear differences which were easy to tell apart. For example, some plants had red flowers and others white flowers, and some plants had short stems and others long stems.

Starting about 1856, Mendel carried out a series of experiments in the garden of his monastery. He carefully isolated certain plants and transferred pollen from one to another. He then collected and sowed the seeds, and when the offspring grew up he counted the different types. In the next ten years or so, he set up hundreds of crosses and produced thousands of offspring.

By counting the offspring, Mendel discovered the ratios which are described on page 176. But he did more than that. He also drew the right conclusions. This is remarkable when you think that he knew nothing about genes – they hadn't been discovered. But he realised that such things must exist – he called them 'factors'. He described how they must be passed from parents to offspring, and we now know that he was right.

In 1866 Mendel published his results in the journal of the local scientific society, but no one took any notice. He even sent a copy to a famous Swiss professor, but he ignored it too. He said that Mendel's experiments were incomplete and that he should plant more peas. In fact Mendel's data were based on more than 21 000 plants.

In 1868 Mendel was made Abbot of his monastery, and he became so busy that he had no more time for research. He died in 1884, unrecognised as a scientist.

Sixteen years later a Dutch biologist called Hugo de Vries was looking through scientific journals in a library when he came across Mendel's paper. He immediately realised its importance and told his colleagues about it. Only then was Mendel's work recognised.

1. What difficulties do you think Mendel might have come up against in his research?
2. From his experiments Mendel was able to make certain predictions about living organisms which were confirmed later. Suggest two such predictions.

Picture 2 Mendel in the garden of the monastery where he carried out his famous experiments on pea plants.

G4
Genetics and society

In this topic we shall learn how the study of genetics can affect our lives.

Picture 1 Three breeds of dog. There are over 100 breeds of dog altogether. They have been produced by selective breeding from a wild wolf-like ancestor.

Picture 3 Sperm can be frozen and stored in 'sperm banks' like the one shown here. Embryos can also be frozen: the embryo is taken from the uterus of a selected female before implantation (or obtained by *in vitro* fertilisation as described on page 101) for future transfer to the uterus of another female.

Impact of genetics on humans

In the previous two sections you have seen how the study of genetics has helped humans understand inheritance. However, genetics has a much wider effect on our lives than we might, at first, realise. Read any national newspaper and you are likely to find articles which have something to do with genetics. Many television programmes, films and books use the theme of genetics as the basis for their story. In this section we will look at two areas of modern genetics often in the news.

Selective breeding

The natural variation which exists in any species of animal or plant can be used as the starting points in a programme to breed organisms with a combination of desirable characteristics.

If you are planning a breeding programme, you have to remember certain things. For example, it's no good trying to cross two different species. Different species can't normally interbreed – it is biologically impossible.[1] However, you can cross two different varieties of the same species – different breeds of dog, for example. In this way you may produce a new variety which combines the best qualities of the two original ones.

Another thing you can do is to stick to one variety and always choose the best individuals for breeding. You might choose the fastest Greyhounds or the biggest Great Danes. In this way you may gradually improve the quality of that variety.

Now for some details, animals first, then plants.

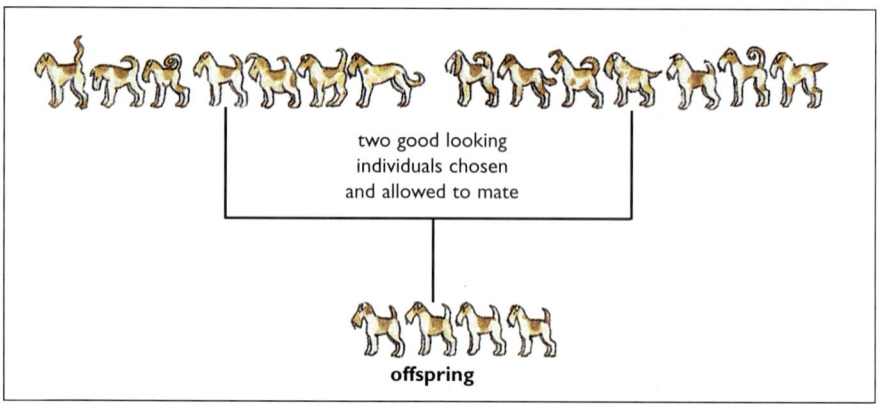

Picture 2 In selective breeding, particular individuals are chosen and allowed to breed. The others are prevented from breeding.

Breeding animals

First you choose a male and a female with the features you want. You then put them in a pen together and let them mate. This is the sort of thing farmers do with sheep.

Another way is to obtain some semen from the male and place it in the vagina of the female. This is called **artificial insemination**.

Artificial insemination is often used for breeding cattle and other farm animals. In the case of cattle, bulls are kept at special centres. Semen is taken from them by a vet, and either frozen or mixed with a preservative for storage. Frozen bull semen can be kept for a very long time and used when needed. Embryos can also be frozen for future use (picture 3).

---

[1] There are exceptions to this general rule. For example, the mule is a cross between a donkey and a horse. However, the mule is sterile and cannot breed.

Genetics and society 183

Breeding plants

First you choose two plants with desirable features. Suppose they are the kind of plants which, left on their own, might pollinate themselves. How can you make sure that one pollinates the other?

The best way is to remove the anthers from one of the plants before it starts producing pollen (see page 56). This is quite easy to do with a needle and forceps. When the carpels of this plant are ripe, you pollinate it with pollen from the other plant, using a small paintbrush or probe (picture 4).

You must make sure that pollen from other plants does not get to your plant. So you cover the plant with a transparent bag, except of course when you are pollinating it.

What has selective breeding done for us?

All our familiar breeds of farm animals, and domestic animals such as cats and dogs, have been produced by selective breeding (picture 5). So have the various varieties of garden plants, such as roses (picture 6).

In the same way plant breeders have produced new varieties of crop plants which are better than the older ones. For example, we now have varieties of wheat and rice which grow more quickly, give more grain and are more resistant to disease, and we have varieties of tomatoes and other fruits which are larger and tastier.

All this is good for humans. Improved crop plants, in particular, have led to enormous advances in agriculture.

Outbreeding and its advantages

When you breed animals or plants, it is best to choose individuals that are not closely related. The offspring produced by crossing unrelated parents are called **hybrids**, and the process by which they are produced is called **hybridisation**. They are usually strong and healthy, and are most likely to reproduce successfully. Breeding from unrelated individuals is called **outbreeding**.

Picture 4 A wheat flower being pollinated by hand. The pollen is transferred by means of a metal probe.

Picture 5 The main breeds of cattle seen in Britain: Friesians (top left), our most common breed, are used mainly for milk; Herefords (top right) are used for beef; Jerseys and Guernseys (bottom left and right) produce very rich milk.

Picture 6 Three varieties of roses. Selective breeding carried out over centuries has produced many different varieties of rose and more are created every year.

Inbreeding and its dangers

Sometimes breeders cross close relatives: a brother and sister perhaps, or father and daughter. This is called **inbreeding**.

Inbreeding is all right if it is only carried out every now and again. But if you go on doing it generation after generation, the offspring start to decline and show various defects. For example, they may be smaller than usual or less resistant to disease, or they may have certain physical abnormalities. Eventually they may fail to reproduce, and the line dies out.

The effects of inbreeding are more noticeable with animals than with plants. So if you want to breed animals, it is particularly important to cross unrelated individuals. This is what the best dog breeders do. Often several different breeders exchange dogs for mating, and in this way the bad effects of inbreeding are avoided. A highly inbred dog may have physical defects such as weak hips or a bad heart. It may have mental defects too. For example, it may suddenly turn savage and attack people.

An example of a highly inbred type of dog – the poodle – is shown in picture 7. The top picture is a portrait of a poodle, painted around 1780. It shows what poodles used to look like. In those days poodles were quite large. It was a working dog and was used for hunting ducks because it was a strong swimmer. Later it was used as a retriever. In the last hundred years or so, breeders have turned this breed into a pet – the miniature poodle shown in the lower picture. This dog is much smaller than its ancestor. It is soft and pretty, easy to keep in a small house or flat, and it fits snugly under its owner's arm. Unfortunately breeding for such a small size has resulted in a number of problems such as kneecaps which slip out of place, and hips which collapse.

It is sad to think that a dog which wins first prize in a show may have serious health problems as a result of the way it has been bred. Fortunately the British Kennel Club has introduced rules and regulations which should reduce the amount of inbreeding in the future. Hopefully the health and fitness of pedigree dogs will then improve.

What about humans? Inbreeding in humans is called **incest**. This applies to matings between brothers and sisters, and between parents and their children. In most countries incest is illegal. Laws against it go back thousands of years, and you can see that there is a good biological reason for them.

Picture 7 The poodle then and now. The top picture is a portrait of a working poodle painted by the artist George Stubbs around 1780. The lower picture is a photograph of a modern miniature poodle.

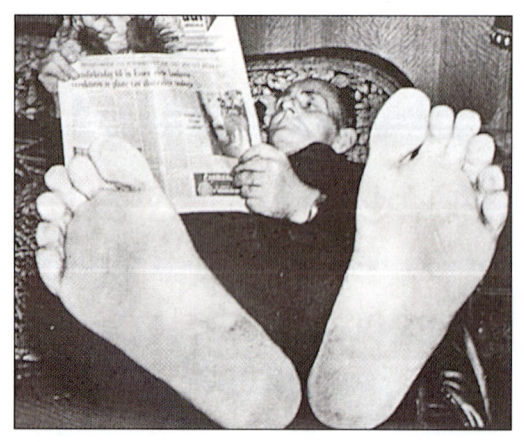

Mutations

Mutations are changes in the genetic information of an organism. Since the information controls the organism's characteristics, any change in the information is likely to lead to an altered phenotype. An organism with an altered phenotype is called a **mutant**.

There are two kinds of mutation. In **gene mutations**, a chemical change occurs in an individual gene. Scientists have shown that there is a change in the DNA molecules in one of the chromosomes (see page 13). The change may be very small indeed, but it may have a great effect on the organism. Haemophilia, a disease where blood takes a very long time to clot, is an example.

In **chromosome mutations**, a major change occurs in one or more of the chromosomes. For example, a person may lack a particular chromosome, or part of one – or an extra one may be present, as in Down's syndrome (see page 185).

Mutations happen from time to time for no apparent reason. However, the rate at which they occur can be greatly increased if the organism is exposed to ionising radiation or to certain chemical substances. This is why these things are so dangerous. Many of the people who survived the two atom bombs which were dropped on Japan at the end of the Second World War received massive doses of atomic radiation. As a result they developed lots of mutations and many of their children were born with defects, far more than in a normal population.

Picture 8 What is unusual about this man? This is one way a mutation can affect a person.

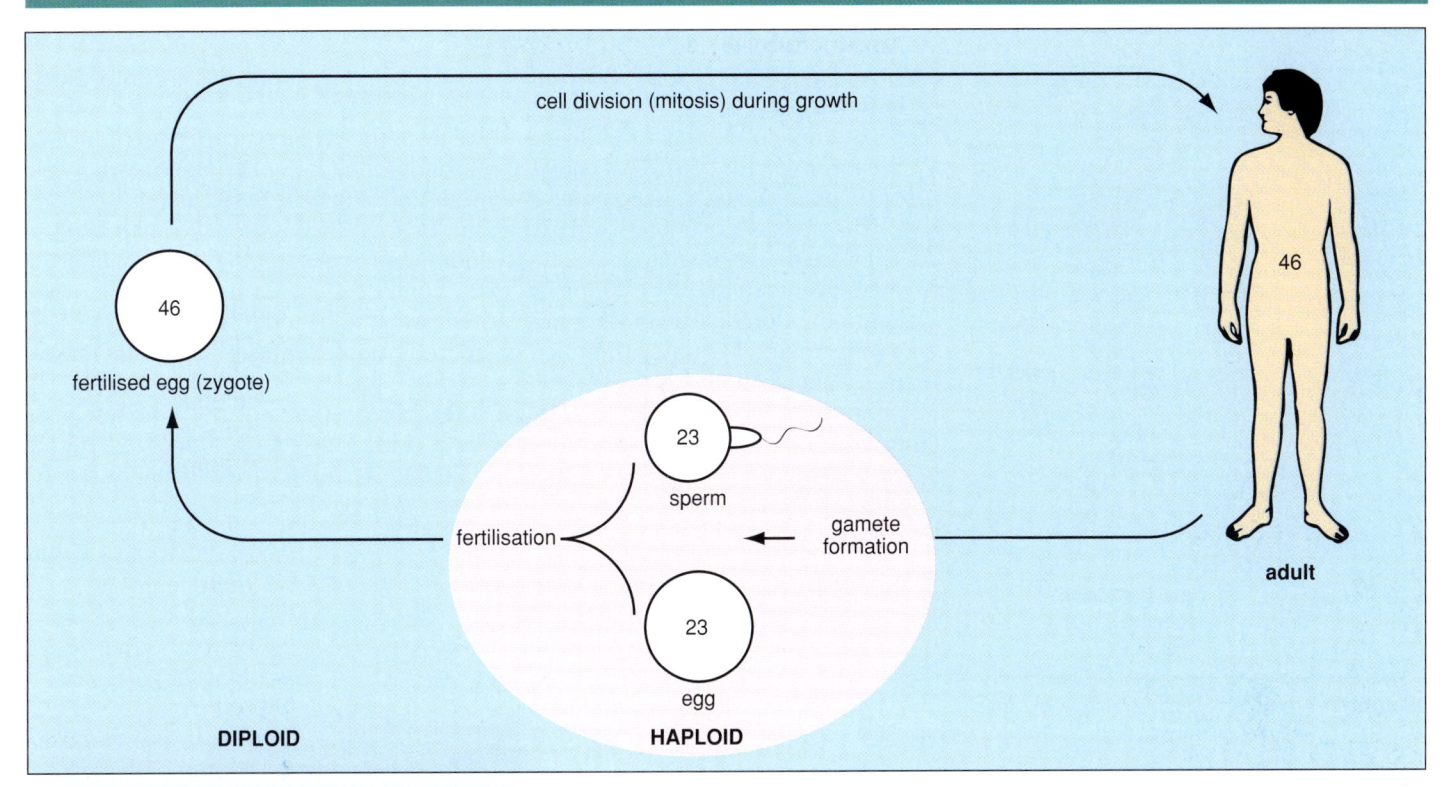

Genetics and society **185**

Picture 9 The human life cycle. The figures refer to the number of chromosomes in each of the cells.

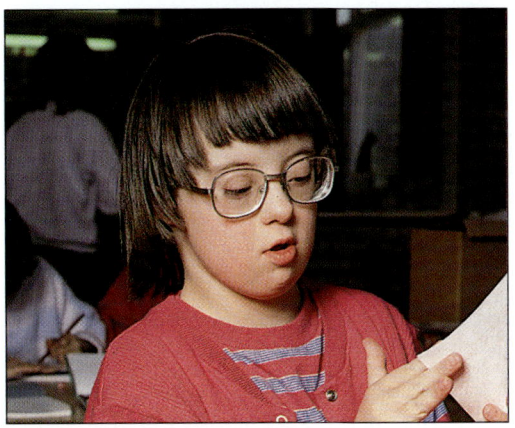

Picture 10 This little girl has Down's syndrome but is able to lead a fairly normal life.

Mutations are not *always* harmful. The man in picture 8 does not suffer because he has an extra finger and toe. Indeed, on rare occasions a mutation may be helpful. Examples of mutations which may be useful to humans include:

- mutant wheat which is resistant to some diseases,
- mutant apples which are extra juicy,
- mutant roses which have an unusual colour.

Chromosome mutations in humans

How do chromosome mutations occur? During the human life cycle the chromosome number in the gametes is reduced from 46 to 23 (picture 9). Abnormal gamete formation, which usually occurs more often in the ovaries of older women, results in some eggs containing an extra chromosome. After fertilisation with a normal sperm the zygote contains one extra chromosome. A person suffering from Down's syndrome has an extra copy of chromosome number 21.

This small change in the number of chromosomes alters the phenotype of the baby. The little girl in picture 10 has an altered physical appearance and is mentally retarded. However, much can be done nowadays to help people with Down's syndrome to overcome their difficulties and lead a full and happy life.

The chance of Down's syndrome occurring is 1 in every 3000 births for a 20-year-old woman, but this rises to 30 in every 3000 births by the time the woman is 40 years old. The chances of abnormal gamete formation increase as the mother gets older.

Amniocentesis

Nowadays doctors can find out if a baby has any abnormal chromosomes before it is born.

A sample of fluid is carefully removed from the amniotic cavity surrounding the fetus (picture 11). This is usually carried out at about the eighteenth week of pregnancy. The fluid contains chemicals and skin cells from the fetus.

The cells are extracted and grown under special conditions for two weeks. They are then stained and examined under a microscope. Any abnormalities in the chromosomes, for example an extra number 21 chromosome, will be visible to the doctor. The mother and father can be told, and if anything serious is wrong an abortion may then be considered. Amniocentesis slightly increases the chance of a miscarriage.

Another technique for examining the chromosomes of the embryo is to extract some of them from the placental cells. This can be done at a much earlier stage in the pregnancy than amniocentesis, but it carries a higher risk of miscarriage.

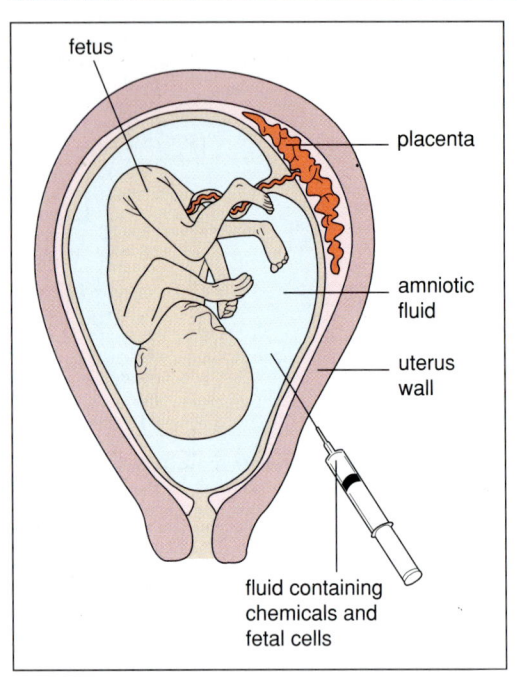

Picture 11 Amniocentesis: the removal of a small sample of amniotic fluid.

Questions

1 Gros Michel is a variety of banana plant. To try to improve the Gros Michel variety, plant breeders crossed it with another type of banana plant. This banana plant had good resistance to Panama disease and leaf spot disease. The table below shows the characteristics of Gros Michel and the new variety of banana.

Characteristic of the banana plant	Gros Michel	New variety
Produces large bunches of fruit	yes	no
Possesses resistance to Panama disease	no	yes
Produces fruit containing no seeds	yes	yes
Possesses resistance to leaf spot disease	no	no

   a Which two characteristics does Gros Michel lack?
   b Suggest two reasons why plant breeders considered the new variety to be an unsuccessful product from the above cross.

2 A rare breed centre decides to collect and breed as many varieties of sheep as it can. The next table provides information on the characteristics of four breeds of sheep.

Breed	Meat yield	Wool quality	Incidence of twins
A	high	poor	1 in 10
B	low	excellent	1 in 2
C	medium	excellent	1 in 5
D	high	good	1 in 2

   a A local sheep farmer wants to increase the size of his flock and improve the wool quality. The rare breed centre is willing to let him have a ram of his choice to breed with his sheep. State the breed he should pick and explain your choice.
   b The rare breed centre wishes to produce a new variety of sheep that would be suitable for both meat and wool production. Which are the two breeds it should use?

3 Cyclamates are artificial sweeteners, about thirty times as sweet as sugar. They used to be added to drinks by the manufacturers. It was then discovered that they could cause 'chromosome aberrations', so they were banned.
   a What do you understand by the term 'chromosome aberration'?
   b What precautions should be taken to prevent potentially dangerous chemicals being added to our food?

4 The man in picture 8 has an extra finger and toe. Can you think of any circumstances in which it might be useful to have an extra finger?

Producing a new variety of wheat

Britain used to import lots of high-quality wheat from Canada and still imports some. Here is an account of how the Canadians developed a new variety of wheat which was particularly well suited to their climate.

In the early 1900s, most Canadian farmers were growing a variety of wheat called **Red Fife**. This produced a lot of grain and the flour was good for bread-making. But Canada often has frosts in late summer which may damage the ripening crops, and Red Fife did not grow fast enough to be sure of avoiding the frosts.

So scientists decided to try to create a fast-growing variety of wheat. They did this by cross-breeding Red Fife with an early-ripening wheat from India. The result was a new variety of wheat which ripened about six to ten days earlier than Red Fife – in good time to beat the frosts. It was called **Marquis**. It was so successful that in a few years more than half the wheat grown in Canada was of this new type. Although no longer grown there it is the standard against which quality Canadian wheats are judged.

In Britain much of our wheat is **winter wheat**: the seeds are sown in the autumn, and the shoots come up before the winter sets in. Growth stops during the winter, and then starts up again the following spring. The advantage of winter wheat is that the young plants are already established by the time spring comes, so the wheat can be harvested earlier.

However, in Canada they have very hard frosts in the winter which would kill the young wheat plants. So most Canadian farmers plant their wheat in the spring. Marquis grows fast enough for the farmer to be sure of harvesting it before the late summer frosts occur.

As well as growing quickly, Marquis gives a high-quality grain. The flour produced from the grain contains a lot of gluten and makes good, well-risen loaves (see page 54).

1. Name one feature of Marquis which makes it particularly suitable for growing in countries with long winters.
2. Name one feature of Marquis which makes its grain particularly useful in bread-making.
3. Describe in detail how the cross between Red Fife and the Indian wheat would have been carried out.
4. What is gluten and why does it help to make 'good, well-risen loaves'?
5. It can take 12 years from when a new variety of wheat is first developed by scientists to when it becomes available to farmers. Why do you think it takes so long?

Capsticks' fleeces are just champion

Cumbrian hill farmers Edmund and Frank Capstick are leading the way in exploiting the full earning potential of wool. Their 450 Rough Fell ewes (females) are not only producing heavier fleeces but wool quality is in the top grade and yielding premium prices.

This year's wool clip was worth £1500 and won them the new reserve champion award in the CIBA Wool Producer of the Year competition. The whole flock is hand-clipped.

"Sheep have to be clipped no matter what the value of the fleece so you might as well have a good fleece to sell as have a bad one," say the Capsticks of Birkhaw, Sedbergh.

The brothers' dedication to producing top-quality wool spans 30 years of stock selection, i.e. choosing the right individuals to breed. Rejecting unsuitable individuals from the ewe flock and meticulous evaluation of fleece quality in stock tups (males) has paid dividends.

But fleece weight has also been addressed by breeding bigger "framier" Rough Fell ewes which are now yielding an average clip of 2.5 kg.

Tups and ewes are selected for white wool with long fibres; lambs showing dark fibres in the neck or body wool are not kept for breeding and all ewes are removed from the flock and sold after three crops.

"This maintains our high standard by selling ewes before coarse hair starts to appear in the fleece," said Edmund Capstick.

This year's clip fell into the British Wool Marketing Board's 714 grade and earned up to 108p/kg for hog fleeces which averaged 3 kg. Most Rough Fell wool this year was earning 102p/kg.

Ewes are hand clipped in late June to early July leaving on more of the wool that has grown since the spring than would be left if the flock was machine-clipped.

"We can often get a cold night, even at shearing time. By leaving a little more fleece on we help to avoid the risk of ewes becoming chilled which can affect milk yield," says Frank Capstick.

Liz Ambler of the British Wool Marketing Board, which organised a flock inspection, said: "The Capsticks are now producing a heavy, top-quality fleece which will always provide them with a clip capable for earning premiums despite market fluctuations."

Improving fleece quality while still retaining the sheep's shape and form has been a constant challenge for the Capsticks. Their swing towards a bigger type of Rough Fell has not only produced more wool but has helped to maintain the size and shape of prime lambs.

"Our mature ewes weigh 120–140 lbs. We achieve 150% lambing and want all our prime lambs away by the end of autumn. We averaged 40.77 kg for all lambs sold this year and had individuals up to 48 kg," said Edmund Capstick.

by Jeremy Hunt

Adapted from *Farmers Weekly* 29 December 1995

Picture 1 Edmund Capstick, champion wool producer of 1995, with one of his Rough Fell sheep.

H1 Living factories

Bacteria and fungi can be used to make a wide range of products.

What is biotechnology?

History books tell us that, even centuries ago, humans made bread and cheese, and brewed beers and wines. These are ancient products of **biotechnology** and, today, form a typical 'ploughman's lunch'. The biotechnological industry is one in which humans use living organisms or cells to convert raw materials into useful substances. In modern biotechnology many useful products are manufactured using a wide range of living organisms.

The **microorganisms** used then, as now, are mainly fungi and bacteria. Other microorganisms, like unicellular algae, are not used to any great extent in biotechnology. In this topic we will look at some important examples.

Alcoholic fermentation

Some organisms can convert glucose into alcohol. This is an example of **anaerobic respiration**, that is respiration occurring in the absence of oxygen (see page 190).

glucose → alcohol + carbon dioxide + energy

This particular reaction is called **alcoholic fermentation**. This distinguishes it from other fermentations, which you will read about later.

The energy released by anaerobic respiration is less than that from aerobic respiration. However, it can supply certain organisms with enough energy to keep them going when oxygen is scarce.

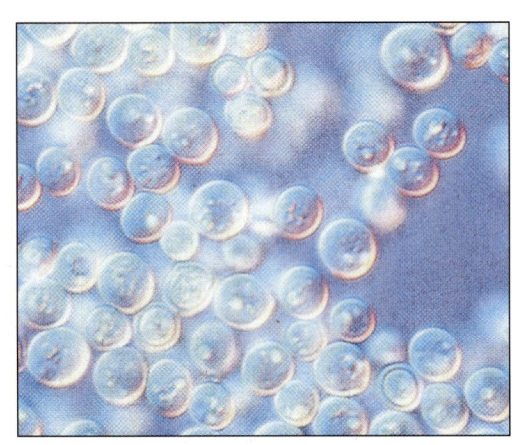

Yeast, the great fermenter

One such organism is yeast (pictures 1 and 2). Yeast is a single-celled fungus which lives on the surface of fruit, feeding on sugar. It multiplies rapidly by **budding**: each cell pinches off new ones and a large number can be formed in a short time (page 60).

For centuries humans have used yeast for making bread and alcoholic drinks such as wine and beer.

Making alcoholic drinks

All you need for making alcohol is a sugar solution and yeast. But to make a pleasant alcoholic drink is not so simple, as any wine-maker will tell you.

Wine is usually made from grapes. The juice contains sugar, and wild yeast grows on the skin. The grapes are crushed and the juice is extracted. The yeast cells multiply, fermenting the sugar and turning it into alcohol (picture 3).

Beer is made from barley. The process is called **brewing**. The partly germinated barley grain contains malt sugar. The grain is mashed with water and the resulting liquid is boiled with hops to give it the right flavour (picture 4). Yeast is then added and fermentation soon gets underway (picture 5).

Wine and beer making are major industries. In Britain over 6000 million litres of beer are drunk each year. Yeast too is manufactured on a large scale – you can buy it from shops. For the pleasure, and problems, which people get from a night in the pub we have to thank this lowly organism.

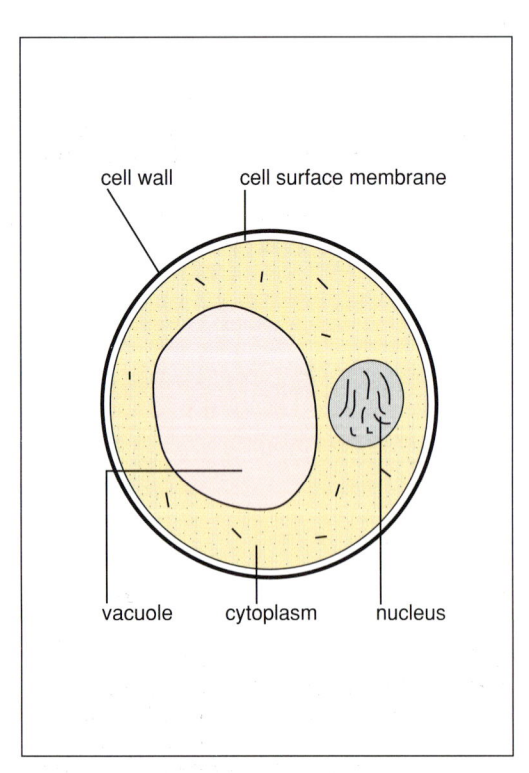

Making bread

Imagine you are a baker. You mix some flour and water with a small amount of sugar and yeast. This makes dough. You then leave the dough in a warm place for an hour or so. The living yeast cells multiply and ferment the sugar, giving off carbon dioxide gas. The gas makes the dough expand (picture 6). The gas is prevented from escaping by the stickiness of the dough (see page 54). When you bake the dough in a hot oven, the heat kills the yeast, and the alcohol evaporates away.

Picture 1 Yeast cells seen under the microscope, greatly magnified.

Picture 2 A yeast cell in detail.

Living factories **189**

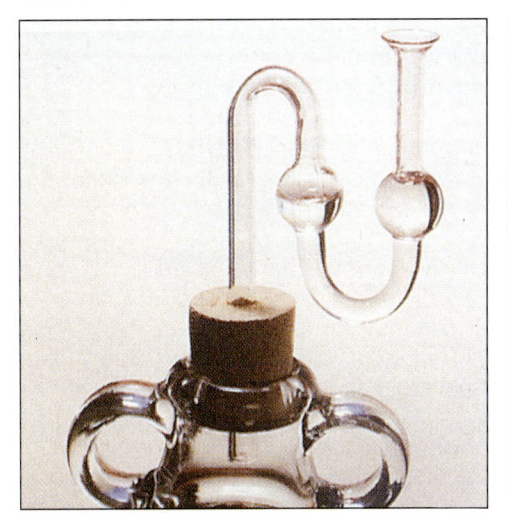

Picture 3 In making wine the jar is fitted with a special kind of valve which allows carbon dioxide to escape but prevents bacteria from getting in.

Picture 4 Hops are climbing plants which are grown in south-east England (Kent). The unpollinated female flowers are gathered and dried, and used in brewing beer.

Picture 5 Beer fermenting in a large tank in a brewery. The carbon dioxide gas given off by the yeast creates a froth on the surface. The men are holding this back so as to view the fermenting mixture underneath.

Fermentations by bacteria

Certain bacteria convert lactose, the sugar in milk, into lactic acid. This occurs anaerobically and is known as **lactic acid fermentation**. The lactic acid curdles the milk, making it go lumpy. **Yoghurt** is made by solidifying the milk in this way. It is then made more creamy and tasty by further bacterial action. It still tastes sour, so fruit juices may be added for flavour and sweetness. The yoghurt should be naturally preserved because of the lactic acid.

To make **cheese**, the solid part of the curdled milk (the **curds**) is separated from the fluid part (the **whey**). One way of doing this is to put the curdled milk in a muslin bag and squeeze out the fluid whey. The paste-like substance left behind is cheese.

At this stage the cheese is white and tasteless. It must now be ripened. This is carried out by microbes, particularly fungi – the sort that bring about decay. They break down the cheese, softening it and giving it its characteristic smell, flavour and appearance (pictures 7 and 8).

Picture 6 Dough before and after rising. Carbon dioxide gas, given off by the yeast, makes the dough expand.

Picture 7
Different types of cheese are ripened by different microbes. Blue cheeses are ripened by moulds which are visible as a network of blue threads. The cheese with large holes in it was ripened by bacteria which gave out carbon dioxide gas which could not escape.

Picture 8 Blue cheese is ripened by a mould (fungus) which grows on it. This machine makes holes in the unripe cheese. The holes allow oxygen to get in and help the mould to spread through the cheese.

Brewing

To manufacture top quality beer, brewers provide the best possible conditions for the growth of yeast.

Malting of the barley must take place first. This involves soaking the barley seeds in water and allowing them to germinate in warm conditions. The enzyme amylase converts the starch in the grain into simple sugars, like glucose and maltose. This provides an excellent food supply for the yeast.

The sugars are then dissolved in hot water and hops are added. These are fruits from a type of mulberry plant and boiling them releases the flavouring for the beer

Alcoholic fermentation is then allowed to take place in carefully controlled conditions. The temperature and pH of the fermentation vessels are monitored and controlled to provide the optimum growing conditions for yeast. Any additives or nutrients that the yeast requires are supplied to the vessel at suitable times during the fermentation process.

Finally, the fermentation vessels are sterilised between each batch to keep out unwanted microbes. These organisms compete with the yeast for food, and can spoil the beer, making it undrinkable.

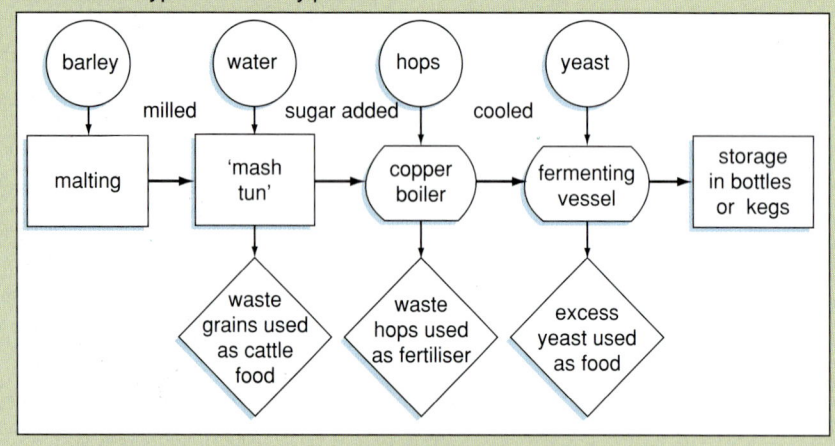

Picture 1 Beer production, getting the best results from yeast.

Aerobic and anaerobic respiration

Respiration provides energy for living cells. You have now read about both aerobic and anaerobic respiration. We should now summarise the differences between them.

During **aerobic respiration**, oxygen is used up and the sugar substrate is completely broken down into carbon dioxide and water. A large amount of energy is released since the breakdown is so complete.

During **anaerobic respiration**, oxygen is not needed and the sugar substrate is broken down to carbon dioxide and lactic acid if it occurs in animal cells, or to carbon dioxide and alcohol if it occurs in yeast. A much smaller amount of energy is released since much of it remains trapped in the end products.

The following organisms can all respire anaerobically: (a) whales, (b) a tapeworm in the human small intestine, (c) bacteria in the mud at the bottom of a lake, (d) the roots of rice plants.

Suggest why it is useful for each of these organisms to be able to respire anaerobically.

Questions

1 The following investigation into respiration was carried out. Dried yeast was mixed with flour and sugar solution to make a dough. The dough was made to fit into a measuring cylinder and the following table shows the volume of the dough over a 40-minute period.

Time (minutes)	0	10	20	30	40
Volume of dough (cm³)	25	27	31	37	40

  a Plot a line graph of the results.
  b Calculate the percentage increase in the volume of the dough, from the start to the end of the investigation.
  c During which 10-minute period was there the greatest increase in volume of the dough?
  d Which substance, produced by the yeast, was responsible for the increase in the volume of the dough?
  e The investigation was carried out at 22°C. Predict the effect on the results if the measuring cylinders had been placed in a water bath at 37°C.

2 As milk sours, there is a change in pH. The table shows changes in pH in a sample of milk over 16 hours at a temperature of 15°C.

Time (hours)	0	4	8	12	16
pH	6.98	6.82	6.66	6.50	6.34

  a Calculate the average decrease in pH per hour.
  b Name the group of organisms which bring about the souring of milk.
  c Give a word equation to describe the fermentation reaction taking place in the milk.

3 The graph shows changes in the number of yeast cells growing in a liquid culture kept at 30°C for 24 hours.

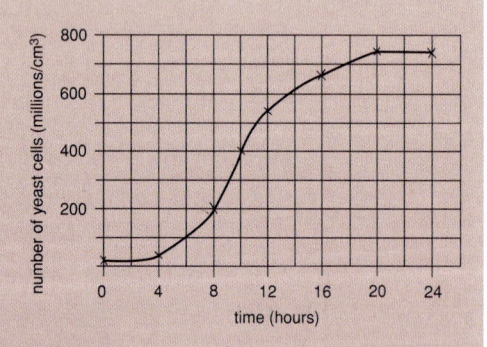

  a During which four-hour period was there the greatest increase in the number of yeast cells?
  b How many hours does it take for the number of yeast cells to stop increasing and become constant? Why does the yeast population stop increasing?
  c At eight hours there are 200 million yeast cells per cm³. How long does it take for there to be double this number?

Industrial fermentation

Microbes such as bacteria and yeasts produce all sorts of things that are useful for humans. Penicillin, insulin and washing powder enzymes are just three examples.

To obtain these products in sufficient amounts, we need to grow microbes on a large scale. This is done by means of an **industrial fermenter**.

One type of fermenter is shown in picture 1. It consists of a large stainless steel vessel. The vessel is filled with a suitable **medium**. This consists of a food solution such as sugar, together with any other substances which the microbes need in order to multiply and grow quickly.

Certain bacteria need only carbohydrate and minerals; others need protein and vitamins as well. Most fungi need carbohydrate, minerals and vitamins, though yeast needs only sugar and minerals.

The right kind of microbes are then added to the medium, and left to multiply.

Paddle-like **stirrers** keep the contents of the vessel moving about. If the microbes are aerobic, they must be given a supply of oxygen. This is done by an **aerator** which bubbles air through the mixture.

Fermenting microbes give off a lot of energy which heats up the medium. This means that the fermentation vessel has to be cooled. Small fermenters can be cooled by a **cooling jacket** surrounding the vessel. Larger fermenters need a **cooling coil** inside.

The vessel, medium and air supply are all sterilised beforehand to prevent any possibility of unwanted microbes getting into the mixture.

When fermentation is complete, the contents of the vessel are collected from a tap at the bottom. The product is then separated from the rest of the mixture and purified.

1 Suggest reasons why it is necessary to stir the contents of the fermentation vessel.

2 Why is it important that unwanted microbes should be kept out of the fermentation vessel?

3 What would happen if you did not cool the fermenter?

4 Suppose you decided to use an industrial fermenter to make beer. What medium would you put in, and what would you add to it?

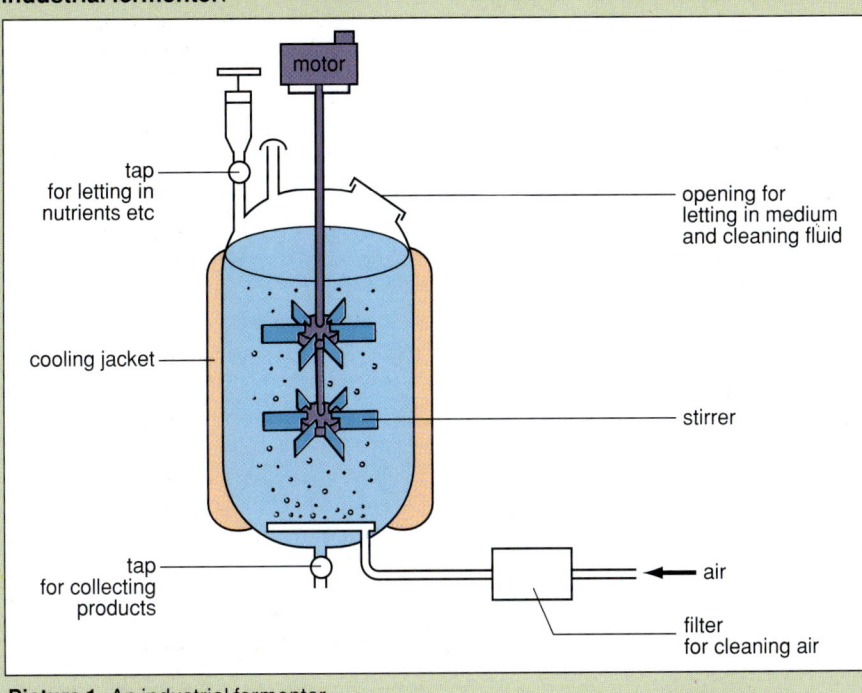

Picture 1 An industrial fermenter.

Batch culture and continuous culture

In the method of fermentation described above, you get the process going, wait for the microbes to grow and then collect the products. You then clean the fermenter and start again. This is called **batch culture** and it is the traditional method used in industrial fermentation.

A more modern method is to use a fermenter with an overflow. Once you have got the process going, the contents of the fermenter overflow and the product is extracted continuously. As fast as the culture overflows, more medium is added to keep pace with the loss. This is called **continuous culture**.

Continuous culture systems are fully automated and go on working day and night.

Continuous culture allows the enzymes or cells to be used for a longer time than those in batch processing. In addition, since the reaction vessel does not have to be emptied, cleaned and sterilised after each batch, there is a saving of time. This makes continuous flow processing much more economic to operate.

1 What are the advantages of continuous culture over batch culture?

2 Most fermentation factories use batch culture and are reluctant to change to continuous culture. Why do you think this is?

3 Why is it correct to regard the rumen of a cow as a continuous culture rather than a batch culture? (See page 89.) What would happen if it was a batch culture?

Producing penicillin, an example of batch culture

A starter culture of the fungus *Penicillium* is added to a liquid medium in a fermenter. The medium contains various sugars. The temperature is kept at a steady 24°C and the oxygen concentration is carefully controlled. The yield of penicillin depends on the oxygen concentration and the relative concentrations of the different sugars.

During the first 24 hours the fungus grows rapidly. After that the sugar content of the medium begins to fall, and the fungus starts producing penicillin. After about a week the concentration of penicillin in the medium reaches a maximum. The culture is then collected and filtered. The liquid medium passes through the filter and the fungus gets left behind. Penicillin is extracted from the medium.

H2 Working with microbes

In this topic we outline safe working practice for microbiology.

How can we handle microbes safely?

Yeast and the bacteria in yoghurt are useful microbes and not harmful to humans. Some types of fungi and bacteria are harmful and can cause diseases in other organisms, including humans. Scientists studying these microbes, and the diseases they cause, must grow them in such a way as to prevent them escaping. They must also be sure that they are growing only the particular microbe that they are investigating. Since contamination of equipment by foreign microbes can happen at any time, **sterile conditions** in the laboratory are vital.

Spores, formed by bacteria to survive poor conditions, can be destroyed by heat and pressure applied together. This enables higher temperatures to be reached. Working instruments, agar jelly and used Petri dishes (see below) are sterilised in this way using an **autoclave**. This is a large pressure cooker which heats water to 121°C. Twenty minutes at this temperature kills bacterial spores, and the equipment becomes sterile.

The activity below outlines how a particular type of bacteria can be cultured.

Activity

Culturing bacteria

CARE Work with bacteria should be carried out only under strict supervision by your teacher.

1. Obtain a Petri dish containing sterile nutrient agar. Keep the lid on whenever possible.
2. Your teacher will give you a plugged tube containing a particular type of bacteria.
3. Sterilise a wire loop by passing it quickly through a small bunsen flame. 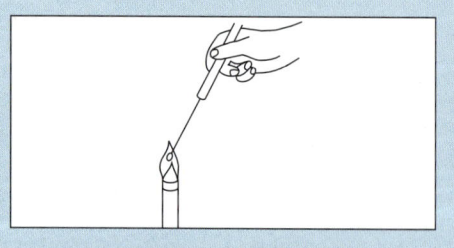
4. Keep hold of the wire loop, and unplug the tube with the same hand. With your other hand, sterilise the neck of the tube by passing it through the flame.

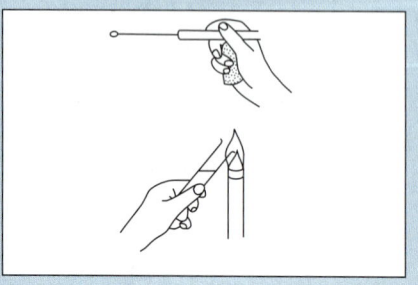

BIOHAZARD — Always wash your hands after working with bacteria.

5. Collect a sample of the bacteria on the wire loop. 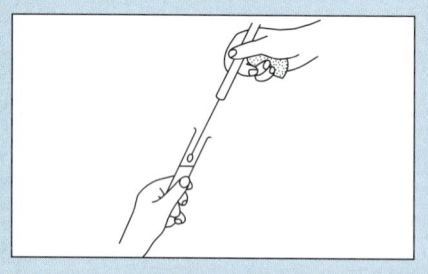
6. Pass the neck of the tube through the flame again, then replace the plug. 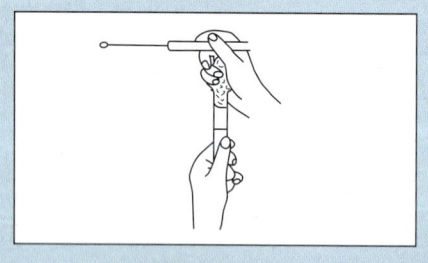
7. Remove the lid of the Petri dish. With the wire loop make a zig-zag streak on the surface of the agar. 
8. Pass the loop through the flame again. Then replace the lid of the Petri dish and fix it firmly with sellotape.
9. Place the Petri dish upside down in an incubator at 30°C.
10. After a day or two examine the dish without removing the lid.

The bacteria should have multiplied to form **colonies**. Each colony consists of thousands of bacteria clumped together.

Different types of bacteria can be recognised by the size, shape and colour of their colonies. How would you describe the colonies in your Petri dish?

Sterilising the wire loop and the neck of the tube helps to prevent contamination with other microbes. What other precautions might you take against contamination?

Why was it necessary to put the Petri dish in an incubator?

The tube which your teacher gave you at the start of this activity contained one particular type of bacteria. This is called a pure culture. Suppose you were given a Petri dish containing colonies of several different types of bacteria. How could you produce a pure culture of one of these types?

Why is it useful to produce pure cultures of bacteria?

Note: Before starting, hands must be washed and the work-bench wiped with disinfectant. Once the work has been completed, hands and bench should be sterilised again.

Microbes and disease

You may think that the world is full of dangerous, disease-causing microbes. In fact many microbes are useful to us whilst others are neither harmful nor useful.

Organisms which cause diseases are called **pathogens**. They can be divided into four main groups.

- **Viruses** cause the common cold, influenza ('flu'), measles, chicken pox, hepatitis B, AIDS and yellow fever.
- **Bacteria** cause Salmonella poisoning (a type of food poisoning), impetigo, tuberculosis, diphtheria, whooping cough, typhoid, tetanus, bacterial dysentery, cholera and syphilis.
- **Protoctists** cause amoebic dysentery and malaria.
- **Fungi** cause athlete's foot and thrush.

In addition, certain diseases are caused by parasitic flatworms and roundworms. For example, bilharzia, a serious disease of the tropics, is caused by a type of flatworm.

Pathogens are spread in many ways.

■ By droplets in the air

When you cough or sneeze, thousands of tiny drops of moisture shoot out of your mouth and nose (picture 1). If you have a disease, these droplets may be teeming with germs. If other people breathe them in, they are likely to catch the disease. The common cold and flu are spread in this way.

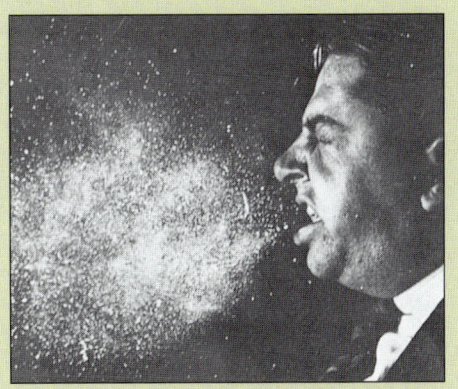

Picture 1 Flash-photo of a sneeze. Thousands of droplets of moisture, containing germs, shoot out of the man's mouth and nose. The droplets may travel at up to 70 miles an hour! A person with tuberculosis may cough up as many as four thousand million bacteria in 24 hours.

■ By dust
Germs stuck to dust particles float through the air and are breathed in by people. Diphtheria and tuberculosis are spread like this.

■ By touch
Sharing hairbrushes and towels with infected people can spread diseases like impetigo and athlete's foot.

■ By faeces
Germs released in the faeces of infected people can get into food and drinking water. Epidemics of typhoid, cholera and dysentery have been caused this way.

■ By animals
Rats, mice, cockroaches and flies can spread diseases to humans. Malaria and yellow fever are spread by the mosquito, and dogs can spread the rabies virus. Rats spread infected fleas in the Middle Ages, causing bubonic plague (the Black Death).

■ By blood
Blood to blood contact in humans can spread both AIDS and viral hepatitis.

1. Explain the reason for each of the following:
   a. A pet which is brought into Britain from overseas is put into quarantine for six months.
   b. If you graze your knee it is sensible to wash it immediately and put a dressing on it.
   c. A surgeon wears a mask over the mouth and nose.
   d. Many of the food items in a supermarket are wrapped in plastic film.
   e. Chlorine is often added to drinking water.

2. Why is it particularly important that the following places should be as free of germs as possible:
   a. operating theatres,
   b. public lavatories,
   c. hotel kitchens,
   d. swimming pools,
   e. doctors' surgeries?

3. Give five examples of places where diseases are likely to spread by people coughing and sneezing.

4. What part is played by each of the following in spreading disease:
   a. flies,
   b. rats,
   c. mosquitoes,
   d. needles,
   e. aeroplanes?

Growing mushrooms

Mushrooms are fungi. The mycelium of a field mushroom is in the soil, and the mushroom itself is its spore-producing body. The mushroom is the only part of the fungus above the ground.

Mushrooms are a popular food, and they have to be mass produced. They do not require light and are grown in places where it is cool and moist such as cellars, sheds, caves and disused mines.

The food on which the fungus develops is usually woody material such as the stalks of wheat and other cereal plants, composted with horse manure. Farm stubble, the stalks of cereal crops left behind after harvesting, is used for growing mushrooms.

Farm stubble used to be burned in the fields after harvesting. However, it is much better to use it for growing mushrooms.

1. Why is it better to use farm stubble for growing mushrooms than to burn it?
2. Why is the stubble composted with horse manure before it is used for growing mushrooms? Do you think it could be used without composting it first?

Picture 1 Truffles are rare and expensive fungi, related to mushrooms, found underground. A great delicacy!

The penicillin fungus

The penicillin fungus, *Penicillium*, feeds on sugary substances on the surface of fruit and other foods. Its life cycle is shown in the picture.

The fungus starts off as a spore. If the spore finds itself on a suitable food source, a thread-like **hypha** grows out. The hypha consists of a chain of cells which grows over the surface of the food, branching this way and that. Eventually the food becomes covered by a tangled mass of hyphae called a **mycelium**. This is visible as a greenish mould on the food.

The hyphae produce digestive enzymes which break down the food into soluble substances. These are then absorbed by the fungus. The hyphae don't penetrate far into the food; they stay near the surface because they need oxygen for respiration.

Eventually the food will run out, so the fungus must move to another source of food. Hyphae grow upwards, and form branches. Spores are pinched off from the tips of the branches. The spores are released and carried away by air currents or on people's fingers. If a spore lands on a suitable surface, a new mould develops and the cycle is repeated.

Picture 1 The structure and life cycle of the penicillin fungus, *Penicillium*.

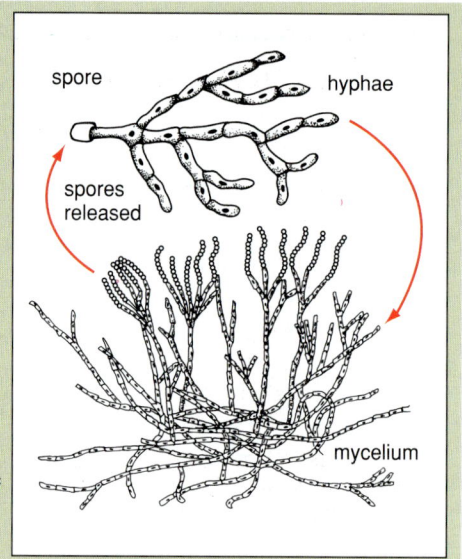

What are bacteria?

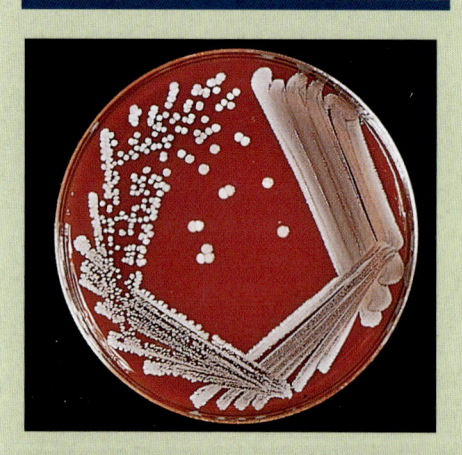

Picture 1 Bacterial colonies growing on an agar plate.

Bacteria are amongst the smallest organisms. You find them almost everywhere: in air, water, soil and inside other organisms. So they are very much part of our environment. Many of them are useful, but some cause serious diseases.

Scientists need to grow bacteria in the laboratory. This is necessary if we are to investigate them, and find ways of fighting the diseases they cause. They can be grown on the surface of a jelly-like material called **agar** to which various food substances are added. In warm conditions, the bacteria multiply to form **colonies** (picture 1).

Each colony consists of thousands of bacteria. If you look at part of a colony under a good light microscope, you can see the individual bacteria as little rods or dots (picture 2). You can see them more clearly if you look at them under the much more powerful electron microscope (picture 3). Different kinds of bacteria have different shapes. Some have whip-like 'hairs' which lash from side to side, propelling the organism along.

If bacteria are grown in a clear liquid medium, they make the liquid go cloudy.

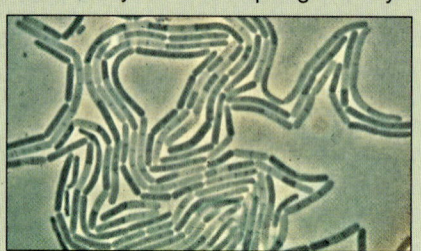

Picture 2 Bacteria under a light microscope.

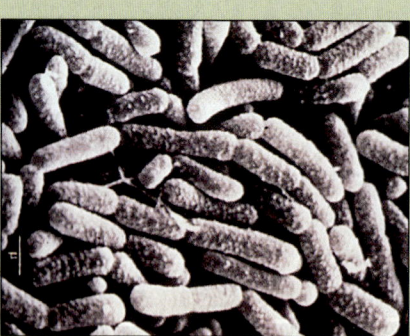

Picture 3 The same type of bacteria under an electron microscope.

Scientists have also studied the *internal structure* of bacteria. They are single cells, but the cell is simpler than those of other organisms and there is no proper nucleus.

Many bacteria are good at surviving bad conditions such as drought, heat, cold and even poisons. They do this by forming a protective coat around themselves. They are then known as **spores**. Inside the spore the bacterial cell becomes dormant – it goes to sleep, as it were. When conditions return to normal, the spore splits open and the bacterial cell comes out (picture 4). The spores of some bacteria can survive for more than fifty years.

Picture 4 On the left is a bacterial spore with a thick protective coat. On the right the coat has split open and the bacterial cell is coming out.

In good conditions bacteria reproduce very quickly (page 60). Their spores and rapid reproduction make disease-causing bacteria difficult to get rid of.

1 In medical research it is important to be able to grow particular kinds of bacteria on their own. Why do you think this is necessary?

2 It is dangerous to eat food which has been left lying around for some time. Which part of the above text helps to explain this?

What are viruses?

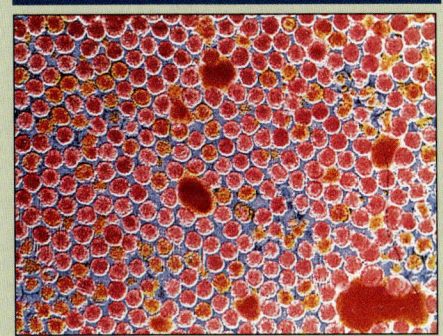

Viruses are much smaller than bacteria. A typical virus has a width of about a ten thousandth of a millimetre. If you lined them up in a row across this page, there would be over two million of them.

Despite their small size, viruses can cause immense harm. All sorts of diseases in humans, domestic animals and crop plants are caused by viruses. The virus disease which has been most in the news in recent years is AIDS, but viruses also cause less serious diseases such as flu and the common cold.

Because viruses are so small, you can only see them with an electron microscope. Four examples are shown in picture 1. Different kinds of viruses have different shapes and this is one way of recognising them.

A virus has a simple structure. It consists of a coiled string of genes surrounded by a wall made of protein. A famous biologist, Sir Peter Medawar, has described them as a piece of bad news wrapped up in protein.

Viruses can only reproduce inside the cells of living organisms. If they are outside the body they usually survive for only a short time.

Inside the victim's cells, the viruses reproduce and make new viruses. Picture 2 shows how they do this. The materials for making the new viruses come from the victim's cell itself. So the virus is a thief, robbing the cell of its contents and killing it in the process. Thousands of new viruses may be released from one cell, and they then attack more cells. No wonder we feel ill when we've got flu.

Different viruses attack different cells. For example, the common cold virus attacks cells in the nose and throat. The much more serious virus that causes AIDS attacks a certain type of blood cell which helps us to fight disease.

Not all viruses reproduce as soon as they get into our cells. Some just stay there and wait, maybe for years. Then suddenly they become active and start multiplying. Until then you don't even know they are there, unless a test is carried out to show that they are.

1. Viruses can be grown in hen's eggs (picture 3) or in tissue cultures. What do we need them for, and why can't they be grown on agar jelly, like bacteria can?

2. Most scientists regard viruses as non-living. Do you think viruses should be regarded as living or non-living things?

3. If viruses survive for only a short time outside the body, how do you think people catch colds from each other?

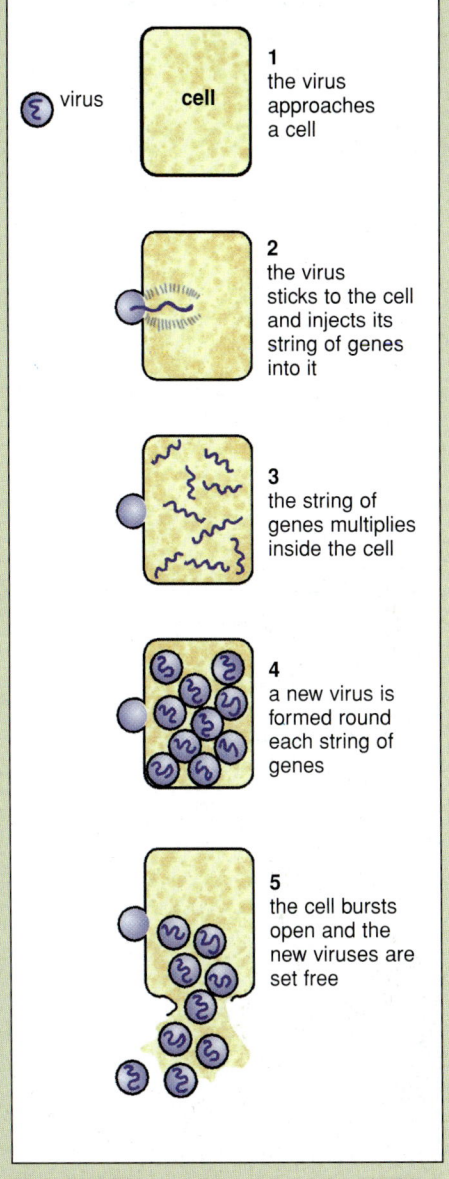

These viruses cause the paralysing disease poliomyelitis.

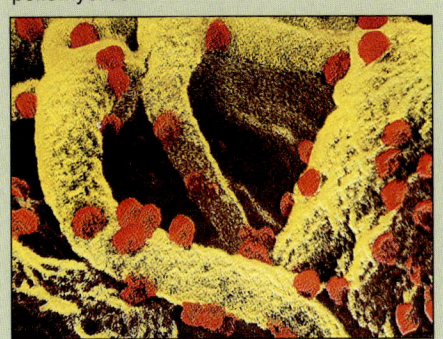

The red objects are the viruses that cause AIDS.

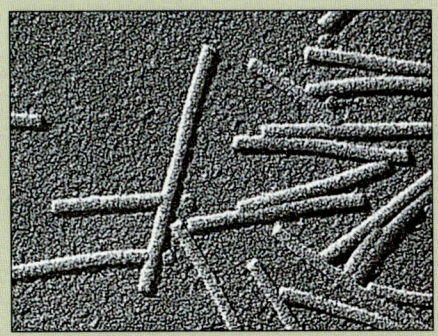

These viruses destroy the leaves of tobacco.

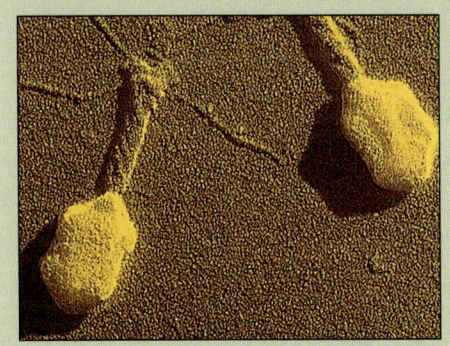

These viruses, known as phage, attack bacteria.

Picture 1 Some examples of viruses.

1. the virus approaches a cell
2. the virus sticks to the cell and injects its string of genes into it
3. the string of genes multiplies inside the cell
4. a new virus is formed round each string of genes
5. the cell bursts open and the new viruses are set free

Picture 2 Viruses can only reproduce inside living cells. Here a virus attacks and destroys a cell.

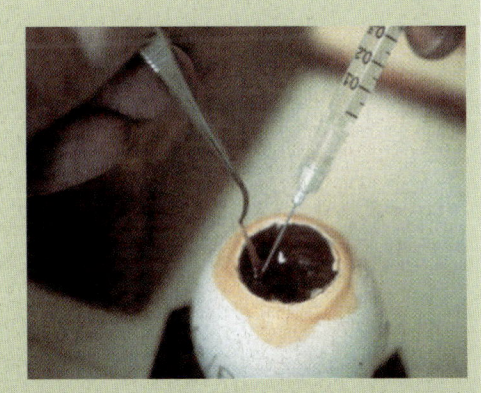

Picture 3 Influenza viruses being injected into a chicken embryo for growing in the laboratory.

H3 Dealing with waste

Bacteria and fungi bring about decay and can be used to get rid of human waste.

Picture 1 The carcass of this buffalo will eventually decay.

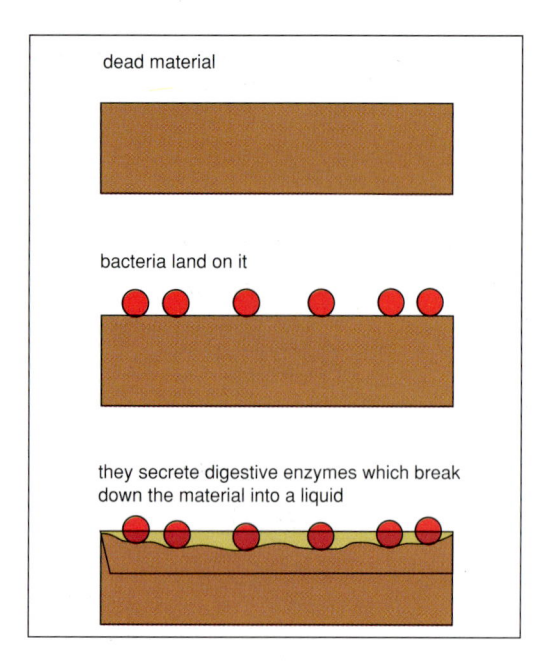

Picture 2 How bacteria bring about decay. Fungi do the same kind of thing.

Picture 3 Fossilised bones of a pterosaur, a flying reptile of 152 million years ago.

What is decay?

After an organism dies, it becomes dead organic matter (detritus). This gradually disintegrates and eventually becomes a liquid consisting of nothing but inorganic substances (picture 1). This is what we mean by **decay**.

Three main things cause decay to happen:

- Immediately after death, the organism's own enzymes start breaking down the body. The organism literally digests itself.
- Various natural processes break the body up. For example, **scavengers** such as birds peck at it, maggots and roundworms wriggle through it and rain softens it.
- Certain microbes, mainly bacteria and fungi, feed on the dead remains and break it down. These **decomposers** are the main agents of decay.

How do decomposers bring about decay?

After an animal or plant has died, it isn't long before some spores of bacteria and fungi land on it. The spores give rise to new individuals. These grow and multiply, spreading quickly through the dead material. A teaspoonful of rotting vegetation may contain over a thousand million bacteria!

To feed on the dead material, the microbes must first break it down into a soluble form, just as we have to digest our food before we can absorb it. Microbes do this by releasing digestive enzymes into the surrounding material (picture 2). The enzymes dissolve the material, and the microbes absorb the soluble products.

Soft remains like skin and muscle decay more quickly than hard structures like bone and wood. A skeleton may remain intact for years after the rest of the body has decayed. Indeed, in certain circumstances bones may become **fossilised** and remain indefinitely (picture 3).

As decay gets under way, the rotting material may get warm. This is because of the heat given out by the millions of respiring microbes. It may also have a foul smell. This is because some of the microbes have special methods of respiration and produce smelly gases such as hydrogen sulphide.

What's needed for decay to occur?

Experiments tell us that these conditions are needed for complete decay to occur:

- **Moisture must be present**

  This is needed for the spores to germinate, and for the microbes to grow and multiply. If a dead body is kept dry, it loses moisture, the skin shrinks and decay does not occur. This process is called **mummification**. The ancient Egyptians used it to preserve the bodies of their kings. Closer to home, it is how hay is made; hay is simply dry grass.

- **It must be warm enough**

  Microbes thrive, and multiply fastest, in a warm environment. Under these circumstances decay will occur quickly. If it is cold, decay is slowed down, and if it is well below freezing it won't happen at all. Extinct mammoths, which died in Siberia thousands of years ago, have been dug out of the ice with their flesh intact and local people cooked the flesh as steaks.

- **Oxygen must be present**

  The microbes which bring about decay need oxygen for their respiration. If oxygen is lacking, they respire without it – that is, **anaerobically** (see page 188). The end products of this process are acids and they stop further decay taking place. So when there is no oxygen present, decay is incomplete. This is how peat is formed. A body left in peat may resist decay. It is also how silage is made.

- **Chemicals which kill the decomposers must not be present**

  A biologist who wants to preserve a specimen will put it in a chemical preservative such as alcohol. In the past this sort of thing has happened naturally when animals have fallen into a tar pit, that's a lake full of an oily liquid. In California there are tar pits containing the undecayed skeletons of extinct sabre-toothed tigers which died about a million years ago.

Making decay occur

To bring about decay, all we need to do is to put some dead material in a place which has all the right conditions for decomposers to flourish. This is what a gardener does when making a **compost heap** (picture 5).

Why is decay important?

If it wasn't for decay, the dead remains of organisms would simply pile up. What a thought!

Decay is important for another reason too. It enables chemical elements such as carbon and nitrogen to circulate in nature. This means that they can be used again and again (see page 40). It's why decaying matter in the form of compost or manure is so good for plants: the locked-up nutrients are released and can be used by plants.

We make use of decay in a number of ways. For example, in a **sewage works** and in **making cheese** (see page 189).

Decay is also important in **getting rid of rubbish**. Things like left-over food, potato peelings and tea leaves can be broken down by decomposers. We call this sort of rubbish **biodegradable**. Thanks to decomposers, the chemicals in these materials can be recycled by nature and used again.

Other kinds of rubbish will not decay, because they are made of substances which microbes cannot live on. They are **non-biodegradable**. They include plastic, polythene and many other artificial materials. If you throw an apple core into a hedge, it will eventually decay and disappear. But if you throw a polythene bag, it will remain there indefinitely – unless some worthy citizen removes it.

Picture 4 These are the remains of a baby mammoth which died thousands of years ago. Because of the extreme cold in Siberia, where it was found, it has been very well preserved.

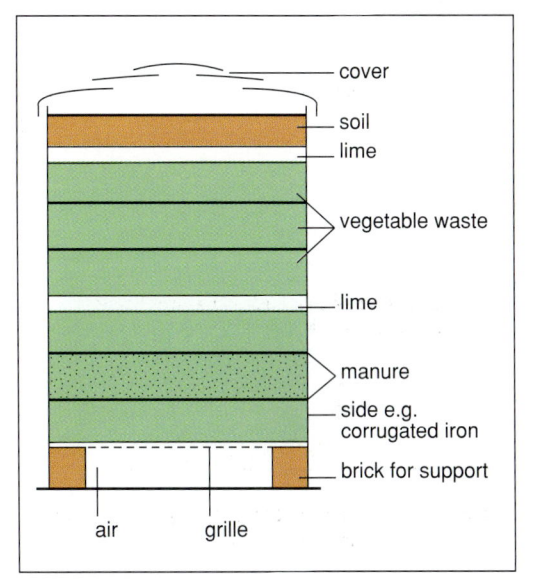

Picture 5 The diagram shows a compost heap in section. In the photograph a gardener tends his compost heap.

Picture 6 Open sewers like this in Pune, India, carry microorganisms which can cause diseases like cholera.

Picture 7 Filter beds in a sewage works. Liquid sewage is sprinkled from long arm-like pipes which rotate slowly over a bed of stones or clinkers. The stones or clinkers are coated with a slimy film of aerobic bacteria and other microbes.

Sewage and its dangers

In previous parts of this book we have mentioned the dangers of not disposing of sewage properly.

The presence of untreated sewage in rivers causes the bacterial population to rise dramatically. They feed on the sewage and in so doing decompose it. However, the bacteria use up all the oxygen in the river and reduce the number of species found. In particular, fish are susceptible to the lowering of the oxygen concentration (see page 45).

Sewage also contains microorganisms from people infected by disease (see page 193). If sewage is not kept completely separate from drinking water, diseases like cholera, dysentery and typhoid can spread (picture 6). This should not normally happen, but after natural disasters, like earthquakes, and wars, sewage pipes may break and their contents mix with the drinking water supplies. This can lead to disease epidemics.

Treatment of sewage

Sewage treatment is carried out in a **sewage works**. The process makes use of bacteria that normally bring about decay. They break down the waste matter into harmless products. Some of the bacteria are aerobic: they need oxygen for respiration. Others are anaerobic: they do not need oxygen. Each type of microbe is only able to break down one substrate. A range of microorganisms is therefore required, since sewage is composed of so many different kinds of waste.

On arrival at the sewage works, the sewage is pumped into a large tank. Here the solids sink to the bottom, forming a sludge. The sludge is broken down by anaerobic bacteria, after which it may be dumped out at sea or disposed of on land. It can also be dried and used as a fertiliser.

Meanwhile the liquid part of the sewage is acted on by aerobic bacteria. They break down any organic material in the liquid, giving off carbon dioxide gas. This process is carried out by mixing the liquid with bacteria in special aerated ponds, or by filtering it through a bed of stones or clinkers coated with bacteria (picture 7). Full breakdown of the sewage can only occur in aerobic conditions, where bacteria are able to covert the organic waste into carbon dioxide, water and simple organic compounds like ammonia.

The liquid that results from this treatment may have lots of bacteria in it. They settle out, forming more sludge.

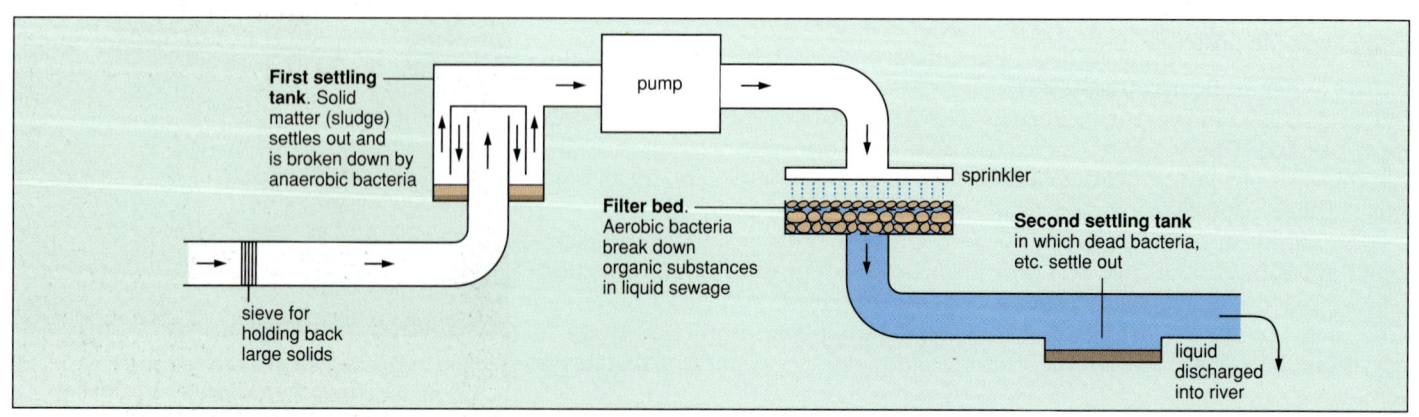

Picture 8 A simplified diagram of a sewage works.

The liquid is now fairly pure water and may be discharged into the sea or a river. If it is discharged into a river, the water can be collected, purified and used again for household supplies. So sewage works enable water to be recycled. If you drink a glass of water in London, it has probably already been through at least three other people!

A simple diagram of a sewage works is shown in picture 8.

Useful products from waste

Sewage disposal is just one example of how microbes can recycle waste. This is really part of a natural process which humans have adapted for their own use. It happens in nature too. For example, bacteria of the nitrogen cycle (see page 40) are able to use organic compounds as energy sources, so they are natural recyclers. Other microorganisms can turn a variety of industrial waste into useful products and so increase its energy value.

Producing fermentation fuels

The anaerobic bacteria in a sewage works give off a gas which is mainly methane. This **biogas** burns well and is used to drive the machinery in modern sewage works.

In developing countries animal and plant waste matter is fermented by anaerobic bacteria in special **biogas digesters** (picture 9). The gas is collected and used for cooking, lighting and other energy-requiring purposes.

In some countries, such as Brazil, alcohol is used as a fuel for cars, either on its own or mixed with petrol as **gasohol**. The alcohol is obtained by fermenting sugar with yeast. The sugar comes mainly from sugar cane plantations but could come from sugar-based waste from industries such as sugar refining.

The advantage of alcohol fuel, obtained from fermentation, is that it is a renewable energy source and does not cause pollution. However, it involves using a lot of land which could be used for growing food crops.

Producing edible protein

Bacteria and fungi, grown in bulk in special chambers, are used as a source of protein food for farm animals and humans. Protein produced this way is called **single cell protein (SCP).** Various waste products are used as food substrates. These include flour waste or wood and paper shavings. Since the bacterial population can grow very rapidly by asexual reproduction (see page 60), they can become a vast source of protein-rich food.

In the case of fungi, the fungal threads are collected and compressed to form a material called **mycoprotein**. Fungal 'chicken' and 'ham' can be made from flavoured mycoprotein, and mycoprotein pies can be bought in food shops.

An advantage of mycoprotein is that it has a high protein and fibre content but no cholesterol. Once again, the waste has been upgraded with an increase in the available protein levels.

Picture 9 An underground biogas digester. What do you think the various people in the picture are doing?

Questions

1. In the manufacture of mycoprotein, sugar and minerals are added to the fungus in a culture chamber. Air is also added along with ammonia, a nitrogen-containing compound.
   a. Suggest why the fungus requires nitrogen.
   b. High temperature steam is passed through the chamber before the fungus is added. Why?
   c. The fungus doubles its mass every 4 hours. Starting with 100 grams, how much is present 24 hours later?
   d. Mycoprotein is composed of 50% protein, 15% fat, 25% fibre and 10% carbohydrate. Illustrate this in a pie chart.

2. The average family throws 5 kilograms of waste paper into the dustbin each week. Calculate how many weeks it would take the average family to discard 90 kilograms of waste paper. Suggest some uses for recycled waste paper.

3. Paper contains mainly cellulose. Suggest a way of turning old newspapers into sugar. What problems would you be likely to have, and what precautions would you need to take?

4. Suggest some precautions that could be taken by people living in an area where the water may have been contaminated by sewage.

H4 Genetic engineering

Scientists have learned how to alter an organism's genes so that they do useful things for us.

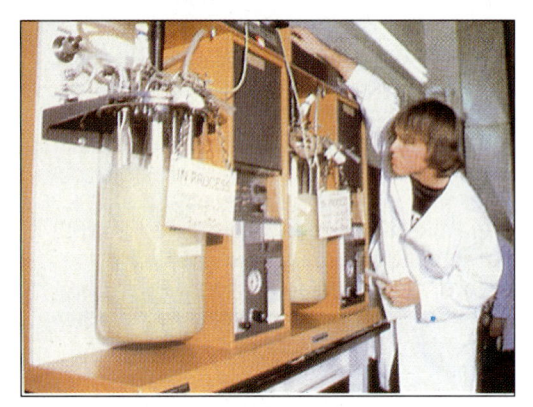

Picture 1 A hormone being produced by genetic engineering.

Manufacturing insulin

Insulin is a hormone which lowers the concentration of sugar in the blood. It is produced by the pancreas. Some people are unable to produce insulin, or at least not enough of it. As a result, they suffer from **diabetes** (see page 109).

People with diabetes have to inject themselves with insulin every day. They therefore need a constant supply of it. For many years insulin has been manufactured by extracting it from the pancreas of cattle and pigs after they have been slaughtered. The insulin is then purified and made suitable for human use.

The trouble with this way of manufacturing insulin is that it is costly, and there are so many people with diabetes that it is difficult to produce enough to go round. Also animal insulin is not quite the same as human insulin, and it may not be as good at combating diabetes.

What makes the human body produce insulin? The answer is that one of our genes tells the pancreas cells to make it. Now suppose we could take this gene out of a human cell and put it in a bacterium. Might the bacterium then make insulin for us?

Not long ago this kind of thing was science fiction, but it has now been done. Scientists have identified the gene that makes human cells produce insulin. They have removed this gene from human cells and transferred it to bacteria. The bacteria multiply rapidly, and the human gene replicates along with the bacteria's own genes. Once inside the bacterial cells, the human gene causes the bacteria to produce insulin.

The procedure just described is illustrated in picture 2. It's an example of **genetic engineering**, a branch of **biotechnology**. Because bacteria multiply so quickly and can be grown in such large numbers, genetic engineering provides a way of producing insulin on a large scale.

Genetically engineered insulin was first tried out on a group of volunteers in a London hospital in 1980. The trial was successful, and this kind of insulin is now widely used, though animal insulin continues to be used as well.

As the population of Britain ages and increases, so does the number of people suffering from diabetes. The demand for insulin gets greater every year. Genetically engineered insulin can keep up with demand and, being human insulin, it should be a successful remedy for diabetes.

Picture 2 The principle of genetic engineering is illustrated here by insulin production.

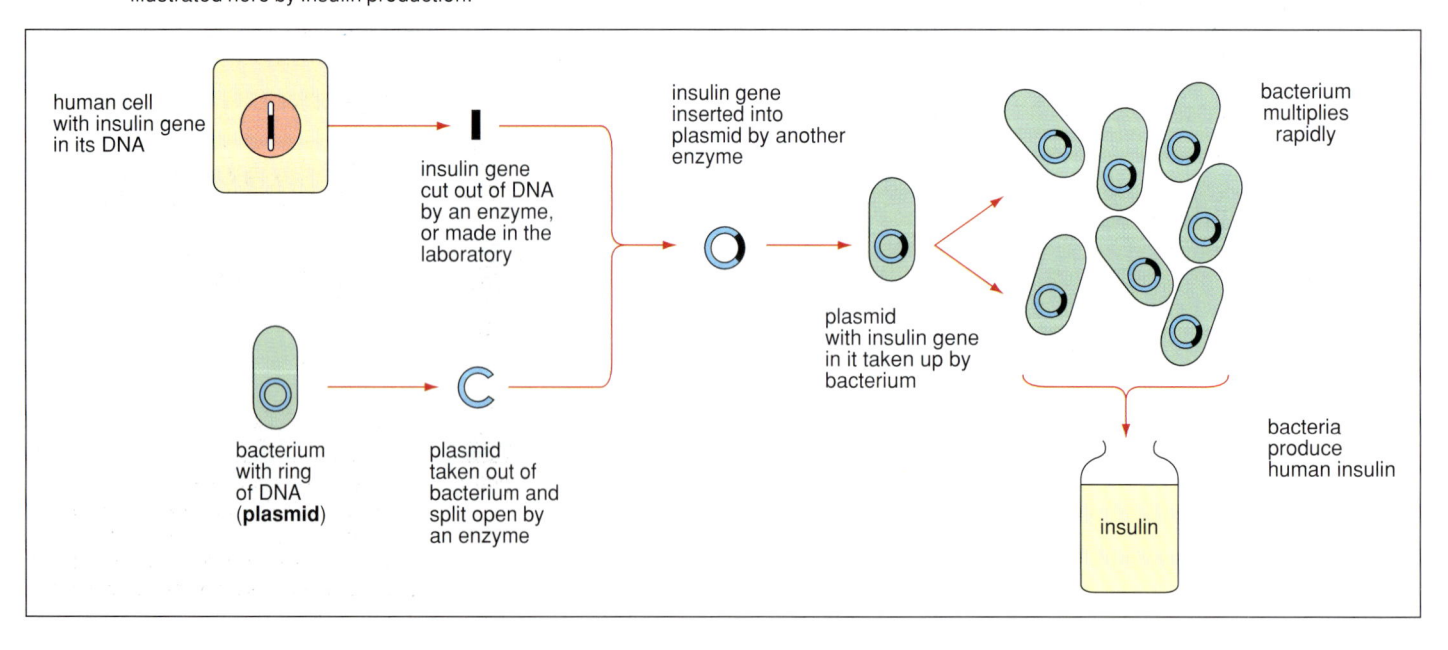

Other products

Genetic engineering is particularly useful when there is no other satisfactory way of making what you want. Such is the case with **growth hormone**.

Lack of growth hormone in a child causes a type of **dwarfism**. It can be put right by giving the child injections of the hormone, but in this case only human growth hormone will do. Animal growth hormone is not suitable.

Growth hormone is produced by the pituitary gland at the base of the brain. Until recently the only way we could get the hormone was by extracting it from the pituitary glands taken from human corpses. Dwarfism is rare – much more so than diabetes. Even so, it was impossible to get enough hormone to go round. Now genetic engineering has come to the rescue. The growth hormone gene has been transferred to bacteria. These bacteria produce the hormone in factories such as the one shown in picture 1.

Manufacturing antibiotics

An **antibiotic** is a substance produced by a microbe which kills, or inactivates, other types of microbe. Microbes produce antibiotics to prevent other microbes competing with them.

The most famous antibiotic is **penicillin**. Its story is told on page 203.

Many other antibiotics besides penicillin are now manufactured from microbes. Some come from fungi, others from bacteria. They are used for treating people with bacterial and fungal diseases (see page 193).

Bacteria that are killed by an antibiotic are described as **sensitive**. Those unaffected by the antibiotic are **resistant**. There is no one antibiotic that is effective against all bacteria and new strains of bacteria are always appearing. These new strains are mutants (formed by mutation, see page 184) and may well be resistant to antibiotics previously used against them. The task of genetic engineering is to continually manufacture a range of new antibiotics in the hope that the mutant strain of bacteria will be sensitive to at least one of them.

In addition, some people may be allergic to certain antibiotics. If a range of antibiotics is available, one that does not cause an allergy in a particular person is likely to be found.

Manufacturing enzymes

Genetic engineering can produce microbes that are able to produce large quantities of enzymes. Once extracted and purified these enzymes have a variety of uses (see pages 122 and 123).

Biological detergents (soap powders) have some of these enzymes added to them. Some stains can be removed from soiled clothes using a very hot wash with a non-biological detergent. But other stains, like egg yolk, blood and grass, can only be removed with the help of enzymes in a biological detergent (picture 3). Protease and lipase enzymes are commonly found in many leading brands. They digest the protein and the fat stains on clothes. The water to wash the clothes is cool, around 40°C. This provides the optimum temperature for the enzymes to work and prevents damage to delicate fibres in the clothing. A cool water wash also saves on heating costs.

Using rennet to make cheese

The first step in cheese-making, the solidifying of the milk, can be carried out by bacteria, as described on page 92. However, milk can also be solidified by treating it with **rennet**, the same substance that is used for turning milk into junket. For years rennet has been used for solidifying milk in cheese-making.

Rennet is the commercial name for the enzyme **rennin** which is found in the stomach of calves (see page 88). Until recently rennin for the cheese industry was obtained from calves' stomachs. But, thanks to genetic engineering, we now have bacteria which can make calves' rennin. Bacterial rennin is used increasingly in making cheese.

1. What are the advantages of using rennin from bacteria rather than calves' rennin in making cheese?
2. Cheese which has been made using bacterial rennin is sometimes called 'vegetarian cheese'. Is this a good name for it? If so, why?

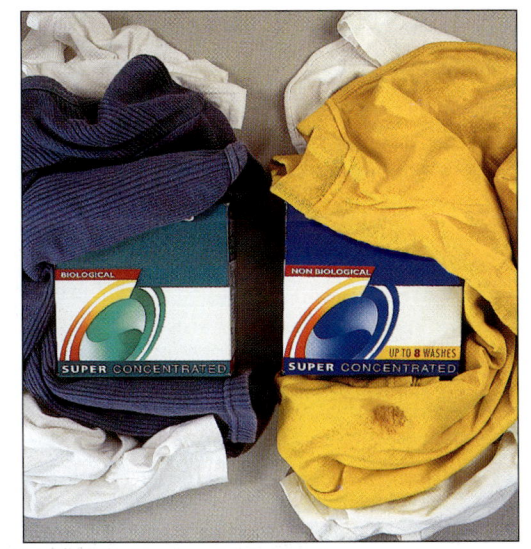

Picture 3 Popular wasing powders come in two types, biological (with added enzymes) and non-biological (no added enzymes). Are there health problems associated with the use of enzymes in washing powder?

Genetic engineering now and in the future

As a result of current genetic engineering, humans have been able to alter the characteristics of some organisms. Scientists have been doing this sort of thing for a long time using selective breeding (see page 182). Improved milk yield of dairy cows and resistance to disease in wheat are two examples of the end products of this slow process. However, genetic engineering, involving the transfer of chromosomal material from one organism to another, is a much quicker way of reaching the desired outcome. Creating an insulin-producing bacterium would have been impossible using selective breeding.

In general, genetic engineering produces bacteria which can:
- produce increased quantities of products,
- speed up processes.

What about the future? You can grow plants in the laboratory from small groups of cells. Now suppose you were to take a gene from bacteria and put it into such cells. The new plants would possess the bacterial gene. Why should we want to do this? You may remember that certain bacteria in the soil can make use of nitrogen from the air (see page 41). This is called **nitrogen-fixation** and it is something that only certain microbes can do. Plants cannot do it, unless they happen to have nitrogen-fixing bacteria inside them.

Now think how useful it would be if we could transfer the genes responsible for nitrogen-fixation into a crop plant such as wheat. The wheat could then use nitrogen from the air. Less fertiliser would be needed, saving money and reducing nitrate pollution.

Scientists have been trying to produce nitrogen-fixing wheat for many years, so far without success. However, other useful genes have been transferred from bacteria to plants. An example is given on the page opposite.

What about humans? Eggs can be taken out of a woman's body, fertilised and then put back again (see page 101). While the egg is out of the body, it might be possible to alter its genes in various ways. For example, harmful genes might be taken out of it, and useful ones put in.

In this way it might be possible to prevent children being born with inherited diseases such as cystic fibrosis and sickle cell disease. This kind of thing is still a long way off, but one day it might become possible.

Immobilisation

Modern biotechnologists have invented a technique in which enzymes are attached to the surface of inert plastic or glass beads. In the case of organisms like yeast, the beads are made of alginate jelly. In both cases the enzymes, or cells, are described as **immobilised**.

The beads are then immersed in substrate solution for batch processing. Alternatively, the substrate can be slowly poured through a column of beads in a continuous flow. The product is removed from the bottom of the column.

These techniques can replace the traditional method of allowing a solution of enzymes or cells to mix freely with a solution of substrate.

The advantages of the immobilised method are:
- the enzyme and product are easily separated,
- the enzyme can be used again, which is useful if it was expensive to produce by genetic engineering,
- the problem of waste disposal is reduced as the enzymes can be recycled.

Overall, immobilisation with continuous flow processing is more efficient and economic than batch processing.

1 What is meant by inert?
2 Are there any advantages in the surfaces being bead-shaped?

Questions

1 Match the statements below with the words or phrases from the list.
   digestive enzymes
   antibiotics
   chromosomal material
   insulin
   a Transferred to bacteria to give them new abilities.
   b Produced by bacteria and used in biological detergents.
   c Used to prevent the growth of bacteria.
   d Produced by gentically engineered bacteria to treat diabetes.

2 Suggest *three* advantages of producing human growth hormone by genetic engineering rather than by extracting it from human corpses.

3 Insulin was the first product of genetic engineering to be made available to the public. Why do you think insulin was chosen? Think of as many possible reasons as you can.

4 There has been some debate as to which is better for treating diabetes, human insulin or animal insulin. If you were comparing them, what sort of things would you look for?

5 Biological washing powders contain protein-digesting enzymes. What advice would you give to the public on how to get the best results with a biological washing powder? Back up your answer with reasons.

6 Why do you think scientists have found it so difficult to produce nitrogen-fixing wheat by genetic engineering?

7 Suggest how genetic engineering might be used to prevent inherited diseases such as cystic fibrosis.

8 Some scientists are worried that bacteria produced by genetic engineering might escape from the laboratory into the environment. What could be the problems if this happened?

Tomato toxin spells end to caterpillar's salad days

A gene responsible for a toxin from a harmless bacterium has been inserted into tomatoes by the Monsanto company so that the engineered fruit can ward off caterpillar-type insects without resorting to artificial pesticides.

'When the insect eats the plant, it ingests that bacterial toxin and dies,' said Dr David Hulst, director of Hulst Research Farm Services in Hughson, California.

The toxin of the bacterium, *Bacillus thuringiensis*, is dangerous only to the caterpillar family, said Dr Hulst. With genetic engineering, this attribute can now be given to a range of crops.

Researchers predict widespread use of this biological control because of growing concern about environmental effects from pesticides that do not always keep insects at or below acceptable levels. Monsanto estimate such genetically engineered tomatoes will be in use in the mid-1990s.

By Roger Highfield

An example of genetic engineering, reproduced from *The Daily Telegraph*, 12 July 1989.

1 How do you think the toxin gene might have been inserted into the tomato plants?
2 What are the possible dangers of inserting this kind of gene into tomato plants?
3 This research was announced in 1989, but it wasn't until the mid-1990s that such genetically engineered tomatoes were in use. Suggest reasons for the long delay.

The story of penicillin

In the late 1920s a Scottish bacteriologist called Alexander Fleming was working at St Mary's Hospital, London. He was growing bacteria on dishes of agar, rather like you may have done in the Activity on page 192.

Normally Fleming covered his bacterial colonies with a lid to prevent them getting contaminated. But one day he accidentally left a dish uncovered. When he examined the dish later, he found that a mould fungus was growing on the agar. But the really interesting thing was that close to the mould the bacterial colonies were absent or had degenerated (picture 2).

The mould turned out to be *Penicillium notatum* which grows on the surface of fruit. Spores of the mould had strayed onto the agar. The mould had then prevented the bacteria from growing.

Fleming at once saw the significance of his discovery. The mould must have produced a substance which acted against the bacteria. If this substance could be extracted from the mould, it might be possible to use it to cure people of bacterial diseases.

It took scientists 12 years to obtain the substance in a usable form. This was achieved by two biochemists, Howard Florey and Ernst Chain. In the early 1940s penicillin, as it came to be called, was tried out on patients in hospital. The results were dramatic. People who were dying of bacterial infections started to recover almost immediately. Since then, penicillin has saved millions of lives.

Penicillin works by preventing bacteria making their cell walls. The result is that newly-formed cells burst open and colonies are prevented from spreading. Penicillin has this effect only on bacteria; it does not affect human cells. This is one of its great advantages.

Today vast amounts of penicillin and other antibiotics are produced in industrial fermenters rather like the one illustrated on page 191.

Picture 1 Alexander Fleming examining one of his culture dishes in the laboratory.

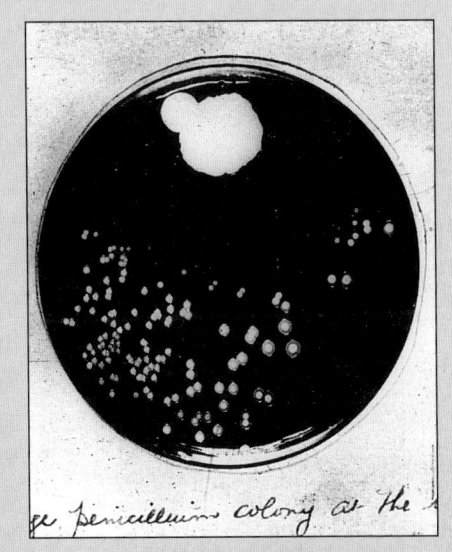

Picture 2 Fleming's culture dish. The bacterial colonies are the small white blobs towards the bottom; the fungus is the much larger white blob at the top. Notice that there are no bacterial colonies close to the fungus. The notes were made by Fleming himself.

1 It is often said that Fleming discovered penicillin by luck. But it wasn't *only* luck. What else was involved?
2 Why do you think it took so long for penicillin to become available in a usable form?
3 How might genetic engineering be used in the manufacture of penicillin?

Index

(Page numbers followed by 'a' refer to activities, those followed by 'c' refer to case studies.)

A
abiotic factors 22-3
abortion 100
absorption 89
acid rain 44
active site 121
adaptation 27c
ADH (anti-diuretic hormone) 106
alcohol
    alcoholic fermentation 188, 190c, 191c
    effect on nervous system 161, 163c
    legal limits 163c
algae 16
alleles 173
    dominant 174
    recessive 174
allergies 149c
    to food additives 84
    to gluten 54c
amino acids 67, 80, 81c
amniocentesis 186
amnion 96
amniotic fluid 96
amoeba 60
amphibians 20
amylase 87, 122, 123c
anaemia 82, 147
animal kingdom 18
annelids 18
anorexia 135c
antagonistic muscles 128
antibiotics 201
    penicillin 194c, 203c
antibodies/antigens 147
    allergies and 149c
    antibodies in breast milk 98
    blood groups and 149c
    fetal antibodies 96
appendix 89
arthritis 132c
arthropods 19
artificial insemination 101, 182
artificial propagation 62-3
asexual reproduction 13, 60-3
assimilation 12
ATP 126
autoclave 192
autotrophic nutrition 12

B
bacteria 16, 192a, 194c
    diseases and 193c
    resistant/sensitive 201
    see also microorganisms
balance 159c
balanced diet 78
batch culture 191c
behaviour
    mating 95c
    rhythmical 110
beri-beri 83
bile and bile salts 89
binary fission 60
binocular vision 153
binomial system 15
biogas 199
biological control
    rabbits/virus disease 37
biosensor 105c

biosphere 38c
biotechnology 11, 188, 200
    see also microorganisms
biotic factors 22
birds 20
birth 97
birth control see contraception
birth rate 36
    post-war bulge 39c
bladder 104
blind spot 151, 154a
blindness 155c
blood 146-8
    circulation 140-3, 144-5c
    clotting 148
    groups 147, 149c
    pressure 143
    transfusions 147, 149c
    vessels 140-1, 143
bone marrow 147
bones see skeleton
Braille 155c
brain 162-3
    drug effects on 163c
bread-making 54c, 188
breast-feeding 98
breeding, selective 182-4
breathing 136-8, 139c
Buchner, Eduard 122c
budding 60, 188
bulimia 135c

C
caecum 89
calcium in diet 82
calorimeter 124
carbohydrates 78-9, 81c, 85c
    energy values 124
carbon cycle 40
carbon dioxide
    anaerobic respiration 188-9, 190c
    carried in blood 146-7
    in exhaled air 136
    global warming and 42
    for photosynthesis 64, 65, 71, 72a
carbon monoxide poisoning 147
carnivores 28
carotene 83
carriers 177
cartilage 129
catalase 120, 122
cells 112-14, 115a
    cell division see mitosis
    tissues/organs 114
cellulase 122
cellulose 67, 78-9, 81c, 114
cell wall 114
central nervous system 160
cervix 92
CFCs 38c, 42, 43
cheese-making 189, 201c
chlorophyll 12, 64, 65-6, 114
chloroplasts 68-9, 114
choice chamber 110
cholesterol 79
chromosomes 113, 173
    cell division and 118, 119
    mutations in 184-5
    sex determination 178
    in sperms and eggs 94, 178, 185
ciliated epithelium 137
circulation 140-3, 144-5c

classification 14-20, 21a
cloning 63, 63c
clotting of blood 148
coal 40
colour vision 153, 154a
communities 22
companion cell 75
competition 37, 39c
conifers 17
conservation 46-8, 49ac
    of plants 51
constipation 91c
consumers 28
continuous culture 191, 201c
contraception 37, 100, 102-3c
controlled experiments 7, 25
coordination 162
cotyledons 52, 54
courtship 95c
crop rotation 46
cross-pollination 57
cuttings 62
cystic fibrosis 177
cytoplasm 113

D
DDT (insecticide) 34, 35c
deafness 158
deamination 104
death rate 36
decay 196
decomposers 30, 196
defaecation 89
denaturation 121
denitrifiers 41
development
    external 98
    internal 96
diabetes 109c, 200
dialysis see kidneys
diaphragm 136
diet (of human) 78-85
    chemistry of 81c, 85c
    dieting 134-5
    of pregnant woman 96, 99c
dietary fibre 78, 89, 91c
diffusion 116
digestion 86-9
    enzymes 87-8
diseases 193c
    anorexia/bulimia 135c
    appendicitis 89
    arthritis 132c
    cancer 166
    heart disease 144c
    inherited 177
    liver cirrhosis 163c
    motor neurone 161
    multiple sclerosis 162
    starvation 135
    vitamin deficiencies 83-4
dispersal of fruits 58
distribution of organisms 24-5, 26a
DNA 13, 184
    nucleoproteins 81c
Down's syndrome 185
drawings and diagrams 10
drugs 163c
    alcohol 161, 163c

E
ear 156-8, 159ac

echinoderm 19
ecological niche 22
ecosystems 22, 49a
    conservation 46-8, 49ac
egg cells 92
    chromosome number 185
ejaculation 93, 94
embryo
    in animals 92, 95
    in plants 52, 57
embryo research 101
emigration 36
endangered species 48
endosperm 54, 57
energy from food 124
    conversion efficiency 32, 33
    food energy values 134-5
    uses of energy 125
environment
    heredity versus 169
environmental issues 11
    air pollution 38c, 42-4
    population growth and 38c
enzymes 120-3
    digestive 87-8, 120
    immobilisation of 202c
    naming of 123c
    and pH 121
    properties of 121
    and temperature 121
    uses of 122, 123c
epidermis 68
epithelium 113
erosion of soil 46
excretion 12-13
    urinary system 104-7, 108-9c
exercise 164-6
    anaerobic respiration and 164
    measuring fitness 165a
    stitch (muscle cramp) 132-3c
experiments 6-7
eye 150-5c
eye colour inheritance 170-2, 173c

F

faeces 89
fallopian tube (oviduct) 92
family planning *see* contraception
farming 32, 33, 49a
    fish farming 34c
    modern methods 46
    selective breeding 182-4, 187c
fats and oils 78, 79, 81c
    emulsification 89
    energy values 124
    saturated/unsaturated 79
fatty acids 79
feeding *see* food and diet; nutrition
fermentation 189
    alcoholic 190c
    lactic acid 189
    producing fuel 199
ferns 17
fertilisation
    in humans 92, 95
    in other animals 93
    in plants 57
    in vitro 101, 101c
fertility drug 101
fetus 96-7
first aid
    for bleeding 148c
    for breathing 139c
    for unconsciousness 162c
fish 20
fitness 166-7

flatworms 18
Fleming, Alexander 201c
flowering plants 17
    flower structure 56, 59a
food additives 84
food chains and webs 28-34, 64
food and diet 78-85
    food from seeds 54, 54c, 63c
    in other organisms 28
    see also diet (in humans); digestion
food energy values 134-5, 188
food poisoning 34
food tests
    for glucose 85a
    for starch 65a
    for vitamin C 85a
food webs 29-30
fossilisation 196
fractures 132-3c
fruits 57
    fruits and dispersal 58
fuels 40, 199
fungi 16
    disease and 60, 193c
    fungal spores 60, 194c
    lichens 17
    penicillin and 191c, 194c, 203c
    see also microorganisms

G

gametes 92, 173
gaseous exchange *see* breathing
gastric glands/juice 88
genes 13, 113, 173
genetics and heredity 170-81
    genetic counselling 177
    genetic engineering 11, 200-3
genotype 175
genus 15
German measles 97
germination 52-3, 54c
glasses (spectacles) 153
global warming 42
glomerulus 105, 106
glycogen 81c, 113
goitre 82
grafting 62
greenhouse effect 42-3
greenhouses 70, 71, 73c
growth 12
    growth hormones 201
    of human fetus 96
guard cells 68
gut 86, 91c

H

habitats 22
haemoglobin 146-7
Harvey, William 145c
hearing 156-8, 159a
heart and circulation 140-3, 144-5c
    fitness and 164-5
heart disease 79, 144
herbivores 28
heredity 170-81
    selective breeding 182-4, 187c
    variation 168-9
heterotrophic nutrition 12
heterozygous 175
hibernation 111
hip dislocation 132c
hip replacement 133c
homozygous 175
Hooke, Robert 112
Hopkins, Frederick Gowland 82
hybridisation 183

hydrochloric acid 88
hyphae 16
hypothesis 6

I

identifying organisms 14-15, 15a, 21a
immigration 36
immobilisation 202c
immunisation
    rubella 97
implantation 95
inbreeding 184
indicator species 44
industry *see* biotechnology
insecticides 34, 35c
insects
    pollination by 57, 59a
insulin 109c, 200
intercostal muscles 136
intestine
    large 89
    small 88
invertebrates 18, 19
iodine (trace element) 82
iron in diet 82

J

joints 129

K

keys 14
kidneys 104-7
    artificial (kidney machine) 107, 108c
    kidney transplant 107, 109c
kingdoms 15, 16-20
knee jerk reflex 161
Krebs, Hans 127
kwashiorkor 79

L

lactic acid 164
lasers 155c
leaf structure 68-9
lichens 17
ligaments 128-9
light
    plants growth and 6-7
    see also photosynthesis
lignin 74
lipase 88, 123c
liver 89, 104
liverworts 17
locomotion *see* movement
long-sightedness 153
lungs 136
lymphocytes 147

M

Malpighi, Marcello 145c
maltase 88, 123c
malting 190c
mammals 20
mating 92, 93
    in humans 94-95
measuring fitness 166
membranes
    cell surface membrane 113
    transport across 116-7
Mendel, Gregor 181c
mesophyll 68
metabolism 120
micronutrients 82-3
microorganisms (microbes) 10, 188
    decomposers 30
    disease and 193-5c

plankton 30
    useful 11, 188-9, 190c, 191c, 194c, 198-9, 200-1
    see also bacteria and fungi
microscope 112, 115a
migration 111
mineral salts 78, 82
    in plants 67, 75
mitosis 118-19
molluscs 19
monoculture 46, 49a
mosses 17
motor neurone disease 161
movement 12
    how we move 128-33c
    in plants 13a
mucus 87
multiple sclerosis 162
muscles 12, 128, 129
mushrooms 193c
mutation 184-5
mycelium 16
myxomatosis 37

N

naming organisms 14
nephron 105
nerves 128
nervous system 160-3
neurotransmitters 161
night-blindness 83, 177
nitrates 40
nitrogen cycle 40-1
nitrogen-fixing bacteria 41, 202
noise levels 158, 159a
nucleic acids 13
    see also DNA
nucleus of cell 113
nutrition 12
    in humans 78-85
    in plants 12, 64-9
    see also diet

O

obesity 134
observing things 6, 9a
oils see fats and oils
oil palm 63c
omnivores 30, 33
optimum 121
organs 114
    transplant operations 107, 109c, 166-7c
osmoregulation 104
osmosis 116, 117c
    in root hairs 77c
outbreeding 183
ovary (human) 92
ovary (plant) 56, 57
oviduct 92
oxygen
    breathing system 136-8, 149c
    carried in blood 146-7
    debt 164
    from photosynthesis 64
    respiration and 12, 125, 126
    for seed respiration 53, 55c
ozone layer 43

P

pacemaker 142
palisade cells 68
pancreas
    role in digestion 88
    role in sugar control 109c
pellagra 83
penicillin 194c, 201, 203c
penis 92

pepsin 88
peptidases 88
peristalsis 87
pesticides 34, 35c
pH 44
    enzyme sensitivity 121
    of soil 23a
    of stomach 88
phagocytes 147
phenotype 175
phloem 69, 74-5, 76c
photosynthesis 12, 50, 64-73, 114
    carbon cycle and 40
    control of 70-3
    leaf structure and 68-9
pituitary gland
    role in growth 200-1
placenta 96, 97
plankton 30, 48
plants
    elements needed 67
    for human use 32-3, 50-1
    leaf structure 68-9
    movement in 13a
    plant kingdom 17
    reproduction (asexual) 60-3
    reproduction (sexual) 56-9
    response to touch 13a
    selective breeding 182-4
plasma 146
platelets 148
plumule 52
poisons
    carbon monoxide 147
    food poisoning 34
    insecticides 34
pollen/pollination 56, 57, 59a
pollen tube 57
pollution
    air pollution 38c, 42-4
    water pollution 45
populations 22, 26c, 36-9
    family planning and 26, 100
predation
    population control and 36-7
predictions 6
pregnancy 96-7
    termination of 100
producers 28
progesterone
    in contraceptive pill 102c
protease 122, 123c
proteins 67,78, 79-80, 81c
    carbon/nitrogen cycles and 40-1
    energy values 124
    gluten 54c
    mycoprotein 197
    single cell protein from fungi 199
    in urine 105
    see also enzymes
protoctists 16, 17
pupil reflex 151, 154a
pulse 143a
pyramid
    of biomass 29
    of energy 29
    of numbers 29

Q

quadrats 24

R

rabbits as pests 37
rabies 193c
radicle 52
radiography 91c

rain forests 47, 71
recovery time 164
red blood cells 146-7
    blood groups and 149c
reflexes 160
    knee jerk reflex 161
    pupil reflex 151, 154a
regeneration 167c
rejection of organ transplants 109c
rennin 88
replacement surgery 167
reproduction 13
    in humans 92-103
    in plants (asexual) 60-3
    in plants (sexual) 56-9
reptiles 20
respiration 12
    aerobic 124-7, 190c
    anaerobic 164, 188-90c, 190c, 191c
    artificial 139c
    breathing 136-8, 139c
    carbon cycle and 40
    effect on atmosphere 126
respirometer 126
response to stimuli 12, 13a
Rhesus blood groups 149c
rickets 82
root hairs 74
roughage see dietary fibre
roundworms 18
rubella 97
runner 61

S

saliva 87
    salivary glands 87
saprobionts 30
scientific method 9c
scurvy 83
seeds 52-4, 54c, 55a
    dispersal of 58
seed coat 57
self-pollination 57
sewage 198-9
sex determination 178
sex drive 100
sexual intercourse 92, 94-5
sexual reproduction 13
    in humans 92-5
    versus asexual reproduction 63
short-sightedness 153
sieve plate 75
single cell protein 199
skeleton 128, 130
    bone injuries 132-3c
    bone structure 130
    replacement surgery 133c
sodium in diet 82
soil
    pH 23a
    water in 74
spare part surgery (replacement surgery) 133c, 166-7c
    see also transplant operations
species 15, 168
spectacles 153
sperm 93-5
    chromosome number 185
    in vitro fertilisation 101, 101c
    sperm bank 101
    vasectomy and 103c
spores 60
    bacterial 194c
stain 112
starch 65a, 78, 81c
    in plants 64, 78, 114
sterile conditions 192

stimulus 12, 110
stoma/stomata 68
stomach 88
sugars 78, 85a
    in plants 64, 67, 74
    in urine 105, 109c

T
teeth 90
tendons 128
test cross 176
test tube babies 101
testes 92
thalidomide 97
thyroid gland 82
tissue typing 109c
tissues 114
trace elements 82
transects 24
translocation 74
transpiration 74
transplant operations 166-7c
trigger stimulus 110
true breeding 175
trypsin 88
tuberculosis 193c
typhoid 193c

U
umbilical cord 96

urea 104, 105
ureter 104, 105
urethra 93, 104
urinary system 104-7, 108-9c
urine 104, 105, 106
uterus 92

V
vacuole 114
vagina 92, 94, 97
variables 7
variation 168-9
variegated 65
vegetarianism 84
    cost aspects 34a
    energy from plants 32, 33
vegetative propagation 60-2
vertebrates 20
villi 89
viruses 193c, 195c
vitamins 78, 82-4

W
washing powders (biological) 201
water
    in diet 80
    functions of 81c
    osmosis 116, 117c

    for photosynthesis 64, 66, 71
    pollution of 45
    regulation by kidneys 105, 106c
    for seed germination 53, 55c
    in the soil 74
    transport in plants 74, 76-7c
weight at birth 99c
wheat 46, 53, 54c, 187c
white blood cells 146, 147
wilting 74
wood 74, 76c

X
xerophthalmia 83
X-rays
    bones 132-3c
    gut 91c
xylem 69, 74, 76c

Y
yeast 122c, 188, 190c
    reproduction in 60
yoghurt 189

Z
zygote 95, 185